Acknowledgments

Many thanks to:

Diana Fitzpatrick for her superb editing,

Terri Hearsh for her excellent book design,

Susan Putney for the eye-catching cover, and

Songbird Indexing Services for the helpful index.

1st edition

Tax Deductions
for Professionals

By Attorney Stephen Fishman

First Edition   JANUARY 2006

Editor   DIANA FITZPATRICK

Cover Design   SUSAN PUTNEY

Book Design   TERRI HEARSH

Proofreading   ROBERT WELLS

Index   SONGBIRD INDEXING SERVICES

Printing   CONSOLIDATED PRINTERS, INC.

Fishman, Stephen.
   Tax deductions for professionals / by Stephen Fishman.-- 1st ed.
     p. cm.
   ISBN 1-4133-0404-4 (alk. paper)
   1. Professions--Taxation--Law and legislation--United States. 2. Professional
corporations--Taxation--United States. 3. Tax deductions--United States. I. Title.

   KF6495.P7F57 2006
   343.7306'7--dc22

                      2005054709

Quantity sales: For information on bulk purchases or corporate premium sales, please
contact the Special Sales Department. For academic sales or textbook adoptions, ask for
Academic Sales, 800-955-4775. Nolo, 950 Parker Street, Berkeley, CA 94710.

Table of Contents

Introduction

1 Tax Deduction Basics

2 Choice of Business Entity

3 Operating Expenses

4 Meal and Entertainment Expenses

5 Car and Local Travel Expenses

6 Long Distance Travel Expenses

11 Medical Expenses

12 Retirement Deductions

13 Inventory

14 More Deductions

15 Hiring Employees and Independent Contractors

16 Professionals Who Incorporate

17 How You Pay Business Expenses

Index

Introduction

Τhis book, the first of its kind, is about tax deductions for all types of professionals, including:

- accountants
- architects
- chiropractors
- consultants
- dentists
- doctors
- engineers
- lawyers
- marriage and family therapists
- optometrists
- pharmacists
- psychologists, and
- veterinarians.

It can be used by professionals who work by themselves, or by those involved in group practices. You can use this book no matter how your practice is legally organized—whether you are a sole proprietor, or are involved in a professional corporation, partnership, or LLC.

A. Why You Need This Book

If you're a professional, no one needs to tell you that taxes are one of your largest expenses. The way to minimize your taxes and maximize your take-home income is to take advantage of every tax deduction available to you.

The IRS will never complain if you don't take all the deductions you're entitled to—and it certainly doesn't make a point of advertising ways to lower your taxes. In fact, many professionals miss out on all kinds of deductions every year simply because they aren't aware of them—or because they neglect to keep the records necessary to back them up.

That's where this book comes in. Specially tailored for the unique needs of professionals, it shows you how you can deduct all or most of your business expenses from your federal taxes—everything from advertising to vehicle depreciation.

This book is not a tax preparation guide—it does not show you how to fill out your tax forms. (By the time you do your taxes, it may be too late to take deductions you could have taken if you had planned the prior year's business spending wisely and kept proper records.) Instead, this book gives you all the information you need to maximize your deductible expenses—and avoid common deduction mistakes. You can (and should) use this book all year long, to make April 15th as painless as possible.

Even if you work with an accountant or another tax professional, you need to learn about tax deductions. No tax professional will ever know as much about your business as you do; and you can't expect a hired professional to search high and low for every deduction you might be able to take, especially during the busy tax preparation season. The information in this book will help you provide your tax professional with better records, ask better questions, obtain better advice—and, just as importantly, evaluate the advice you get from tax professionals, websites, and other sources.

If you do your taxes yourself (as more and more small businesspeople are doing, especially with the help of tax preparation software), your need for knowledge is even greater. Not even the most sophisticated tax preparation program can decide which tax deductions you should take or tell you whether you've overlooked a valuable deduction.

B. The Ever-Changing Tax Laws

Congress is constantly amending the tax laws—and the changes in the last few years have been particularly significant. This book (which will be updated annually) covers all the latest tax laws through the end of 2005. Some recent significant tax changes that are covered in this book include:

- an increase in the standard mileage deduction for the last four months of 2005 (see Chapter 5)
- $5,000 of business start-up expenses may now be deducted during a business's first year (see Chapter 10)
- extension of the $105,000 Section 179 deduction (see Chapter 9)

- the Section 179 deduction for SUVs has been limited to $25,000 (see Chapter 9)
- a new deduction for domestic manufacturing activities (see Chapter 14)
- a new deduction for upgrading the energy efficiency of commercial buildings (see Chapter 8), and
- new Roth 401(k) retirement plans (see Chapter 12).

C. Icons Used in This Book

 This icon alerts you to a practical tip or good idea.

 This is a caution to slow down and consider potential problems.

 This refers you to other sources of information about a particular topic covered in the text.

 This icon tells you where in the text you can read more about a particular topic.

 This icon means that you may be able to skip some material that doesn't apply to your situation.

 This icon lets you know when you may need the advice of a professional, usually a lawyer or tax professional.

Chapter 1

Tax Deduction Basics

The tax code is full of deductions for professionals—from automobile expenses to wages for employees. Before you can start taking advantage of these deductions, however, you need a basic understanding of how businesses pay taxes and how tax deductions work. This chapter gives you all the information you need to get started. It covers:

- how tax deductions work (Section A)
- how to calculate the value of a tax deduction (Section B), and
- what professionals can deduct (Section C).

A. How Tax Deductions Work

A tax deduction (also called a tax write-off) is an amount of money you are entitled to subtract from your gross income (all the money you make) to determine your taxable income (the amount on which you must pay tax). The more deductions you have, the lower your taxable income will be and the less tax you will have to pay.

1. Types of Tax Deductions

There are three basic types of tax deductions: personal deductions, investment deductions, and business deductions. This book covers only business deductions—the large array of write-offs available to business owners, including professionals.

Personal Deductions

For the most part, your personal, living, and family expenses are not tax deductible. For example, you can't deduct the food that you buy for yourself and your family. There are, however, special categories of personal expenses that may be deducted, subject to strict limitations. These include items such as home mortgage interest, state and local taxes, charitable contributions, medical expenses above a threshold amount, interest on education loans, and alimony. This book does not cover these personal deductions.

Investment Deductions

Many professionals try to make money by investing money. For example, they might invest in real estate or play the stock market. They incur all kinds of expenses, such as fees paid to money managers or financial planners, legal and accounting fees, and interest on money borrowed to buy investment property. These and other investment expenses (also called expenses for the production of income) are tax deductible, subject to strict limitations. Investment deductions are not covered in this book.

Business Deductions

Because a professional practice is a profit-making enterprise, it is a business for tax purposes. People in business usually must spend money on their business—for example, for office space, supplies, and equipment. Most business expenses are deductible, sooner or later, one way or another. And that's what this book is about: How professionals may deduct their business expenses.

2. You Pay Taxes Only on Your Profits

The federal income tax law recognizes that you must spend money to make money. Virtually every professional, however small his or her practice, incurs some expenses. Even a professional with a low overhead practice (such as a psychologist) must pay for office space and insurance. Of course, many professionals incur substantial expenses, even exceeding their income.

If you are a sole proprietor (or owner of a one-person LLC taxed as a sole proprietorship), you are not legally required to pay tax on every dollar your practice takes in (your "gross income"). Instead, you owe tax only on the amount left over after your practice's deductible expenses are subtracted from your gross income (this remaining amount is called your "net profit"). Although some tax deduction calculations can get a bit complicated, the basic math is simple: the more deductions you take, the lower your net profit will be, and the less tax you will have to pay.

EXAMPLE: Karen, a sole proprietor, earned $100,000 this year from her child psychology practice. Fortunately, she doesn't have to pay income tax on the entire $100,000—her gross business income. Instead, she can deduct from her gross income various business expenses, including a $10,000 office rental deduction (see Chapter 3) and a $5,000 deduction for insurance (see Chapter 14). These and her other expenses amount to $20,000. She can deduct the $20,000 from her $100,000 gross income to arrive at her net profit: $80,000. She pays income tax only on this net profit amount.

The principle is the same if your practice is a partnership, LLC, LLP, or S corporation: business expenses are deducted from the entity's profits to determine the entity's net profit for the year, which is passed through the entity to the owners' individual tax returns.

EXAMPLE: Assume that Karen is a member of a three-owner LLC, and is entitled to one-third of the LLC's income. She doesn't pay tax on the gross income the LLC receives, only on its net income after expenses are deducted. This year, the LLC earned $400,000 and had $100,000 in expenses. She pays tax on one-third of the LLC's $300,000 net profit.

If your practice is organized as a C corporation, it too pays tax only on its net profits.

3.   You Must Have a Legal Basis for Your Deductions

All tax deductions are a matter of legislative grace, which means that you can take a deduction only if it is specifically allowed by one or more provisions of the tax law. You usually do not have to indicate on your tax return which tax law provision gives you the right to take a particular deduction. If you are audited by the IRS, however, you'll have to provide a legal basis for every deduction the IRS questions. If the IRS concludes that your deduction wasn't justified, it will deny the deduction and charge you back taxes, interest, and penalties.

B. The Value of a Tax Deduction

Most taxpayers, even sophisticated professionals, don't fully appreciate just how much money they can save with tax deductions. Only part of any deduction will end up back in your pocket as money saved. Because a deduction represents income on which you don't have to pay tax, the value of any deduction is the amount of tax you would have had to pay on that income had you not deducted it. So a deduction of $1,000 won't save you $1,000—it will save you whatever you would otherwise have had to pay as tax on that $1,000 of income.

1. Federal and State Income Taxes

To determine how much income tax a deduction will save you, you must first figure out your marginal income tax bracket. The United States has a progressive income tax system for individual taxpayers with six different tax rates (often called tax brackets), ranging from 10% of taxable income to 35% (see the chart below). The higher your income, the higher your tax rate.

You move from one bracket to the next only when your taxable income exceeds the bracket amount. For example, if you are a single taxpayer, you pay 10% income tax on all your taxable income up to $7,300. If your taxable income exceeds $7,300, the next tax rate (15%) applies to all your income over $7,300—but the 10% rate still applies to the first $7,300. If your income exceeds the 15% bracket amount, the next tax rate (25%) applies to the excess amount, and so on until the top bracket of 35% is reached.

The tax bracket in which the last dollar you earn for the year falls is called your "marginal tax bracket." For example, if you have $150,000 in taxable income, your marginal tax bracket is 28%. To determine how much federal income tax a deduction will save you, multiply the amount of the deduction by your marginal tax bracket. For example, if your marginal tax bracket is 28%, you will save 28¢ in federal income taxes for every dollar you are able to claim as a deductible business expense (28% x $1 = 28¢). The following table lists the 2005 federal income tax brackets for single and married individual taxpayers and shows the tax savings for each dollar of deductions.

2005 Federal Personal Income Tax Brackets		
Tax Bracket	Income If Single	Income If Married Filing Jointly
10%	Up to $7,300	Up to $14,600
15%	$7,301 to $29,700	$14,601 to $59,400
25%	$29,701 to $71,950	$59,401 to $119,950
28%	$71,951 to $150,150	$119,951 to $182,800
33%	$150,151 to $326,450	$182,801 to $326,450
35%	All over $326,450	All over $326,450

Income tax brackets are adjusted each year for inflation. For current brackets, see IRS Publication 505, *Tax Withholding and Estimated Tax.* You can obtain this and all other IRS publications by calling the IRS at 800-TAX-FORM, visiting your local IRS office, or downloading the publications from the IRS Internet site at www.irs.gov.

You can also deduct your business expenses from any state income tax you must pay. The average state income tax rate is about 6%, although seven states (Alaska, Florida, Nevada, South Dakota, Texas, Washington, and Wyoming) don't have an income tax.

2. Social Security and Medicare Taxes

Everyone who works—whether a business owner or an employee—is required to pay Social Security and Medicare taxes. The total tax paid is the same, but the tax is paid differently depending on whether you are an employee of an incorporated practice or a self-employed owner of a partnership, LLC, or LLP. Employees pay one-half of these taxes through payroll deductions; employers must pony up the other half and send the entire payment to the IRS. Self-employed professionals must pay all of these taxes themselves. These differences don't mean much when you're an employee of a business you own, since the money is coming out of your pocket whether it is paid by the employee or employer.

These taxes are levied on the employment income of employees, and on the self-employment income of business owners. They consist of a 12.4% Social Security tax on income up to an annual limit; in 2006, the limit was $94,200. Medicare taxes are not subject to any income limit and are levied at a 2.9% rate. This combines to a total 15.3% tax on employment or self-employment income up to the Social Security tax ceiling. After the ceiling is reached, the tax goes down to 2.9%.

Like income taxes, self-employment taxes are paid on the net profit you earn from a business. Thus, deductible business expenses reduce the amount of self-employment tax you have to pay by lowering your net profit.

3.   Total Tax Savings

When you add up your savings in federal, state, and self-employment taxes, you can see the true value of a business tax deduction. For example, if you're single and your taxable business income (whether as an employee of an incorporated practice or a self-employed owner of a partnership, LLC, or LLP) is below the Social Security tax ceiling, a business deduction can be worth as much as 28% (in federal taxes) + 15.3% (in self-employment taxes) + 6% (in state taxes). That adds up to a whopping 49.3% savings. If you buy a $1,000 computer for your practice and you deduct the expense, you save about $493 in taxes. In effect, the government is paying for almost half of your business expenses.

Additional business deductions are worth less if your income is above the Social Security tax ceiling, since you don't have to pay the 12.4% Social Security tax. For example, if you're in the 33% income tax bracket, an additional deduction will be worth 33% (in federal taxes) + 6% (in state taxes) + 2.9% in Medicare taxes. This adds up to 41.9%. Still not bad.

This is why it's so important to know all the business deductions you are entitled to take and to take advantage of every one.

> ⚠️ **Don't buy things just to get a tax deduction.** Although tax deductions can be worth a lot, it doesn't make sense to buy something you don't need just to get a deduction. After all, you still have to pay for the item, and the tax deduction you get in return will only cover a portion of the cost. For example, if you buy a $3,000 computer you don't really need, you'll probably be able to deduct less than half the cost. That means you're still out over $1,500—money you've spent for something you don't need. On the other hand, if you really do need a computer, the deduction you're entitled to is like found money—and it may help you buy a better computer than you could otherwise afford.

C. What Professionals Can Deduct

Professionals are business owners, and as such they can deduct four broad categories of business expenses:

- start-up expenses
- operating expenses
- capital expenses, and
- inventory costs.

This section provides an introduction to each of these categories (they are covered in greater detail in later chapters).

> **⚠ You must keep track of your expenses.** You can deduct only those expenses that you actually incur. You need to keep records of these expenses to (1) know for sure how much you actually spent; and (2) prove to the IRS that you really spent the money you deducted on your tax return, in case you are audited. Accounting and bookkeeping are discussed in detail in Chapter 20.

1. Start-Up Expenses

The first money you will have to shell out will be for your practice's start-up expenses. These include most of the costs of getting your practice up and running, like license fees, advertising costs, attorney and accounting fees, travel expenses, market research, and office supplies expenses. Start-up costs are not currently deductible—that is, you cannot deduct them all in the year in which you incur them. However, you can deduct up to $5,000 in start-up costs in the first year you are in business. You must deduct amounts over $5,000 over the next 15 years. (See Chapter 10 for a detailed discussion of deducting start-up expenses.)

> **EXAMPLE:** Cary, an optometrist who has recently graduated from optometry school, decides to open his own practice. Before Cary's optometry office opens for business, he has to rent space, hire and train employees, and obtain all necessary optometric equipment. These start-up expenses cost Cary $50,000. Cary may deduct $5,000

of this amount the first year he's in business. The remainder may be deducted over the first 180 months that he's in business—$3,000 per year for 15 years.

2.   Operating Expenses

Operating expenses are the ongoing day-to-day costs a business incurs to stay in business. They include such things as rent, utilities, salaries, supplies, travel expenses, car expenses, and repairs and maintenance. These expenses (unlike start-up expenses) are currently deductible—that is, you can deduct them all in the same year in which you pay them. (See Chapter 3.)

> **EXAMPLE:** After Cary's optometry office opens, he begins paying $5,000 a month for rent and utilities. This is an operating expense that is currently deductible. When Cary does his taxes, he can deduct from his income the entire amount he paid for rent and utilities for the year.

3.   Capital Expenses

Capital assets are things you buy for your practice that have a useful life of more than one year, such as land, buildings, equipment, vehicles, books, furniture, and patents you buy from others. These costs, called capital expenses, are considered to be part of your investment in your business, not day-to-day operating expenses.

Large businesses—those that buy at least several hundred thousand dollars of capital assets in a year—must deduct these costs by using depreciation. To depreciate an item, you deduct a portion of the cost in each year of the item's useful life. Depending on the asset, this could be anywhere from three to 39 years (the IRS decides the asset's useful life).

Small businesses can also use depreciation, but they have another option available for deducting many capital expenses—they can currently deduct up to $105,000 in capital expenses per year under a provision of the tax code called Section 179. Section 179 is discussed in detail in Chapter 9.

EXAMPLE: Cary spent $5,000 on examining chairs for his office. Because the chairs have a useful life of more than one year, they are capital assets that he will either have to depreciate over several years or deduct in one year under Section 179.

Certain capital assets, such as land and corporate stock, never wear out. Capital expenses related to these costs are not deductible; the owner must wait until the asset is sold to recover the cost. (See Chapter 9 for more on this topic.)

4.   Inventory

Inventory is merchandise that a business makes or buys to resell to customers. It doesn't matter whether you manufacture the merchandise yourself or buy finished merchandise from someone else and resell the items to customers. Inventory doesn't include tools, equipment, or other items that you use in your practice; it refers only to items that you buy or make to sell.

Whether professionals sell inventory for tax purposes can be a tricky question. Materials that are an indispensable and inseparable part of the rendering of a service are not inventory—for example, gold that a dentist places in patients' teeth is not inventory.

You must deduct inventory costs separately from all other business expenses—you deduct inventory costs as you sell the inventory. Inventory that remains unsold at the end of the year is a business asset, not a deductible expense. (See Chapter 13 for more on deducting inventory.)

EXAMPLE: In addition to providing optometric services, Cary stocks and sells eyeglasses to his patients. In his first year in practice, Cary spent $15,000 on his inventory of eyeglasses, but sold only $10,000 worth of them. He can deduct only $10,000 of the inventory costs for the year.

■

Chapter 2

Choice of Business Entity

This chapter is about how your tax life is affected by the form of business entity you use to conduct your professional practice. If you're already in practice, you will learn the pros and cons of the business form you have chosen—and you may decide to convert to another type of entity or tax treatment. If you're just starting your practice, you will need to figure out which business entity and tax treatment is best for you.

A. Types of Business Entities

Every business has a legal form, including a professional practice. If you're in practice right now, your business almost certainly falls into one of the following categories:
- sole proprietorship
- partnership
- corporation
- limited liability company (LLC), or
- limited liability partnership (LLP).

The sole proprietorship and partnership are the default business entities—they come into existence automatically unless a business's owners take the steps necessary to form one of the other entities.

The following chart gives you an idea of the breakdown for the types of business entities professionals use. (It does not include professionals who provide health services—doctors, dentists, and so on.) Note that the numbers in the chart reflect 2002 tax filings. LLCs have been growing in popularity each year, so they may be somewhat underrepresented in the chart.

Tax Returns Filed by Professionals—2002	
Type of Entity	**Number of Tax Returns Filed in 2002**
Sole Proprietors	2,672,400
Partnerships (including LLPs)	50,639
LLCs	71,399
C Corporations (2001 returns)	709,837
S Corporations	480,120

1.   Sole Proprietorship

The majority of professionals who practice by themselves are sole proprietors. Many have attained this legal status without even realizing it. Quite simply, if you start running a professional practice by yourself and do not incorporate or form an LLC or LLP, you are automatically a sole proprietor.

A sole proprietorship is a one-owner business. Unlike a corporation, LLC, general partnership, or LLP, it is not a separate legal entity. The business owner (proprietor) personally owns all the assets of the business and is in sole charge of its operation. Most sole proprietors run small operations, but a sole proprietor can hire employees and nonemployees, too. Indeed, some sole proprietors have large operations with many employees.

You don't have to do anything special or file any papers to set up a sole proprietorship, other than the usual license, permit, and other regulatory requirements your state and/or locality imposes on any business. Of course, if you're in a profession that requires a license to practice, you must comply with the applicable requirements or the state may force you to close your proprietorship.

Sole proprietorships are the most common form of business entity used by professionals. One big reason for their popularity is that they are by far the simplest and cheapest way to organize a one-owner business.

If you practice by yourself, a sole proprietorship may well be your best bet. As far as taxes are concerned, it's an excellent choice because it provides pass through taxation, which most professionals prefer. (See Section C.) You also won't have to file a separate tax return for your practice, which saves time and money.

Sole proprietorships do have one big drawback: They offer no limited liability. Corporations, LLCs, and LLPs provide limited liability, which is the main reason why many professionals use them. However, when you practice by yourself, the limited liability you'll obtain by forming a corporation, LLC, or LLP is often more illusory than real.

Thus, sticking with the unflashy, simple, and cheap sole proprietorship is a perfectly rational choice. Remember, however, that if you stop practicing by yourself and form a group practice, you can no longer be a sole proprietor. You'll automatically become a partner in a partnership unless you form an LLC, LLP, or corporation—which is highly advisable.

For detailed guidance about how to form and run a sole proprietorship, refer to *Working for Yourself: Law & Taxes for Independent Contractors, Freelancers & Consultants,* by Stephen Fishman (Nolo).

2.   Limited Liability Company (LLC)

The limited liability company, or LLC, is the newest type of business form in the United States. The LLC is a unique hybrid: a cross between a partnership and corporation. It provides the flexibility, informality, and tax attributes of a partnership and the limited liability of a corporation. However, a few states (California, Oregon, and Rhode Island) bar most types of professionals from using them. In these states, professionals seeking the desirable attributes of an LLC will usually choose either an LLP or an S corporation instead.

In most states, professionals who form LLCs must adhere to restrictions similar to those for professional corporations (see Section 4, below). All the owners must be licensed to perform the professional services carried on by the LLC and ownership cannot be transferred to unlicensed individuals. Thus, for example, all the owners of a dental LLC must be licensed dentists, and no dentist-owner may transfer his LLC ownership to a nondentist.

To form an LLC, one or more people must file articles of organization with their state's business filing office. Although not required by all states, it is highly desirable to adopt a written LLC operating agreement laying out how the LLC will be governed. If you don't prepare an operating agreement, the default provisions of your state's LLC laws will apply.

LLCs provide limited liability and partnership tax treatment—an ideal combination for many professionals. If you're in a group practice, the LLC should be on the top of your list when choosing your business entity.

On the other hand, if you are in solo practice, you won't gain much by forming an LLC. As far as taxes go, you'll still be treated like a sole proprietorship by the IRS. More importantly, the limited liability a solo practitioner obtains by using an LLC may prove to be more mythical than real.

> **For a complete discussion on how to form limited liability companies,** see *Form Your Own Limited Liability Company,* by Anthony Mancuso (Nolo).

3. Limited Liability Partnership (LLP)

Professionals in all states now have the option of forming a special type of partnership called a limited liability partnership (LLP) (also called a "registered limited liability partnership"). LLPs are much the same as regular general partnerships except for one crucial advantage—they limit the partners' liability for malpractice claims and, in some states, debts incurred by the partnership.

Professionals in some states—California, for example—use LLPs because state law prohibits them from forming LLCs, another popular entity that provides limited liability. LLPs are limited to professionals in certain occupations—typically people who work in the medical, legal, and accounting fields, and a few other professions in which a professional-client relationship exists. In some states, engineers, veterinarians, and acupuncturists are also allowed to form LLPs. Not all categories of licensed professionals can form an LLP—it depends on your state.

At least two partners are needed to form an LLP, and the partners must usually be licensed in the same or related professions. LLPs don't come into existence automatically like general partnerships (see Section 5, below, for more on general partnerships). In most states, creating an LLP requires registration with the state government, annual filings, and administrative fees.

Form an LLP if you want to have an LLC, but your state doesn't allow people in your profession to use them. If your state allows you to use either an LLC or LLP, don't choose an LLP without first carefully checking your state's laws to see if LLPs provide the same degree of limited liability protection as LLCs. If they don't, form an LLC.

4.   Corporation

A corporation is a legal form in which you can organize and conduct a business and share in the profits or losses. In the past, most states prohibited many types of professionals—for example, doctors and lawyers—from forming a corporation because they feared they would be used to limit their liability for malpractice. Now, all states permit professionals to form a special kind of corporation called a "professional corporation" or "professional service" corporation. The professional corporation has the basic attributes of a regular corporation with certain restrictions about ownership and the type of work it can do. (All further references to corporations include professional corporations and professional service corporations.)

The list of professionals who must form professional corporations varies from state to state, but usually includes:

- accountants
- engineers
- lawyers
- psychologists
- social workers
- veterinarians, and
- health care professionals such as doctors, dentists, nurses, physical therapists, optometrists, opticians, and speech pathologists.

Most states impose restrictions on who may own a professional corporation and the work it can do. Typically, a professional corporation must be organized for the sole purpose of performing professional services, and all shareholders must be licensed to render that service. For example, in a medical corporation, all the shareholders must be licensed physicians.

A professional corporation is a state law classification—it has nothing to do with the IRS or taxes. A professional corporation can be either a C or S corporation for tax purposes, as described below. A professional corporation is also not the same as a "personal service corporation" (PSC). A PSC is an IRS classification that has nothing to do with the professional corporation rules of your state (see Section D2 for more on PSCs).

Although the word "corporation" tends to conjure up images of huge business corporations (like IBM or Microsoft), in reality, most corporations—especially those owned by professionals—are small operations. In fact, in many professional corporations, there is only one shareholder who is also often the sole employee—that is, a single person directs and runs the corporation and owns all the corporate stock.

A corporation has a legal existence completely separate from its owners—indeed, it is considered to be a "person" for legal purposes. It can hold title to property, sue and be sued, have bank accounts, borrow money, hire employees, and do anything else in the business world that a human being can do. If you incorporate your practice, the corporation becomes the "owner" of the business and you own the corporation in the form of stock ownership and ordinarily work as its employee.

You create a corporation by filing the necessary forms with and paying the required fees to your appropriate state agency—usually the office of the secretary of state or corporations commissioner. Each state specifies the forms to use and the filing cost. You will need to check your state law to determine if you must form a professional corporation and make sure you meet any special requirements for professional corporations. You'll also need to choose a name for your corporation, adopt corporate bylaws, set up your corporate records, and "capitalize" your corporation—issue stock in return for money, property, and/or services provided to the corporation.

Many professionals, particularly those in the health care field, have incorporated their practices. Many of these corporations were formed before LLCs became widely available and corporations were the only game in town if a professional wanted limited liability. Even if they want to, the shareholders of many of these corporations can't convert them to another type of entity because the tax costs would be prohibitive. (See Section E, below.)

However, although their popularity has diminished somewhat since the advent of the LLC, professionals continue to form corporations. S corporations are especially popular because they can provide savings on Social Security and Medicare taxes. C corporations are often chosen because they provide the best deductions for fringe benefits—a very important consideration for many high-income professionals. But you can obtain these same benefits by forming an LLC and electing to have it taxed as an S or C corporation. (See Section C, below, for more on S and C corporations.)

Perhaps the most important reason corporations continue to be used is habit. People like what they're used to and everyone is used to corporations. They have been around for over 100 years and are well understood by businesspeople, courts, lawyers, and tax professionals. LLCs are much newer and have more legal uncertainties.

For more information on corporations and how to incorporate, refer to *Incorporate Your Business*, by Anthony Mancuso (Nolo). There are also incorporation services that will incorporate your business for you. Among the best known is The Company Corporation at www.corporate.com.

5. Partnership

In the past, almost all professionals who practiced with others were partners in a general partnership. However, most professionals abandoned the general partnership form when other types of business entities (like professional corporations, LLCs, and LLPs) were created that limited their personal liability for malpractice claims and debts— something a partnership does not do.

A partnership is a form of shared ownership and management of a business. A general partnership automatically comes into existence whenever two or more people enter into a venture together to earn a profit and don't choose to form some other business entity. As with sole proprietorships, it is not necessary to file any papers to form a general partnership. The partners contribute money, property, and/or services to the partnership and in return receive a share of the profits it earns. The partnership form is extremely flexible because the partners may agree to split the profits and manage the business in virtually any way they want. (We refer to general partnerships simply as "partnerships.")

Unlike a sole proprietorship, a partnership has a legal existence distinct from its owners (the partners). It can hold title to property, sue and be sued, have bank accounts, borrow money, hire employees, and do anything else in the business world that a human being can do. Because a partnership is a separate legal entity, property acquired by a partnership is property of the partnership and not of the partners individually. This differs from a sole proprietorship where the proprietor-owner individually owns all the sole proprietorship property.

Because partnerships provide no limited liability to their owners, professionals abandoned them in droves when professional corporations and LLCs became available. Indeed, as the chart at the beginning of this chapter shows, the partnership has become nearly extinct among professionals.

If you are in a partnership right now, you should seriously think about forming an LLC, LLP, or corporation so that you can limit your personal liability for acts by the other people in your group practice. However, if limited liability is not important to you—for example, because you have plenty of insurance—a partnership is just as good for a group practice as an LLC or LLP.

 For a detailed discussion of partnerships including how to write partnership agreements, see *The Partnership Book*, by Denis Clifford and Ralph Warner (Nolo).

B. Limiting Your Liability

The most important consideration in choosing your business structure (or deciding whether or not to stick with what you have) is usually liability—that is, the extent a business's owners are personally responsible for paying for their business's debts and business-related lawsuits. Indeed, this issue is seen as so important that the corporation, LLC, and LLP were created for the express purpose of limiting their owners' liability.

It's likely that you're as concerned about your liability as anybody else. For this reason, you might think that you should form a corporation or limited liability company. After all, these business forms are supposed to provide "limited liability"—protection from debts and lawsuits. Indeed, many people seem to believe that forming a corporation, LLP, or LLC is like having a magic shield against liability. However, the sad truth is that there are many holes in the limited liability shield offered by the corporation, LLP, and LLC.

1.   What Is Liability?

Liability means being legally responsible for a debt or for doing something that injures someone, such as committing professional malpractice or injuring someone in a traffic accident. If you are personally liable for a debt or wrong and a person sues you and obtains a judgment against you, you'll have to pay the judgment yourself. If you don't pay, the person who obtained the judgment can take your personal property to pay it (subject to certain limits). Thus, you could end up losing your personal bank accounts, personal property (like your car), and even your house.

On the other hand, if only your business is liable for a debt or wrongdoing, you have no legal obligation to use personal funds to pay a person who obtains a judgment against your business. But, of course, your business assets can by taken to satisfy a judgment against your business.

Obviously, business owners, including professionals, don't want to put their personal assets at risk if they get sued for malpractice or other alleged wrongdoing, or if their practice incurs debts. It was to help avoid personal liability and encourage people to invest in businesses that the corporation was created. Much later, the limited liability company was established to provide the same degree of limited liability without the expense and bother of forming and running a corporation. LLPs were also established to give professionals limited liability. Corporations, LLCs, and LLPs are all "limited liability entities."

The "default" business entities—the sole proprietorship and partnership—provide no limited liability at all—you are personally liable for your business's debts and wrongdoing by you or anyone else who works in your practice. If you want limited liability, you must take the necessary steps to form a corporation, LLC, or LLP under your state law.

⚠️ **Liability has nothing to do with taxation or the way a business entity is taxed.** For example, the owners of a partnership will have unlimited liability even if they choose to have their partnership taxed as a corporation. You must actually form a limited liability business entity under the applicable state law to benefit from its limited liability attributes.

2.   Liability for Professional Malpractice

The single greatest liability exposure most professionals face is for malpractice. A single medical malpractice lawsuit, for example, can result in a judgment for millions. Even if you're innocent, defending a malpractice lawsuit can cost hundreds of thousands of dollars. Can a limited liability entity help you avoid personal liability for malpractice? Yes, but not as much as you might think.

Your Own Malpractice

No limited liability entity—whether a corporation, LLC, or LLP—protects you against personal liability for your own malpractice, or other personal wrongdoing. If your business doesn't have enough assets to pay a judgment obtained against you, your personal assets can be taken. Thus, your personal assets will always be on the line if you are sued for malpractice. This is why professionals should always have malpractice insurance.

> **EXAMPLE:** Janet, a civil engineer, forms a professional corporation of which she is the sole shareholder. She helps design a bridge that collapses, killing dozens of commuters. Even though Janet is incorporated, she could be held personally liable (along with her corporation) for any damages caused by her alleged malpractice in designing the bridge. Both Janet's personal assets and those of her corporation are at risk.

Malpractice by Others

What if somebody else in your practice gets sued for malpractice? If your practice is a partnership, each partner is personally liable for any wrongful acts committed by a copartner in the ordinary course of partnership business. Thus, you will be personally liable for malpractice claims against your copartners, even if you were not personally involved. This makes the partnership a bad choice for professionals who practice together. It is by far the most important reason that most professionals don't practice as regular partnerships.

In contrast, if your practice is a corporation, LLC, or LLP, you won't be personally liable for malpractice by your fellow co-owners (or employees) as long as you weren't personally involved in the alleged wrongdoing. Many states require that certain types of professionals have malpractice insurance to obtain this limited liability. The rules vary from state to state—you should learn yours.

> **EXAMPLE:** Louis is a doctor involved in an incorporated medical practice with Susan and Florence. One of Louis's patients claims he committed malpractice and sues Louis personally and also sues the group. While both the group and Louis can be held liable, the other doctors in the group, Susan and Florence, cannot be held personally liable for Louis's malpractice. This means their personal assets are not at risk.

Thus, if you're involved in a group practice with other professionals, it's *highly advisable* to form a limited liability entity. You don't want to be held personally liable for someone else's malpractice.

On the other hand, if you practice alone, a limited liability entity won't help you at all when it comes to malpractice liability, because there is no co-owner whose malpractice you need to be insulated from.

3.   Liability for Business Debts

In addition to liability for malpractice, you could be personally liable for debts incurred by your practice.

Sole Proprietors and Partnerships

When you're a sole proprietor, you are personally liable for all the debts of your business. This means that a business creditor—a person or company to whom you owe money for items you use in your inventing business—can go after all your assets, both business and personal. This may include, for example, your personal bank accounts, stocks, your car, and even your house. Similarly, a personal creditor—a person or company to whom you owe money for personal items—can go after your business assets, such as business bank accounts and equipment.

Partners are personally liable for all partnership debts and lawsuits, the same as sole proprietors. However, partnership creditors are required to proceed first against the partnership property. If there isn't enough to satisfy the debts, they can then go after the partners' personal property.

In addition, each partner is deemed to be the agent of the partnership when conducting partnership business in the usual way. This means you'll be personally liable for partnership debts your partners incur while carrying on partnership business, whether you knew about them or not.

Limited Liability Entities

Corporations and LLCs were created to enable people to invest in businesses without risking all their personal assets if the business failed or became unable to pay its debts. (In some states, LLPs provide no protection at all against partnership debts; in others, they provide the same protection as an LLC or corporation.)

If you're talking about a large corporation or LLC, then limited liability for debts really does exist. For example, if you buy stock in Microsoft, you don't have to worry about Microsoft's creditors suing you. But it usually doesn't work that way for small corporations or small LLCs— especially newly established ones without a track record of profits and good credit history.

Major creditors, such as banks, don't want to be left holding the bag if your business goes under. To help ensure payment, they will want to be able to go after your personal assets as well as your business assets. As a result, if you've formed a corporation or LLC, they will demand that you personally guarantee business loans, credit cards, or other extensions of credit—that is, sign a legally enforceable document pledging your personal assets to pay the debt if your business assets fall short. This means that you will be personally liable for the debt, just as if you were a sole proprietor or partner.

Not only do banks and other lenders universally require personal guarantees, other creditors do as well. For example, you may be required to personally guarantee payment of your office lease and even leases for expensive equipment. Standard forms used by suppliers often contain personal guarantee provisions making you personally liable when your company buys equipment and similar items.

You can avoid having to pledge a personal guarantee for some business debts. These will most likely be routine and small debts. But, of course, once someone gets wise to the fact that your business is not paying its bills, they won't extend you any more credit. If you don't pay your bills and obtain a bad credit rating, no one may be willing to let you buy things for your business on credit. Other creditors might be careless and not require a personal guarantee.

Piercing the Corporate Veil

Another way you can be personally liable even though you've formed a corporation is through a legal doctrine called "piercing the corporate veil." Under this legal rule, courts disregard the corporate entity and hold its owners personally liable for any harm done by the corporation *and* for corporate debts. Corporate owners are in danger of having their corporation pierced if they treat the corporation as their "alter ego," rather than as a separate legal entity—for example, they fail to contribute money to the corporation or issue stock, they take corporate funds or assets for personal use, they commingle corporate and personal funds, or they fail to observe corporate formalities such as keeping minutes and holding board meetings. The same type of piercing can probably be used against LLC owners.

---

4. Other Types of Liability

Malpractice and business debts aren't the only type of liability you need to be worried about. Other forms of liability include:

- Premises liability: responsibility for injuries or damages that occur at your office or other place of business.
- Infringement liability: when someone claims that you have infringed on a patent, copyright, trademark, or trade secret.
- Employer liability: liability for injuries or damages caused by an employee while he or she was working for you.

If you're a sole proprietor or partner in a partnership, you'll be personally liable for these types of lawsuits. Theoretically, you're not personally liable if you form a corporation or LLC. (In some states, LLPs are also supposed to provide protection from these types of liability; in others, they protect only against malpractice liability by others in your practice.)

However, remember that you're always personally liable for your own negligence or intentional wrongdoing. You can be personally liable under a negligence theory for all the different types of lawsuits outlined above. Here are some examples of how you could be sued personally even though you've formed a corporation, LLC, or LLP:

- An employee accidentally injures someone while running an errand for you. The injured person sues you personally for damages claiming you negligently hired, trained, and/or supervised the employee.
- Someone sues you, claiming you've infringed upon a patent, trade secret, or copyright. Even if you've formed a corporation or LLC, you can be personally liable for such claims.
- The person in charge of your payroll fails to properly withhold and pay income and Social Security taxes for your employees. You can be personally liable even if you weren't personally involved.

In all these cases, forming a corporation, LLC, or LLP will prove useless to protect you from personal liability.

5.   The Role of Insurance

If incorporating or forming an LLC or LLP won't relieve you of all your personal liability, what are you supposed to do to protect yourself from business-related lawsuits? There's a very simple answer: get insurance. Your insurer will defend you in such lawsuits and pay any settlements or damage awards up to your policy limits. This is what all wise business owners do, whether they are sole proprietors, partners, LLP owners, LLC members, or corporation owners. Liability and many other forms of business insurance are available to protect you from the types of lawsuits described above. Liability insurance premiums are deductible as a business expense.

Note carefully, however, that insurance won't protect you from liability for business debts—for example, if you fail to pay back a loan or default on a lease. This is where bankruptcy comes in.

Type of Entity	Limited Liability Against Lawsuits?	Limited Liability Against Debts?
Sole Proprietorship	No	No
Partnership	No	No
LLC	Yes	Yes
LLP	Yes	Maybe
Corporation	Yes	Yes

C. The Four Ways Business Entities Are Taxed

Businesses are not all taxed alike. There are four different types of tax treatment available:

- sole proprietorship tax treatment
- partnership tax treatment
- S corporation tax treatment, and
- C corporation tax treatment.

You get to choose which type of tax treatment you want. This is one of the most important business decisions you'll ever make because there are big differences among the available choices. For example, if you choose S or C corporation treatment, you'll be your practice's employee and have to have your income and Social Security taxes withheld from your salary. In contrast, you're not an employee if your practice receives sole proprietorship or partnership tax treatment. Nothing is withheld from your pay, so you'll have to pay estimated taxes four times a year. There are also important differences as to how profits can be allocated among a group practice's owners, how losses can be deducted, and even the likelihood of an IRS audit. These and other differences are compared in Section D, below. First, you need to understand how the different forms of tax treatment work.

1. Tax Treatment Choices

Whenever a business entity is created or comes into existence, it automatically receives a form of tax treatment by default. However, except for sole proprietorships, business entities have some leeway to change from their default treatment to another type of tax treatment.

A multiowner LLC, LLP, or partnership is automatically taxed as a partnership by default, but may choose to be taxed as a C corporation or S corporation. This is easily accomplished by filing a document called an election with the IRS. Once this is done, as far as the IRS is concerned, the LLC, LLP, or partnership is now the same as a corporation and it files the tax forms for that type of entity. However, the great majority of LLCs, LLPs, and partnerships stick with their default partnership tax treatment.

Corporations are taxed as C corporations by default, but may change to S corporation tax treatment by filing an S corporation election. This is extremely common. A one-owner LLC is taxed as a sole proprietorship by default but can elect to be taxed as a C or S corporation by filing an election. This is not common, however. The sole proprietorship is the only entity that can't change its tax treatment—it must retain the sole proprietorship taxation treatment that it receives by default.

The table below shows all the choices available for each type of entity.

Type of Entity	Tax Treatment Choices
Sole proprietorship	Sole proprietorship taxation (default treatment)
Partnership, LLP, multiowner LLC	Partnership taxation (default treatment); or C corporation taxation; or S corporation taxation
One-owner LLC	Sole proprietorship taxation (default treatment); or C corporation taxation; or S corporation taxation
Corporation	C corporation taxation (default treatment); or S corporation taxation

2. Sole Proprietorship Taxation

When you're a sole proprietor (or single-member LLC with sole proprietor tax treatment), you and your business are one and the same for tax purposes. Sole proprietorships don't pay taxes or file tax returns. Instead, you must report the income you earn or losses you incur on your own personal tax return (IRS Form 1040). If you earn a profit, the money is added to any other income you have—for example, interest income or your spouse's income if you're married and file a joint tax return—and that total is taxed.

Although you are taxed on your total income regardless of its source, the IRS still wants to know about the profitability of your business. To show whether you have a profit or loss from your sole proprietorship, you must file IRS Schedule C, *Profit or Loss From Business*, with your tax return. On this form, you list all your business income and deductible expenses. If you have more than one business, you must file a separate Schedule C for each one.

> **EXAMPLE:** Irina is a sole proprietor dentist with no one else in her practice. This year, she had $250,000 in dental income and $150,000 in expenses, giving her a $100,000 profit. She files Schedule C with her personal tax return (IRS Form 1040) listing the expenses and income from her practice. She reports her $100,000 profit on her Form 1040 and pays personal income tax on it, as well as Social Security and Medicare taxes. To figure her taxes, she adds her dental income to any other taxable income she has for the year—for example, investment income—and pays taxes on it at personal tax rates.

Sole proprietors must use the sole proprietor form of taxation. If a sole proprietor wants a different type of tax treatment, he must form a business entity such as a corporation or LLC.

In addition, LLCs with one owner are automatically treated like sole proprietorships for tax purposes. However, they have the option of switching to a C or S corporation taxation.

3.   Partnership Taxation

The next basic form of business taxation is partnership taxation. This form of taxation applies to partnerships, LLPs, and multimember LLCs. When they are first formed, these entities all automatically use partnership taxation; and the great majority continues to use it throughout their existence. However, they have the option to switch to other forms of taxation.

Under partnership tax treatment, the business entity is a "pass through" entity for tax purposes—that is, it ordinarily pays no taxes itself. Instead, the profits, losses, deductions, and tax credits of the business are passed through the business to the owner's individual tax returns. If the business has a profit, the owners pay income tax on their ownership share on their individual returns at their individual income tax rates. If the business incurs a loss, it is likewise shared among the owners who may deduct it from other income on their individual returns, subject to certain limitations.

Unlike a sole proprietorship, a partnership is considered to be separate from the partners for the purposes of computing income and deductions. The partnership files its own tax return on IRS Form 1065. Form 1065 is not used to pay taxes; rather, it is an "information return" that informs the IRS of the partnership's income, deductions, profits, losses, and tax credits for the year. Form 1065 also includes a separate part called Schedule K-1 in which the partnership lists each partner's share of the items listed on Form 1065. A separate Schedule K-1 must be provided to each partner. Each partner reports on his individual tax return (Form 1040) his share of the partnership's net profit or loss as shown on Schedule K-1. Ordinary business income or loss is reported on Schedule E, *Supplemental Income or Loss*. However, certain items must be reported on other Schedules—for example, capital gains and losses must be reported on Schedule D and charitable contributions on Schedule A.

> **EXAMPLE:** Irina decides to join her dental practice with her friend Leo's dental practice. They practice together as general partners. The partnership earns $500,000 in income in one year and has $200,000 in deductible expenses. The $300,000 annual profit the partnership earns is passed through the partnership to Leo and Irina's individual tax returns—each gets 50% of the profit or $150,000. They each must pay personal income tax on their share of the profits. Their profit is added to any other income they have and is taxed at their individual tax rates.

4.   S Corporation Taxation

S corporations are taxed much like partnerships. Like a partnership, an S corporation is a pass through entity—income and losses pass through the corporation to the owners' personal tax returns.

S corporations also report their income and deductions much like partnerships. An S corporation files an information return (Form 1120S) reporting the corporation's income, deductions, profits, losses, and tax credits for the year. Like partners, shareholders must be provided a Schedule K-1 listing their shares of the items on the corporation's Form 1120S. The shareholders file Schedule E with their personal tax returns (Form 1040) showing their share of corporation income or losses.

No business entity starts out with the S corporation form of taxation. Instead, you must obtain it by filing an election with the IRS. The most common way to obtain S corporation taxation is to form a regular C corporation and then file an election to be taxed as an S corporation with the IRS. This simply involves filing IRS Form 2253 with the IRS. However, S corporation status is allowed only if:

- the corporation has no more than 100 shareholders
- none of the corporation's shareholders are nonresident aliens—that is, noncitizens who don't live in the United States
- the corporation has only one class of stock—for example, there can't be preferred stock giving some shareholders special rights, and
- none of the corporation's shareholders are other corporations or partnerships.

These restrictions apply whether you form a C corporation and change it to an S corporation, or form an LLC, LLP, or partnership and elect S corporation tax treatment. They do not pose a problem for the vast majority of professionals.

The other way to obtain S corporation status is to form a partnership, LLP, or LLC and file an S corporation election with the IRS. This isn't usually done because professionals who have LLCs, LLPs, or partnerships usually prefer their default partnership tax treatment. However, if you already have an LLC, LLP, or partnership, and S corporation tax treatment sounds attractive to you, you should consider filing an S corporation election. But see a tax professional before making this important decision. (See Section E.)

5.   C Corporation Taxation

Under the C corporation form of taxation, the business is treated as a separate taxpaying entity. Profits and losses do not pass through to the owners' individual tax returns as they do with the sole proprietorship, partnership, and S corporation forms of taxation. Instead, C corporations must pay income taxes on their net income and file their own tax returns with the IRS using Form 1120 or Form 1120-A.

In effect, when one or more professionals form a C corporation, they create two or more separate taxpayers—the corporation and themselves, the shareholders. This separate tax identity has both advantages and disadvantages.

A C corporation pays income tax only on its net profit for the tax year, and it pays this at its own corporate tax rates, not the personal tax rates of its owners. It gets to deduct from its income all of its ordinary and necessary business expenses, including employee salaries, most fringe benefits, bonuses, and operating expenses like office rent. However, dividends distributed to the shareholders are not deductible (which, in theory, can lead to double taxation—see Section D2).

C corporation shareholders don't pay personal income tax on income the incorporated business earns until it is distributed to them (as individual income) in the form of salary, bonuses, or dividends. They also don't get to deduct the corporation's business expenses on their personal returns. They belong to the corporation.

> **EXAMPLE:** Bill forms a C corporation—Bill, Inc.—to own and operate his medical practice. He owns all the stock in the corporation. The corporation takes in $500,000 in income. It pays out $300,000 in operating expenses and salaries for Bill's employees, and pays Bill a $100,000 salary. Bill, Inc. had a net profit for the year of $100,000 ($500,000 income − $400,000 expenses = $100,000 net profit.) It must pay taxes on its profit at the applicable corporate tax rate. Bill, Inc. files its own tax return and pays the tax from its own funds. Bill, the individual and employee of Bill, Inc., must file his own personal income tax return and pay income taxes on his $100,000 salary at individual income tax rates.

All corporations are initially taxed as C corporations and stay that way unless they file an election to be taxed as an S corporation with the IRS. In addition, partnerships, LLPs, and LLCs can elect to be taxed like C corporations. This is not commonly done, but is an option you should consider if you already have an LLC, LLP, or partnership and would like to obtain the benefits of C corporation tax treatment without going to the trouble of actually forming a corporation. See a tax professional first, however, because once you choose C corporation treatment it may be prohibitively expensive to switch back. (See Section E.)

D. Comparing Tax Treatments

No single type of tax treatment is best for every professional. To help you intelligently choose the tax treatment for your practice, this section compares how the four tax treatments differ in nine crucial areas:

- tax deductions
- tax rates
- owners' employment status
- fringe benefits
- allocating profits and losses
- deducting business losses
- retaining earnings in the business
- state taxes, and
- IRS audit rates.

1. Tax Deductions

Does your form of taxation change the type of tax deductions you may take for your practice? Mostly, no. Tax deductions are largely the same no matter how a business is taxed. Any business may deduct the ordinary and necessary expenses it incurs, as well as take depreciation for long-term business assets. This covers almost all the deductions in this book.

However, some deductions differ for C and S corporations, as compared with sole proprietor and partnership taxation:

- C and S corporations need not pay tax on all or part of the dividends they receive from stock they own in other corporations
- C and S corporations get much better treatment for charitable deductions of inventory or scientific property (see Chapter 13), and
- there are major differences in the way capital gains and losses are taxed (see IRS Publication 544, *Sales and Other Dispositions of Assets*, for details).

In addition, C corporation employees need not pay tax on many types of fringe benefits, including health insurance and other medical benefits (see Chapter 16).

2. Tax Rates

Wouldn't it be nice if you could lower your tax rate by changing your tax treatment? Many business owners can do this (at least in part) by using C corporation tax treatment. Unfortunately, professionals are ordinarily not among them. Instead, most professionals end up paying income tax on their profits at personal tax rates no matter what form of tax treatment they choose. For this reason, tax rates are usually not an important consideration when professionals choose their tax treatment.

If your practice has sole proprietorship, partnership, or S corporation tax treatment, you are taxed on any profits you receive from the business at your personal income tax rate.

The 2005 personal income tax rates are listed in the following chart (they are adjusted each year to account for inflation).

2005 Federal Personal Income Tax Brackets		
Tax Bracket	Income If Single	Income If Married Filing Jointly
10%	Up to $7,300	Up to $14,600
15%	$7,301 to $29,700	$14,601 to $59,400
25%	$29,701 to $71,950	$59,401 to $119,950
28%	$71,951 to $150,150	$119,951 to $182,800
33%	$150,151 to $326,450	$182,801 to $326,450
35%	All over $326,450	All over $326,450

C corporations have their own income tax rates (shown in the chart below). At certain income levels, these rates are lower than those for individuals—for example, a single individual must pay a 28% tax on income from $71,951 to $100,000, while a C corporation pays only a 25% tax on this amount. C corporations have these lower rates to help them keep money in the business for expansion purposes. If you can use these lower corporate rates, it can be advantageous to keep profits in the corporation rather than paying them to yourself in the form of salary, bonus, or fringe benefits.

| Regular C Corporation Income Tax Rates ||
Taxable Income	Tax Rate
Up to $50,000	15%
$50,001-$100,000	25%
$100,001-$335,000	34%
$335,001-$10,000,000	39%
$10,000,001-$15,000,000	35%
$15,000,001-$18,333,333	38%
All over $18,333,333	35%

Few professionals are able to take advantage of these C corporation tax rates. Instead, professionals with C corporations ordinarily make sure that their corporations pay little or no tax at all and instead pay income tax only on their employee compensation at their personal tax rates. There are two reasons for this:

- the 35% flat tax rate for personal service corporations, and
- double taxation.

Both issues are discussed in detail below.

Personal Service Corporations

Special tax rules apply to C corporations (or LLCs, LLPs, or partnerships that elect to be taxed as C corporations) owned by people engaged in occupations involving professional services. The IRS calls such corporations "personal service corporations," or PSCs. These corporations pay corporate tax at a flat rate of 35% on all their net income. The reasoning behind this rule is that professionals who form C corporations shouldn't have a tax advantage over professionals who have other types of business entities. Therefore, they must pay tax on all their income at the highest individual tax rate.

Personal Service Corporation Income Tax Rates	
Taxable Income	**Tax Rate**
All over $0	35%

EXAMPLE: The Walter Marvin Professional Corporation is a C corporation owned by Marvin. His company has a $100,000 profit for the year. It must pay corporate income tax on the whole $100,000 at the flat 35% rate because his corporation is a personal service corporation.

A C corporation will be classified as a personal service corporation if substantially all the stock is owned by corporate employees engaged in the following activities or professions:
- health services
- law
- accounting
- engineering
- architecture
- consulting
- actuarial science, or
- performing arts.

Health services include medical services provided by physicians, nurses, dentists, physical therapists, and other similar health care professionals. Veterinarians are included as well. (Rev. Rul. 91-30.) Consulting means getting paid to give a client your advice or counsel. You're not a consultant if you get paid only if the client buys something from you or from someone else through you. Thus, consulting does not include sales or brokerage services.

These categories include the great majority of C corporations formed by professionals. Fortunately, the vast majority of PSCs make sure their corporation has no net profit for the year by taking out any profits in the form of salary or bonuses (on which they pay tax on their personal returns at individual rates). Or, they have their corporation provide them with fringe benefits which are not taxable at all (see Section 4). Thus, few PSCs actually pay income taxes at the 35% rate. In fact, they usually don't pay any taxes at all.

The IRS can disregard your PSC status altogether if it determines that your principal purpose for forming the PSC was to obtain corporate tax benefits. (IRC § 269A(a).) If this occurs, the IRS can treat you as if you never incorporated for tax purposes and may reallocate income to you. You could also lose tax benefits you obtained by forming the PSC, such as tax savings from health and accident insurance plans, medical reimbursement plans, and employer pension plans.

This IRS rule is intended to prevent professionals from forming PSCs solely to obtain tax benefits. It applies, however, only to PSCs that perform services for just one client or patient. Thus, it's usually not an issue because most PSCs are formed to provide services to a large number of patients or clients.

> **EXAMPLE:** Sally is a medical doctor employed by Acme Hospital. Sally wants to obtain the benefit of a medical reimbursement plan, but Acme doesn't have one. So, she forms a professional corporation that she wholly owns and has it provide her, its only employee, with a plan. Sally has Acme hire her corporation, Sally, Inc., to work for it, instead of hiring her as an individual. Acme pays Sally, Inc., which then pays Sally, its employee. Sally works only for Acme Hospital. If Sally is audited, the IRS could disregard her corporation and treat her as a sole proprietor, thereby denying her the tax benefits she obtained through her corporation's medical reimbursement plan.

Avoiding PSC Status

To be classified as a PSC for IRS purposes, a C corporation must have:
- employees who spend 95% or more of their time performing health, law, engineering, architecture, accounting, actuarial science, performing arts, or consulting services, and
- stock that is at least 95% (by value) owned by employees who perform such professional services for the corporation. (Temp. Reg. §1.448-1T(e)(4),(5).)

One way to avoid having your C corporation classified as a PSC is to engage in more than one line of business. The corporation won't be a PSC if the second business requires at least 5% of the corporation's employees' time and doesn't involve one of the PSC services listed above. For example, one CPA firm avoided PSC status by purchasing its office building and carefully documenting that more than 5% of its employees' time was spent managing the building.

Another strategy (that is less likely to work) is to have 5% or more of the stock owned by people who are not corporate employees. For example, the owners might transfer some stock to their relatives to avoid the 95% threshold. However, in most states the stock in professional corporations may be owned only by the professionals who work for the corporation.

The rule may also apply to a professional who is a member of a partnership, LLC, LLP, or corporation and who forms a PSC which he substitutes for himself in the entity.

EXAMPLE: Andre is a dentist who practices in an LLC, with Tom and Mike. Andre wants to obtain tax-advantaged benefits that he can get only as an employee of a professional corporation. He forms a professional corporation and becomes its only employee. He then transfers his interest in the LLC to his corporation. The corporation is now part-owner of the LLC, not Andre personally. As Andre's employer, the corporation has Andre provide dental services to the LLC, and pays him a salary and benefits, such as a medical reimbursement plan. Because Andre is an employee, he need not pay income tax on these fringe benefits, and they may be deducted as a business expense by his corporation—making them tax free. This all sounds great, but the IRS could disregard Andre's corporation because (1) it's a PSC, (2) it performs all its services for one entity (the LLC), and (3) its principal purpose was to give Andre tax benefits he couldn't get otherwise (such as a medical reimbursement plan).

You can avoid any risk of having the IRS disregard your PSC status if you perform your services for more than one client or patient. For example, Sally from the first example above would have been safe had her PSC performed services for two or more hospitals at the same time. You can also avoid the rule if you can show the IRS you had a significant nontax reason for forming your PSC—for example, to obtain limited liability.

⚠️ **For PSCs, don't go it alone.** Be sure to consult your tax advisor before forming a professional corporation if it will be a PSC and you'll perform substantially all your services for one client or entity.

Double Taxation

If you're the owner of a C corporation (or choose that method of taxation for your LLC, LLP, or partnership), any direct payment of your corporation's profits to you will be considered a dividend by the IRS and taxed twice. First, the corporation will pay corporate income tax on the profit at corporate rates on its own return, and then you'll pay personal income tax on what you receive from the corporation. This is called "double taxation."

Income from dividends (payments of earnings from corporations to their shareholders) used to be taxed at ordinary income tax rates, which currently range from 10% to 35% (see the chart at the beginning of this section). Under tax changes that took effect in 2003, however, qualified dividends are taxed at a maximum of 15% for the years 2003 through 2008. Unless Congress acts again, the tax on dividends will rise to a maximum of 38.6% in 2009 and 39.6% in 2011. (For those in the 10% or 15% tax bracket, the tax rate on qualified dividends is 5%. In 2008, the 5% rate will drop to zero, but then will go back up to 10% in 2009.)

When you add the 15% personal tax on dividends to the 35% corporate income tax most professional C corporations must pay, you have a total 50% tax. Ouch! In practice, however, the effective tax rate is slightly lower than 50%.

> **EXAMPLE:** Al has incorporated his consulting business, which is taxed as a C corporation. He owns all the stock and is the company's president and sole employee. In one recent year, the corporation earned $150,000 in gross income. The corporation paid Al an $80,000 salary and had $20,000 in deductible operating expenses, resulting in a $50,000 profit for the year. Al had his corporation pay him the $50,000 in the form of a dividend. The $50,000 is taxed twice: First, the corporation pays $17,500 tax on it at the corporate rate (35% because Al's corporation is a personal service corporation). This leaves $32,500 of the $50,000 to distribute to Al. Al pays personal income tax on the $32,500 at the 15% dividends tax rate—a $4,875 tax. The total tax is $22,375. This amounts to an effective tax rate of 48%.

In real life, however, double taxation is rarely a problem for professionals who have C corporations (or LLCs, LLPs, or partnerships taxed that way). Ordinarily, you'll be an employee of your corporation and the salary, benefits, and bonuses you receive will be deductible expenses for corporate income tax purposes. If you handle things right, your employee compensation will eat up all or most the corporate profits so there's little or no taxable income left on which your corporation will have to pay income tax. In accounting parlance, the corporation's income is "zeroed out." You'll only pay income tax once—personal income tax on your employee compensation.

> **EXAMPLE:** Assume that Al from the above example has his corporation pay him $80,000 in salary and a $50,000 year-end employee bonus. He is paid no dividend. The corporation's total deductible expenses are now $150,000 ($80,000 salary + $20,000

operating expenses + $50,000 bonus = $150,000). The corporation's deductible expenses are equal to its $150,000 gross income for the year, leaving zero taxable income. As a result, the corporation pays no income taxes. Al must only pay personal income tax on his salary and bonus, just as any other employee would. The $50,000 distributed to Al as an employee bonus is taxed as ordinary income (not a dividend) at his marginal (top) income tax rate, which is 28%. Thus, Al only has to pay $14,000 in personal income tax on the bonus. Obviously, this is far less than the $22,375 in total corporate and individual income tax that would have had to been paid if the $50,000 distribution was a dividend.

When you own your own C corporation, whether alone or with one or more co-owners, you get to decide how much to pay yourself, and what form your payments will take. Obviously, you'll want to pay yourself enough to avoid double taxation. However, your decision about how much to pay yourself is subject to review by the IRS in the event of an audit. The IRS allows only corporate owner-employees to pay themselves a reasonable salary for work they actually perform. Any amounts that are deemed unreasonable are treated as disguised dividends by the IRS and are subject to double taxation. (See Chapter 16 for a detailed discussion of how much you can pay yourself when you are an incorporated professional-employee.)

Double taxation can become all too real for C corporations (or LLCs, LLPs, or partnerships taxed that way) that own assets that appreciate in value over time, such as real estate or patents. If a C corporation with such assets liquidates (goes out of business), the property must be treated as if it were sold by the corporation for its fair market value. The corporation must pay income taxes on the gain—that is, on the amount the property's fair market value exceeds its basis (cost). Moreover, if the property is distributed to the shareholders on liquidation, they will have to pay tax on the amount that the property's fair market value exceeds the tax basis of their shares. The same holds true if the property is sold and the money distributed to the shareholders.

EXAMPLE: Charles, Inc., is a C corporation solely owned by Charles, a podiatrist. The corporation has owned a small office building for over ten years. The building is worth $250,000, but has only a $50,000 basis. Charles liquidates his corporation and has it transfer ownership of the building to him. Charles's basis in his corporate stock is $75,000. He has a $175,000 capital gain he must pay personal income tax on ($250,000 building value – $75,000 corporate basis = $175,000 gain). His corporation has a $200,000 gain it must pay income tax on ($250,000 building value – $50,000 building basis = $200,000 gain). Thus, there is a double tax—to Charles and his corporation.

In contrast, the owners of an entity taxed as a partnership or S corporation can ordinarily distribute appreciated assets to themselves tax-free upon liquidation. This makes these tax treatments far superior for businesses that own assets that appreciate in value over time.

If you're a sole proprietor, you already personally own all your business assets, so the issue of asset distributions does not arise.

3.   Owners' Employment Status

Should you be an employee of your practice or a self-employed business owner? The answer to this question has important consequences because employees and self-employed people are treated differently for many tax purposes. Each type of employment status has its pros and cons; neither is best for every professional. You choose your employment status when you choose your tax treatment. If you choose S or C corporation tax treatment, you'll be an employee. If you choose any other tax treatment, you'll be self-employed. You should understand the ramifications of this decision before you make it.

Sole Proprietor and Partnership Tax Treatment

If your practice is taxed as a sole proprietorship or partnership, you are not an employee of your business entity. Instead, you are a business owner—also called self-employed. Your business doesn't have to pay payroll taxes on your income or withhold income tax from your pay. It need not file employment tax returns, or pay state or federal unemployment taxes. You need not be covered by workers' compensation insurance. All this can save hundreds of dollars per year.

However, you do have to pay self-employment taxes—that is Social Security and Medicare taxes—on your business income, called self-employment income by the IRS. This consists of a 12.4% Social Security tax on the first $94,200 in income in 2006, and a 2.9% Medicare tax on all self-employment income, no matter how much. Thus, a total 15.3% tax must be paid up to the ceiling amount. The Social Security tax ceiling is adjusted annually for inflation. These taxes must be paid four times a year (along with income taxes) in the form of estimated taxes. Self-employment taxes are equivalent to the total Social Security and Medicare tax (FICA tax) paid for an employee.

> **EXAMPLE:** Mel is a sole proprietor dentist. In 2006,his net self-employment income was $195,000. He must pay a 15.3% self-employment tax on the first $94,200 of his self-employment income, and a 2.9% Medicare tax on the remainder. His total self-employment tax is (15.3% x $94,200) + (2.9% x $100,800) = $17,336.

S Corporation Tax Treatment

As far as employment status goes, things work very differently for professionals who choose S corporation status. Although an S corporation is taxed much like a partnership, it is still a corporation—a separate legal entity. An S corporation shareholder who performs more than minor services for the corporation will be its employee for tax purposes, as well as a shareholder. In effect, an active shareholder in a corporation wears at least two hats: as a shareholder (owner) of the corporation, and as an employee of that corporation. If the corporation is small, as most professional corporations are, the shareholder/employee normally serves as an officer and director of the corporation as well. So, one person can be wearing four hats.

A shareholder/employee must be compensated for his services to the practice with a reasonable salary and any other employee compensation the corporation wants to provide. The shareholder/employee must report his S corporation's earnings on his personal income tax return, and pay his share of Social Security and Medicare taxes on any employee salary he's paid. The corporation must withhold federal income and employment tax from the shareholder/employee's pay, and pay state and federal unemployment taxes and Social Security and Medicare taxes on the employee's behalf.

The Social Security and Medicare tax rate for an employee is the same as for a self-employed business owner; however, it's paid differently. Half the total tax is deducted by the employer from the employee's pay, and half is paid by the employer itself. When you own the business that is paying these taxes, it makes no practical difference that half is paid by the employer—you are the employer.

> **EXAMPLE:** Assume that Mel (from the above example) has formed an S corporation of which he's the sole shareholder. Because he performs dental services for the corporation, he is its employee for tax purposes. In one recent year, the corporation paid Mel $195,000 in employee salary. The corporation withholds half of Mel's Social Security and Medicare taxes from his wages and pays the other half itself. The total tax is $17,336 just like when Mel was a sole proprietor.

Also, most states require that each employee be provided with workers' compensation insurance coverage. However, some states dispense with this requirement if the corporation has only a few employees. Unemployment insurance and workers' compensation coverage costs at least several hundred dollars per employee.

Clearly, being classified as an S corporation employee has many disadvantages for a professional. But it also has one potential big advantage: S corporation tax treatment can provide a way to take some money out of your corporation without paying employment taxes. This is because you do not have to pay employment tax on distributions (dividends) from your S corporation—that is, on earnings and profits that pass through the corporation to you as a shareholder, not as an employee in compensation for your services. The larger your distribution, the less employment tax you'll pay. The S corporation is the only business form that makes it possible for its owners to save on Social Security and Medicare taxes. This is the main reason S corporations have been, and remain, popular with professionals.

EXAMPLE: Assume that Mel's S corporation pays him only a $90,000 salary. The remaining $105,000 of the corporation's profits are passed through the S corporation and reported as an S corporation distribution on Mel's personal income tax return, not as employee salary. Because it is not viewed as employee wages, neither Mel nor his corporation need to pay Social Security or Medicare tax on this amount. Mel and his corporation only pay a total of $13,770 in employment taxes (15.3% x $90,000 = $13,770) instead of $17,336—a tax savings of $3,566.

If you took no salary at all, you would not owe any Social Security and Medicare taxes. As you might expect, however, this is not allowed. The IRS requires S corporation shareholder-employees to pay themselves a reasonable salary—at least what other businesses pay for similar services. (See Chapter 16, Section B, for a detailed discussion of what constitutes a reasonable salary.)

C Corporation Tax Treatment

When you form a C corporation (or choose that method of taxation for your LLC, LLP, or partnership) and actively work in the business, you become your corporation's employee, with the same tax consequences as described for an S corporation employee above. However, C corporation shareholder/employees can't save on taxes by paying themselves corporate distributions instead of employee salaries. This is because a C corporation is a tax-paying entity and cannot deduct distributions made to shareholders. Thus, it must pay corporate income tax on the distributions—ordinarily at a 35% rate (see Section D, above). Moreover, the shareholders must pay a 15% income tax on such distributions.

EXAMPLE: Assume that Mel (from the above examples) has a C corporation. It pays him $90,000 in employee wages and a $105,000 shareholder distribution. Mel and his corporation must pay $13,770 in employment taxes on Mel's wages (15.3% x $90,000 = $13,770), just like when Mel had an S corporation in the previous example. However, because it's a C corporation (and a personal services corporation), Mel's corporation must pay $36,750 in corporate income taxes on the $105,000 Mel left in his corporate bank account to be distributed to him as a dividend (35% x $100,500 = $36,750). The dividend is not deductible by the corporation as a business expense, and Mel must pay a 15% income tax on it. Only $68,250 was left to be distributed to Mel as a dividend after his corporation paid its taxes, so Mel must pay a $10,238 tax on the amount (15% x $68,250 = $10,238). The total tax on the $105,000 distribution is $46,988.

Had Mel paid himself the $100,000 as employee salary instead (for a $190,000 total salary), it would have been subject to a $2,900 Medicare tax, and $29,993 in personal income taxes. No corporate income tax would be due because the salary could be deducted by Mel's corporation as a business expense. The total tax on the $100,000 would only be $32,893

However, being a C corporation employee, instead of a self-employed business owner or S corporation employee, has significant tax advantages when it comes to fringe benefits.

4. Fringe Benefits

Fringe benefits are things like health, disability, and life insurance; paid vacations; a company car; and reimbursement of medical expenses not covered by insurance. This is the one major area where C corporation tax treatment is far superior to the other tax regimes.

C Corporation Tax Treatment

When you form a C corporation (or elect to have your LLC, LLP, or partnership taxed as a C corporation) and actively work in the business, you become your corporation's employee. Being a corporate employee, instead of a self-employed business owner, has significant tax advantages when it comes to fringe benefits. The tax law allows a C corporation to provide its employees with many types of fringe benefits which it can deduct from the corporation's income as a business expense. But the employees need not include the value of the fringe benefits in their taxable income, effectively making them tax-free. This can save many thousands of dollars in taxes. No other business entity can do this.

Possible tax-free employee fringe benefits include:

- health, accident, and dental insurance for you and your family
- disability insurance
- reimbursement of medical expenses not covered by insurance
- deferred compensation plans
- working condition fringe benefits such as company-owned cars
- group term life insurance, and
- death benefit payments up to $5,000.

EXAMPLE: Marilyn incorporates her optometric practice, of which she is the only employee. Marilyn's corporation provides her with health insurance and a medical reimbursement plan for uninsured medical expenses for her and her family at a cost of $10,000 per year. The entire cost can be deducted from the corporation's income for corporate income tax purposes, but is not included as income on Marilyn's personal tax return. In effect, no tax need be paid on the $10,000.

Sole Proprietorship, Partnership, and S Corporation Tax Treatment

Professionals taxed as sole proprietors, S corporation owners, and partners, may deduct 100% of their health insurance premiums from their personal income tax, including their own health insurance premiums and those for their spouses and dependents. But this is a special personal deduction, not a business deduction. Thus, it doesn't reduce their income for Social Security and Medicare tax purposes.

These professionals get no other tax advantaged fringe benefits. If the entity provides the owner with another type of fringe benefit, its value must be included in the owner's personal tax return and income tax paid on it. For example, if an entity taxed as a partnership provides an owner with disability insurance, the owner must include the value of the insurance in his taxable income for the year. But there is one way around this: the business owner can hire his or her spouse as an employee and provide the spouse with benefits. (See Chapter 11.)

 See Chapter 16 for a detailed discussion of fringe benefits for professionals who are taxed as C corporations.

5. Allocating Profits and Losses

Partnerships, LLPs, and LLCs taxed like partnerships (as most are) have a tax advantage when it comes to allocating profits and losses. Unlike corporations, they have great flexibility on how to allocate profits and losses among the owners. For example, one owner could get 75% of the profits and the other 25%, even though they are each equal owners of the LLC or partnership. Professionals involved in group practices find this flexibility very attractive because it allows them to be creative in fashioning their compensation. For example, partnership or LLC profits can be distributed according to each owner's collections or receipts, shared equally, shared according to each owner's percentage of ownership, based on complex formulas involving points or units, or based on a combination of methods—for example, distributions could be based partly on ownership percentages and partly on collections. Or, they can use a less rational approach: Partners or LLC members can simply get together at the end of the year and decide how much each person should get of the firm's net profits for the year. However, there are limits on how creative LLCs, LLPs, and partnerships can get. Complex IRS rules ("substantial economic effect rules") permit the IRS to disregard a partnership allocation of profits or losses if it's done only to avoid taxes.

You don't have the same flexibility with an S or C corporation. Any profits taken out of a corporation as dividends must be distributed to the shareholders in proportion to their ownership share. For example, if there are two shareholders and each owns 50% of the stock, they must each receive, and pay income tax on, a 50% share of any corporate dividend. The only way to provide disproportionate distributions is to pay some employee-shareholders more salary or other employee compensation than others. But there is a limit on how much employee compensation a C corporation shareholder/employee may reasonably be paid. And, it's preferable to pay S corporation shareholders as little employee compensation as possible to avoid employment taxes. (See Chapter 16.)

6.   Deducting Business Losses

Some professional practices lose money. Though this is not common, it can occur. How you can deduct these losses will depend on what type of tax treatment you have for your business. And though the problem of having losses doesn't occur often with professional businesses, the differences between the tax treatments and how you can deduct the losses is significant.

Sole Proprietorship and Partnership Tax Treatment

Just as income passes through a sole proprietorship or partnership to the owners' personal tax returns, so do losses. Thus, subject to some important limitations, losses from an entity taxed as a sole proprietorship (sole proprietorship or single-member LLC) or an entity taxed as a partnership (LLC, LLP, or partnership) can be deducted from any other income the owners have. They can even be deducted from income earned in prior years that has already been taxed, or saved up and used in future years. This makes sole proprietorship or partnership tax treatment ideal for a business that expects to lose money, which professionals just starting out sometimes do.

> **EXAMPLE 1:** Lisa holds a full-time job as an engineer. She decides to establish a part-time consulting business she operates as a sole proprietor. During her first year as a sole proprietor, she incurs $11,000 in expenses and earns $1,000 in consulting fees, giving her a $10,000 loss from her consulting business. She reports this loss on IRS Schedule C, which she files with her personal income tax return (Form 1040). Because Lisa is a sole proprietor, she can deduct this $10,000 loss from any income she has, including her $100,000 annual salary from her engineering job. This saves her about $4,000 in taxes for the year.

> **EXAMPLE 2:** Jack and Johanna are a married couple who file a joint income tax return. Johanna earns $80,000 a year from her job. Jack is a lawyer employed by an insurance company. He quits his job and starts his own legal practice. He forms a one-owner LLC, which

is taxed as a sole proprietorship. In his first year in business, his company earns $20,000 and has $40,000 in expenses. The entire $20,000 business loss passes through the LLC to Jack and Joanna's personal joint tax return. They subtract the $20,000 loss from their total taxable income for the year, which consists of Joanna's $80,000 salary. This leaves them with $60,000 in income for the year. Because they are in the 25% income tax bracket, they've saved $5,000 in federal income tax (25% x $20,000 = $5,000).

However, there are some limitations on the amount of losses an owner of an entity taxed as a partnership can deduct on his personal tax return. The most important limit is that the deduction for losses cannot exceed the owner's basis in a partnership, LLP, or LLC taxed like a partnership. "Basis" means your total investment in the business for tax purposes. In general, a business owner cannot deduct a loss that exceeds his cash contribution to the entity, plus income previously recognized from the entity, reduced by any losses or deductions that were previously deducted. Importantly, owners of entities taxed as partnerships may also add to their basis their share of all the entity's liabilities—loans and other debts—which can greatly increase their basis and allow them to deduct more losses.

EXAMPLE: Ralph and Norton, both chiropractors, decide they want to join their practices. They form an LLC taxed like a partnership. They each own a 50% interest in the LLC and equally share all partnership profits and losses. They each contribute $10,000 to the LLC. The LLC also obtained a $50,000 bank loan to cover its first-year operating expenses. Ralph and Norton each have a $35,000 basis in the LLC ($10,000 cash contribution + 50% of the $50,000 loan = $35,000). The LLC loses $50,000 the first year. Ralph and Norton may each deduct $25,000 of the loss on their personal returns. This leaves them each with a $10,000 basis. If the LLC loses $50,000 the next year, they will each be able to deduct only $10,000 of the loss, and will end up with a zero basis.

S Corporation Tax Treatment

S corporation shareholders (or owners of LLCs, LLPs, or partnerships taxed that way) may also deduct their share of business losses from their personal incomes. However, unlike owners of partnership tax entities, S corporations shareholders may not add S corporation liabilities to their basis. The only liabilities that may be added to an S corporation shareholder's basis are shareholder loans that the shareholder makes to the corporation. Thus, if Ralph and Norton from the above example had formed an S corporation, they each would have only a $10,000 starting basis and could deduct only that amount of their first year loss. As a result, partnership tax treatment has a big advantage over S corporation tax treatment when it comes to deducting losses.

C Corporation Tax Treatment

If a C corporation has a loss for the tax year, it is "trapped" in the corporation—it stays in the corporation and can only be deducted on the corporation's tax return. Losses do not pass through to the shareholders' personal returns as is the case with pass through entities. Thus, the shareholders don't get to deduct the losses from their personal income from other sources. This makes the C corporation form of taxation the worst possible for a money-losing business. However, few professionals incur losses, so this factor is usually not so important when choosing their tax treatment.

7. Retaining Earnings in Your Business

If you want to keep earnings in your business without paying personal income tax on those earnings, you will not want to choose partnership tax treatment. Each owner of a practice that is taxed as a partnership must pay taxes on her entire share of profits, even if the entity chooses to reinvest the profits in the business rather than distributing them to the owners. This results in "phantom income"—income you must pay tax on even though you never received it.

> **EXAMPLE:** Mario, Paula, and Ralph jointly own a group optometric practice organized as an LLC and taxed like a partnership. This

year, they had $300,000 in profits, which they share equally. They
would like to keep $100,000 of their profits in the business to help
purchase new equipment and a building for their practice. They are
free to do this, but they will still all be taxed on their full share of
the LLC's $300,000 profit, even though it is not distributed to them.
Thus, they each have to pay tax on $100,000—their individual
shares of the $300,000 profit—even though they actually receive
only $67,000 from their LLC and leave the remaining $100,000 in
their LLC bank account.

The same thing happens to sole proprietors. They pay tax on all their
business profits, even those they leave in their business.

C corporation tax treatment is the only form of taxation that allows
business owners to retain earnings in the business without having to pay
personal income taxes on them. This allows you to split the income your
business earns with your corporation. Unfortunately, income splitting
is not nearly as advantageous for professionals as it is for most other
business owners. This is because a professional corporation taxed as a C
corporation usually qualifies as a personal service corporation that must
pay a flat 35% income tax on all its income (see Section D, above). This
is equal to the top income tax rate for individuals. (Of course, this rule
also applies to LLCs, LLPs, and partnerships that choose to be taxed as C
corporations.)

Tax Savings Through Income Splitting

It is still possible to save some money through income splitting because
you don't have to pay Social Security and Medicare taxes on profits you
retain in a C corporation. These consist of a 12.4% Social Security tax on
salaries paid to employees, including yourself, up to an annual ceiling
amount ($94,200 in 2006), and a 2.9% Medicare tax on all employee
income. Whether you'll save money, and how much, depends on your
personal income tax bracket. If you are in one of the top two individual
tax brackets (35% or 33%), you have a combined 37.9% tax rate on your
employee compensation (35% income tax + 2.9% Medicare tax = 37.9%
combined tax). If you keep money in your corporation instead of taking
it out as employee compensation, the corporation will just have to pay

a 35% corporate income tax, so you save 2.9% in taxes. But, if your top bracket is 33%, you'll save only 0.9%.

> **EXAMPLE:** Betty, a single doctor, owns and operates an incorporated medical practice taxed as a C corporation. In one year, the corporation pays Betty a $350,000 salary, which placed her in the top 35% income tax bracket. After paying all its annual expenses, Betty's corporation is left with a net profit of $100,000. Rather than pay herself the $100,000 as an employee bonus, Betty decides to leave the money in her corporation and use it for future expansion. The corporation pays 35% corporate income tax on these retained earnings. Had Betty taken the $100,000 as a bonus, she would have had to pay a 35% personal income tax on it, plus she and her corporation would have had to split the 2.9% Medicare tax. Not having to pay the Medicare tax saved $2,900 (2.9% x $100,000 = $2,900).

Professional corporations in the fields of health, law, accounting, architecture, or consulting may keep up to $150,000 of their C corporation earnings in their corporate bank account without penalty. Professionals who don't practice in these fields may keep up to $250,000 in a C corporation. You can use this money to expand your practice, buy equipment, or pay yourself employee benefits, such as health insurance and pension benefits.

If you keep more than the $150,000 or $250,000 limit, you'll become subject to an extra 15% tax called the "accumulated earnings tax." This tax is intended to discourage you from sheltering too much of your corporation's earnings. However, you can avoid the 15% if you can show the IRS that the excess accumulations are held for reasonably anticipated needs of the business, not just to avoid taxes. In practice, though, few small corporations need to, or are able to, accumulate more than the $150,000 or $250,000 limit.

Personal Holding Company Penalty Tax

If five or fewer professionals own 50% or more of a C corporation's stock, it can become subject to the personal holding company tax. This is an extra 15% penalty tax on the corporation's income. The tax can be imposed if at least 60% of the corporation's undistributed income for the tax year is "personal holding company income." This is income derived from passive sources such as interest, royalties, dividends, and rents. Unfortunately for professionals, income from professional services can also be personal holding company income.

Amounts received for professional services are personal holding company income if:

- they are paid under a written or oral contract in which the client (rather than the corporation) can designate (by name or description) the particular employee who is to perform the services, and
- the designated employee owns 25% or more of the corporation's stock. (IRC § 543(a)(7).)

> **EXAMPLE:** Sally is the sole owner of her C corporation. Her company is hired by Acme, Inc., to perform consulting services. The contract specifies that Sally, and Sally alone, may perform the services. All the income Sally's company earns from the contract is personal holding company income. If all her corporation's personal holding company income for the year amounts to 60% or more of her company's total income, the 15% personal holding company holding tax will be triggered.

Many professional corporations meet the five-owner/50% ownership test and thus can be subject to the personal holding company penalty if they are not careful. (You can't get around the ownership test by giving corporate stock to other business entities or relatives.)

Fortunately, it's relatively easy to avoid the personal holding company penalty tax. First, you should make sure that no agreement you make with any client requires that the services be performed by any employee of your corporation who owns 25% or more of the company stock. It's also advisable to include in your client agreement a provision that your corporation, not the client, has the right to designate the person who will perform the services.

If you are considering incorporating your practice (or changing your LLC, LLP, or partnership to C corporation tax treatment), you should be careful about assigning your personal service contracts to your new corporation. It could trigger the personal holding company tax. Fortunately, the IRS permits newly incorporated businesses in this fix to avoid the tax in many cases by paying out a "deficiency dividend." However, the corporation will still be subject to interest and other penalty payments. It's wise for any professional who incorporates an existing practice to check with a tax professional to make sure they will not run afoul of the personal holding company penalty tax.

8.   State Taxes

Depending on where you practice, state taxes might be an important factor in your choice of business entity. Some states impose higher taxes on businesses than others.

All states, except Nebraska and South Dakota, impose corporate income based on the amount of taxable income earned in the state by the corporation. The rates vary from state to state. But some states also charge franchise taxes—for example, California exacts a hefty $800 "minimum franchise tax" per year after the first year a corporation is in business.

Most states tax sole proprietorships, partnerships, LLCs, and LLPs the same way the IRS does. The owners pay taxes to the state on their personal returns, and—the entity itself does not pay a state tax. But some states impose special taxes on pass through entities. For instance, California levies a tax on LLCs that make over $250,000 per year; the tax ranges from about $900 to $11,000. A similar tax is imposed on California S corporations. Illinois, Massachusetts, and Pennsylvania charge LLCs $200, $500, and $360, respectively, as annual report filing fees.

In addition, some states (including California, Delaware, Illinois, Massachusetts, New Hampshire, Pennsylvania, and Wyoming) impose an annual LLC fee that is not income-related. This may be called a "franchise tax," an "annual registration fee" or a "renewal fee." In most states, the fee is about $100; but California exacts an $800 "minimum franchise tax" per year from LLCs and LLPs as well. Before forming any business entity, find out what taxes or fees your state charges. You should be able to find this at the website of your state's secretary of state, department of corporations, or department of revenue or tax.

9.   IRS Audit Rates

Does how your business is taxed affect your chances of being audited by the IRS? The short answer is Yes! The following chart shows the most recently reported IRS audit rates for all types of businesses.

IRS Audit Rates		
	2003 Audit Rate	**2004 Audit Rate**
Sole Proprietors		
Income under $25,000	3.00%	3.15%
$25,000 to $100,000	1.33%	1.47%
$100,000 and over	1.47%	1.86%
Partnerships (includes most LLCs)	0.35%	0.26%
S Corporations	0.30%	0.19%
C Corporations		
Assets under $250,000	0.22%	0.18%
$250,000 to $1 million	0.63%	0.34%
$1 million to $5 million	1.50%	0.60%
$5 million to $10 million	3.25%	1.90%

This chart shows that sole proprietors have a much greater chance of being audited by the IRS than businesses operated through partnerships or corporations. In 2004, 1.86% of sole proprietors earning more than $100,000 from their business were audited. In contrast, only 0.19% of S corporations and 0.18% of C corporations with less than $250,000 in assets were audited. Thus, sole proprietors earning over $100,000 were ten times more likely to be audited than most corporations! A similar disparity holds true for partnerships.

Only corporations with assets worth more than $10 million were audited more often than sole proprietors. These statistics undoubtedly reflect the IRS's belief that sole proprietors habitually underreport their income, take deductions to which they are not entitled, or otherwise cheat on their taxes. Also, the IRS believes sole proprietors have greater opportunity to cheat on tax returns because they are often self-prepared. In contrast, tax returns for corporations, partnerships, and LLCs are usually prepared by tax professionals who know they can be punished by the IRS if they prepare a false return.

However, the IRS promises that audits for corporations and partnerships will increase in the next few years. Moreover, audit rates for all types of businesses are relatively low; so this factor alone probably shouldn't dictate your choice of business entity.

E. Should You Change Your Business Entity or Tax Treatment?

Neither your choice of business entity under state law, nor the tax treatment for your business under federal tax law, is engraved in stone. You can always switch to another form of tax treatment, another business entity form, or both. Indeed, many professionals start out as sole proprietors and then switch to a corporation, LLC, or LLP when they take on partners and want limited liability.

Whether you should make a change depends on what your goals are and what type of entity and tax treatment you have now. There is no business entity or form of tax treatment that is right for every professional.

The following chart can help you decide if you should convert to a different entity, or simply change your tax treatment (which is easier to do). For example, if you want limited liability, the chart shows that you must have a C or S corporation or an LLC or LLP (with any type of tax treatment). If you want to combine your limited liability with lower Social Security and Medicare taxes, you can choose an S corporation, or an LLC or LLP with S corporation tax treatment. If, instead, you want limited liability and maximum deductions for fringe benefits, you'll want a C corporation, or an LLC or LLP with C corporation tax treatment. But no entity will give you limited liability, lower Social Security and Medicare taxes, and maximum deductions for benefits.

Choice of Business Entity Decision Matrix

	Limited liability	Maximum deductions for fringe benefits	Reduce Social Security and Medicare taxes	Deduct business losses	Retain earnings in business	Reduce IRS audit chances	Simplicity and low cost
C corporation	✓	✓			✓	✓	
S corporation	✓		✓			✓	
Multiowner LLC or LLP with partnership tax treatment	✓			✓		✓	
LLC or LLP with C corporation tax treatment	✓	✓			✓	✓	
LLC or LLP with S corporation tax treatment	✓		✓	✓		✓	
Partnership with partnership tax treatment						✓	
Partnership with C Corporation tax treatment			✓	✓		✓	
Partnership with S Corporation tax treatment		✓			✓	✓	
Sole Proprietorship				✓			✓
One-Owner LLC with Sole Proprietorship tax treatment	✓			✓			

1.   The Cost of Converting to Another Business Form

As a general rule, unincorporated professionals will have little tax cost in converting to a sole proprietorship, partnership, LLC, or LLP. However, there can be exceptions. Thus, before doing such a conversion, you should consult a tax professional.

Converting to a corporation can be tax free if IRS rules are followed. (See IRC § 351.) However, in some cases, there can be serious tax consequences, particularly for professionals whose main business asset is their accounts receivable. Tax will be due if the business liabilities transferred to (or assumed by) the corporation exceed the owner's tax basis in the transferred business assets.

> **EXAMPLE:** Felix is a sole proprietor architect who decides to incorporate his practice. By far his largest business asset is his practice's accounts receivable—the money owed to him by his clients—which amounts to $100,000. However, under standard tax rules, he has a zero basis in such accounts receivable. His only other business asset is $10,000 in cash. He transfers the receivables and cash to the corporation along with $100,000 in liabilities. The amount of transferred liabilities exceeds the basis in his business assets by $90,000. Felix will have to pay tax on the $90,000 excess.

This result can be avoided with careful planning. For example, Felix from the above example could retain his accounts receivable and pay personal income tax on them as they are paid. Or, Felix could lend money to his dental practice prior to incorporation so that the basis in the transferred assets exceeds the amount of liabilities. Thus, it's essential that your tax advisor approve your incorporation plans before you file articles of incorporation to convert an existing sole proprietorship, partnership, LLC, or LLP to a corporation.

There are often significant tax costs if you want to convert out of a C corporation. Indeed, if you already have a C corporation, you may be stuck with it. To convert a corporation to a sole proprietorship, LLC, LLP, or partnership, it must be dissolved and its assets liquidated. Both the C corporation and its shareholders may end up owing substantial taxes when the corporation is dissolved. For example, the corporation may owe taxes if it owns assets that appreciated over its existence, such as real property. The shareholders may also have to pay income tax if the amount or cash value of the property they receive on liquidation exceeds their individual basis in their shares.

Dissolution isn't necessary when a C corporation is converted to an S corporation. But there could still be substantial tax problems—for example, collection of accounts receivable could be subject to double taxation. In addition, the S corporation may have to pay tax on "built-in gains" if it sells assets within ten years after electing S status. Built-in gains are the amount that the fair market value of the corporation's assets exceeded their tax basis when the S election was made.

> **EXAMPLE:** Jack and Jane, both chiropractors, organized their practice as a C corporation in 1996. In 2006, they had their corporation elect S status. The corporation owned a small office building. The building's basis was $200,000, but its fair market value in 2006 was $300,000. If the building is sold anytime before 2017, the corporation will have to pay a special 35% corporate level tax on its $100,000 built-in gain. Assume the building is sold in 2010 for $400,000. The corporation must pay a $35,000 tax on the built-in gain. Jack and Jill will then have to pay personal income tax on the remaining $165,000 of the $200,000 gain on the 2010 sale.

Again, consult a tax professional before converting a corporation.

 Refer to *LLC or Corporation?* by Anthony Mancuso (Nolo) for a good overview of the tax and other consequences of converting to a different business entity.

2. Changing Your Tax Treatment

As discussed above, it's possible to change the way your business is treated for tax purposes without changing your business form. This can be much cheaper and easier than converting to another business entity.

LLCs, Partnerships, LLPs

Partnerships, multiowner LLCs, and LLPs automatically receive partnership tax treatment when they are created. However, they can change to S corporation tax treatment or C corporation treatment. LLCs with only one owner receive sole proprietorship tax treatment when they are created. They can also switch to S or C corporation treatment. You do this by making an "election" to receive corporation tax treatment with the IRS.

Most businesses don't make this election because most LLCs, LLPs, and partnerships want to be taxed like partnerships (or sole proprietor-ships in the case of one-owner LLCs). However, you might choose to be taxed as an S corporation if you want to save on employment taxes. Or, you might want to be taxed like a C corporation because you want maximum deductions for fringe benefits.

If you want to make an election to change your tax treatment, you simply check the appropriate box on IRS Form 8832, *Entity Classification Election,* and file it with the IRS. The election can be made at any time. Once you file the form, your LLC, LLP, or partnership will be treated exactly like a C corporation by the IRS (most states also recognize the election for state tax purposes). You'll have to file corporate tax returns and will have all the benefits and burdens of C corporation tax treatment described above. If you want your LLC, LLP, or partnership to be taxed like an S corporation, you may do so by filing an S corporation election with the IRS, IRS Form 2553. But you must meet all the conditions for S corporation status to be treated as one (see Section C, above).

Your business will still be an LLC, LLP, or partnership for all other non-tax purposes. Thus, for example, a partnership will not provide limited liability to its owners even if it's taxed like a corporation by the IRS.

> **EXAMPLE:** Tony and Mitch, both Michigan orthodontists, co-own an LLC taxed like a partnership. They both decide they want to take advantage of the tax-free fringe benefits available to C corporations. There are two ways they can do this: (1) they can dissolve their LLC and form a new corporation in Michigan; or (2) they can simply file an election with the IRS to have their LLC taxed like a C corporation. They decide to do it the easy way and file the election. As far the IRS is concerned, the Tony and Mitch LLC is now a C corporation. It is a separate taxpaying entity and must file its own corporate tax returns. Tony and Mitch are now employees of their practice for tax purposes. They must have income and employment taxes withheld from their pay and they will be qualified to receive tax-free employee fringe benefits.

⚠ Electing a new tax treatment has the same tax consequences as converting to a different type of business entity. For example, a partnership, LLP, or multiowner LLC that elects corporation tax treatment is deemed to have liquidated for tax purposes and contributed all its assets and liabilities to the corporation in exchange for stock. (IRS Reg. 301.7701-

3(g)(1)(i).) This can have costly tax consequences as described above. The moral: Be sure to consult with your tax advisor before making an election to have your LLC, LLP, or partnership taxed like a corporation.

If it turns out you don't like your corporation tax treatment, you can change back to partnership tax treatment by making another election; but, you must ordinarily wait five years to do so. (Treas. Reg. 301.7701-3(c)(1)(iv).) Moreover, electing to change back to partnership tax treatment could result in added taxes because it will be treated as a constructive corporate liquidation for federal income tax purposes that can be taxable to both the liquidating corporation and its shareholders. Again, consult a tax advisor before making a change.

Corporations

Corporations also have the ability to change how they are taxed. All corporations automatically receive C corporation tax treatment when they are created. But a C corporation that meets the requirements may choose S corporation status by filing an election with the IRS as described above. It's also possible for an S corporation to revoke its S corporation status and return to C corporation tax treatment.

3. Automatic Conversion of Your Business Entity

In some cases, your business will automatically convert to one of the two default entities: the sole proprietorship or partnership. This can happen without you even knowing it. For example, if a sole proprietor starts to practice with one or more other professionals instead of on his own, he will automatically become a partner in a partnership unless the partners elect to form a corporation, LLC, or LLP. The new partnership will automatically receive partnership tax treatment.

Similarly, if a partnership, LLC, LLP, or corporation breaks up and all the former owners start to practice on their own, they will each automatically become sole proprietors and receive sole proprietor tax treatment.

If you don't want to be a sole proprietor or partner in a partnership, you need to take steps to form another entity. Ideally, you should do this before an automatic conversion occurs.

Chapter 3

Operating Expenses

This chapter covers the basic rules for deducting business operating expenses—the bread and butter expenses virtually every professional incurs for things like rent, supplies, and salaries. If you don't maintain an inventory or buy expensive equipment, these day-to-day costs will probably be your largest category of business expenses (and your largest source of deductions).

A. Requirements for Deducting Operating Expenses

There are so many different kinds of business operating expenses that the tax code couldn't possibly list them all. Instead, if you want to deduct an item as a business operating expense, you must make sure the expenditure meets certain requirements. If it does, it will qualify as a deductible business operating expense. To qualify, the expense must be:

- ordinary and necessary
- a current expense
- directly related to your business, and
- reasonable in amount. (IRC § 162.)

Your Practice Must Have Begun

You must be *carrying on* a business to have deductible operating expenses. Costs you incur before your practice is up and running are not currently deductible operating expenses, even if they are ordinary and necessary. However, up to $5,000 in start-up expenses may be deducted the first year you're in business, with the remainder deducted over the next 15 years. (See Chapter 10 for a discussion of start-up expenses.)

1. Ordinary and Necessary

The first requirement is that the expense must be ordinary and necessary. This means that the cost is common and "helpful and appropriate" for your business (*Welch v. Helvering*, 290 U.S. 111 (1933)). The expense doesn't have to be indispensable to be necessary; it need only help your business in some way—even if it's minor. A one-time expenditure can be ordinary and necessary.

> **EXAMPLE:** Connie, a dentist, buys a television set and installs it in her dental office waiting room so patients can watch TV while waiting for their appointments. Although having a TV set in her waiting room is not an indispensable item for Connie's dental business, it is helpful; some patients might choose Connie instead of another dentist because they can watch TV while they wait. Therefore, the TV is an ordinary and necessary expense for Connie's dental practice.

It's usually fairly easy to figure out whether an expense passes the ordinary and necessary test. Some of the most common types of operating expenses include:

- rent for an outside office
- employee salaries and benefits
- equipment rental
- legal and accounting fees
- car and truck expenses
- travel expenses
- meal and entertainment expenses
- supplies and materials
- publications
- subscriptions
- repair and maintenance expenses
- business taxes
- interest on business loans
- licenses
- banking fees
- advertising costs
- home office expenses
- business-related education expenses
- postage
- professional association dues

- business liability and property insurance
- health insurance for employees
- office utilities, and
- software used for business.

Generally, the IRS won't second-guess your claim that an expense is ordinary and necessary, unless the item or service clearly has no legitimate business purpose.

> **EXAMPLE:** An insurance agent claimed a business deduction for part of his handgun collection because he had to go to "unsafe job sites" to settle insurance claims, and there was an unsolved murder in his neighborhood. The tax court disallowed the deduction explaining, "A handgun simply does not qualify as an ordinary and necessary business expense for an insurance agent, even a bold and brave Wyatt Earp type with a fast draw who is willing to risk injury or death in the service of his clients." (*Samp v. Comm'r*, T.C. Memo 1981-1986.)

2. Current Expense

Only current expenses are deductible as business operating expenses. Current expenses are for items that will benefit your practice for less than one year. These are the costs of keeping your business going on a day-to-day basis, including money you spend on items or services that get used up, wear out, or become obsolete in less than one year. A good example of a current expense is your practice's monthly phone bill, which benefits your business for one month. In contrast, buying a telephone for your practice would be a capital expense (not a current expense) because the phone will benefit your business for more than one year. Other common capital expenses include cars, business equipment, computers, and real estate.

Current expenses are currently deductible—that is, they are fully deductible in the year in which you incur them. Because all business operating expenses are current expenses, they are also all currently deductible. However, the annual deductions for some operating expenses (notably home offices) are limited to the amount of profits you earn from the business in that year. (See Chapter 7 for more on the home office deduction.) Items you buy for your practice that last for more than one year (capital expense items) must be depreciated over several years or deducted in one year under § 179. (See Chapter 9 for more on deducting long-term assets.)

3.   Business-Related

An expense must be directly related to your practice to be deductible as a business operating expense. This means that you cannot deduct personal expenses. For example, the cost of a personal computer is a deductible operating expense only if you use the computer for business purposes; it is not deductible if you use it to pay personal bills or play computer games. If you buy something for both personal and business use, you can deduct only the business portion of the expense. For example, if you buy a cellular phone and use it half of the time for business calls and half of the time for personal calls, you can deduct only half of the cost of the phone as a business expense.

Many expenses have both a personal and business component, which can make it difficult to tell if an expense is business-related. Because of this, the business-related requirement is usually the most challenging factor in determining whether an expense qualifies as a deductible business operating expense.

Even the most straightforward costs can present difficulties. For example, it's usually easy to tell whether postage is a personal or business expense. If you mail something for your practice, it's a business expense; if you mail something unrelated to your business, it's a personal expense. But even here, there can be questions. For example, should a doctor be allowed to deduct the postage for postcards he sends to his patients while he is on vacation in Europe? (Yes—the tax court said the postage was deductible as an advertising expense; *Duncan v. Comm'r*, 30 T.C. Memo 386 (1958).)

The IRS has created rules and regulations for some of the more common operating expenses that often involve a difficult crossover of personal and business. Some of these rules help by laying out guidelines for when an expense is and isn't deductible. Others impose record-keeping and other requirements to prevent abuses by dishonest taxpayers. Most of the complexity in determining whether an expense is deductible as a business operating expense involves understanding and applying these special rules and regulations.

The expenses that present the most common problems (and are subject to the most comprehensive IRS rules and regulations) include:

- home office expenses (see Chapter 7)
- meals and entertainment (see Chapter 4)
- travel (see Chapters 5 and 6)
- car and truck expenses (see Chapter 5)
- business gifts (see Chapter 14)
- bad debts (see Chapter 14)
- employee benefits (see Chapter 12)
- interest payments (see Chapter 14)
- health insurance (see Chapter 11)
- casualty losses (see Chapter 14)
- taxes (see Chapter 14), and
- education expenses (see Chapter 14).

Through these rules and regulations, the IRS provides guidance on the following types of questions:

- If you rent an apartment and use part of one room as a business office, should you be allowed to deduct all or a portion of the rent as a business operating expense? How much of the room has to be used as an office (and for what period of time) for it to be considered used for business rather than personal purposes? (See Chapter 7 for information on the home office deduction.)
- Can you deduct the money you spend on a nice suit to wear to your office? (See Chapter 14 for information about deducting business clothing.)
- Can you deduct the cost of driving from home to your office? (See Chapter 5 for rules about deducting commuting expenses.)
- Can you deduct the cost of a lunch with a former client? Does it matter whether you actually talk about business at the lunch? (See Chapter 4 for rules about deducting meals and entertainment.)

4.   Reasonable

Subject to some important exceptions, there is no limit on how much you can deduct, as long as the amount is reasonable and you don't deduct more than you spend. As a rule of thumb, an expense is reasonable unless there are more economical and practical ways to achieve the same result. If the IRS finds that your deductions were unreasonably large, it will disallow them or at least disallow the portion it finds unreasonable.

Whether a deduction is reasonable depends on the circumstances, but certain areas are hot buttons for the IRS—especially car, entertainment, travel, and meal expenses. There are strict rules requiring you to fully document these deductions. (See Chapters 4, 5, and 6 for more on car, travel, and meal and entertainment expenses.) The reasonableness issue also comes up when a business pays excessive salaries to employees to obtain a large tax deduction. For example, a professional might hire his 12-year-old son to answer phones and pay him $50 an hour—clearly an excessive wage for this type of work.

For some types of operating expenses, the IRS limits how much you can deduct. These include:

- the home office deduction, which is limited to the profit from your business (although you can carry over and deduct any excess amount in future years) (see Chapter 7)
- business meals and entertainment, which are only 50% deductible (see Chapter 4)
- travel expenses, which are limited depending on the length of your trip and the time you spent on business while away (see Chapter 6), and
- business gifts, which are subject to a $25 maximum per individual per year (see Chapter 14).

B.   Operating Expenses That Are Not Deductible

Even though they might be ordinary and necessary, some types of operating expenses are not deductible under any circumstances. In some cases, this is because Congress has declared that it would be morally wrong or otherwise contrary to sound public policy to allow people to deduct these costs. In other cases, Congress simply doesn't want to allow the deduction. These nondeductible expenses include:

- fines and penalties paid to the government for violation of any law— for example, tax penalties, parking tickets, or fines for violating city housing codes (IRC § 162(f))
- illegal bribes or kickbacks to private parties or government officials (IRC § 162(c))
- lobbying expenses or political contributions; however, a business may deduct up to $2,000 per year in expenses to influence local legislation (state, county, or city), not including the expense of hiring a professional lobbyist (such lobbyist expenses are not deductible)
- two-thirds of any damages paid for violation of the federal antitrust laws (IRC § 162(g))
- professional accreditation fees, including bar exam fees, medical and dental license fees paid to get initial licensing, and accounting certificate fees paid for the initial right to practice accounting
- charitable donations by any business other than a C corporation (these donations are deductible only as personal expenses; see Chapter 14)
- country club, social club, or athletic club dues (see Chapter 4)
- federal income taxes you pay on your business income (see Chapter 14)
- certain interest payments (see Chapter 14).

C. Tax Reporting

It's very easy to deduct operating expenses from your income taxes. You simply keep track of everything you buy (or spend money on) for your practice during the year, including the amount spent on each item. Then you record the expenses on your tax return. If you are a sole proprietor, you do this on IRS Schedule C, *Profit or Loss From Business*. To make this task easy, Schedule C lists common current expense categories— you just need to fill in the amount for each category. For example, if you spend $1,000 for advertising during the year, you would fill in this amount in the box for the advertising category. You add up all of your current expenses on Schedule C and deduct the total from your gross business income to determine your net business income—the amount on which you are taxed.

If you are a limited liability company owner, partner in a partnership, or S corporation owner, the process is very similar, except you don't use Schedule C. LLCs and partnerships file IRS Form 1065, and their owners' share of expenses is reported on Schedule K-1. S corporations use Form 1120S. Each partner, LLC member, and S corporation shareholder's share of these deductions passes through the entity and is deducted on the owner's individual tax return on Schedule E. Regular C corporations file their own corporate tax returns.

■

Chapter 4

Meal and Entertainment Expenses

A professional practice isn't conducted solely in an office. Your most important business meetings, client contacts, and marketing efforts can take place at restaurants, golf courses, or sporting events. The tax law recognizes this and permits you to deduct part of the cost of business-related entertainment. However, taxpayers have abused this deduction in the past, so the IRS has imposed strict rules limiting the types of entertainment expenses you can deduct and the amount of the deduction you can take.

A. What Is Business Entertainment?

You may deduct only half of the total amount you spend on business entertainment activities. Because ordinary and necessary business activities are usually fully deductible, you want to be able to distinguish between regular business activities and entertainment.

The basic rule is that entertainment involves something fun, such as:

- dining out
- going to a nightclub
- attending a sporting event
- going to a concert, movie, or the theater
- visiting a vacation spot (a ski area or beach resort, for example), or
- taking a hunting, yachting, or fishing trip.

Although eating out might fall into other categories of business operating expenses depending on the circumstances, it is by far the number one business entertainment expense.

1. Activities That Aren't Entertainment

Entertainment does not include activities that are for business purposes only and don't involve any fun or amusement, such as:

- providing supper money to an employee working overtime
- paying for a hotel room used while traveling on business, or
- transportation expenses incurred while traveling on business.

In addition, meals or other entertainment expenses related to advertising or promotions are not considered entertainment. As a rule, an expense for a meal or other entertainment item will qualify as advertising if you make it available to the general public—for example, if a dentist provides free coffee and soft drinks to patients in his waiting room, the cost would not be considered an entertainment expense. These kinds of advertising and promotion costs are fully deductible business operating expenses (see Chapter 14).

2.   Meals Can Be Travel or Entertainment

A meal can be a travel expense or an entertainment expense, or both. The distinction won't affect how much you can deduct—both travel (overnight) and entertainment expenses are only 50% deductible. But different rules apply to the two categories.

A meal is a travel expense if you eat out of necessity while away from your "tax home" on a business trip (see Chapter 6 for more on your tax home). For example, any meal you eat alone while on the road for business is a travel expense. On the other hand, a meal is an entertainment expense if you treat a client, customer, or other business associate, and the purpose of the meal is to benefit your practice. A meal is both a travel and an entertainment expense if you treat a client or other business associate to a meal while on the road. However, you may deduct this cost only once—whether you choose to do it as an entertainment or a travel expense, only 50% of the cost is deductible (see Section C).

B.   Who You Can Entertain

You must be with one or more people who can benefit your business in some way to claim an entertainment expense. This could include current or potential:

- clients
- customers
- suppliers
- employees (see Chapter 15 for special tax rules for employees)
- independent contractors
- agents

- partners, or
- professional advisors.

This list includes almost anyone you're likely to meet for business reasons. Although you can invite family members or friends along, you can't deduct the costs of entertaining them, except in certain limited situations (see Section C).

C. Deducting Entertainment Expenses

Entertainment expenses, like all business operating expenses, are deductible only if they are ordinary and necessary. This means that the entertainment expense must be common, helpful, and appropriate for your practice. Taxpayers used to have to show only that the entertainment wasn't purely for fun, and that it benefited their business in some way. This standard was so easy to satisfy that the IRS imposed additional requirements for deducting these expenses.

Before the IRS made the standard tougher, you could deduct ordinary and necessary entertainment expenses even if business was never discussed. For example, you could deduct the cost of taking a client to a restaurant, even if you spent the whole time drinking martinis and talking about sports (the infamous "three-martini lunch"). This is no longer the case—now you must discuss business with one or more business associates either before, during, or after the entertainment if you want to claim an entertainment deduction (subject to one exception: see Section C4, below).

Who's going to know? The IRS doesn't have spies lurking about in restaurants, theaters, or other places of entertainment, so it has no way of knowing whether you really discuss business with a client or other business associate. You're pretty much on the honor system here. However, be aware that if you're audited, the IRS closely scrutinizes this deduction because many taxpayers cheat when they take it. You'll also have to comply with stringent record-keeping requirements. (See Chapter 20.)

1.   Business Discussions Before or After Entertainment

The easiest way to get a deduction for entertainment is to discuss business before or after the activity. To meet this requirement, the discussion must be "associated" with your practice—that is, it must have a clear business purpose, such as developing new business or encouraging existing client relationships. You don't, however, have to expect to get a specific business benefit from the discussion. Your business discussion can involve planning, advice, or simply exchanging useful information with a business associate.

You automatically satisfy the business discussion requirement if you attend a business-related convention or meeting to further your business. Business activities—not socializing—must be the main purpose for the convention. Save a copy of the program or agenda to prove this.

Generally, the entertainment should occur on the same day as the business discussion. However, if your business guests are from out of town, the entertainment can occur the day before or the day after the business talk.

> **EXAMPLE:** Mary and Jack are a wealthy couple seeking to build a fancy vacation home. They travel from their home in Boston to New York City to meet with Al, a well-known architect. The couple arrives on Tuesday evening and Al treats them to dinner at a nice restaurant that night. The following morning, Mary and Jack go to Al's office to discuss the building project and look at some preliminary designs. Al can deduct the dinner they had the night before as an entertainment expense.

You can get a deduction even if the entertainment occurs in a place like a nightclub, theater, or loud sports arena where it's difficult or impossible to talk business. This is because your business discussions occur before or after the entertainment, so the IRS won't be scrutinizing whether or not you actually could have talked business during your entertainment activity.

EXAMPLE: Following lengthy negotiations at a client's office, you take the client to a baseball game to unwind. The cost of the tickets is a deductible business expense.

The entertainment can last longer than your business discussions, as long as you don't spend just a small fraction of your total time on business. Thus, it's not sufficient simply to ask an associate "How's business?" You must have a substantial discussion. Also, your business-related discussions don't have to be face-to-face—they can occur over the telephone or even by email. If you have an email discussion, be sure to save the individual emails.

2.   Business Discussions During Meals

Another way you can deduct entertainment expenses is to discuss business during a meal at a restaurant. To get the deduction, you must show that:

- the main purpose of the combined business discussion and meal was the active conduct of business—you don't have to spend the entire time talking business, but the main character of the meal must be business
- you did in fact have a business meeting, negotiation, discussion, or other bona fide business transaction with your guest or guests during the meal, and
- you expect to get income or some other *specific business benefit* in the future from your discussions during the meal—thus, for example, a casual conversation where the subject of business comes up won't do; you have to have a specific business goal in mind.

EXAMPLE: Ivan, a sole proprietor consultant, has had ongoing email discussions with a prospective client who is interested in hiring him. Ivan thinks he'll be able to close the deal and get a contract signed in a face-to-face meeting. He chooses a lunch meeting because it's more informal and the prospective client will like getting a free lunch. He treats the client to a $40 lunch at a nice restaurant. During the lunch, they finalize the terms of a contract for Ivan's consulting services and come to a handshake agreement. This meal clearly led to a specific business benefit for Ivan, so he can deduct half of the cost of both his and his client's lunch as an entertainment expense.

You don't necessarily have to close a deal, sign a contract, or otherwise obtain a specific business benefit to get a deduction. But you do have to have a *reasonable expectation* that you can get some specific business benefit through your discussions at the meal—for example, obtaining a new client or investment in your practice.

No Deductions for Business Discussions During Other Kinds of Entertainment

As a general rule, you can't get a business entertainment deduction by claiming that you discussed business during an entertainment activity other than a meal. In the IRS's view, it's usually not possible to engage in serious business discussions at entertainment venues other than restaurants because of the distractions. Examples of places the IRS would probably find not conducive to serious talk include:

- nightclubs, theaters, or sporting events
- cocktail parties or other large social gatherings
- hunting or fishing trips
- yachting or other pleasure boat outings, or
- group gatherings at a cocktail lounge, golf club, athletic club, or vacation resort that includes people who are not business associates.

This means, for example, that you usually can't claim that you discussed business during a golf game, even if your foursome consists of you and three business associates. In the IRS's view, golfers are unable to play and talk business at the same time. On the other hand, you could have a business discussion before or after a golf game—for example, in the clubhouse. This might seem ridiculous, but it is the rule.

3. Entertaining at Home

The cost of entertaining at your home is deductible if it meets either of the above two tests. However, the IRS will be more likely to believe that you discussed business during home entertainment if only a small number of people are involved—for example, if you have a quiet dinner party. A larger gathering—a cocktail party, for example—will probably qualify as an entertainment expense only if you have business discussions before or after the event. (For example, you sign a contract with a client during the afternoon and invite him to your house for a large party with your business associates and family.) You can't, however, deduct the costs of inviting nonbusiness guests to your house (see Section B, above).

No Deduction for Lawyer's Birthday Parties

Every year, Joseph Flaig, a successful personal injury lawyer, held birthday parties for himself. He rented a banquet hall and invited over 1,000 people, including present and former clients and insurance adjusters. The guests were treated to a buffet dinner where champagne was served and an orchestra played dance music. Flaig claimed the $5,000 to $7,000 he spent on these parties was a deductible business entertainment expense because he engaged in brief chit chat with clients and potential clients and occasionally had them sign legal documents. The IRS and tax court disagreed. They concluded that the contacts Flaig had with clients at his parties were too insignificant to qualify as business discussions. The parties were primarily personal and social in nature, and therefore not deductible as entertainment expenses. (*Flaig v. Comm'r.*, T.C. Memo 1984-150.)

---

4. Entertainment in Clear Business Settings

An exception to the general rule that you must discuss business before, during, or after entertainment is when the entertainment occurs in a clear business setting. For example, this exception applies to:

- the price of renting a hospitality room at a convention where you discuss your services or products, or
- entertainment that occurs under circumstances where there is no meaningful personal relationship between you and the people you entertained—for example, you entertain local business or civic leaders at the opening of a new hotel to get publicity for your practice, rather than to form business relationships with them.

D. Calculating Your Deduction

Most expenses you incur for business entertainment are deductible, including meals (with beverages, tax, and tips), your transportation expenses (including parking), tickets to entertainment or sporting events, catering costs of parties, cover charges for admission to night clubs, and rent paid for a room where you hold a dinner or cocktail party.

You are allowed to deduct only 50% of your entertainment expenses, including taxes and tips. For example, if you spend $50 for a meal in a restaurant, you can deduct $25. You must, however, keep track of everything you spend and report the entire amount on your tax return. The only exceptions to the 50% rule are transportation expenses, which are 100% deductible, and certain meals for employees (see Section D).

If you have a single bill or receipt that includes some business entertainment as well as other expenses (such as lodging or transportation), you must allocate the expense between the cost of the entertainment and the cost of the other services. For example, if your hotel bill covers meals as well as lodging, you'll have to make a reasonable estimate of the portion that covers meals. It's best to try and avoid this hassle by getting a separate bill for your deductible entertainment.

1. Expenses Must Be Reasonable

Your entertainment expenses must be reasonable—the IRS won't let you deduct entertainment expenses that it considers lavish or extravagant. There is no dollar limit on what is reasonable; nor are you barred from entertaining at deluxe restaurants, hotels, nightclubs, or resorts.

Whether your expenses will be considered reasonable depends on the particular facts and circumstances—for example, a $250 expense for dinner with a client and two business associates at a fancy restaurant would probably be considered reasonable if you closed a business deal during the meal. Because there are no concrete guidelines, you have to use common sense.

2. Going "Dutch"

You can deduct entertainment expenses only if you pay for the activity. If a client picks up the tab, you obviously get no deduction. If you split the expense, you must subtract what it would have normally cost you for the meal from the amount you actually paid, and then deduct 50% of that total. For example, if you pay $20 for lunch and you usually pay only $5, you can deduct 50% of $15, or $7.50.

If you go Dutch a lot and are worried that the IRS might challenge your deductions, you can save your grocery bills or receipts from eating out for a month to show what you usually spend. You don't need to keep track of which grocery items you eat for each meal. Instead, the IRS assumes that 50% of your total grocery receipts are for dinner, 30% for lunch, and 20% for breakfast.

3. Expenses You Can't Deduct

There are certain expenses that you are prohibited from deducting as entertainment.

Entertainment Facilities

An "entertainment facility" is any property you own, rent, or use for entertainment—for example, a yacht, hunting lodge, fishing camp, swimming pool, car, airplane, apartment, hotel suite, or home in a vacation resort. You may not deduct any expense for the use of an entertainment facility, including expenses for depreciation and operating costs such as rent, utilities, maintenance, or security.

However, you can deduct out-of-pocket expenses that you incur while providing entertainment at an entertainment facility—for example, costs for food and beverages, catering, gas, and fishing bait. These are not expenses for the use of an entertainment facility itself. However, these expenses are subject to the requirements discussed in Sections B and C.

> **EXAMPLE:** Bill, an attorney, takes a valued client on an afternoon fishing trip. He rents a fishing boat and fishing equipment, and has a caterer provide a nice lunch for the trip. Bill may not deduct the cost of renting the fishing boat because it is an entertainment facility. But, if he has a business discussion with the client before, during, or after the trip, he may deduct his out-of-pocket expenses, including the cost of the catered lunch, fishing equipment, and bait.

Nonbusiness Guests' Expenses

You may not deduct the cost of entertaining people who are not business associates. If you entertain business and nonbusiness guests at an event, you must divide your entertainment expenses between the two and deduct only the business part.

> **EXAMPLE:** You take three clients and six friends to dinner. Because there were ten people at dinner, including you, and only four were business related, 40% of this expense qualifies as business entertainment. If you spend $200 for the dinner, only $80 would be deductible. And because entertainment expenses are only 50% deductible, your total deduction for the event is $40.

Ordinarily, you cannot deduct the cost of entertaining your spouse or the spouse of a business associate. However, there is an exception: You can deduct these costs if you can show that you had a clear business purpose (rather than a personal or social purpose) in having the spouse or spouses join in.

> **EXAMPLE:** You take a client visiting from out of town to dinner with his wife. The client's wife joins you because it's impractical (not to mention impolite) to have dinner with the client and not include his wife. Your spouse joins the party because the client's spouse is present. You may deduct the cost of dinner for both spouses.

Club Dues and Membership Fees

In the good old days, you could deduct dues for belonging to a country club or other club where business associates gathered. This is no longer possible. The IRS says you cannot deduct dues (including initiation fees) for membership in any club if one of the principal purposes of the club is to:

- conduct entertainment activities for members, or
- provide entertainment facilities for members to use.

Thus, you cannot deduct dues paid to country clubs, golf and athletic clubs, airline clubs, hotel clubs, or clubs operated to provide members with meals. However, you can deduct other expenses you incur to entertain a business associate at a club.

> **EXAMPLE:** Jack, a doctor, is a member of the Golden Bear Golf Club in Columbus, Ohio. His annual membership dues are $10,000. One night Jack invites another doctor in the community to dinner at the club's dining room where they discuss Jack buying his practice. Jack pays $100 for the dinner. Jack's $10,000 annual dues are not deductible, but his costs for the dinner are.

You can deduct dues to join business-related tax-exempt organizations or civic organizations as long as the organization's primary purpose isn't to provide entertainment. Examples include professional associations such as a medical or bar association, as well as organizations like the Kiwanis or Rotary Club, business leagues, chambers of commerce, and trade associations.

4.   Entertainment Tickets

You can deduct only the face value of an entertainment ticket, even if you paid a higher price for it. For example, you cannot deduct service fees that you pay to ticket agencies or brokers, or any amount over the face value of tickets that you buy from scalpers. However, you can deduct the entire amount you pay for a ticket if it's for an amateur sporting event run by volunteers to benefit a charity.

Ordinarily, you or an employee must be present at an entertainment activity to claim it as a business entertainment expense. This is not the case, however, with entertainment tickets. You can give tickets to clients or other business associates rather than attending the event yourself, and still get a deduction. If you don't go to the event, you have the option of treating the tickets as a gift. You can get a bigger deduction this way sometimes. Gifts of up to $25 are 100% deductible (see Chapter 14), so with tickets that cost less than $50, you get a bigger deduction if you treat them as a gift. If they cost more, treat them as an entertainment expense.

> **EXAMPLE:** You pay $40 to a scalper for a ticket to a college basketball game that has a face value of only $30. You give the ticket to a client, but don't attend the game yourself. By treating the ticket as a gift, you may deduct $25 of the expense. If you treated it as an entertainment expense, your deduction would be limited to 50% of $30 or $15. However, if you paid $100 for a ticket with a $60 face value, you would be better off treating it as an entertainment expense. This way you would be able to deduct 50% of $60 or $30. If you treated the ticket as a gift, your deduction would be limited to $25.

You may also deduct the cost of season tickets at a sports arena or theater. But, if you rent a skybox or other private luxury box, your deduction is limited to the cost of a regular nonluxury box seat. The cost of season tickets must be allocated to each separate event.

> **EXAMPLE:** Jim, an accountant, spends $5,000 for two season tickets to his local professional football team. The tickets entitle him and a guest to attend 18 games. He must allocate the cost game-by-game. If, during the course of the football season. He ends up giving tickets for nine games to clients and uses the others for himself and his wife: he may deduct 50% of the total cost as a business entertainment expense.

5.   Meals for Employees

Ordinarily, meal and entertainment expenses for your employees are only 50% deductible, just like your own meal and entertainment expenses. However, you or your practice may take a 100% deduction for employee meals:

- provided as part of a company recreational or social activity—for example, a picnic for your employees
- provided on business premises for your convenience—for example, you provide lunch because your employees must remain in the office to be available to work, or
- if the cost is included as part of the employee's compensation and reported as such on his or her W-2.

E.   Expenses Reimbursed by Clients

If a client reimburses you for entertainment expenses, you don't need to count the reimbursement that you receive as income as long as you give the client an adequate accounting of your expenses and comply with the accountable plan rules. Basically, this requires that you submit all your documentation to the client in a timely manner, and return any excess payments. Accountable plans are covered in detail in Chapter 17. If you comply with the rules, the client gets to deduct 50% of the expenses and you get 100% of your expenses paid for by somebody else. This is a lot better then getting only a 50% entertainment expense deduction. The reimbursement should not be listed by the client on any Form 1099-MISC a client is required to send to the IRS showing the amount paid to you for your services during the year.

> **EXAMPLE:** Philip, a sole proprietor marketing consultant, takes several people out to lunch to discuss ways to obtain publicity for a client. He bills his client $500 for the lunches and provides all the proper documentation. The client reimburses Philip $500. Philip gets no deduction for the lunches, but he also doesn't have to include the

$500 reimbursement in his income for the year; his client may deduct 50% of the expense as a business entertainment expense.

On the other hand, if you don't properly document your expenses, any reimbursement you obtain from your client must be reported as income on your tax return and should be included in any 1099-MISC form the client provides the IRS reporting how much you were paid (see Chapter 15). The client can still deduct the reimbursement as compensation paid to you. The client's deduction is not subject to the 50% limit because the payment is classified as compensation, not reimbursement of entertainment expenses. You may deduct the expenses on your own return, but your deduction will be subject to the 50% limit.

> **EXAMPLE:** Assume that Philip from the above example fails to make an adequate accounting of his meal expenses to his client, but the client still reimburses him for the full $500. The client may deduct the entire $500, and must include this amount in the 1099-MISC form it provides the IRS reporting how much it paid Philip during the year. Philip must include the $500 as income on his tax return and pay tax on it. He may list the $500 as an entertainment expense on his personal tax return, but his deduction is limited to $250.

If you obtain no reimbursement from your client, you can deduct the cost as a business entertainment expense on your own tax return, but your deduction will be subject to the 50% limit. You must keep adequate records of your entertainment expenses even if your client doesn't reimburse you for them.

F.   Reporting Entertainment Expenses to the IRS

How entertainment expenses are reported to the IRS and deducted depends on how your practice is organized and how the expenses are paid.

1. Sole Proprietors

If you're a sole proprietor, you must list your entertainment expenses on Schedule C, *Profit or Loss From Business.* The Schedule contains a line just for this deduction. You list the total amount and then subtract from it the portion that is not deductible—50%.

2. Partnerships, LLCs, and LLPs

If you've formed a partnership, LLC, or LLP, you can pay entertainment expenses from your business's bank account or by using a business credit card, or you can pay them from your personal funds or by using your personal credit card.

It's best, and simplest, to pay entertainment expenses with business funds or a business credit card. Expenses paid with partnership, LLC, or LLP funds are listed on the information return the entity files with the IRS, not your personal tax return.

If you pay for entertainment expenses with your personal funds or credit card, you can always be reimbursed by your practice. If you provide an adequate accounting and follow the accountable plan rules, the reimbursement will not be taxable income to you. Your practice deducts the reimbursement on its return, you don't list it on your personal return. Alternatively, you may be able to forgo reimbursement and deduct the expense on your personal return; but special requirements must be satisfied to do this. (See Chapter 17.)

3. Corporations

If you've formed a corporation and it pays for your entertainment expenses, the corporation deducts them on its own tax return. Things are more complicated if you personally pay for entertainment expenses, because you will ordinarily be your corporation's employee and special rules apply to expenses paid by employees. (See Chapter 17.)

Be Careful How You List Entertainment Expenses on Tax Returns

Unlike the Schedule C filed by sole proprietors, the tax returns filed by partnerships, LLCs, LLPs, and corporations do not contain a specific line to report the amount of deductible entertainment expenses. They should be listed as "meals and entertainment" on a separate "Other Expenses" schedule.

Be careful never to lump together expenses for meals and entertainment with other expenses such as those for business travel, lodging, or continuing education. Some taxpayers put all these expenses into a single expense category called "travel and entertainment." This is a mistake because, while meal and entertainment expense are only 50% deductible, expenses for business travel, lodging, and continuing education are 100% deductible. Both your financial statements and tax returns should use separate expense categories for "travel and lodging," "continuing education," "employee benefits," and "meals and entertainment."

Chapter 5

Car and Local Travel Expenses

That expensive car parked in your garage not only looks great—it could also be a great tax deduction. If, for example, you drive 10,000 miles per year for your practice, you can get a federal income tax deduction of at least $4,050 (based on 2005 rates). You might be able to deduct even more, depending on how you choose to deduct your car expenses.

This chapter shows you how to deduct expenses for local transportation—that is, business trips that don't require you to stay away from home overnight. These rules apply to local business trips using any means of transportation, but this chapter focuses primarily on car expenses, the most common type of deduction for local business travel.

Overnight trips (whether by car or other means) are covered in Chapter 6.

Transportation expenses are a red flag for the IRS. Transportation expenses are the number one item that IRS auditors look at when they examine small businesses. These expenses can be substantial—and it is easy to overstate them—so the IRS will look very carefully to make sure that you're not bending the rules. Your first line of defense against an audit is to keep good records to back up your deductions. This is something no accountant can do for you—you must develop good record-keeping habits and follow them faithfully to stay out of trouble with the IRS.

A. Deductible Local Transportation Expenses

Local transportation costs are deductible as business operating expenses if they are ordinary and necessary for your business, trade, or profession. The cost must be common, helpful, and appropriate for your business. (See Chapter 3 for a detailed discussion of the ordinary and necessary requirement.) It makes no difference what type of transportation you use to make the local trips—car, van, SUV, limousine, motorcycle, taxi, bus, or train—or whether the vehicle you use is owned or leased. You can deduct these costs as long as they are ordinary and necessary and meet the other requirements discussed below.

Attorneys may be barred from deducting advanced client costs. Your local travel costs might not be deductible if they constitute advanced client costs you incur while performing legal services for a client. See Chapter 17.

1.   Travel Must Be for Business

You can only deduct local trips that are for business—that is, travel to a business location. Personal trips—for example, to the supermarket or the gym—are not deductible as business travel expenses. A business location is any place where you perform business-related tasks, such as:

- the place where you have your principal place of business, including a home office
- other places where you work, including temporary work sites
- places where you meet with clients or patients
- the bank where you do business banking
- a local college where you take professional continuing education classes
- the store where you buy business supplies, or
- the place where you keep business inventory.

Starting a New Practice

The cost of local travel you do before you start your practice, such as travel to investigate starting your practice, is not a currently deductible business operating expense. It is a start-up expense subject to special deduction rules. (See Chapter 10 for more on start-up expenses.)

You don't have to do all the driving yourself to get a car expense deduction. Any use of your car by another person qualifies as a deductible business expense if:

- it is directly connected with your practice
- when required, it is properly reported by you as income to the other person (and, if you have to, you withhold tax on the income)—for example, where an employee uses your car for personal purposes (see Section F), or
- you are paid a fair market rental for the use of your car.

Thus, for example, you can count as business mileage a car trip your employee, spouse, or child takes to deliver an item for your practice or for any other business purpose.

2. Commuting Is Not Deductible

Most professionals have an outside office where they work on a regular basis. Unfortunately, you can't deduct the cost of traveling from your home to your regular place of business. These are commuting expenses, which are a nondeductible personal expense.

Commuting occurs when you go from home to a permanent work location—either your:

- office or other principal place of business, or
- another place where you have worked or expect to work for more than one year.

> **EXAMPLE:** Kim, a consultant, runs her business from an office in a downtown office building. Every day, she drives 20 miles to and from her suburban home to her office. None of this commuting mileage is deductible. But she may deduct trips from her office to a client's office, or any other business-related trip that starts from her office.

Even if a trip from home has a business purpose—for example, to deliver important papers to your office—it is still considered commuting and is not deductible. (You may, however, deduct the cost of renting a trailer or any other extraordinary expenses you incur to haul inventory or supplies from your home.)

Nor can you deduct a commuting trip because you make business calls on your cell phone, listen to work-related tapes, or have a business discussion with an associate or employee during the commute. Also, placing an advertising display on your vehicle won't convert a commute to a business trip.

Because commuting is not deductible, where your office or other principal workplace is located has a big effect on the amount you can deduct for local business trips. You will get the fewest deductions if you work solely in an outside office. You lose out on many potential business miles this way because you can't deduct any trips between your home and your office.

As explained below, you can get the most deductions for local business trips if you have a home office.

You Have a Home Office

If you have a home office that qualifies as your principal place of business, you can deduct the cost of any trips you make from home to another business location. For example, you can deduct the cost of driving from home to your outside office, a client's office, or to attend a business-related seminar. The commuting rule doesn't apply if you work at home because, with a home office, you never commute to work (you're there already).

Your home office will qualify as your principal place of business if it is the place where you earn most of your income or perform the administrative or management tasks for your practice. (See Chapter 7 for more on the home office deduction.) If your home office qualifies as your principal place of business, you can vastly increase your deductions for business trips.

> **EXAMPLE:** Kim (from the above example) maintains a home office where she does the administrative work for her consulting practice; she also has an outside office where she does her other work. She can deduct all her business trips from her home office, including the 20-mile daily trip to her outside office. Thanks to her home office, she can now deduct 100 miles per week as a business trip expense, all of which was a nondeductible commuting expense before she established her home office.

You Go to a Temporary Business Location

Travel between your home and a temporary work location is not considered commuting and is therefore deductible. A temporary work location is any place where you realistically expect to work less than one year.

> **EXAMPLE:** Sally is a sole proprietor engineer. Her office is in a downtown office building, and she does not have a home office. She is hired by Acme Corp. to perform consulting work. This requires that she drive to Acme's offices, 50 miles away from her home. The project is expected to last three months. Sally may deduct the cost of driving from home to Acme Corporation's offices.

Temporary work locations are not limited to clients' offices. Any place where you perform business-related tasks for less than one year is a temporary work location. This may include a bank, post office, office supply store, school, or similar places.

> **EXAMPLE:** Jim is an optometrist with his own practice and has no home office. One day he travels from home to his local lens supplier to pick up some lenses for his office. This is not commuting and is deductible.

However, a place will cease to be a temporary work location if you continue to go there for more than one year.

> **EXAMPLE:** Jim goes from his house to his lens supplier to pick up lenses every month, year after year. The lens supplier is no longer a temporary work location, and his trips there from home are nondeductible commuting expenses.

You can convert a nondeductible commute into a deductible local business trip by making a stop at a temporary work location on your way to your office. Stopping at a temporary work location converts the entire trip into a deductible travel expense.

> **EXAMPLE:** Eleanor's business office is in a downtown building. She has no home office. One morning, she leaves home, stops off at a client's office to drop off some work, and then goes to her office. The entire trip is deductible because she stopped at a temporary work location on her way to her office.

Keep in mind, though, that making such stops is necessary only if you don't have a home office. If Eleanor had a home office, the commuting rule wouldn't apply and the trip would be deductible with or without the stop.

Deductions for Local Business Travel

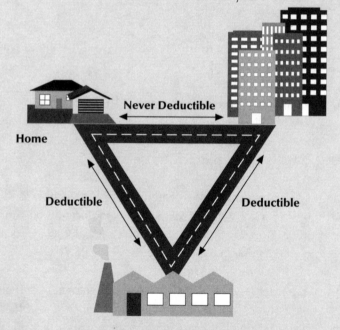

Office
Place you expect to work for more than one year

Home

Never Deductible

Deductible

Deductible

Temporary Work Location
If you have regular outside or home office, trips to and from home are deductible only if temporary work location is outside metropolitan area of home.

Business Mileage Self-Test

See if you can figure out how many business miles were driven in each of the following examples.

1. John, a salesman with no home office, drives 25 miles to his downtown office in the morning, works all day, and then drives 25 miles back home. After dinner, he drives 30 miles to meet a client and then drives directly back home that night. Total business miles _____.

   Answer: 60. The trip to and from home to his office is nondeductible commuting, but the trip from home to the client and back is deductible because the client's office is a temporary work location for John.

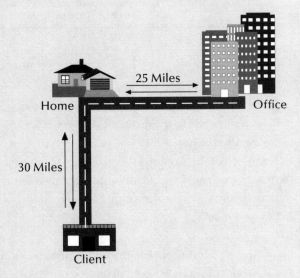

2. Sue is a freelance writer who works from home. She drives five miles to the grocery store and then heads off to the library five miles away to do research for an article. She then drives from the library back home, a distance of ten miles. Total business miles _____.

Business Mileage Self-Test (continued)

Answer: 20. This is a good example of how you can convert a personal trip into a business trip. Sue's trip to the grocery store isn't deductible, but her journey to the library is. Because the grocery store is en route to the library, she gets to deduct all ten miles (five to the grocery store; five to the library). It's ten miles back to her house from the library, so she gets a total of 20 business miles.

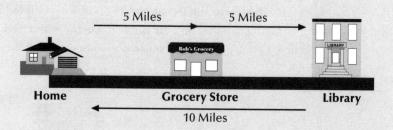

3. Nick is a bookie who works out of his car. One day he drives 20 miles from home to the racetrack. He then drives 15 miles from the track to the homes of three customers to make collections. At the end of the day, he drives ten miles to get back home. That evening, he drives 15 miles from home to the house of an associate for a business meeting and then drives back home. Total business miles _____.

Answer: 15. Because Nick has no fixed business location, he may not deduct travel from home to his first business location or back to home from his last business location. Thus, he cannot deduct the 20-mile trip to the track or the ten miles back home from the customer's house. Nor could he deduct the 30 miles round trip later that night from home to the business meeting. He can only deduct the mileage for the two middle collection calls that he made.

Business Mileage Self-Test (continued)

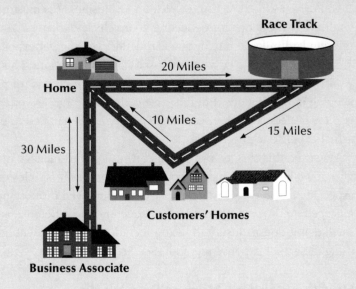

4. Gloria runs her home construction business from an outside office. She has no home office. One day she drives from home to a site 30 miles away where her company is building a house and then drives back home at the end of the day. The project is expected to last six months. Total business miles _____.

Answer: 60. Gloria is working at a temporary work location. Her travel from home to the building site is not considered commuting.

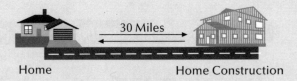

B. The Standard Mileage Rate

If you drive a car, SUV, van, or pick-up for business (as most people do), you have two options for deducting your vehicle expenses: You can use the standard mileage rate or you can deduct your actual expenses.

Let's start with the easy one: the standard mileage rate. This method works best for people who don't want to bother with a lot of record keeping or calculations. But this ease comes at a price—it often results in a lower deduction than you might otherwise be entitled to using the actual expense method.

However, this isn't always the case. The standard mileage rate may give you a larger deduction if you drive many business miles each year, especially if you drive an inexpensive car. But, even if the standard mileage rate does give you a lower deduction, the difference is often so small that it doesn't justify the extra record keeping you will have to do using the actual expense method. (See Section C, below.)

1. How the Standard Mileage Rate Works

Under the standard mileage rate, you deduct a specified number of cents for every business mile you drive. The IRS sets the standard mileage rate each year.

Usually, there is a single standard mileage rate for the entire year. However, due to the rapid rise in gas prices in the second half of 2005, there are two rates for 2005. For January 1, 2005 through August 31, the rate is 40.5 cents per mile for business mileage. For the period September 1 through December 31, the rate goes up to 48.5 cents per mile. The standard mileage rate for 2006 is 44.5 cents per mile. The rates are the same whether you own or lease your car.

Standard Mileage Rates for 2005 and 2006	
January 1–August 31, 2005	40.5 cents
September 1–December 31, 2005	48.5 cents
2006	44.5 cents

To figure out your deduction, simply multiply your business miles by the applicable standard mileage rate. Because there are two different standard mileage rates for 2005, you'll have to do two separate calculations—one for the first eight months of the year and another for the last four months. You then combine the two to determine your total deduction for the year.

> **EXAMPLE:** Ed, a doctor, drove his car a total of 10,000 miles for business in 2005. He drove 6,052 business miles from January through August, and 3,948 miles from September through December. His deduction for the first eight months of the year is $2,451) (40.5 cents x 6,052 = $2,451). His deduction for the last four months is $1,915 (48.5 cents x 3,948 = $1,915). His total deduction for 2005 is $4,366.

The big advantage of the standard mileage rate is that it requires very little record keeping. You only need to keep track of how many business miles you drive, not the actual expenses for your car, such as gas, maintenance, or repairs.

If you choose the standard mileage rate, you cannot deduct actual car operating expenses—for example, maintenance and repairs, gasoline and its taxes, oil, insurance, and vehicle registration fees. All of these items are factored into the rate set by the IRS. And you can't deduct the cost of the car through depreciation or Section 179 expensing because the car's depreciation is also factored into the standard mileage rate (as are lease payments for a leased car).

The only expenses you can deduct (because these costs aren't included in the standard mileage rate) are:

- interest on a car loan
- parking fees and tolls for business trips (but you can't deduct parking ticket fines or the cost of parking your car at your place of work), and
- personal property tax that you paid when you bought the vehicle based on its value—this is often included as part of your auto registration fee.

Auto loan interest is usually the largest of these expenses. Unfortunately, many people fail to deduct it because of confusion about the tax law. Taxpayers are not allowed to deduct interest on a loan for a car that is for personal use, so many people believe they also can't deduct interest on a business car. This is not the case. You may deduct interest on a loan for a car you use in your business. But there is one exception—if you're an employee, you may not deduct interest on a car loan even if you use the car 100% for your job.

If you use your car for both business and personal trips, you can deduct only the business use percentage of interest and taxes.

> **EXAMPLE:** Ralph uses his car 50% for his medical practice and 50% for personal trips. He uses the standard mileage rate to deduct his car expenses. He pays $3,000 a year in interest on his car loan. He may deduct 50% of this amount, or $1,500, as a business operating expense in addition to his business mileage deduction.

2. Requirements to Use the Standard Mileage Rate

Not everyone can use the standard mileage rate. You won't be able to use it (and will have to use the actual expense method instead) if you can't meet the following requirements.

First-Year Rule

You must use the standard mileage rate in the first year you use a car for business or you are forever foreclosed from using that method for that car. If you use the standard mileage rate the first year, you can switch to the actual expense method in a later year, and then switch back and forth between the two methods after that, provided the requirements listed below are met. For this reason, if you're not sure which method you want to use, it's a good idea to use the standard mileage rate the first year you use the car for business. This leaves all your options open for later years. However, this rule does not apply to leased cars. If you lease your car, you must use the standard mileage rate for the entire lease period if you use it in the first year.

There are some restrictions on switching back to the standard mileage rate after you have used the actual expense method. You can't switch back to the standard mileage rate after using the actual expense method if you took accelerated depreciation, a Section 179 deduction, or bonus depreciation on the car. You can switch back to the standard mileage rate only if you used the straight line method of depreciation during the years you used the actual expense method. This depreciation method gives you equal depreciation deductions every year, rather than the larger deductions you get in the early years using accelerated depreciation methods.

However, these restrictions on depreciation are often academic. Because of the severe annual limits on the depreciation deduction for passenger automobiles, it often makes no difference which depreciation method you use—you'll get the same total yearly deduction. So using straight line depreciation poses no hardship. Keep in mind, however, that if you switch to the actual expense method after using the standard mileage rate, you'll have to reduce the tax basis of your car by a portion of the standard mileage rate deductions you already received. This will reduce your depreciation deduction. (See Section C3, below, for more on vehicle depreciation deductions.)

Five-Car Rule

You can't use the standard mileage rate if you have five or more cars that you use for business simultaneously. When the IRS says "simultaneously," it means simultaneously. You're barred from using the standard mileage rate only if you operate five or more cars for business at the exact same time.

3. Calculating the Depreciation Included in the Standard Mileage Rate

If you've taken the standard mileage deduction for your car for any year, you won't have a separate depreciation deduction because it is included in the single standard mileage rate. To determine how much depreciation you've taken, multiply the total business miles you drove the car by the amount of the standard mileage rate that accounts for depreciation. These amounts are shown in the following table:

Year	Amount of Depreciation Included in Standard Mileage Rate (Per Business Mile)
2006	17 cents
2005	17 cents
2003-2004	16 cents
2001-2002	15 cents
2000	14 cents
1994-1999	12 cents

(For earlier years, see IRS Publication 463, *Travel, Entertainment, Gift, and Car Expenses.*)

> **EXAMPLE:** Reginald drove his car 10,000 miles for his architecture practice in 2003, 2004, and 2005. His annual depreciation was $1,700 in 2005 (17 cents x 10,000 = $1,700). He had $1,600 depreciation in both 2004 and 2003, giving him $4,900 total depreciation. He must reduce the basis of the car by this amount to determine its adjusted basis. He paid $15,000 for the car, so its adjusted basis is $10,100.

C. The Actual Expense Method

Instead of using the standard mileage rate, you can deduct the actual cost of using your car for business. This requires much more record keeping, but it can result in a larger deduction. However, because of the very low caps on depreciation deductions for automobiles (see Section 3, below), the amount of the increased deduction you get by using the actual expense method is often quite small. You may well conclude that it does not justify the additional record keeping required.

Business Travel by Motorcycle

You must use the actual expense method if you ride a motorcycle— the standard mileage rate is only for passenger vehicles. However, the limits on depreciation for passenger automobiles discussed in Section 3, below, do not apply to bicycles or motorcycles. You may depreciate these items just like any other business property. Or, if you wish, you can deduct the full cost of a motorcycle or bicycle in the year that you purchase it under Section 179. (See Chapter 9 for more on Section 179.)

1.   How the Actual Expense Method Works

As the name implies, under the actual expense method, you deduct the actual costs you incur each year to operate your car, plus depreciation. If you use this method, you must keep careful track of all the costs you incur for your car during the year, including:

- gas and oil
- repairs and maintenance
- depreciation of your original vehicle and improvements (see Section 3, below)
- car repair tools
- license fees
- parking fees for business trips
- registration fees
- tires
- insurance
- garage rent
- tolls for business trips
- car washing
- lease payments
- interest on car loans
- towing charges, and
- auto club dues.

> ### Watch Those Tickets
>
> You may not deduct the cost of driving violations or parking tickets, even if you were on business when you got the ticket. Government fines and penalties are never deductible as a matter of public policy.

When you do your taxes, add up the cost of all these items. For everything but parking fees and tolls, multiply the total cost of each item by the percentage of time you use your car for business. For parking fees and tolls that are business-related, include (and deduct) the full cost. The total is your deductible transportation expense for the year.

> **EXAMPLE:** In one recent year, Laura drove her car 8,000 miles for her consulting practice and 8,000 miles for personal purposes. She can deduct 50% of the actual costs of operating her car, plus the full cost of any business-related tolls and parking fees. Her expenses amount to $10,000 for the year, so she gets a $5,000 deduction, plus $500 in tolls and parking for business.

If you have a car that you use only for business, you may deduct 100% of your actual car costs. Be careful, though. If you own just one car, it's usually hard to claim that you use it only for business. The IRS is not likely to believe that you walk or take public transportation everywhere except when you're on business. Your argument might be more persuasive if you live in a city with a developed transportation system, such as Chicago, New York City, or San Francisco, and you drive your car only when you go out of town on business. But be prepared for the IRS to question your deduction. And if you're a sole proprietor, the IRS will know how many cars you own because sole proprietors who claim transportation expenses must provide this information on their tax returns. (See Section F, below, for more on tax reporting.)

2. Record-Keeping Requirements

When you deduct actual car expenses, you must keep records of all the costs of owning and operating your car. This includes not only the number of business miles and total miles you drive, but also gas, repair, parking, insurance, tolls, and any other car expenses. Record keeping for car expenses is covered in Chapter 20.

3. Vehicle Depreciation Deductions

Using the actual expense method, you can deduct the cost of your vehicle. However, you can't deduct the entire cost in the year when you purchase your car. Instead, you must deduct the cost a portion at a time over several years, using a process called depreciation. (For more on depreciation generally, see Chapter 9.) Although the general concept of depreciation is the same for every type of property, special rules apply to depreciation deductions for cars. These rules give you a lower deduction for cars than you'd be entitled to using the normal depreciation rules. Because of these rules, it can take a very long time to fully depreciate an automobile—as much as 20 years or more in the case of an expensive car. As a result, few people ever fully depreciate an automobile—they usually sell it or trade it in first.

This section focuses on the depreciation rules for passenger automobiles, as defined by the IRS. To understand the depreciation rules discussed in this section, you will need to be familiar with the general depreciation rules covered in Chapter 9.

Is Your Vehicle a Passenger Automobile?

First, you must figure out whether your vehicle is a passenger automobile as defined by the IRS. A passenger automobile is any four-wheeled vehicle made primarily for use on public streets and highways that has an unloaded gross weight of 6,000 pounds or less. The vehicle weight includes any part or other item physically attached to the automobile, or usually included in the purchase price of an automobile. This definition includes virtually all automobiles.

However, if your vehicle is an SUV, van, or truck, or has a truck base (as do most SUVs), it is a passenger automobile only if it has a gross loaded vehicle weight of 6,000 pounds or less. The gross loaded weight is based on how much the manufacturer says the vehicle can carry and is different from unloaded weight—that is, the vehicle's weight without any passengers or cargo.

You can find out your vehicle's gross loaded and unloaded weight by looking at the metal plate in the driver's side door jamb, looking at your owner's manual, checking the manufacturer's website or sales brochure, or asking an auto dealer. The gross loaded weight is usually called the Gross Vehicle Weight Rating (GVWR for short). The gross unloaded weight is often called the "curb weight."

Vehicles that would otherwise come within the passenger automobile definition are excluded if they are not likely to be used more than a minimal amount for personal purposes—for example, ambulances, hearses, taxis, and other vehicles used in a transportation business.

Passenger Automobiles Are Listed Property

All passenger automobiles are "listed property"—property that is often used for personal purposes. As explained in Chapter 9, the IRS imposes more stringent requirements on deductions for listed property to discourage fraudulent deduction claims. Because passenger automobiles are listed property, you must keep mileage records showing how much you use your car for business and personal purposes and you must file IRS Form 4562, *Depreciation and Amortization*, with your annual tax return. (See Chapter 20.)

Other Vehicles That Are Listed Property

Passenger automobiles are not the only vehicles that are listed property. Trucks, buses, boats, airplanes, motorcycles, and any other vehicles used to transport persons or goods are also listed property. The listed property rules apply to these vehicles even if they weigh more than 6,000 pounds and therefore don't qualify as passenger automobiles. However, some types of vehicles are not subject to the listed property rules, including vehicles not likely to be used more than a minimal amount for personal purposes (such as ambulances and taxis) and any vehicle with a loaded gross vehicle weight of over 14,000 pounds that is designed to carry cargo.

What You Can Depreciate

You can depreciate your entire investment in a car (also called your basis). If you buy a passenger automobile and use it for business that same year, your basis is its cost. You may depreciate the entire cost, even if you financed part of the purchase with a car loan. The cost also includes sales taxes, destination charges, and other fees the seller charges. It does not, however, include auto license and registration fees. This assumes you use the car 100% for business. If you use it less than 100%, you may only depreciate an amount equal to your percentage of business use. For example, if you use your car 50% for business, you may depreciate only 50% of the cost.

If you trade in your old car to a dealer to purchase a new car, your basis in the car you purchase is equal to the adjusted basis of the trade-in car, plus the cash you pay (whether out of your own pocket or financed with a car loan).

> **EXAMPLE:** Brenda buys a new car for her consulting practice. The car has a $20,000 sticker price. She trades in her old car and pays the dealer $15,000, all of which she finances with a car loan from her bank. Her trade-in has an adjusted basis of $7,000. Her basis in the new car is $22,000 ($7,000 + $15,000), even though the sticker price on the new car was only $20,000.

If you convert a car that you previously owned for personal use to a business car, your basis in the car is the lower of what you paid for it (at the time you purchased it for personal use) or its fair market value at the time you convert it to business use. Your basis will usually be its fair market value, as this is usually the lower number. You can determine the fair market value by checking used car value guides, such as the *Kelley Blue Book*.

Used car price guides often give more than one value—for example, the Kelley Blue Book gives a private party value and a retail value. Using the highest value will give you the largest deduction. The best known used car price guides (available free on the Internet) are:

- *Kelley Blue Book*: www.kbb.com
- Edmunds: www.edmunds.com
- NADAguides: www.nadaguides.com.

Look at more than one guide, because the prices can vary.

Depreciation Limits for Passenger Automobiles

Passenger automobiles have a five-year recovery period (but it takes six calendar years to depreciate a car; see Chapter 9). As a result, you'd think it would take at most six years to fully depreciate a car. Unfortunately, this is usually not the case. Depreciating a passenger automobile is unique in one very important way: The annual depreciation deduction for automobiles is limited to a set dollar amount each year. The annual limit applies to all passenger vehicles, no matter how much they cost. Because the limits are so low, it can take many years to fully depreciate a car, far longer than the six years it takes to depreciate other assets with a five-year recovery period.

Starting in 2003, the IRS established two different sets of deduction limits for passenger automobiles: one for passenger automobiles, other than trucks and vans, and slightly higher limits for trucks and vans that qualify as passenger automobiles (based on their weight) and are built on a truck chassis. This includes minivans and sport utility vehicles built on a truck chassis (as long as they meet the weight limit).

The charts below show the maximum annual depreciation deduction allowed for passenger automobiles and trucks and vans placed in service in 2005. The limits for vehicles placed in service before 2005 are different. They were much higher for the first year during the years 2002 through 2004 because bonus depreciation could be used to boost the depreciation deduction by 50% or 30%. (You can triple these limits if you buy an electric car after May 6, 2003.) The second chart shows the limits for passenger automobiles that are trucks and vans as defined above. Both charts assume 100% business use of the vehicle. You can find all the deduction limits in IRS Publication 946, *How to Depreciate Property*, and Publication 463, *Travel, Entertainment, Gift, and Car Expenses*.

Depreciation Limits for Passenger Automobiles Placed in Service During 2005	
1st tax year	$2,960
2nd tax year	$4,700
3rd tax year	$2,850
Each succeeding year	$1,675

Depreciation Limits for Trucks and Vans Placed in Service During 2005	
1st tax year	$3,260
2nd tax year	$5,200
3rd tax year	$3,150
Each succeeding year	$1,875

The depreciation limits are not reduced if a car is in service for less than a full year. This means that the limit is not reduced when the automobile is either placed in service or disposed of during the year.

EXAMPLE: Mario pays $50,000 for a new passenger automobile on June 1, 2005 and uses it 100% for his psychiatric practice. He may deduct a maximum of $2,970 in 2005; $4,700 in 2006; $2,850 in 2007; and $1,675 thereafter.

The deduction limits in the above table are based on 100% business use of the vehicle. If you don't use your car solely for business, the limits are reduced based on your percentage of personal use.

EXAMPLE: Mario uses his new car 60% for his practice. His first-year deduction is limited to $1,776 (60% x $2,960 = $1,776).

Your total depreciation deduction depends on the percentage of the time you use your car for business. For example, if you drive 5,000 miles for business and 5,000 for personal purposes in a year, you'll have 50% business use and you'll qualify for only 50% of the total allowable depreciation deduction for that year. So, if the total allowable deduction was $2,960, you'd get only $1,480. Obviously, you want to have as many business miles as possible. A little-known IRS rule can help you rack up more business mileage. When you determine your business mileage for purposes of your depreciation deduction, you may include miles you drove for investment or other income-producing purposes—for example, to visit a rental property or attend an investment seminar. This rule applies only when you figure your total allowable automobile depreciation deduction.

Depreciation Methods

You may use regular depreciation or Section 179 expensing (provided certain requirements are met), or both, to deduct the cost of a passenger automobile used for business. However, your total deduction cannot exceed the annual limits listed in the charts in the previous section. Because the dollar limits on automobile depreciation are so low, there is usually no advantage gained by using Section 179 to take this deduction instead of regular depreciation. It won't increase your deduction and will count against the $105,000 annual Section 179 limit. The only exception is when you are depreciating an extremely inexpensive car.

The following table shows how much of the cost of an automobile may be depreciated each year using the three different depreciation methods and applying the midyear convention. (If more than 40% of all the depreciable property you placed in service during the year was placed in service during the last quarter of the year, you'll have to use the midquarter convention; see Chapter 9.) You must use the slower straight-line method if you use your car less than 51% for business and you must continue to use this method even if your business use rises over 50% in later years. Although automobiles have a five-year recovery period, they are depreciated over six calendar years.

Automobile Depreciation Table

Year	200% Declining Balance Method (midyear convention)	150% Declining Balance Method (midyear convention)	Straight-Line Method (midyear convention)
1	20%	15%	10%
2	32%	25.5%	20%
3	19.2%	17.85%	20%
4	11.5%	16.66%	20%
5	11.5%	16.66%	20%
6	5.76%	8.33%	10%

Restrictions on Section 179

You may use Section 179 to expense a passenger automobile's cost only if you use it at least 51% of the time for business. You can't get around this rule by using it over 50% for business in the first year and less in subsequent years. If your use goes below 50% during any year in the six-year recovery period, you'll have to repay the Section 179 deduction to the IRS—a process called recapture. (See Chapter 9 for more about recapture.)

In addition, you cannot use Section 179 if you convert a personal passenger automobile to business use. The Section 179 deduction is also subject to an income limit—you can't deduct more than your total business income for the year. (See Chapter 9.) If you elect to use Section 179, you must use it before you take regular depreciation.

EXAMPLE 1: Mario buys a $20,000 car in February 2005 and uses it 80% of the time for his psychiatric practice. The maximum 2005 depreciation deduction for his car is $2,960. However, because he uses the car only 80% for business, his deduction is limited to $2,368 (80% x $2,960). He may use regular depreciation, Section 179 expensing, or both, to deduct the $2,368. Using the fastest form of depreciation—the 200% declining balance method—results in a $4,000 deduction (20% x $20,000 tax basis in the car). However, Mario may deduct only $2,368 of this amount. He decides not to use Section 179 because it won't increase his deduction and will count against the $105,000 annual Section 179 limit. (See Chapter 9.)

EXAMPLE 2: Billie buys a used Yugo in February 2005 and uses it 100% for her accounting practice. The car cost $5,000—her tax basis for depreciation purposes. Using the fastest form of regular depreciation (200% declining balance method), the most Billie could deduct the first year is $1,000 (20% x $5,000), which is far less than the $2,960 annual limit for auto depreciation. She decides to combine depreciation with Section 179 expensing instead. First, she deducts $1,960 using Section 179, then she deducts the remaining $1,000 using regular depreciation. This way, she gets to use the full $2,960 auto depreciation deduction, instead of just $1,000.

How Long Do You Depreciate an Auto?

Because of the annual limits on depreciation and Section 179 deductions for passenger automobiles, you won't be able to deduct the entire cost of a car worth more than $15,535 over the six-year recovery period. Don't worry—as long as you continue to use your car for business, you can keep taking annual deductions after the six-year recovery period ends, until you recover your full basis in the car. The maximum amount you can deduct each year is determined by the date you placed the car in service and your business use percentage.

EXAMPLE: In 2005, Kim pays $30,000 for a car she uses 100% for business. Her depreciable basis in the car is $30,000. Her maximum depreciation deductions for the car over the next six years are as follows:

2005	$ 2,960
2006	4,700
2007	2,850
2008	1,675
2009	1,675
2010	1,675
Total	$ 15,535

At the end of the five-year depreciation period, she has $14,465 in unrecovered basis. Even though the depreciation period is over, she may continue to deduct $1,675 each year until she recovers the remaining $14,465 (assuming she continues to use the car 100% for business). This will take another nine years.

Heavy Deductions for Heavy Metal: Expensing SUVs and Other Weighty Vehicles

The depreciation limits discussed above apply only to passenger automobiles—that is, vehicles with a gross loaded weight of less than 6,000 pounds. (See Subsection a, above.) Vehicles that weigh more than this are not subject to the limits. Until 2004, this created a great deduction opportunity for professionals who purchased SUVs they used over 50% for business: They could deduct as much as $102,000 of the cost in one year using the Section 179 deduction.

However, allowing these huge deductions for Hummers and other SUVs bought for business purposes caused such an uproar that Congress limited the Section 179 deduction for SUVs to $25,000. The limit applies to any SUV placed in service after October 22, 2004.

For these purposes, an SUV is any four-wheeled vehicle primarily designed or used to carry passengers over public streets, roads, or highways, that has a gross vehicle weight of 6,000 to 14,000 pounds. However, the $25,000 limit does not apply to any vehicle:

- designed to have a seating capacity of more than nine persons behind the driver's seat
- equipped with a cargo area of at least six feet in interior length that is an open area or designed for use as an open area, but is enclosed by a cap and not readily accessible directly from the passenger compartment, or
- that has an integral enclosure, fully enclosing the driver compartment and load carrying device, does not have seating rearward of the driver's seat, and has no body section protruding more than 30 inches ahead of the leading edge of the windshield.

Thus, for example, the $25,000 limit does not apply to most pick-ups or vans that weigh more than 6,000 pounds. (It doesn't apply to any vehicle that weighs more than 14,000 pounds.)

Although the Section 179 deduction for SUVs weighing over 6,000 pounds is limited to $25,000, this is still a very good deal compared to the allowable deduction for passenger automobiles. For example, a person who buys a $50,000 SUV that weighs 6,000 pounds and is used 100% for business can deduct $35,000 of the cost the first year ($25,000 Section 179 deduction + $10,000 regular depreciation using the 200% declining balance method and half-year convention). But, a person who buys a $50,000 passenger automobile can deduct only $2,960 the first year. If the SUV was used only 60% for business, $21,000 could still be deducted the first year (60% of the $35,000 amount for 100% business use). The first-year deduction for a 60% business use passenger automobile is only $1,776. Note that an SUV must be used at least 51% of the time for business to take any Section 179 deduction.

Auto Repairs and Improvements

Auto repairs and maintenance costs are fully deductible in the year they are incurred. You add these costs to your other annual expenses when you use the actual expense method. (You get no extra deduction for repairs when you use the standard mileage rate.) If you fix your car yourself, you may deduct the cost of parts and depreciate or deduct tools, but you get no deduction for your time or labor.

Unlike repairs, improvements to your car must be depreciated over several years, not deducted all in the year when you pay for them. What's the difference between a repair and an improvement? Good question. Unlike a repair, an improvement:

- increases the value of your car
- makes the car more useful, or
- lengthens your car's useful life.

EXAMPLE 1: Doug spends $200 to repair the carburetor for his car that he uses for his medical practice. This is a current expense, because the repair doesn't increase the value of his car or lengthen its useful life. The repair merely allows the car to last for a normal time.

EXAMPLE 2: Doug spends $2,000 on a brand-new engine for his car. This is a capital expense because the new engine increases the car's value and useful life.

This rule can be difficult to apply because virtually all repairs increase the value of the property being repaired. Just remember that an improvement makes your vehicle more valuable than it was before it was worked on, while a repair simply restores the car's value to what it was worth before it broke down.

Improvements are depreciated separately from the vehicle itself—that is, they are treated as a separate item of depreciable property. The same rules, however, apply to depreciating improvements as for regular auto depreciation. Depreciation of the original automobile and the later improvements are combined for purposes of the annual depreciation limits. The recovery period begins when the improvement is placed in service.

Car Repair Tool Costs Are Deductible

If you work on your car yourself, you may deduct the cost of your car repair tools. Your tools must be deducted separately from your auto expenses. If they are only worth $100 or so, you can currently deduct them as a business operating expense. If they are worth more, you must depreciate them or expense them under Section 179. If your tools are older or you haven't kept your receipts for tools you bought this year, you'll have to estimate their fair market value. Take a look in your garage and see what you have to deduct.

---

4. Leasing a Car

If you lease a car that you use in your practice, you can use the actual expense method to deduct the portion of each lease payment that reflects the business percentage use of the car. You cannot deduct any part of a lease payment that is for commuting or personal use of the car.

> **EXAMPLE:** John pays $400 a month to lease a Lexus. He uses it 50% for his dental practice and 50% for personal purposes. He may deduct half of his lease payments ($200 a month) as a local transportation expense for his sales business.

Leasing companies typically require you to make an advance or down payment to lease a car. You can deduct this cost, but you must spread the deduction out equally over the entire lease period.

With the standard mileage method, you don't deduct any portion of your lease payments. Instead, this cost is covered by the standard mileage rate set by the IRS. (See Section B, above, for more on the standard mileage rate.)

Is it Really a Lease?

Some transactions that are called "auto leases" are really not leases at all. Instead, they are installment purchases—that is, you pay for the car over time, and by the end of the lease term you own all or part of the car. You cannot deduct any payments you make to buy a car, even if the payments are called lease payments. Instead, you have to depreciate the cost of the car as described in Section 3, above.

Leasing Luxury Cars

If you lease what the IRS considers to be a luxury car for more than 30 days, you may have to reduce your lease deduction. The purpose of this rule is to prevent people from leasing very expensive cars to get around the limitations on depreciation deductions for cars that are purchased. (See Section 3, above.) A luxury car is currently defined as one with a fair market value of more than $17,500.

The amount by which you must reduce your deduction (called an "inclusion amount") is based on the fair market value of your car and the percentage of time that you use it for business. The IRS recalculates it each year. You can find the inclusion amount for the current year in the tables published in IRS Publication 463, *Travel, Entertainment, Gift, and Car Expenses.* For example, if you leased a $40,000 car in 2004 and used it solely for business in 2006, you would have to reduce your car expense deduction by $204 for the year. If you used the car only 50% for business, the reduction would be $120. The inclusion amount for the first year is prorated based on the month when you start using the car for business.

Should You Lease or Buy Your Car?

When you lease a car, you are paying rent for it—a set fee each month for the use of the car. At the end of the lease term, you give the car back to the leasing company and own nothing. As a general rule, leasing a car instead of buying it makes economic sense only if you absolutely must have a new car every two or three years and drive no more than 12,000 to 15,000 miles per year. If you drive more than 15,000 miles a year, leasing becomes an economic disaster because it penalizes you for higher mileage.

There are numerous financial calculators available on the Internet that can help you determine how much it will cost to lease a car compared to buying one. Be careful when you use these calculators—they are designed based on certain assumptions, and different calculators can give different answers. For a detailed consumer guide to auto leasing created by the Federal Reserve Board, go to the Board's website at www.federalreserve.gov/pubs/leasing.

D. How to Maximize Your Car Expense Deduction

Sam and Sue, both accountants, drive their cars 10,000 miles for their practices each year. This year, Sam got a $4,050 auto deduction, while Sue got $5,500. Why the difference? Sue took some simple steps to maximize her deduction. You can get the largest deduction possible by following these tips.

1. Use the Method That Gives the Largest Deduction

Many taxpayers choose the standard mileage rate because it's easier—it requires much less record keeping than the actual expense method. However, you'll often get a larger deduction if you use the actual expense method. The American Automobile Association estimated that the average cost of owning a car in 2005 was 56 cents per mile. This is substantially more than the IRS allows you to deduct under the standard mileage rate for 2005 (40.5 cents per mile for the first eight months of the year and 48.5 cents per mile for the last four months). Of course, this is just an average; your expenses could be lower, depending on the value of your car and how much you spend for repairs, gas, and other operating costs. The only way to know for sure which method gives you the largest deduction is to do the numbers.

EXAMPLE: In January 2005, Vicky buys a $20,000 car. During the year, she drives it 10,000 miles for her consulting practice (7,000 miles from January through August, and 3,000 from September through December) and 5,000 miles for personal purposes. She keeps track of all of her car expenses during the year. When she does her taxes, she compares the deduction she would receive using the actual expense method and the standard mileage rate. To do so, she completes the tables shown below.

Actual Expense Method Worksheet

Business/Personal Use

Total Mileage for Business		$ 10,000
Total Mileage for Year	÷	15,000
Business %	=	67%

Actual Annual Expenses

Gas and Oil		$ 3,400
Insurance	+	1,500
Repairs and Maintenance	+	500
Registration	+	50
Wash and Wax	+	200
Other	+	50
Total Actual Expenses	=	$ 5,700
Business %	X	67%
Business Total		= $ 3,149
Depreciation Deduction (67% x $2,960)		+ 1,983
Interest (total x business %)		+ 1,500
Personal Property Taxes (total x business %)		+ 350
Parking and Tolls		+ 1,800
Total Auto Deduction		= $ 8,782

Standard Mileage Rate Worksheet

Business Mileage

1/1/05-8/31/05	$ 6,052	
9/1/05-12/31/05	+ $ 3,948	
Total Mileage for Business		$10,000
Total Mileage for Year		÷ 15,000
Business %		= 67%

Standard Mileage Rate

1/1/05-8/31/05 (40.5¢ x 6,052)	$ 2,451	
9/1/05-12/31/05 (48.5¢ X 3,948)	+ 1,915	
Total Standard Mileage Deduction		= $ 4,366
Interest (total x business %)		+ 1,500
Personal Property Taxes (total x business %)		+ 350
Parking and Tolls		+ 1,800
Total Auto Deduction		= $ 8,016

There are circumstances when the standard mileage rate might give you a better deduction than the actual expense method. If you drive a car that's not worth much, either because it's old or an inexpensive model, you might come out ahead. Why? Because you get the same fixed deduction rate no matter how much the car is worth. Seventeen cents of the 2005 and 2006 standard mileage rate is for depreciation. With an inexpensive car, you might benefit from using the standard mileage rate, because the car's actual depreciation will be less than the 17-cent fixed amount.

EXAMPLE: Max buys a $1,000 used car in January 2005 and uses it exclusively in his chiropractic practice. Using the actual expense rate, he could get a $1,000 deduction for depreciation the first year (assuming he used Section 179 to deduct the entire purchase price of the car). This is $2,400 less than the $3,400 depreciation deduction he can get using the standard mileage rate (17 cents x 20,000 miles = $3,400). He'll do even better in 2006 and later—he would get no depreciation at all under the actual expense method, but he still gets 17 cents a mile using the standard mileage rate.

2. Use Two Cars for Business

If you use the actual expense method, you might think you would get a larger deduction by using one car 100% of the time for business instead of having two cars that you use less than 100% for business. This is usually not the case—two cars are usually better than one, because you can get a larger total depreciation deduction by depreciating two cars.

> **EXAMPLE:** Biff owns two cars. He needs to drive 20,000 miles for business during the year and 10,000 miles for personal purposes. Let's see how big a deduction he gets using one car versus two.

One Business Car

	Car 1	Car 2
Total Miles	20,000	10,000
Business Miles	20,000	0
Business %	100%	0
Total Costs	$6,500	$5,000
Total Auto Deduction	$6,500	0

Two Business Cars

	Car 1	Car 2
Total Miles	20,000	10,000
Business Miles	15,000	5,000
Business %	75%	50%
Total Costs	$6,500	$5,000
Total Auto Deduction	$4,875	$2,500

By using two cars instead of one, but driving the same total number of miles, Biff gets a $7,375 deduction, compared with only a $6,500 deduction for one car.

The IRS requires you to have a good reason for using two cars instead of one for your business. It shouldn't be hard to come up with one—for example, you don't want to put too many miles on each car, or one car carries more cargo and the other gets better gas mileage.

Of course, if you use the standard mileage rate, it makes no difference how many cars you drive—your deduction is based solely on your total business mileage.

3.   Keep Good Records

More than anything else, keeping good records is the key to the local transportation deduction. The IRS knows that many people don't keep good records. When they do their taxes, they make wild guesses abut how many business miles they drove the previous year. This is why IRS auditors are more suspicious of this deduction than almost any other.

Record keeping for the transportation deduction doesn't have to be too burdensome. If keeping records of gas, oil, repairs, and all your other car expenses is too much trouble (and it can be a pain in the neck), use the standard mileage rate (assuming you qualify for it). That way, you'll only need to keep track of how many miles you drive for business. Indeed, you might not even have to keep track of your business miles for the entire year; instead you may be able to use a sample period of thee months or one week a month. Remember that keeping track of your actual expenses often gives you a larger deduction. It's up to you to decide which is more important: your time or your money.

See Chapter 20 for a detailed discussion of how to keep car and mileage records.

E.   Other Local Transportation Expenses

You don't have to drive a car or other vehicle to get a tax deduction for local business trips. You can deduct the cost of travel by bus or other public transit, taxi, train, ferry, motorcycle, bicycle, or any other means. However, all the rules limiting deductions for travel by car discussed in Section A2, above, also apply to other transportation methods. This means, for example, that you can't deduct the cost of commuting from your home to your office or other permanent work location. The same record-keeping requirements apply as well.

F. Reporting Transportation Expenses on Schedule C

If you're a sole proprietor, you will list your car expenses on Schedule C, *Profit or Loss From Business.* Schedule C asks more questions about this deduction than almost any other deduction (reflecting the IRS's general suspicion about auto deductions).

Part IV of Schedule C is reproduced below. If you answer "no" to question 45, you cannot claim to use your single car 100% for business (unless you are an unusual case—see Section C1 above). If you answer "no" to questions 47a or 47b, you do not qualify for the deduction.

Part IV **Information on Your Vehicle.** Complete this part **only** if you are claiming car or truck expenses on line 9 and are not required to file Form 4562 for this business. See the instructions for line 13 on page C-4 to find out if you must file Form 4562.

43 When did you place your vehicle in service for business purposes? (month, day, year) ▶ ..../......../.......

44 Of the total number of miles you drove your vehicle during 2004, enter the number of miles you used your vehicle for:

a Business .... **b** Commuting .... **c** Other ....

45 Do you (or your spouse) have another vehicle available for personal use?. . . . . ☐ Yes ☐ No

46 Was your vehicle available for personal use during off-duty hours? . . . . ☐ Yes ☐ No

47a Do you have evidence to support your deduction? . . . . ☐ Yes ☐ No

b If "Yes," is the evidence written? . . . . ☐ Yes ☐ No

Report Your Interest Expenses Separately

If you deduct the interest you pay on a car loan, you have the option of reporting the amount in two different places on your Schedule C: You can lump it in with all your other car expenses on line 9 of the schedule titled "Car and truck expenses," or you can list it separately on line 16b as an "other interest" cost. Reporting your interest expense separately from your other car expenses reduces the total car expense shown on your Schedule C. This can help avoid an IRS audit.

G. When Clients Reimburse You

Professionals who undertake local travel while performing services for a client often have their expenses reimbursed by the client. You need not include such reimbursements in your income if you provide an adequate accounting of the expenses to your client and comply with the accountable plan rules. Basically, this requires that you submit all your documentation to the client in a timely manner, and return any excess payments. Accountable plans are covered in detail in Chapter 17. Record keeping rules for business driving are covered in Chapter 20.

> **EXAMPLE:** Erica, a sole proprietor accountant, is hired by Acme Corp. to handle an audit. She keeps a complete mileage log showing that she drove 500 miles while working on the audit. Acme reimburses Erica $250 for the business mileage. Erica need not include this amount in her income for the year. Acme may deduct it as a business expense.

If you do not adequately account to your client for these expenses, you must include any reimbursements or allowances in your income. They should also be included in any 1099-MISC form the client provides the IRS reporting how much you were paid (see Chapter 15). The client can still deduct the reimbursement as compensation paid to you. You may deduct the expenses on your own return, but you'll need documentation to back them up in the event of an audit.

> **EXAMPLE:** Assume that Erica doesn't keep proper track of her mileage. At the end of the year, she estimates that she drove 500 miles on Acme's behalf. Acme reimburses Erica $250, but concludes she didn't adequately account for her expenses under the IRS rules. It deducts the $250 on its tax return as compensation paid to Erica, and includes the $250 on the 1099-MISC form it sends the IRS the following February reporting how much it paid her. Erica deducts the $250 on her return as a business expense. Two years later, Erica is audited by the IRS. When the auditor asks her for her records showing how many miles she drove while representing Acme, Erica tells him she doesn't have any. The auditor disallows the deduction.

H. Professionals With Business Entities

If your practice is legally organized as a corporation, LLC, partnership, or LLP, there are special complications when it comes to deducting car expenses. Moreover, you have the option of having your practice own (or lease) the car you use, instead of using your personal car for business driving.

 This section doesn't apply to professionals who are sole proprietors or owners of one-person LLCs taxed as sole proprietorships. There is no separate legal entity to get between them and their business expense deductions. Moreover, sole proprietors don't have company cars because they personally own all their business assets.

1. Using Your Own Car

If you use your own car for business driving, how your expenses may be deducted depends on whether your practice is a corporation, LLC, partnership, or LLP.

LLCs, Partnerships, and LLPs

If you have organized your practice as an LLC, partnership, or LLP, it is probably taxed as a partnership (see Chapter 2). Usually, you'll seek reimbursement for your deductible car and other local travel expenses from your business entity. You can use either the standard mileage rate or actual expense method to calculate your expenses.

As long as you comply with the record-keeping rules for car expenses and your reimbursement is made under an accountable plan, any reimbursement you receive will not be taxable income. Basically, you must submit all your documentation to the practice in a timely manner and return any excess payments. Accountable plans are covered in detail in Chapter 17.

The practice can deduct the amount of the reimbursed car expenses on its tax return (Form 1065) and reduce its taxable profit for the year. Or, in many cases, the practice will obtain reimbursement from the client on whose behalf you did your local business travel (see Section G.)

EXAMPLE: Rick, a partner in a CPA firm organized as an LLC, uses his personal car for local business driving. He uses the standard mileage rate and keeps careful track of all of his business mileage. He submits a request for reimbursement to the firm, along with his mileage records. He was entitled to a $4,050 reimbursement from his firm. This money is not taxable income to Rick, and the firm may list it on its tax return as a business expense, or seek reimbursement from Rick's clients.

Instead of seeking reimbursement, you can deduct car expenses on your personal tax return, provided either of the following is true:

- You have a written partnership agreement or LLC operating agreement which provides that the expense will not be reimbursed by the partnership or LLC.
- Your practice has an established routine practice of not reimbursing the expense.

Absent such a written agreement or established practice, *no personal deduction may be taken*. You must seek reimbursement from the partnership, LLP, or LLC instead. If you take a personal deduction for your car expenses, your practice does not list them on its tax return, and they do not reduce your practice's profits. But they will reduce your taxable income. (See Chapter 17.)

You deduct your unreimbursed car expenses (and any other unreimbursed business expenses) on IRS Schedule E (Part II) and attach it to your personal tax return. You must attach a separate schedule to Schedule E listing the car and other business expenses you're deducting.

EXAMPLE: Assume that Rick's CPA firm has a written policy that all the partners must personally pay for their own car expenses. Instead of seeking reimbursement, Rick lists his $4,050 car expense on his own tax return, Schedule E, reducing his taxable income by that amount. The CPA firm does not list the expense on its return, thus it does not reduce the firm's income.

Corporations

If your practice is legally organized as a corporation (whether a C or S corporation), you are probably working as its employee. Special rules govern all business expense deductions by employees. Your best option is to have your corporation reimburse you for your car expenses. You get reimbursement in the same way as described above for LLCs and partnerships. You must comply with all the documentation rules for car expenses and the accountable plan requirements. If you do, your corporation gets to deduct the expense and you don't have to count the reimbursement as taxable income. If you fail to follow the rules, any reimbursements must be treated as employee income subject to tax (but you may deduct your expenses as described below). (See Chapter 17.)

2.   Using a Company Car

If your business entity buys a car that you use (that is, your business holds the title to the car, not you personally), the dollar value of your business driving is a tax-free working condition fringe benefit provided to you by your practice. In addition, the practice gets to deduct all of its actual car expenses on its tax return—for example, depreciation, interest on a car loan, maintenance, fuel it pays for, and insurance costs.

You get no personal deduction for these expenses; but, of course, if your practice is a pass-through entity, the deduction on its return will reduce the amount of taxable profit passed on to your tax return. However, you can personally deduct the actual cost of fuel or maintenance you pay for yourself, and the cost of anything else you buy for the car. You can't use the standard mileage rate to figure your costs. You must keep track of your mileage using one of the methods described in Chapter 20; and, if you personally buy fuel or other items for the car, you must comply with all the documentation rules for car expenses covered in that chapter.

> **EXAMPLE:** John, a veterinarian, is a one-third owner of a group practice organized as an LLC. The LLC buys a $20,000 car that John uses 100% for business driving. He keeps careful track of his mileage. In 2005, he drove the car 6,000 miles. The LLC may deduct on its tax return all the expenses it incurs from owning the car:

interest on car loan	$1,100
depreciation	2,960
fuel	1,200
maintenance	1,000
insurance	1,000
Total	$7,260

John's LLC lists the $7,260 as a deduction on its tax return. As a result, instead of reporting a $300,000 annual profit, it has a $292,740 profit. John pays income and self-employment tax on his distributive share of this amount, which is one-third. John gets no personal deduction for these expenses, but he may personally deduct as a business expense the cost of fuel he paid for using his own money. This gives him a $400 deduction. John need not pay any tax on the value of having the car because it is a tax-free working condition fringe benefit provided to him by the LLC.

Things get more complicated if, as is often the case, you use a company car for both business and personal driving. The dollar value of your personal use of the car is treated as a taxable fringe benefit. The amount must be added to your annual compensation and income, Social Security, and Medicare taxes must be paid on it.

EXAMPLE: Assume that John (from the above example) uses his company car 60% for business driving and 40% for personal driving. His LLC still gets the $7,260 deduction for its car expenses. However, the dollar value of John's personal driving is a taxable fringe benefit that must be added to his annual compensation. If the value of his personal driving was $5,000, he has to pay income and self-employment tax on this amount. He still gets to deduct the cost of fuel he paid for when he drove the car for business.

Here's the key question: How do you place a dollar value on your personal use of a company car? This determines how much money must be added to your income for such use. You can use three different methods to figure this out, and they may yield very different results.

Percentage of Actual Annual Lease Value

You can determine the value of your personal use of a company car by figuring out how much it would cost to lease the car for a year and then multiplying that amount by the percentage of your personal use. To determine the annual lease cost of a car yourself, you can contact auto leasing companies or do other similar research.

> **EXAMPLE:** Linda, a shareholder-employee of an accounting practice organized as a C corporation, has her company purchase a 2005 Lexus that she uses for 50% of the time for business and 50% of the time for personal purposes. It would cost Linda's company $9,600 a year ($800 per month) to lease the Lexus. Half of this amount is a tax-free working condition fringe benefit, the other half ($4,800) must be added to Linda's employee wages. Linda must pay income and employment tax on that amount.

IRS Annual Lease Value Table

Figuring out how much it costs to lease a car requires time and effort. The IRS has an easier way: It has created a table listing what it has determined to be the annual cost of leasing a car, based on its fair market value. To use the table, here's what you do:

- Figure out the fair market value of the car at the time it was provided to the employee by your company. If the car is new, the fair market value is its cost, plus tax, title, and other purchase expenses. If the car isn't new, the fair market value is what you'd pay to buy it from a third party in an arm's-length transaction in the area where the vehicle was purchased. You can use used car guides such as the *Kelley Blue Book* to determine the fair market value.
- Look up on the IRS *Annual Lease Value Table* the lease value for a car in your car's price range. The table is contained in IRS Publication 15-B, *Employer's Tax Guide to Fringe Benefits.*
- Multiply the car's annual lease value by the percentage of personal use during the year. The result is the amount that must be included in the employee's compensation as a taxable fringe benefit.

EXAMPLE: Jim's law corporation, of which he is the sole shareholder/employee, provides him with a car. In 2005, he used the car 60% of the time for his law practice, and 40% of the time for personal purposes. The car, a used Honda Accord, has a fair market value of $20,000. According to the IRS *Annual Lease Value Table*, it has an annual lease value of $5,600. Jim multiplies this amount by his personal use percentage (40%), to determine the value of his personal use—$2,240 (40% x $5,600 = $2,240). This amount must be added to Jim's employee compensation for 2005.

You must use the *Annual Lease Value Table* from the first day you drive a company car, or it can't be used at all. However, if the cents-per-mile method is used (see below), you can switch to the table method if you no longer qualify for the other method.

The *Annual Lease Value Table* does not include the value of fuel the company pays for. Its value must be added separately to your compensation. If the company reimburses you for gas, or you use a company credit card to pay for it, you generally value the fuel at the amount reimbursed or the amount charged.

EXAMPLE: Assume that Jim's law firm provided him with a company credit card to buy gas for his company car. He spent $1,500 for gas for the car during the year. Jim's personal use percentage of the car was 40%, so $600 must be added to Jim's employee wages (40% x $1,500 = $600).

It's important to understand that the IRS's table assumes that the company pays for maintenance and insurance for the car. As a result, the annual lease costs in the table are somewhat higher than under a normal lease, where the lessee pays for maintenance and insurance. You can't reduce the amounts in the table, even if you pay for maintenance and insurance. The higher amounts in the table increase the amount that must be added to your taxable compensation. Thus, either you shouldn't personally pay for maintenance or insurance, or you shouldn't use the table; use the car's actual lease value instead.

Cents-Per-Mile Method

The cents-per-mile method is the easiest way to determine the value of your personal use of a company car. You simply multiply the total miles the employee drove the car for personal purposes during the year by the standard mileage rate—40.5 cents for the first eight months of 2005 and 48.5 cents for the last four months of the year or 44.5 cents for 2006. For example, if you drive a company car 3,000 miles for personal purposes during the first eight months of 2005 and 1,000 miles for personal purposes during the last four months, $2,915 must be added your compensation (40.5 cents x 3,000 miles) + (48.5 cents x 1,000 miles) = $2,915.

However, this method may be used only for cars whose fair market value is below a threshold established by the IRS. In 2005, the threshold was $14,800 for passenger automobiles, and $16,300 for trucks and vans (including minivans and SUVs built on a truck chassis). The cents-per-mile rule may not be used for a car worth more than this on the first day it was made available to you or anyone else in the company. Obviously, this low threshold makes the cents-per-mile method unavailable for many company cars.

Even if a company car falls within the IRS threshold, the cents-per-mile method may be used only if you meet one of the following tests.

Regular use in trade or business test. To pass this test, you must be able to show that either:

- at least 50% of the vehicle's total annual mileage is for business, or
- based on all of the facts and circumstances, the vehicle is used regularly in your business. (Infrequent business use of the vehicle, such as for occasional trips to the airport or between your multiple business premises, is not regular use of the vehicle in your business.)

Mileage test. To pass the mileage test, you must be able to show either:

- The car is actually driven at least 10,000 miles during the year. If you own or lease the vehicle only part of the year, you may reduce the 10,000 miles requirement proportionately.
- The vehicle is used during the year primarily by company owners or employees.

If you pass one of the tests, you may use the cents-per-mile method, but only if you begin using the method on the first day the car is made available to you (or anyone else in your practice) for personal use. You must continue to use the cents-per-mile rule for all subsequent years, unless the car no longer passes either of the tests.

The cents-per-mile rate includes the value of fuel provided by the employer. If the employee provides his or her own gas, you can reduce the rate by up to 5.5 cents. For example, in 2005, the rate would be reduced to 35 cents. This will reduce the amount that must be added to your taxable compensation.

Cars Leased by the Company

If your company leases a car it provides you, all the rules above still apply. But it's much easier to figure out the value of your personal use of the car—simply multiply the annual lease payments by the percentage of personal use.

> **EXAMPLE:** ABC Medical Corporation leases a Mercedes at a cost of $12,000 per year for the use of Dr. Welby, one of ABC's shareholder/ employees. This year, Welby uses the car 30% for business and 70% for personal driving. ABC must add 70% of $12,000, or $8,400, to Welby's employee compensation for the year. ABC gets to deduct all of its lease payments as a business expense.

Is Using a Company Car a Good Idea?

As a general rule, if your group practice is a pass-through entity—an LLC, partnership, LLP, or S corporation—you'll be better off if you use your own car instead of a company car. This is because of the very low annual caps on car depreciation (see Section C). For example, first-year depreciation for a passenger automobile is limited to $2,960 in 2005, no matter how much the car costs. However, these caps are not taken into account when you determine the annual lease value of the car. They are not included in the IRS *Annual Lease Value Table*. Thus, the annual lease value is too large compared with the actual deductions allowed for a car. As a result, you'll have to pay more for your personal use of the car than you would if you used your own car and didn't have to determine the lease value. The more the car costs, the greater the difference will be.

I.   Should You Trade In or Sell Your Old Car?

Whether you sell or trade in a car you use for business can have a big effect on your taxes. The general rule is:
- sell the car if the sale results in a loss for tax purposes (as it usually does)
- trade in the car instead of selling it if you'd earn a profit on the sale.

These guidelines apply whether you individually own the car you use for business, or the car is owned by your practice.

To determine whether you would earn a profit or incur a loss on the sale of a business car, you subtract the car's adjusted basis from its sales price. For example, if your car has an adjusted basis of $15,000 and you sell it for $20,000, you will have $5,000 in profit. If you sold the car for $10,000, you'd have a $5,000 loss.

The depreciation allowed on a business vehicle reduces its tax basis, thus it has a major effect on whether you earn a profit or incur a loss when the vehicle is sold. Usually, a car is sold at a loss because its true resale value is less than the depreciation allowed by the IRS.

1.   When to Sell

A loss on the sale of a business car is good taxwise because you can deduct it from your other income. So you should sell your car instead of trading it in if the sales price is less than your adjusted basis.

> **EXAMPLE:** Adolf purchased a $30,000 car in 2005 and used it 100% for business every year. In 2007, his adjusted basis is $22,400 ($30,000 − $7,600 depreciation). The most he can sell the car for is $15,000. He should sell the car rather than trade it in because the sale will result in a $7,400 business loss that he can deduct from his income.

The above example assumes you use the car 100% for business. If you use it less than 100%, you may deduct only the business portion of your loss. To do this, you treat your car as if it were two separate vehicles: a business car and a personal car. You'll have two different basis numbers—one for your business use of the car, and one for your personal use. You separately determine your business and personal profit or loss when you sell the car. A business loss is deductible, a personal loss is not. However, both business and personal profit on an auto sale are taxed.

> **EXAMPLE:** Assume that Adolf (from the above example) used his $30,000 car for business only 75% of the time. His starting business basis is $22,500 (75% x $30,000 = $22,500). His starting personal basis is $7,500 (25% x $30,000 = $7,500). He took a total of $7,600 in depreciation during the years he used the car for business. Depreciation is a business deduction, so it is subtracted only from his business basis. This leaves him with a $14,900 business basis ($22,500 – $7,600 = $14,900). He still has his original $7,500 personal basis. If he sells the car, he must deduct his $14,900 business basis from 75% of the sales price, and deduct his personal basis from the remaining 25%. If the sales price is $15,000, he must deduct $14,900 from $11,250 (75% of the $15,000 sales price), leaving him with a $3,650 business loss. He also deducts his $7,500 personal basis from 25% of the sales price ($3,750), leaving him with a $3,750 personal loss. He may deduct the $3,650 business loss, but he may not deduct the $3,750 personal loss.

If, like most people, you don't use your car the same amount for business each year, you'll have to calculate your business use percentage for the entire time you used the car. You do this by adding up all your business and personal miles and then dividing the business miles by the total of all your miles.

> **EXAMPLE:** Shoshona purchased a car in 2002 and used it for both business and personal driving as follows:

Year	Business Miles	Personal Miles	Total Miles
2002	8,543	4,260	12,803
2003	9,288	3,702	12,990
2004	11,684	4,633	16,317
2005	7,307	5,953	13,260
Total	36,822	18,548	55,370

36,822 business miles divided by 55,370 total miles = 0.67. Thus, Shoshona used her car a total of 67% of the time for business from 2002 through 2005.

2.   When to Trade In

It's better to trade in your car if you're going to earn a profit on the sale. A profit on a sale is bad taxwise because you'll have to pay tax on it. If you use your car for both business and personal driving, you must pay tax on both your business and personal profit. You'll avoid earning a taxable profit if you trade in your car instead of selling it.

When you trade in your car, instead of ending up with money in your pocket (that you would have to pay tax on), the adjusted basis of your trade-in car becomes part of the tax basis of the new car (see Section C3, above). In addition, if you owe sales tax on the purchase of a new car, many states make you pay tax only on the purchase price less the value of the trade in. If, instead, you sell the old car and apply the proceeds to the purchase of a new car, you would have to pay sales tax on the full purchase price.

> **EXAMPLE:** Eva purchased a car in 2005 and used it 100% for her law practice every year. She paid $20,000 for the car and had taken $7,660 in depreciation by 2007. Her car's adjusted basis is $12,340 ($20,000 – $7,660 = $12,340). A friend offers her $15,000 for the car. Should she sell it? No! If she sells the car for $15,000, she'll have a $2,660 gain that she'll have to pay tax on ($15,000 – $12,340 = $2,660). Instead of selling the car, she should trade it in for another car (assuming she gets a decent value on her trade-in). This way she'll have no profit to pay tax on. Instead, her $12,340 adjusted basis in the old car will become part of the basis of the new car. If the new car costs $25,000 and she pays $10,000 cash plus her trade-in, the new car's basis will be $22,340—the cash she paid for the new car plus the basis of her old car.

In the above example, the amount Eva received on her trade-in was equal to what she would have received if she sold her car to her friend. However, if you can get substantially more selling your car than on a trade-in, you may be better off selling it. Why? The tax benefits of the trade-in may not equal the extra amount received on the sale.

Subject to the two exceptions below, you can sell your old car to anyone and deduct the business portion of your loss. You may sell to a car dealer, but you cannot purchase another car from the dealer at the same time—this would be considered a trade-in by the IRS.

Exception 1: You cannot sell your old car to a close relative and deduct your loss. For these purposes, a close relative is any lineal descendent or ancestor, such as parents, children, siblings, or grandparents. However, aunts, uncles, nieces, nephews, and cousins are not included in this exception.

Exception 2: You cannot sell your car to a business entity, such as a corporation or LLC, in which you are the majority owner, and deduct your loss. Thus, you can't form an LLC, sell your car to it at a loss, and then deduct the loss from your taxes.

■

Chapter 6

Long Distance Travel Expenses

I f you travel overnight for business, you can deduct your airfare, hotel bills, and other expenses. If you plan your trip right, you can even mix business with pleasure and still get a deduction. However, IRS auditors closely scrutinize these deductions. Many taxpayers claim them without complying with the stringent rules the IRS imposes. To avoid unwanted attention, you need to understand the limitations on this deduction and keep proper records.

A. What Is Business Travel?

For tax purposes, business travel occurs when you travel away from your tax home for your business on a temporary basis. You don't have to travel any set distance to get a travel expense deduction. However, you can't take this deduction if you just spend the night in a motel across town. You must travel outside your city limits. If you don't live in a city, you must go outside the general area where your business is located.

You must stay away overnight or at least long enough to require a stop for sleep or rest.

> **EXAMPLE:** Phyllis, an engineer with her own firm based in Los Angeles, flies to San Francisco to meet potential clients, spends the night in a hotel, and returns home the following day. Her trip is a deductible travel expense.

You cannot satisfy the rest requirement by merely napping in your car.

> **EXAMPLE:** Frederick Barry, a consulting engineer, worked with clients in a three-state area by making one-day trips to each client. He frequently left home at 6:30 a.m. and did not return until midnight. During the day, he habitually stopped in a rest area and closed his eyes for 20 minutes to refresh himself for the remaining drive. The tax court said that Barry's trips did not constitute tax-deductible long distance travel because he was not away from home long enough to require substantial sleep or rest. (*Barry v. Comm'r,* 54 T.C. 115.)

If you don't stay overnight (or long enough to require sleep or rest), your trip will not qualify as business travel. However, this does not necessarily mean that you can't take a tax deduction. Local business trips, other than commuting, are deductible. However, you may only deduct your transportation expenses—the cost of driving or using some other means of transportation. You may not deduct meals or other expenses like you can when you travel for business and stay overnight.

EXAMPLE: Philip drives from his office in Los Angeles to a client meeting in San Diego and returns the same day. His 200-mile round trip is a deductible local business trip. He may deduct his expenses for the 200 business miles he drove, but he can't deduct the breakfast he bought on the way to San Diego.

 For a detailed discussion of tax deductions for local business travel, see Chapter 5.

1. Where Is Your Tax Home?

Your tax home is the entire city or general area where your principal place of business is located. This is not necessarily the place where you live.

EXAMPLE: Tim is a lawyer/lobbyist who maintains his office in Washington, DC. However, his family lives in New York City. He spends weekends with his family in New York and stays in a hotel during the week when he works in Washington. Tim's tax home is in Washington, DC. This means that when he travels back and forth between his Washington office and his New York home, his trips are nondeductible commuting. In addition, he gets no travel expense deductions while staying in Washington—for example, he can't deduct his hotel room or meals as a business travel expense. Because Washington, DC, is his tax home, he's not traveling while staying there.

The IRS doesn't care how far you travel for business. You'll get a deduction as long as you travel outside your tax home's city limits and stay overnight. Thus, even if you're just traveling across town, you'll qualify for a deduction if you manage to stay outside your city limits.

> **EXAMPLE:** Pete, a tax advisor, has his office in San Francisco. He travels to Oakland for an all day meeting with a client. At the end of the meeting, he decides to spend the night in an Oakland hotel rather than brave the traffic back to San Francisco. Pete's stay qualifies as a business trip even though the distance between his San Francisco office and the Oakland client meeting is only eight miles. Pete can deduct his hotel and meal expenses.

If you don't live in a city, your tax home covers the general area where it is located. This general area is anywhere within about 40 miles of your tax home.

Multiple Work Locations

If you work in more than one location, your tax home is your main place of business. To determine this, consider:

- the total time you spend in each place
- the level of your business activity in each place, and
- the amount of income you earn from each place.

> **EXAMPLE:** Lee, a dentist, has his own dental office in Houston, Texas. In addition, he works in his father's dental office in Dallas, Texas. He spends three weeks a month in Houston and one week in Dallas. He makes $150,000 per year from his Houston practice and $50,000 per year from his work in Dallas. Houston—where he spends more time and makes more money—is his tax home.

Temporary Work Locations

You may regularly work at your tax home and also work at another location. It may not always be practical to return from this other location to your tax home at the end of each workday. Your overnight stays at these temporary work locations qualify as business travel as long as your work there is truly temporary—that is, it is reasonably expected to last no more than one year. If that is the case, your tax home does not change and you are considered to be away from home for the entire period you spend at the temporary work location.

> **EXAMPLE:** Betty is a self-employed sexual harassment educator. She works out of her home office in Chicago, Illinois. She is hired to conduct sexual harassment training and counseling for a large company in Indianapolis, Indiana. The job is expected to last three months. Betty's assignment is temporary, and Chicago remains her tax home. She may deduct the expenses she incurs traveling to and staying in Indianapolis.

On the other hand, if you reasonably expect your work at the other location to last more than one year, that location becomes your new tax home and you cannot deduct your expenses while there as travel expenses.

> **EXAMPLE:** Carl, a CPA who is a partner in an accounting firm with several offices in the Northwest, ordinarily works from the firm's Seattle office and lives in Seattle. However, the firm's Boise, Idaho, office is short-staffed, so Carl goes there to help handle the workload. He expects he'll have to work out of the Boise office for at least 12 months. He lives in a Boise hotel. Boise is now Carl's tax home and he may not deduct his expenses while staying there as travel expenses, even though he lives in Seattle. Thus, he may not deduct his hotel or food expenses. However, he may deduct his travel expenses if he travels to and from Boise to Seattle for a business purpose.

If you go back to your tax home from a temporary work location on your days off, you are not considered away from home while you are in your hometown. You cannot deduct the cost of meals and lodging there. However, you can deduct your expenses, including meals and lodging, while traveling between your temporary work location and your tax home. You can claim these expenses up to the amount it would have cost you to stay at your temporary work location. In addition, if you keep your hotel room during your visit home, you can deduct that cost.

2.   Your Trip Must Be for Business

Your trip must be primarily for business to be deductible, and you must
have a business intent and purpose before leaving on the trip. You
have a business purpose if the trip benefits your business in some way.
Examples of business purposes include:

- finding new clients, patients, or new markets for your services
- dealing with existing clients or patients
- learning new skills to help in your practice
- contacting people who could help your practice, such as potential
  investors, or
- checking out what the competition is doing.

It's not sufficient merely to claim that you had a business purpose
for your trip. You must be able to prove this by showing that you spent
at least part of the time engaged in business activities while at your
destination. Acceptable business activities include:

- visiting or working with existing or potential clients or patients, and
- attending professional seminars or conventions where the agenda
  is clearly connected to your practice.

On the other hand, business activities do not include:

- sightseeing
- recreational activities that you attend by yourself or with family or
  friends, or
- attending personal investment seminars or political events.

Use common sense when deciding whether to claim that a trip is
for business. If you're audited, the IRS will likely question any trip that
doesn't have some logical connection to your existing professional
practice.

Travel for a New Business or Location

You must actually be in business to have deductible business trips.
Trips you make to investigate a potential new business or to actually
start or acquire a new business are not currently deductible business
travel expenses. However, they may be deductible as business start-up
expenses, which means you can deduct up to $5,000 of these expenses
the first year you're in business if your total start-up expenses are less
than $50,000. (See Chapter 10 for more on start-up expenses.)

Travel as an Education Expense

You may deduct the cost of traveling to an educational activity directly related to your business.

> **EXAMPLE:** Louis, an architect, travels from his home in Philadelphia to a conference in London on how to make buildings bomb-proof. The cost is a deductible travel expense.

However, you can't take a trip and claim that the travel itself constitutes a form of education and is therefore deductible.

> **EXAMPLE:** Assume that Louis travels from Philadelphia to London just to see the sights and become more familiar with British architecture. This trip is not a deductible travel expense. (See Chapter 14 for more on education expenses.)

Visiting Professional Colleagues

Visiting professional colleagues or competitors may be a legitimate business purpose for a trip. But you can't just socialize with them. You must use your visit to learn new skills, check out what your competitors are doing, seek investors, or attempt to get new clients or patients.

B. What Travel Expenses Are Deductible

Subject to the limits covered in Section C below, virtually all of your business travel expenses are deductible. These fall into two broad categories: your transportation expenses and the expenses you incur at your destination.

> ⚠ **Attorneys may be barred from deducting advanced client costs.** Your travel costs might not be deductible if they constitute advanced client costs you incur while performing legal services for a client. See Chapter 17.

Transportation expenses are the costs of getting to and from your destination—for example:

- fares for airplanes, trains, or buses
- driving expenses, including car rentals
- shipping costs for your personal luggage, equipment, or other things you need for your practice, and
- meals, beverages, and lodging expenses you incur while en route to your final destination.

If you drive your personal car to your destination, you may deduct your costs by using the standard mileage rate or deduct your actual expenses. You may also deduct your mileage while at your destination. (See Chapter 5 for more on deducting car expenses.)

You may also deduct the expenses you incur to stay alive (food and lodging) and do business while at your destination. Destination expenses include:

- hotel or other lodging expenses for business days
- 50% of meal and beverage expenses (see Section C, below)
- taxi, public transportation, and car rental expenses at your destination
- telephone, Internet, and fax expenses
- computer rental fees
- laundry and dry cleaning expenses, and
- tips you pay on any of the other costs.

You may deduct 50% of entertainment expenses if you incur them for business purposes. You can't deduct entertainment expenses for activities that you attend alone because this solo entertainment obviously wouldn't be for business purposes. If you want to deduct the cost of a nightclub or ball game while on the road, be sure to take a business associate along. (See Chapter 4 for a detailed discussion of the special rules that apply to deductions for entertainment expenses.)

1.   Traveling First Class or Steerage

To be deductible, business travel expenses must be ordinary and necessary. This means that the trip and the expenses you incur must be helpful and appropriate for your business, not necessarily indispensable. You may not deduct lavish or extravagant expenses, but the IRS gives you a great deal of leeway here. You may, if you wish, travel first class, stay at four-star hotels, and eat at expensive restaurants. On the other hand, you're also entitled to be a cheapskate—for example, you could stay with a friend or relative at your destination to save on hotel expenses and still deduct meals and other expenses.

2.   Taking People With You

You may deduct the expenses you pay for a person who travels with you only if he or she:
   • is your employee
   • has a genuine business reason for going on the trip with you, and
   • would otherwise be allowed to deduct the travel expenses.

   These rules apply to your family as well to nonfamily members. This means you can deduct the expense of taking your spouse, child, or other relative only if the person is your employee and has a genuine business reason for going on a trip with you. Typing notes or assisting in entertaining clients is not enough to warrant a deduction; the work must be essential to your practice.

   However, this doesn't mean that you can't take any deductions at all when you travel with your family. You may still deduct your business expenses as if you were traveling alone—and you don't have to reduce your deductions, even if others get a free ride with you. For example, if you drive to your destination, you can deduct the entire cost of the drive, even if your family rides along with you. Similarly, you can deduct the full cost of a single hotel room even if you obtain a larger, more expensive room for your whole family.

> **EXAMPLE:** Yamiko, an engineer, travels from New Orleans to Sydney, Australia, to meet with a client. She takes her husband and young son with her. The total airfare expense for her and her family is $2,500. She may deduct the cost of a single ticket: $1,000. She spends $250 per night for a two-bedroom hotel suite in Sydney. She may deduct the cost of a single room for one person: $100 per night.

C. How Much You Can Deduct

If you spend all of your time at your destination on business, you may deduct 100% your expenses (except meal expenses, which are only

50% deductible—see Section 6, below). However, things are more complicated if you mix business and pleasure. Different rules apply to your transportation expenses and the expenses you incur while at your destination ("destination expenses").

1.   Travel Within the United States

Business travel within the United States is subject to an all or nothing rule: You may deduct 100% of your transportation expenses only if you spend more than half of your time on business activities while at your destination. If you spend more time on personal activities than on business, you get no transportation deduction. In other words, your business days must outnumber your personal days. You may also deduct the destination expenses you incur on the days you do business. Expenses incurred on personal days at your destination are nondeductible personal expenses. (See Section 5, below, for the rules used to determine what constitutes a business day.)

> **EXAMPLE:** Tom works in Atlanta. He takes the train for a business trip to Houston. He spends six days in Houston, where he spends all his time on business and spends $400 for his hotel, meals, and other living expenses. On the way home, he stops in Mobile for three days to visit his parents and spends $100 for lodging and meals there. His round-trip train fare is $250. Tom's trip consisted of six business days and three personal days, so he spent more than half of the trip on business. He can deduct 100% of his train fare and the entire $400 he spent while on business in Houston. He may not, however, deduct the $100 he spent while visiting his parents. His total deduction for the trip is $650.

If your trip is primarily a vacation—that is, you spend over half of your time on personal activities—the entire cost of the trip is a nondeductible personal expense. However, you may deduct any expenses you have while at your destination which are directly related to your business. This includes such things as phone calls or faxes to your office, or the cost of renting a computer for business work. It doesn't include transportation, lodging, or food.

> **EXAMPLE:** Tom (from the above example) spends two days in Houston on business and seven days visiting his parents in Mobile. His entire trip is a nondeductible personal expense. However, while in Houston he spends $50 on long distance phone calls to his office—this expense is deductible.

As long as your trip is primarily for business, you can add a vacation to the end of the trip, make a side trip purely for fun, or go to the theater and still deduct your entire airfare. What you spend while having fun is not deductible, but you can deduct all of your business and transportation expenses.

> **EXAMPLE:** Bill, an engineer, flies to Miami for a four-day trial. He spends three extra days in Miami swimming and enjoying the sights. Because he spent over half his time on business—four days out of seven—the cost of his flight is entirely deductible, as are his hotel and meal costs during the trial. He may not deduct his hotel, meal, or other expenses during his vacation days.

2. Travel Outside the United States

Travel outside the United States is subject to more flexible rules than travel within the country. The rules for deducting your transportation expenses depend on how long you stay at your destination.

Trips of up to Seven Days

If you travel outside the United States for no more than seven days, you can deduct 100% of your airfare or other transportation expenses, as long as you spend part of the time on business. You can spend a majority of your time on personal activities, as long as you spend at least some time on business. Seven days means seven consecutive days, not counting the day you leave but counting the day you return to the United States. You may also deduct the destination expenses you incur on the days you do business. (See Section 5, below, for the rules used to determine what constitutes a business day.)

EXAMPLE: Billie, a urologist, flies from Portland, Oregon, to Vancouver, Canada. She spends four days sightseeing in Vancouver and one day at a seminar on urologic surgery. She may deduct 100% of her airfare, but she can deduct her lodging, meal, and other expenses from her stay in Vancouver only for the one day she attended the seminar.

Trips for More Than Seven Days

The IRS does not want to subsidize foreign vacations, so more stringent rules apply if your foreign trip lasts more than one week. For these longer trips, the magic number is 75%: If you spend more than 75% of your time on business at your foreign destination, you can deduct what it would have cost to make the trip if you had not engaged in any personal activities. This means you may deduct 100% of your airfare or other transportation expense, plus your living expenses while you were on business and any other business-related expenses.

EXAMPLE: Sean, an international business consultant, flies from Boston to Dublin, Ireland. He spends one day sightseeing and nine days in client meetings. He has spent 90% of his time on business, so he may deduct 100% of his airfare to Dublin and all of the living and other expenses he incurred during the nine days he was in Dublin on business. He may not deduct any of his expenses (including hotel) for the day he spent sightseeing.

If you spend more than 50%—but less than 75%—of your time on business, you can deduct only the business percentage of your transportation and other costs. You figure out this percentage by counting the number of business days and the number of personal days to come up with a fraction. The number of business days is the numerator (top number), and the total number of days away from home is the denominator (bottom number). For ease in determining the dollar amount of your deduction, you can convert this fraction into a percentage.

What Is Foreign Travel?

Different deduction rules apply to travel within the United States and foreign travel, so it's important to know which is which. For IRS purposes, foreign travel means travel outside of the United States. Thus, for example, a trip to Puerto Rico would be a foreign trip, even though it is a United States possession. Travel outside the United States does not include travel from one point in the United States to another point in the U.S.

If you travel by plane, train, or other public transportation, any place in the United States where your plane or other means of transportation makes a scheduled stop is a point in the U.S. Your foreign trip begins at the last scheduled stop in the United States.

EXAMPLE: Ben flies from Chicago to Miami, changes planes, and then flies to Puerto Rico. The flight from Chicago to Miami is within the United States, so the domestic travel rules apply. The flight from Miami to Puerto Rico is outside the United States, so the foreign travel rules apply. Ben then returns to Chicago on a nonstop flight from Puerto Rico. All of the return trip is outside the United States because there are no scheduled stops in the U.S.

If you travel by private car to a foreign destination, the portion of the trip that is within the United States is governed by the domestic travel rules.

EXAMPLE: Bart travels by car from Denver to Mexico City and returns. His travel to and from the U.S. border back to Denver is travel within the United States. The foreign travel rules apply only to the portion of his trip inside Mexico.

If you travel by private airplane, any trip (or portion of a trip) for which both takeoff and landing are in the United States is travel within the United States, even if part of the flight is over a foreign country.

EXAMPLE: Brenda flies her private plane nonstop from Seattle to Juneau, Alaska. Because she took off and landed in the United States, the trip is within the United States for tax purposes—even though she had to fly over Canada on the way to Juneau. However, if she makes a scheduled stop in Vancouver, Canada, both legs of the flight are considered travel outside the United States and are subject to the foreign travel rules.

EXAMPLE: Sam flies from Las Vegas to London, where he spends six days on business and four days sightseeing. He spent 6/10 of his total time away from home on business. The fraction 6/10 converts to 60% (6 ÷ 10 = 0.60). He therefore spent 60% of his time on business. He can deduct 60% of his travel costs—that is, 60% of his round-trip airfare, hotel, and other expenses. The trip cost him $3,000, so he gets an $1,800 deduction.

If you spend less than 51% of your time on business on foreign travel that lasts more than seven days, you cannot deduct any of your costs.

Side Trips

Expenses you incur if you stop at a nonbusiness (personal) destination en route to, or returning from, your business destination are not deductible. For example, if you stop for three vacation days in Paris on your way to a week-long client meeting in Bangladesh, you may not deduct your expenses from your Paris stay.

Determining how much of your airfare or other transportation costs are deductible when you make side trips is a three-step process:

- determine the percentage of the time you spent on vacation
- multiply this vacation percentage by what it would have cost you to fly round trip from your vacation destination to the United States, and
- subtract this amount from your total airfare expense to arrive at your deductible airfare expense.

EXAMPLE: Jason, a psychotherapist, lives in New York. On May 5, he flew to Paris to attend a psychotherapy conference that began that same day. The conference ended on May 14. That evening, he flew from Paris to Dublin to visit friends until May 21, when he flew directly home to New York. The entire trip lasted 18 days, 11 of which were business days (the nine days in Paris and the two travel days) and seven of which were vacation days. He spent 39% of his time on vacation (7/18 = 39%). His total airfare was $2,000. Round-trip airfare from New York to Dublin would have been $1,000. To determine his deductible airfare, he multiplies $1,000 by 39% and then subtracts this amount from his $2,000 airfare expense: 1,000 x

39% = 390; $2,000 – $390 = $1,610. His deductible airfare expense
is $1,610.

3.   Conventions

Your travel to, and stay at, a convention is deductible in the same
manner as any other business trip, as long as you satisfy the following
rules.

Conventions Within North America

You may deduct the expense of attending a convention in North America
if your attendance benefits your practice. You may not, however, deduct
any expenses for your family.

How do you know if a convention benefits your practice? Look at the
convention agenda or program (and be sure to save a copy). The agenda
does not have to specifically address what you do in your practice,
but it must be sufficiently related to show that your attendance was for
business purposes. Examples of conventions that don't benefit your
practice include those for investment, political, or social purposes.

You probably learned in school that North America consists of the
United States, Canada, and Mexico. However, for convention expense
purposes, North America includes much of the Caribbean and many
other great vacation destinations, including:

- American Samoa
- Baker Island
- Barbados
- Bermuda
- Canada
- Costa Rica
- Dominica
- Dominican Republic
- Grenada
- Guam
- Guyana
- Honduras
- Howland Island

- Jamaica
- Jarvis Island
- Johnston Island
- Kingman Reef
- Marshall Islands
- Mexico
- Micronesia
- Midway Islands
- Northern Mariana Islands
- Palau
- Palmyra
- Puerto Rico
- Saint Lucia
- Trinidad and Tobago
- United States (the 50 states and Washington, DC)
- U.S. Virgin Islands, and
- Wake Island.

Foreign Conventions

More stringent rules apply if you attend a convention outside of North America (as defined above). You can take a deduction for a foreign convention only if:

- the convention is directly related to your practice (rather than merely benefiting it), and
- it's as reasonable for the convention to be held outside of North America as in North America.

To determine if it's reasonable to hold the convention outside of North America, the IRS looks at the purposes of the meeting and the sponsoring group, the activities at the convention, where the sponsors live, and where other meetings have been or will be held.

The sponsors of conventions for professionals held outside the U.S. usually try to come up with a reason justifying the location—for example, the American Bar Association held a convention in London during which the American lawyers studied the British legal system by attending trials at the famed Old Bailey Courthouse.

4. Travel by Ship

You can deduct travel by ship if a convention or other business event is conducted on board a ship, or if you use a ship as a means of transportation to a business destination. The following additional rules apply to travel by sea.

Shipboard Conventions and Seminars

Forget about getting a tax deduction for a pure pleasure cruise. You may, however, be able to deduct part of the cost of a cruise if you attend a convention, seminars, or similar meetings directly related to your practice while on board. Personal investment or financial planning seminars don't qualify.

But there is a major restriction: You must travel on a U.S.-registered ship that stops only in ports in the United States or its possessions, such as Puerto Rico or the U.S. Virgin Islands. If a cruise sponsor promises you'll be able to deduct your trip, investigate carefully to make sure it meets these requirements.

If you go on a cruise that is deductible, you must file a signed note with your tax return from the meeting or seminar sponsor listing the business meetings scheduled each day aboard ship and certifying how many hours you spent in attendance. Make sure to get this statement from the meeting sponsor. Your annual deduction for attending conventions, seminars, or similar meetings on ships is limited to $2,000.

Transportation by Ship

You can get a deduction if you use an ocean liner, cruise ship, or other means of water travel solely as a means of transportation to a business destination. This isn't very common these days, but it can be done. In this event, your deduction for each travel day is limited to an amount equal to twice the highest amount federal workers are paid each day (called the per diem rate) for their living expenses while traveling inside the U.S. on government business. You can find the latest rates at www .gsa.gov. (Look for the link to "Per Diem Rates" in the "Featured Topics" section. You want the rates listed in the column entitled "Maximum per diem rate".)

EXAMPLE: In 2005, Caroline travels by ocean liner from New York to London. Her expense for the six-day cruise is $5,000. However, she may deduct only twice the highest 2005 federal per diem amount for each day of the cruise. This amount is $259, so she can only deduct $518 per day. Caroline's deduction for the cruise cannot exceed $3,108 (6 days x $518 = $3,108).

In addition, if your bill includes separately stated amounts for meals and entertainment while on the ship, you can deduct only 50% of these expenses. For example, if Caroline's bill showed that she was charged $2,000 for food and entertainment while on the trip, she could deduct only $1,000.

Does this mean you can take a long pleasure cruise to a business destination and get a deduction for each day? No—the regular foreign travel rules apply to ship travel. A foreign trip that lasts more than 14 days is deductible only if you spend more than half of the time on business.

EXAMPLE: Marcia embarks on a 30-day cruise from Los Angeles to Tokyo, where she attends a three-day business conference. She then flies back to Los Angeles. Her entire trip took 34 days, three of which were for business. Because she spent less than 50% of her time on business, the entire trip is a nondeductible personal expense.

5. Calculating Time Spent on Business

To calculate how much time you spend on business while on a business trip, you must compare the number of days you spend on business with the days you spend on personal activities. All of the following are considered business days:

- any day in which you work for more than four hours
- any day when you must be at a particular place for your practice— for example, to attend a client meeting—even if you spend most of the day on personal activities

- any day when you spend more than four hours on business travel—travel time begins when you leave home and ends when you reach your hotel, or vice versa
- any day when you drive 300 miles for business (you can average your mileage). For example, if you drive 1,500 miles to your destination in five days, you may claim five 300-mile days, even if you drove 500 miles on one of the days and 100 miles on another
- any day when your travel and work time together exceeds four hours
- any day when you are prevented from working because of circumstances beyond your control—for example, a transit strike or terrorist act, and
- any day sandwiched between two work days if it would have cost more to go home than to stay where you are—this rule can let you count weekends as business days. (See Section D below.)

EXAMPLE: Mike, a sole proprietor architect who hates flying, travels by car from his home in Reno, Nevada, to Cleveland, Ohio, for a meeting with a potential client. He makes the 2,100-mile drive in six days, arriving in Cleveland on Saturday night. He has his meeting with the client for one hour on Monday. The investor is intrigued with Mike's ideas, but wants him to come up with a preliminary design. Mike works on this for five hours on Tuesday and three hours on Wednesday, spending the rest of his time resting and sightseeing. He has his second client meeting on Thursday, which lasts two hours. He sightsees the rest of the day and then drives straight home on Friday. Mike's trip consisted of 15 business days: 11 travel days, one sandwiched day (the Sunday before his first meeting), two meeting days, and one day when he worked more than four hours. He had one personal day—the day when he spent only three hours working.

Be sure to keep track of your time while you're away. You can do this by making simple notes on your calendar or travel diary. (See Chapter 20 for a detailed discussion of record keeping while traveling.)

6.   50% Limit on Meal Expenses

The IRS figures that whether you're at home or away on a business trip, you have to eat. Because home meals ordinarily aren't deductible, the IRS won't let you deduct all of your food expenses while traveling. Instead, you can deduct only 50% of your meal expenses while on a business trip. There are two ways to calculate your meal expense deduction: You can keep track of your actual expenses or use a daily rate set by the federal government.

Deducting Actual Meal Expenses

If you use the actual expense method, you must keep track of what you spend on meals (including tips and tax) en route to and at your business destination. When you do your taxes, you add these amounts together and deduct half of the total.

> **EXAMPLE:** Frank goes on a business trip from Santa Fe, New Mexico, to Reno, Nevada. He gets there by car. On the way, he spends $200 for meals. While in Reno, he spends another $200. His total meal expense for the trip is $400. He may deduct half of this amount, or $200.

If you combine a business trip with a vacation, you may deduct only those meals you eat while on business—for example, meals you eat while attending client meetings or doing other business-related work. Meals that are part of business entertainment are subject to the rules on entertainment expenses covered in Chapter 4.

You do not necessarily have to keep all your receipts for your business meals, but you need to keep careful track of what you spend, and you should be able to prove that the meal was for business. See Chapter 20 for a detailed discussion of record keeping for meal expenses.

Using the Standard Meal Allowance

When you use the actual expense method, you must keep track of what you spend for each meal, which can be a lot of work. So the IRS provides an alternative method of deducting meals: Instead of deducting your actual expenses, you can deduct a set amount for each day of your business trip. This amount is called the standard meal allowance. It covers your expenses for business meals, beverages, tax, and tips. The amount of the allowance varies depending on where and when you travel.

The good thing about the standard meal allowance is that you don't need to keep track of how much you spend for meals and tips. You only need to keep records to prove the time, place, and business purpose of your travel. (See Chapter 4 for more on meal and entertainment expenses.)

The bad thing about the standard meal allowance is that it is based on what federal workers are allowed to charge for meals while traveling, and is therefore relatively modest. In 2006, the daily rates for domestic travel ranged from $39 per day for travel in the least expensive areas to up to $64 for high-cost areas, which includes most major cities. While it is possible to eat on $64 per day in places like New York City or San Francisco, you won't have a very good time. If you use the standard meal allowance and spend more than the allowance, you get no deduction for the overage.

Not Everyone Can Use the Standard Meal Allowance

The standard meal allowance may not be used by an employer to reimburse an employee for travel expenses if the employee:

- owns more than 10% of the stock in an incorporated practice, or
- is a close relative of a 10% or more owner—a brother, sister, parent, spouse, grandparent, or other lineal ancestor or descendent.

In these instances, the employee must deduct actual meal expenses for business-related travel to be reimbursed by the employer. Thus, if you've incorporated your business and work as its employee, you must keep track of what you spend on meals when you travel for business and are reimbursed for your expenses by your corporation.

The rates are generally higher for travel outside the continental United States—that is, Alaska, Hawaii, and foreign countries. For example, in 2005 the allowance for London, England, was $142 and $169 for Tokyo, Japan. In contrast, travelers to Baghdad were permitted only $15 per day; it's apparently very cheap to eat in Baghdad.

The standard meal allowance includes $3 per day for incidental expenses—tips you pay to porters, bellhops, maids, and transportation workers. If you wish, you can use the actual expense method for your meal costs and the $3 incidental expense rate for your tips. However, you'd have to be a pretty stingy tipper for this amount to be adequate.

The standard meal allowance is revised each year. You can find the current rates for travel within the United States on the Internet at www .gsa.gov (look for the link to "Per Diem Rates" in the "Featured Topics" section) or in IRS Publication 1542. The rates for foreign travel are set by the U.S. State Department and can be found at www.state.gov/m/a/als/ prdm. When you look at these rate listings, you'll see several categories of numbers. You want the "M & IE Rate"—short for meals and incidental expenses. Rates are also provided for lodging, but these don't apply to nongovernmental travelers.

You can claim only the standard meal allowance for business days. If you travel to more than one location in one day, use the rate in effect for the area where you spend the night. You are allowed to deduct 50% of the standard meal allowance from your taxes as a business expense.

> **EXAMPLE:** Art travels from Los Angeles to Chicago for a three-day business conference. Chicago is a high-cost locality, so the daily meal and incidental expense rate (M&IE) is $64. Art figures his deduction by multiplying the daily rate by five and multiplying this by 50%: 5 days x $64 = $320; $320 x 50% = $160.

If you use the standard meal allowance, you must use it for all of the business trips you take during the year. You can't use it for some trips and then use the actual expense method for others. For example, you can't use the standard allowance when you go to an inexpensive destination and the actual expense method when you go to a pricey one.

Because the standard meal allowance is so small, it's better to use it only if you travel exclusively to low-cost areas or if you are simply unable or unwilling to keep track of what you actually spend for meals.

You Don't Have to Spend Your Whole Allowance

When you use the standard meal allowance, you get to deduct the whole amount, regardless of what you spend. If you spend more than the daily allowance, you are limited to the allowance amount. But if you spend less, you still get to deduct the full allowance amount. For example, if you travel to New York City and live on bread and water, you may still deduct $25.50 for each business day. This strategy will not only save you money, you'll lose weight as well.

D. Maximizing Your Business Travel Deductions

Here are some simple strategies you can use to maximize your business travel deductions.

1.   Plan Ahead

Plan your itinerary carefully before you leave to make sure your trip qualifies as a business trip. For example, if you're traveling within the United States, you must spend more than half of your time on business for your transportation to be deductible. If you know you're going to spend three days on business, arrange to spend no more than two days on personal activities so this rule is satisfied. If you're traveling overseas for more than 14 days, you'll have to spend at least 75% of your time on business to deduct your transportation—you may be able to do this by using strategies to maximize your business days. (See Section 3, below.)

2.   Make a Paper Trail

If you are audited by the IRS, there is a good chance you will be questioned about business travel deductions. Of course, you'll need to have records showing what you spent for your trips. (See Chapter 20 for a detailed discussion on record keeping.) However, you'll also need documents proving that your trip was for your existing business. You can do this by:

- making a note in your calendar or daily planner of every client meeting you attend or other business-related work you do—be sure to note the time you spend on each business activity
- obtaining and saving business cards from anyone you meet while on business
- noting in your calendar or daily planner the names of all the people you meet for business on your trip
- keeping the program or agenda from a convention or training seminar you attend, as well as any notes you made
- after you return, sending thank-you notes to the business contacts you met on your trips—be sure to keep copies, and
- keeping copies of business-related correspondence or emails you sent or received before the trip.

3.   Maximize Your Business Days

If you mix business with pleasure on your trip, you have to make sure that you have enough business days to deduct your transportation costs. You'll need to spend more than 50% of your days on business on domestic trips and more than 75% for foreign trips of more than 14 days.

You don't have to work all day for that day to count as a business day: Any day in which you work at least four hours is a business day, even if you goof off the rest of time. The day will count as a business day for purposes of determining whether your transportation expenses are deductible, and you can deduct your lodging, meal, and other expenses during the day, even though you only worked four hours.

You can easily maximize your business days by taking advantage of this rule. For example, you can:

- work no more than four hours in any one day whenever possible
- spread your business over several days—for example, if you need to be present at three meetings, try to spread them over two or three days instead of one, and
- avoid using the fastest form of transportation to your business destination—travel days count as business days, so you'll add business days to your trip if you drive instead of fly. Remember, there's no law that says you have to take the quickest means of transportation to your destination.

4. Take Advantage of the Sandwich Day Rule

IRS rules provide that days when you do no business-related work count as business days when they are sandwiched between workdays, as long as it was cheaper to spend that day away than to go back home for the off days. If you work on Friday and Monday, this rule allows you to count the weekend as business days, even though you did no work.

> **EXAMPLE:** Kim, an optometrist, flies from Houston to Honolulu, Hawaii, for an optometrist convention. She arrives on Wednesday and returns the following Wednesday. She does not attend any convention activities during the weekend and goes to the beach instead. Nevertheless, because it was cheaper for her to stay in Hawaii than to fly to Houston just for the weekend and then back to Hawaii, she may count Saturday and Sunday as business days. This means she can deduct her lodging and meal expenses for those days (but not the cost of renting a surfboard).

Converting a Vacation Into a Business Trip

Here are three strategies you can use to legally convert a non-deductible personal vacation into a deductible business trip:

- **Combine your vacation with a continuing professional education program.** Travel to take continuing education courses required for your profession is deductible. Sign up for a program in a desirable location and take the family along with you.
- **Visit a colleague.** Travel to attend meetings with professional colleagues for business purposes—not to socialize—is tax deductible. Document your visit with letters and email.
- **Hold a board meeting.** If your practice is incorporated, you can hold your annual board meeting in a desirable location and deduct your travel expenses. You must really hold a board meeting and have documentation to prove it—corporate minutes and a written agenda.

If you use any of these strategies and take your family with you, your family's expenses are not deductible, unless a family member provides essential services to your practice. However, your travel expenses are deductible, provided you follow the rules covered above. For example, if you travel within the United States, you must spend at least 51% of your total days on business to deduct your transportation expenses. If you spend over half your days on nonbusiness activities, virtually none of your expenses are deductible. The rules differ for foreign travel.

EXAMPLE: Ralph, a Chicago surgeon, attends an educational program on new surgical techniques in Miami and takes his wife and two children with him. He and his family spend seven days in Miami. While his family has fun, Ralph attends the surgery seminar for four hours a day for four days. He spends the other three days relaxing with his family. Ralph spent four of seven days on business, which is more than 50% of his total time in Miami. Thus, he gets to deduct his airfare to and from Miami and his hotel and meal expenses for his four business days. He and his family stayed in a two bedroom hotel suite, but he can deduct only what it would have cost for a one-bedroom room.

E. How to Deduct Travel Expenses

How you deduct your travel expenses depends on how your practice is legally organized. If you're a sole proprietor, you deduct your expenses on your personal tax return. However, if your practice is an LLC, partnership, or LLP, your expenses may have to be deducted on the business entity's return, not your personal tax return. If your practice is a corporation, any personal deduction will be limited.

1. Sole Proprietors

If you're a sole proprietor, you list your travel expenses on Schedule C, *Profit or Loss From Business*. Travel expenses other than meals are listed on line 24a. Meals are listed on lines 24b-d. You list the full amount of meal expenses, but deduct only 50% of the total.

2. LLCs, Partnerships, and LLPs

If your practice is organized as an LLC, partnership, or LLP, it will ordinarily be taxed as a partnership (see Chapter 2). If you are, you will have to seek reimbursement of your deductible travel expenses from your practice, unless you fall within the exception discussed below. The amount of the reimbursement is not taxable income to you, provided you comply with all required record-keeping rules for car expenses and the reimbursement is made under an accountable plan. Basically, this requires that you submit all your documentation to the practice in a timely manner, and return any excess payments. Accountable plans are covered in detail in Chapter 17.

The amount of the reimbursed travel expenses is listed on the partnership's tax return (Form 1065) and reduces its taxable profit for the year.

EXAMPLE: Rick, a partner in a group medical practice organized as an LLC, flies from Chicago to St. Paul to attend a two-day seminar on new surgical techniques. He incurs $1,500 in travel expenses and keeps careful track of all his expenses. After he gets back, he submits a request for reimbursement from the LLC, along with an expense report and all required receipts. The LLC pays him $1,500. This money is not taxable income to Rick and the LLC may list it on its tax return as a business expense.

There is one exception to the reimbursement rule which allows you to deduct travel expenses on your personal tax return if either:
- a written partnership agreement or LLC operating agreement provides that the expense will *not* be reimbursed by the partnership or LLC, or
- your practice has an established routine practice of not reimbursing the expense.

Absent such a written statement or practice, *no personal deduction may be taken*. Reimbursement from the partnership, LLP, or LLC must be sought instead. If you take a personal deduction for your travel expenses, your practice does not list them on its tax return, and they do not reduce your practice's profits. But they will reduce your taxable income. (See Chapter 17.)

You deduct your unreimbursed travel expenses (and any other unreimbursed business expenses) on IRS Schedule E (Part II) and attach it to your personal tax return. Don't use Schedule C. You must attach a separate schedule to Schedule E listing the car and other business expenses you're deducting.

EXAMPLE: Assume that Rick's LLC has a written policy that all the partners must personally pay for their own travel expenses. Instead of seeking reimbursement, Rick lists his $1,500 travel expense on his own tax return, Schedule E, reducing his taxable income by that amount. The LLC does not list the expense on its return, thus it does not reduce the practice's income.

3.   Corporations

If your practice is legally organized as a corporation (whether a C or S corporation), you will ordinarily be its employee. Special rules govern all business expense deductions by employees. Your best option is to have your corporation reimburse you for your travel expenses. This process is the same as described above for LLC and partnerships. If you comply with all the documentation rules for car expenses and accountable plan requirements, your corporation gets to deduct the expense on its tax return and you don't have to count the reimbursement as income. If you fail to follow the rules, any reimbursements must be treated as employee income subject to tax (but you may deduct your expenses as described below).

Alternatively, you can forgo reimbursement from your corporation and deduct your travel expenses on your personal tax return. However, this is not a good option because employees can deduct unreimbursed employee expenses only as miscellaneous itemized deductions on Form 1040, Schedule A. Thus, they are deductible only if an employee itemizes his or her deductions and only to the extent that these deductions, along with any other miscellaneous itemized deductions, exceed 2% of the employee's adjusted gross income. Additional deduction limits are imposed on higher-income employees—in 2005, employees earning more than $145,950. (See Chapter 17.)

F.   Travel Expenses Reimbursed by Clients

Professionals who travel while performing services for a client often have their expenses reimbursed by the client. You need not include such reimbursements in your income if you provide an adequate accounting of the expenses to your client and comply with the accountable plan rules. Basically, this requires that you submit all your documentation to the client in a timely manner and return any excess payments. Accountable plans are covered in detail in Chapter 17. Record-keeping rules for long distance travel are covered in Chapter 20.

EXAMPLE: Farley, an architect, incurs $5,000 in travel expenses while working on a new shopping center for a client. He keeps complete and accurate records of his expenses which he provides to his client. His client reimburses him the $5,000. Farley need not include the $5,000 in his income for the year and Farley's client may deduct the reimbursement as a business expense.

If you do not adequately account to your client for these expenses, you must include any reimbursements or allowances in your income, and they should also be included in any 1099-MISC form the client is required to provide the IRS reporting how much you were paid (see Chapter 17). The client can still deduct the reimbursement as compensation paid to you. You may deduct the expenses on your own return, but you'll need documentation to back them up in the event of an audit.

■

Chapter 7

The Home Office Deduction

T he federal government helps out business owners by letting them deduct their home office expenses from their taxable income. If, like many professionals, you regularly work at home, you may able to claim the home office deduction. Even if you have an outside office where you do the bulk of your work, you still may be able to use this deduction. However, if you plan on taking the deduction, you need to learn how to do it properly. There are strict requirements you must follow and how you claim the deduction will depend in part on what type of business entity you have.

A. Qualifying for the Home Office Deduction

To take the home office deduction, you must have a home office—that is, an office or other workplace in your home that you use regularly and exclusively for business. Your "home" may be a house, apartment, condominium, mobile home, or even a boat. You can also take the deduction for separate structures on your property that you use for business, such as an unattached garage, workshop, studio, barn, or greenhouse. If you qualify, you can deduct your expenses for your home office.

> **EXAMPLE:** Rich is a sole proprietor attorney who rents a law office in a downtown office building. However, he also regularly performs law-related work in the basement of his San Francisco rental home, which he has converted into a home office. If he meets the requirements discussed below, he can deduct his home office expenses, including a portion of his rent, from his law practice income. This saves him over $2,000 per year on his income and self-employment taxes.

It's easier now to claim the home office deduction. If you've heard stories about how difficult it is to qualify for the home office deduction, you can breathe more easily. Changes in the tax law that took effect in 1999 make it much easier for businesspeople to qualify for the deduction. So even if you haven't qualified for the deduction in the past, you may be entitled to take it now.

1.   Three Threshold Requirements

There are three threshold requirements that everyone must meet to qualify for the home office deduction. You must:
- be in business
- use your home office exclusively for business (unless you store inventory in your home—see Section 2, below), and
- use your home office for your business on a regular basis.

If you get past this first hurdle, then you must also meet *any one* of the following five requirements:
- your home office is your principal place of business
- you regularly and exclusively use your home office for administrative or management activities for your practice and have no other fixed location where you perform such activities
- you meet patients, clients, or customers at home
- you use a separate structure on your property exclusively for business purposes, or
- you store inventory or product samples at home.

These rules apply whether you are a sole proprietor, partner in a partnership or LLP, limited liability company (LLC) owner, or if you have formed a C or S corporation. However, if you are an employee of a corporation that you own and operate, or have formed a multimember LLC, LLP, or partnership, there are some additional requirements (see Sections C and D, below).

You Must Be in Business

You may take the home office deduction only for a business. You can't take the deduction for a hobby or other nonbusiness activity that you conduct out of your home. Nor can you take it if you perform personal investment activities at home—for example, researching the stock market.

You don't have to work full time in a business to qualify for the home office deduction. If you satisfy the requirements, you can take the deduction for a side business that you run from a home office. The side business can even be related to your regular business. For example, a surgeon who established a biopsy lab in his home was able to claim the home office deduction for the lab because the lab was a separate business from his surgical practice. (*Hoye v. Comm'r*, T.C. Memo 1990-57.)

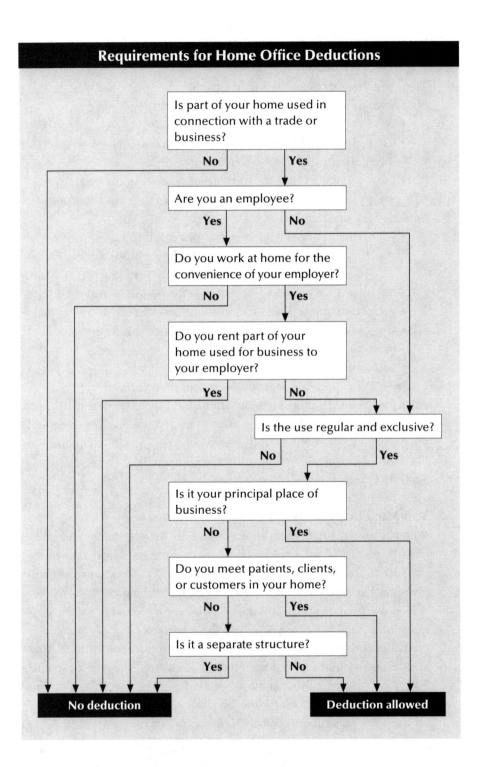

Requirements for Home Office Deductions

Is part of your home used in connection with a trade or business?

- No
- Yes

Are you an employee?

- Yes
- No

Do you work at home for the convenience of your employer?

- No
- Yes

Do you rent part of your home used for business to your employer?

- Yes
- No

Is the use regular and exclusive?

- No
- Yes

Is it your principal place of business?

- No
- Yes

Do you meet patients, clients, or customers in your home?

- No
- Yes

Is it a separate structure?

- Yes
- No

No deduction

Deduction allowed

However, you must use your home office regularly, and the total amount you deduct cannot exceed your profit from the business. (See Section B2, below, for more on the profit limitation.)

You can use the same home office for two or more businesses. But, to take the home office deduction for any of your businesses, *each* business for which you use your home office must separately qualify for the deduction.

> **EXAMPLE:** Lester, a veterinarian, who practices from a building outside his home, has a sideline business selling dog training videos. He conducts the video business from an office in a bedroom in his home. He also occasionally uses the bedroom office to perform work for his veterinary practice. His use of the home office for his video business qualifies for the home office deduction, but his use for his veterinary practice does not support the deduction because it fails to satisfy any of the five additional requirements covered in Section A2, above. As a result, Lester gets no home office deduction at all.

Exclusive Business Use

You can't take the home office deduction unless you use part of your home exclusively for your business. In other words, you must use your home office *only for your business.* The more space you devote exclusively to your business, the more your home office deduction will be worth. (See Section B, below.) This requirement doesn't apply if you store inventory at home. (See Section 2e.)

If you use part of your home—such as a room or garage—as your business office, but you also use that same space for personal purposes, you won't qualify for the home office deduction.

> **EXAMPLE:** Johnny, an accountant, has a den at home furnished with a desk, chair, bookshelf, filing cabinet, and a bed for visiting guests. He uses the desk and chair for both business and personal reasons. The bookshelf contains both personal and business books, the filing cabinet contains both personal and business files, and the bed is used only for personal reasons. Johnny can't claim a home office deduction for the den because he does not use it, or any part of it, exclusively for business purposes.

How Big (or Small) Can Your Home Office Be?

Your home office can be as big or small as you want or need. You are not required to use as small a space as possible. If you like plenty of office space, you can spread out and even use more than one room. But, remember, you may use your home office space only for business. You aren't even supposed to use it for personal business, such as writing personal checks. You must also use all your home office space regularly.

Although the IRS probably won't be inspecting your home office, your deduction must still make sense in the event you are audited. If you live in a one-bedroom apartment and claim the entire bedroom as a home office, you'll need to have an answer ready when the IRS asks where you sleep.

In one case, a psychologist who lived in San Francisco claimed a home office deduction for one-quarter of her apartment. However, the entire apartment was a 400-square-foot studio, consisting of an open area (approximately 13 feet by 15 feet) furnished with a desk and a couch, and a small dining area and kitchen (each approximately seven feet by eight feet). Given the layout of this tiny apartment, neither the IRS nor the tax court bought the psychologist's claim that she used 100 square feet exclusively for her psychology practice. (*Mullin v. Comm'r*, T.C. Memo 2001-121.)

The easiest way to meet the exclusive use test is to devote an entire room in your home to your business—for example, by using an extra bedroom as your office. However, not everybody has a room to spare—and the IRS recognizes this. You can still claim the deduction even if you use just part of a room as your office, as long as you use that part exclusively for business.

EXAMPLE: Paula, a sole proprietor consulting engineer, keeps her desk, chair, bookshelf, computer, and filing cabinet in one part of her den and uses them exclusively for her engineering practice. The remainder of the room—one-third of the space—is used to store a bed for houseguests. Paula can take a home office deduction for the two-thirds of the room that she uses exclusively as an office.

If you use the same room (or rooms) for your office and for other purposes, you'll have to arrange your furniture and belongings so that a portion of the room is devoted exclusively to your business. Place only your business furniture and other business items in the office portion of the room. Business furniture includes anything that you use for your business, such as standard office furniture like a desk and chair. Depending on your business, it could include other items as well—for example, a psychologist might need a couch, and a consultant might need a seating area to meet with clients. One court held that a financial planner was entitled to have a television in his home office because he used it to keep up on financial news. Be careful what you put in this space, however. In another case, the IRS disallowed the deduction for a doctor because he had a television in the part of his living room that he claimed as his home office. The court wouldn't buy the doctor's claim that he only watched medical programs.

The IRS does not require you to physically separate the space you use for business from the rest of the room. However, doing so will help you satisfy the exclusive use test. For example, if you use part of your living room as an office, you could separate it from the rest of the room with folding screens or bookcases.

Although you must use your home office exclusively for business, you and other family members or visitors may walk through it to get to other rooms in your residence.

As a practical matter, the IRS doesn't have spies checking to see whether you're using your home office just for business. However, complying with the rules from the beginning means you won't have to worry if you are audited.

When the IRS Can Enter Your Home

IRS auditors may not enter your home unless you or another lawful occupant gives them permission. The only exception is if the IRS obtains a court order to enter your home, which is very rare. In the absence of such a court order, an IRS auditor must ask permission to come to your home to verify your home office deduction. You don't have to grant permission for the visit—but if you don't, the auditor will probably disallow your deduction.

Regular Business Use

It's not enough to use a part of your home exclusively for business; you must also use it regularly. For example, you can't place a desk in a corner of a room and claim the home office deduction if you almost never use the desk for your practice.

Unfortunately, the IRS doesn't offer a clear definition of regular use. The agency has stated only that you must use a portion of your home for business on a continuing basis—not just for occasional or incidental business. One court has held that 12 hours of use a week is sufficient. (*Green v. Comm'r,* 79 T.C. 428 (1982).) You might be able to qualify with less use—for example, an hour a day—but no one knows for sure. It's a good idea to keep track of how much you use your home office. Your record doesn't have to be fancy—notes in an appointment book are sufficient.

2.   One of Five Additional Requirements

Using a home office exclusively and regularly for business is not enough to qualify for the home office deduction: You also must satisfy any one of the additional five requirements described below. Moreover, if your practice is a corporation, you must meet the convenience of the employer test covered in Section 3, below.

Principal Place of Business

One way to satisfy the additional home office deduction requirement is to show that you use your home as your principal place of business. How you accomplish this depends on where you do most of your work and what type of work you do at home.

If you only work at home

If, like a growing number of professionals, you do all or almost all of your work in your home office, your home is clearly your principal place of business and you'll have no trouble qualifying for the home office deduction.

> **EXAMPLE:** Linda, a sole proprietor architect, uses one bedroom of her two-bedroom apartment as the only office for her architecture practice. Except on the relatively rare occasions when she meets with clients in their offices or goes to building sites, she performs all her work in her home office. This office clearly qualifies as her principal place of business.

Working in multiple locations

If you work in more than one location, your home office still qualifies as your principal place of business if you perform your most important business activities—those activities that most directly generate your income—at home.

> **EXAMPLE:** Charles is a consultant who performs marketing research for his clients. He spends 30 to 35 hours per week in his home office performing research and writing reports, and five to ten hours a week meeting with clients in their offices. The essence of Charles's business is marketing research—this is how he generates his income. Therefore, his home qualifies as his principal place of business because that's where he performs his research activities.

If you perform equally important business activities in several locations, your principal place of business is where you spend more than half of your time. If there is no such location, you don't have a principal place of business.

> **EXAMPLE:** Sue is a psychologist who meets with her patients both in an outside office and at home. She spends 25 hours per week in her home office and 15 hours at her outside office. Her home office qualifies as her principal place of business.

Administrative Work

Of course, most professionals spend the bulk of their time working away from home, usually in an outside office. Thus, their home offices cannot qualify as their principal place of business under the test discussed above. Fortunately, legal changes that took effect in 1999 make it possible for such people to qualify for the home office deduction. Under the rules, your home office qualifies as your principal place of business for purposes of the home office deduction, even if you work primarily outside your home, if:

- you use the office regularly and exclusively to perform administrative and/or management activities for your business, and
- there is no other fixed location where you conduct substantial administrative or management activities.

Administrative and management activities include, but are not limited to:

- billing clients or patients
- keeping books and records
- ordering supplies
- setting up appointments, and
- writing reports.

This means that you can qualify for the home office deduction even if your home office is not where you generate most of your income. It's sufficient that you regularly use it for the administrative and management activities you perform for your business. As long as you have no other fixed location where you regularly do these activities—for example, an outside office—you'll get the deduction.

You don't have to personally perform at home all the administrative or management activities your business requires to qualify for the home office deduction. Your home office can qualify for the deduction even if:

- you have others conduct your administrative or management activities at locations other than your home—for example, another company does your billing from its place of business
- you conduct administrative or management activities at places that are not fixed locations for your business, such as in a car or a hotel room
- you occasionally conduct minimal administrative or management activities at a fixed location outside your home, such as your outside office.

Moreover, you can qualify for the deduction even if you have suitable space to conduct administrative or management activities outside your home, but choose to use your home office for those activities instead.

> **EXAMPLE 1:** Sally is a sole proprietor attorney with a flourishing criminal defense practice. She has a small office she shares with several other attorneys, but spends most of her work time in court, local jails, and in her car. Sally employs an outside firm to bill her clients and perform the other bookkeeping her practice requires. Sally also has a home office she uses to perform most of the administrative and management tasks she does herself, such as setting up appointments, writing briefs and memos, and ordering supplies. Sally also performs some of these tasks, such as making appointments, while in court or in her car on the way to or from court. She rarely uses her outside office for these tasks. Sally's home office qualifies as her principal place of business for purposes of the home office deduction. She conducts administrative or management activities for her business as an attorney there and has no other fixed location where she conducts substantial administrative or management activities for this business. The fact that she occasionally performs some administrative tasks in her car or in court does not disqualify her for the deduction because they are not fixed locations for her law practice. Likewise, she doesn't lose the deduction because she has an outside company do her billing.

EXAMPLE 2: Paul is a sole proprietor anesthesiologist. He spends the majority of his time administering anesthesia and postoperative care in three local hospitals. One of the hospitals provides him with a small shared office where he could conduct administrative or management activities. Paul very rarely uses the office the hospital provides; instead, he uses a room in his home that he has converted to an office. He uses this room exclusively and regularly to contact patients, surgeons, and hospitals regarding scheduling; prepare for treatments and presentations; maintain billing records and patient logs; satisfy continuing medical education requirements; and read medical journals and books.

Paul's home office qualifies as his principal place of business for deducting expenses for its use. He conducts administrative or management activities for his business as an anesthesiologist there and he has no other fixed location where he conducts a substantial portion of these activities. His choice to use his home office instead of the one provided by the hospital does not disqualify his home office from being his principal place of business. The fact that he performs substantial nonadministrative or nonmanagement activities at fixed locations outside his home—that is, at hospitals—also does not disqualify his home office from being his principal place of business.

Unfortunately, not all professionals find it convenient, or even possible, to perform all or most of their administrative or management tasks out of their home offices. They must use their outside offices for making appointments, doing record keeping, or similar work. These professional will not qualify for the home office deduction under the rule described in this section, even if they have home offices they regularly and exclusively use to perform some administrative tasks.

Meeting Clients or Customers at Home

All is not necessarily lost if your home office does not qualify as your principal place of business. You can still take the home office deduction for any part of your home that you use exclusively to meet with clients, customers, or patients. You must physically meet with others in this home location; phoning or emailing them from there is not sufficient.

And the meetings must be a regular and integral part of your business; occasional meetings don't qualify.

It's not entirely clear how often you must meet clients at home for those meetings to be considered regular. However, the IRS has indicated that meeting clients one or two days a week is sufficient. Exclusive use means you use the space where you meet clients only for business. You are free to use the space for business purposes other than meeting clients—for example, doing your business bookkeeping or other paperwork. But you cannot use the space for personal purposes, such as watching television.

> **EXAMPLE:** June, an attorney, works three days a week in her city office and two days in her home office, which she uses only for business. Her home office does not qualify as her principal place of business under either of the tests discussed in Subsections a and b, above—she does not generate most of her income from home, and she does not use her home office to perform most of the administrative and management tasks for her practice. However, she meets clients at her home office at least once a week. Because she regularly meets clients at her home office, she qualifies for the home office deduction even though her city office is her principal place of business.

Many professionals such as doctors, lawyers, and accountants, can qualify for the home office deduction under this rule because it's easy for them to meet with clients or patients at home. If you want to do this, encourage clients or customers to visit you at home and keep a log or appointment book showing all of their visits. Also, you should place your home office phone number and address on your business cards and stationery.

Using a Separate Structure

You can also deduct expenses for a separate freestanding structure, such as a studio, garage, or barn, if you use it exclusively and regularly for your business. The structure does not have to be your principal place of business or a place where you meet patients, clients, or customers.

Exclusive use means that you use the structure only for business—for example, you can't use it to store gardening equipment or as a guesthouse. Regular use is not precisely defined, but it's probably sufficient to use the structure ten or 15 hours a week.

> **EXAMPLE:** Deborah is a sole proprietor accountant who spends 40 hours per week working in her outside office. This office is her principal place of business, and she does not meet with clients at home or perform most of her administrative and management work there. Nevertheless, Deborah qualifies for the home office deduction: She has a pool house in her back yard that she has converted into a home office that she uses ten to 15 hours per week on her accounting work. Because she uses the separate pool house structure regularly and exclusively for her accounting practice, she gets the home office deduction.

Storing Inventory or Product Samples

You can also take the home office deduction if you sell retail or wholesale products and you store inventory or product samples at home. However, you must meet all the following tests.

- you sell products at wholesale or retail as your trade or business
- you keep the inventory or product samples in your home for use in your trade or business
- your home is the only fixed location of your trade or business
- you use the storage space on a regular basis, and
- the space you use is a separately identifiable space suitable for storage.

> **EXAMPLE:** Lisa is an optometrist who also maintains a large stock of eyeglasses she sells to her patients, or anyone else who wants to buy them. She rents a home and regularly uses half of her small attached garage to store part of her eyeglass inventory. Lisa can deduct the expenses for the storage space under the home office deduction.

3. Special Requirement for Employees

If you have formed a corporation to own and operate your practice, you're probably working as its employee. (See Chapter 16.) To qualify for the home office deduction as an employee, you must satisfy all the requirements discussed above. In addition, you must be able to show that you maintain your home office for the convenience of your employer—that is, your corporation. An employee's home office is deemed to be for an employer's convenience if it is:

- a condition of employment
- necessary for the employer's business to properly function, or
- needed to allow the employee to properly perform his or her duties.

The convenience of employer test is not met if using a home office is for your convenience or because you can get more work done at home. For example, you won't pass the test if you have an outside office but like to take work home with you.

When you own the business that employs you, you ordinarily won't be able to successfully claim that a home office is a condition of your employment—after all, as the owner of the business, you're the person who sets the conditions for employees, including yourself. Thus, you'll have to satisfy either the necessity or performance tests.

If there is no other office where you do your work, you should be able to successfully claim that your home office is necessary for your business to properly function and/or for you to perform your employee duties.

It will be more difficult to establish necessity if you have an outside office. Nevertheless, business owners in this situation have successfully argued that their home offices were necessary—for example, because their corporate offices were not open or not usable during evenings, weekends, or other nonbusiness hours, or were too far from home to use during off-hours.

Renting Your Home Office to Your Corporation

If you're an employee of your professional corporation and you can't meet the convenience of the employer test or the other requirements for the home office deduction, you have another option: Forget about the home office deduction and rent your home office to your C corporation. You won't save any income tax this way, but you can still save on Social Security and Medicare taxes.

Here's how it works.

- You rent your home office to your C corporation for a fair market rental.
- Your C corporation deducts the rent as a business expense on its tax return (Form 1120).
- You report the rent you receive as ordinary income on your personal tax return, and pay income tax on it.

Ordinarily, a landlord may deduct his rental expenses such as mortgage interest, depreciation, and utilities. However, a special tax rule prohibits an employee who rents part of his home to his employer from deducting such expenses. (IRC § 280A(c)(6).) So, you can forget about taking any deductions for your rental expenses to reduce your income taxes.

However, you still save on Social Security and Medicare taxes because the rental income you receive is not subject to these taxes. For the rent to be deductible by the corporation, however, there must be a legitimate business reason for this rental arrangement. This would be the case if your home office was your only office, or if you could otherwise show a legitimate need for it.

> **EXAMPLE:** Rod, an accountant who works out of his home, has formed a C corporation. Rod does not qualify for the home office deduction because he does not use his office exclusively for his accounting business. He charges his corporation $10,000 per year for the use he makes of his office for his accounting practice. Rod gets no home office deduction, but his corporation deducts the rent on its own tax return. He reports the $10,000 on his personal tax return as rental income, but takes no deductions for rental expenses

such as depreciation and utilities. Rod saves nothing on his income taxes, but he and his corporation need not pay Social Security and Medicare taxes on the $10,000 rental payment. This saves $1,530 in taxes that would have had to have been paid if the $10,000 were paid to Rod as employee salary.

This strategy only works for C corporations because they are not subject to the home office deduction rules (although their employees are). It won't work with an S corporation because the home office rules apply to pass-through entities. As a result, an S corporation can't deduct rent paid for a home office that doesn't satisfy all the rules discussed in Section A, above.

You need to be careful not to charge your corporation too much rent. Amounts the IRS deems excessive may be recharacterized as constructive dividends that are not deductible by the corporation. They will, therefore, be subject to corporate income tax which professional corporations usually pay at a 35% rate. (See Chapter 2.) To avoid this, the rent you charge your corporation should be the same as you would charge a stranger.

B. Calculating the Home Office Deduction

This is the fun part—figuring out how much the home office deduction will save you in taxes.

1. How Much of Your Home Is Used for Business?

To calculate your home office deduction, you need to determine what percentage of your home you use for business. The law says you can use "any reasonable method" to do this. Obviously, you want to use the method that will give you the largest home office deduction. To do this, you want to maximize the percentage of your home that you claim as your office. There is no single way to do this for every home office. Try both methods described below and use the one that gives you the largest deduction.

When Is an Office Part of a Home?

Kenneth Burkhart, a professional photographer, purchased a two-story building with a full basement. The building was originally constructed and used as a three-flat apartment building with a separate apartment in the basement and on each of the two upper floors. Burkhart converted the upper two floors into a single residence for his use and converted the basement to a studio and darkroom for his photography business.

Was the studio part of his residence or a separate apartment? This was not an idle question. The home office deduction rules apply only to offices or other workspaces that are part of a business owner's "dwelling."

Courts faced with this issue look at whether the area used for business is physically and functionally part of the business owner's residence. In this case, the court noted that Burkhart had removed the basement's outside entrance, kitchen, bathroom, and sleeping area. Because the basement could only be reached from the upper floors of the building, the court reasoned that the upper floors and the basement had become a single "house," similar to millions of other family homes with two upper floors and a basement. Thus, Burkhart's studio was part of his dwelling and was subject to the home office deduction rules. (*Burkhart v. Comm'r*, T.C. Memo 1989-417.)

Some tax experts advise not to claim more than 20% to 25% of your home as an office unless you store inventory at home. However, home business owners have successfully claimed much more. In one case, for example, an interior decorator claimed 74% of his apartment (850 of 1,150 square feet) as a home office. He was audited, but the IRS did not object to the amount of space he claimed for his office. (*Visin v. Comm'r*, T.C. Memo 2003-246.) In another case, a professional violinist successfully claimed a home office deduction for her entire living room, which took up 40% of her one-bedroom apartment. She used the room solely for violin practice. (*Popov v. Comm'r*, 246 F.3d 1190 (9th Cir. 2002).) It is probably true, though, that the larger your home office deduction, the greater your chances of being audited.

Square Footage Method

The most precise method of measuring your office space is to divide the square footage of your home office by the total square footage of your home. For example, if your home is 1,600 square feet and you use 400 square feet for your home office, 25% of the total area is used for business. Of course, you must know the square footage of your entire home and your office to make this calculation. Your home's total square footage may be listed on real estate documents or plans; you'll have to measure your office space yourself. You don't need to use a tape measure; you can just pace off the measurements.

You are allowed to subtract the square footage of common areas such as hallways, entries, stairs, and landings from the total area that you are measuring. You can also exclude attics and garages from your total space if you don't use them for business purposes. You aren't required to measure this way, but doing so will give you a larger deduction because your overall percentage of business use will be higher.

Room Method

Another way to measure is the room method. You can use this method only if all of the rooms in your home are about the same size. Using this method, you divide the number of rooms used for business by the total number of rooms in the home. Don't include bathrooms, closets, or other storage areas. You may also leave out garages and attics if you don't use them for business. For example, if you use one room in a five-room house for business, your office takes up 20% of your home.

The room method often yields a larger deduction. Even though IRS Form 8829, *Expenses for Business Use of Your Home,* (the form sole proprietors file to claim the home office deduction), seems to require you to use the square footage method, this isn't the case. As long as all of the rooms in your home are about the same size, you can use the room method. Using the room method will often result in a larger deduction.

EXAMPLE: Rich, a sole proprietor lawyer, rents a six-room house in San Francisco and uses one bedroom as his home office. Using the square footage method, Rich measures his entire house and finds it is 2,000 square feet. His home office is 250 square feet. Using these figures, his home office percentage is 12.5% (250 divided by 2,000 = 12.5%). However, he wants to do better than this, so he measures his common areas, such as hallways and stairways, which amount to 200 square feet. He subtracts this amount from the 2,000 total square feet, which leaves 1,800 square feet. This gives him a home office percentage of 14% (250 divided by 1,800 = 14%).

Rich then tries the room method to see whether this provides a better result. His house has six rooms—three bedrooms, a living room, a dining room, and a kitchen. He doesn't count the bathroom, garage, or attic. Because he uses one entire room as his home office, he divides one by six, leaving 16.7% as his home office percentage. Rich uses this amount to figure his home office deduction.

2.   What Expenses Can You Deduct?

The home office deduction is not one deduction, but many. Most costs associated with maintaining and running your home office are deductible. However, because your office is in your home, some of the money you spend also benefits you personally. For example, your utility bill pays to heat your home office, but it also keeps the rest of your living space warm. The IRS deals with this issue by dividing home office expenses into two categories: direct expenses, which benefit only your home office; and indirect expenses, which benefit both your office and the rest of your home.

Direct Expenses

You have a direct home office expense when you pay for something just for the home office portion of your home. This includes, for example, the cost of painting your home office, carpeting it, or paying someone to clean it. The entire amount of a direct home office expense is deductible.

> **EXAMPLE:** Jean pays a housepainter $400 to paint her home office. She may deduct this entire amount as a home office deduction.

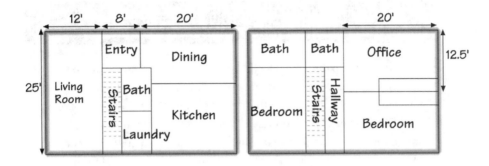

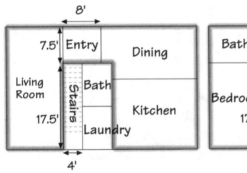

You Can Deduct Business Expenses Even If You Don't Qualify for the Home Office Deduction

Many business owners believe that they can't deduct any expenses they incur while working at home unless they qualify for the home office deduction. This is a myth that has cost many taxpayers valuable deductions. Even if you don't qualify for, or take the home office deduction, you can still take tax deductions for expenses you incur while doing business at home. These are expenses that arise from the fact that you are doing business, not from the use of the home itself.

- **Telephone expenses.** You can't deduct the basic cost of a single telephone line into your home, but you can deduct the cost of long-distance business calls and special phone services that you use for your business (such as call waiting or message center). You can also deduct the entire cost of a second phone line that you use just for business.

- **Business equipment and furniture.** The cost of office furniture, copiers, fax machines, and other personal property you use for your business and keep at home is deductible, whether or not you qualify for the home office deduction. If you purchase these items specifically for your home business, you can expense them (deduct them in one year) under Section 179 or depreciate them over several years. If you convert personal property you already own to business use, you may depreciate the fair market value. If you're a sole proprietor, you deduct these costs directly on Schedule C, *Profit or Loss From Business*. You don't have to list them on the special tax form used for the home office deduction. If you use the property for both business and personal reasons, the IRS requires you to keep records showing when the item was used for business or personal reasons—for example, a diary or log with the dates, times, and reasons the item was used. See Chapter 20 for a detailed discussion.

- **Supplies.** Supplies for your business are currently deductible as an operating expense if they have a useful life of less than one year. Otherwise, you must depreciate them or expense them under Section 179.

Virtually anything you buy for your office that becomes obsolete, wears out, or gets used up is deductible. However, you may have to depreciate permanent improvements to your home over 27.5 years, rather than deduct them in the year when you pay for them. Permanent improvements are changes that go beyond simple repairs, such as adding a new room to your home to serve as your office. (See Chapter 9.)

Indirect Expenses

An indirect expense is a payment for something that benefits your *entire home*, including both the home office portion and your personal space. You may deduct only a portion of this expense—the home office percentage of the total.

> **EXAMPLE:** Instead of just painting her home office, Jean decides to paint her entire home for $1,600. She uses 25% of her home as an office, so she may deduct 25% of the cost, or $400.

Most of your home office expenses will be indirect expenses, including:

- **Rent.** If you rent your home or apartment, you can use the home office deduction to deduct part of your rent—a substantial expense that is ordinarily not deductible. Your tax savings will be particularly great if you live in a high-rent area.

> **EXAMPLE:** Sam uses 20% of his one-bedroom Manhattan apartment as a home office for his consulting business. He pays $2,000 per month in rent, and may therefore deduct $400 of his rent per month ($4,800 per year) as a home office expense. This saves him over $2,000 in federal, state, and self-employment taxes.

- **Mortgage interest and property taxes.** Whether or not you have a home office, you can deduct your monthly mortgage interest and property tax payments as a personal itemized income tax deduction on your Schedule A (the tax form where you list your personal income tax deductions). But if you have a home office, you have the option of deducting the home office percentage of your mortgage interest and property tax payments as part of your home office deduction. If you do this, you may not deduct this amount on your

Schedule A (you can't deduct the same item twice). The advantage of deducting the home office percentage of your monthly mortgage interest and real estate tax payments as part of your home office deduction is that it is a business deduction, not a personal deduction; as such, it reduces the amount of your business income subject to self-employment taxes, as well as reducing your income taxes. The self-employment tax is 15.3%, so you save $153 in self-employment taxes for every $1,000 in mortgage interest and property taxes you deduct as part of your home office deduction.

EXAMPLE: Suzy, a sole proprietor child therapist, uses 20% of her three-bedroom Tulsa home as a home office. She pays $10,000 per year in mortgage interest and property taxes. When she does her taxes for the year, she may deduct $2,000 of her interest and taxes as part of her home office deduction (20% of $10,000). She adds this amount to her other home office expenses and decreases her business income for both income tax and self-employment tax purposes. The extra $2,000 business deduction saves her $306 in self-employment tax (15.3% x $2,000). She may deduct the remaining $8,000 of mortgage interest and property tax as a personal deduction on her Schedule A.

- **Depreciation.** If you own your home, you're also entitled to a depreciation deduction for the office portion of your home. See Chapter 9 for a detailed discussion of depreciation.
- **Utilities.** You may deduct your home office percentage of your utility bills for your entire home, including electricity, gas, water, heating oil, and trash removal. If you use a disproportionately large amount of electricity for your home office, you may be able to deduct more.
- **Insurance.** Both homeowner's and renter's insurance are partly deductible as indirect home office expenses. However, special insurance coverage you buy just for your home office—for example, insurance for your computer or other business equipment—is fully deductible as a direct expense.
- **Home maintenance.** You can deduct the home office percentage of home maintenance expenses that benefit your entire home, such as housecleaning of your entire house, roof and furnace repairs,

and exterior painting. These costs are deductible whether you hire someone or do them yourself. If you do the work yourself, however, you can deduct only the cost of materials, not the cost of your own labor. Termite inspection, pest extermination fees, and snow removal costs are also deductible. However, the IRS won't let you deduct lawn care unless you regularly use your home to meet clients or customers. Home maintenance costs that don't benefit your home office—for example, painting your kitchen—are not deductible at all.

- **Casualty losses.** Casualty losses are damage to your home caused by such things as fire, floods, or theft. Casualty losses that affect your entire house—for example, a leak that floods your entire home—are deductible in the amount of your home office percentage. Casualty losses that affect only your home office—for example, a leak that floods only the home office area of the house—are fully deductible direct expenses. Casualty losses that don't affect your home office—for example, if only your kitchen floods—are not deductible as business expenses. However, they may be deductible as itemized personal deductions.

- **Condominium association fees.** These fees (often substantial) are partly deductible as an indirect expense if you have a home office.

- **Security system costs.** Security system costs are partly deductible as an indirect expense if your security system protects your entire home. If you have a security system that protects only your home office, the cost is a fully deductible direct expense.

Mileage Deductions for Leaving the House

If your home office is your principal place of business, you can deduct the cost of traveling from your home to other work locations for your business. For example, you can deduct the cost of driving to perform work at a client's or customer's office. If you don't have a home office, these costs are not deductible. The mileage deductions obtained from driving to and from a home office can often exceed the value of the home office deduction itself. See Chapter 5 for a detailed discussion of the business mileage deduction.

- **Computer equipment.** Computers and peripheral equipment (such as printers) are deductible whether or not you qualify for the home office deduction. However, if you don't qualify for the home office deduction, you must prove that you use your computer more than half of the time for business by keeping a log of your usage. (See Chapter 20 for more information on this requirement.) If you qualify for the home office deduction, you don't need to keep track of how much time you spend using your computer for business.
- **Supplies and materials.** Office supplies and materials you use for your home business are not part of the home office deduction. They are deductible whether or not you qualify for the home office deduction.

Types of Home Expenses		
Expense	**Description**	**Deductibility**
Direct	Things you buy only for your home office	Deductible in full
Indirect	Things you buy to keep your entire home up and running	Deductible based on the percentage of home used as a business office
Unrelated	Things you buy only for parts of your home not used for business	Not deductible

Profit Limit on Deductions

You cannot deduct more than the net profit you earn from your home office. If you run a successful business out of your home office, this won't pose a problem. But if your business earns very little or loses money, the limitation could prevent you from deducting part or even all of your home office expenses in the current year.

> **EXAMPLE:** Gilbert Parker worked full time for a large accounting firm, but in his spare time he was writing a book. Parker set aside a portion of his home as an office he used exclusively for writing. Like many beginning authors, he earned no money from writing. He thought that he could at least get a tax deduction for his writing

Sam Creates a Home Office

Sam, a financial planner, converts one of the bedrooms of his two-bedroom condominium into a home office. He goes on something of a shopping spree, purchasing the following items:

- carpeting for his office
- a separate telephone for the office
- office supplies, such as stapler and paper
- a new desk for his office
- a new computer for his office (and one for his family).

He also moves a fancy chair he already owns to his office and uses it solely for his business. In the meantime, Sam's wife has their kitchen repainted and hires a cleaning person to clean the entire condo twice a month. Sam and his wife pay $2,000 each month on mortgage interest, real estate taxes, and homeowner's insurance.

The chart below shows which of these expenses are direct and indirect home office expenses, business operating expenses that are deductible whether or not Sam qualifies for the home office deduction, long-term asset expenses that are also deductible without regard to the home office deduction, and expenses that are not deductible.

Direct Home Office Expenses (100% Deductible)	Indirect Home Office Expense (Deductible in Amount of Home Office Percentage)	Business Operating Expenses	Long-Term Asset Expenses	Not Deductible
Carpet for home office	Mortgage interest and real estate taxes	Office supplies	Office desk	Carpet for living room
	Utilities (electricity and heat)	Business telephone	Office chair	Computer for children
	Cleaning service		Computer for business	
	Homeowner's insurance			

efforts by deducting his home office expenses, totaling $6,571, $4,904, and $5,444 over three years. He used these deductions to reduce the income tax he had to pay on his salary from his day job. However, both the IRS and the tax court held he could not deduct these expenses. Although he had a legitimate home office, Parker wasn't entitled to a home office deduction because he earned no money from writing. (*Parker v. Comm'r*, T.C. Memo 1984-233.)

Gilbert Parker ran afoul of the most significant limitation on the home office deduction: the net profit limitation.

If your deductions exceed your profits, you can deduct the excess in the following year and in each succeeding year until you deduct the entire amount. There is no limit on how far into the future you can deduct these expenses; you can claim them, even if you no longer live in the home where they were incurred. So, whether or not your business is making money, you should keep track of your home office expenses and claim the deduction on your tax return.

The profit limitation applies only to the home office deduction. It does not apply to business expenses that you can deduct under other provisions of the tax code.

If you're a sole proprietor, your profit (for these purposes) is the gross income you earn from your business minus your business deductions other than your home office deduction. You must also subtract the home office portion of your mortgage interest, real estate taxes, and casualty losses.

Tax preparation software can calculate your profit for home office deduction purposes, but it's a good idea to understand how it works. First, start with your gross income from your business—all the money you earn. Next, figure out how much money you earn from using your home office. If you do all of your work at home, this will be 100% of your business income. But if you work in several locations, you must determine the portion of your gross income that comes from working in your home office. To do this, consider how much time you spend working in your home office and the type of work you do at home.

Then, subtract from this amount:

- the business percentage of your mortgage interest and real estate taxes (you'll have these expenses only if you own your home), plus any casualty losses, and

- all of your business expenses that are not part of the home
  office deduction—for example, car expenses, travel, insurance,
  depreciation of business equipment, business phone, supplies, or
  salaries. You must deduct these separately from the home office
  deduction, even if you incurred them while doing business at home.
  The remainder is your net profit—the most you can deduct for using
your home office.

EXAMPLE: Sam runs a part-time consulting business out of his home
office, which occupies 20% of his home. In one year, his gross income from the business was $4,000. He had $1,000 in expenses other
than his home office deduction and he paid $10,000 in mortgage
interest and real estate taxes for the year. His home office deduction
for the year is limited to $1,000. He calculates this as follows:

Gross income from business:	$4,000
Minus business portion of mortgage interest and taxes	
($10,000 x 20% = $2,000)	− 2,000
Balance:	2,000
Minus direct business expenses	− 1,000
Home office deduction limitation	$1,000

Sam's total home office expenses for the year amount to $4,000;
this includes $2,000 in mortgage interest and real estate taxes, plus
$2,000 in other expenses, such as utilities and depreciation of his
home. Sam first deducts those home office expenses that are not
deductible as personal itemized deductions—everything other
than mortgage interest, real estate taxes, and casualty losses. These
expenses were $2,000; he may deduct only $1,000 of this amount
because his home office deduction profit limit is $1,000. Because
he has reached his profit limit, Sam can't deduct as a home office
deduction any portion of his $2,000 mortgage interest and real
estate tax expenses. However, he may deduct these entire amounts
as personal itemized deductions on Schedule A. Sam may deduct
the $1,000 in unused home office expenses the following year, if he
has sufficient income from his business.

If your business is organized as a partnership, LLC, or corporation, the income limit still applies to your home office deduction. Your income when computing your allowable deduction is based on the gross income from your business allocable to your home office, minus all other deductions of the LLC, partnership, or corporation. IRS Publication 587, *Business Use of Your Home*, contains a worksheet you can use to figure this amount.

Special Concerns for Homeowners

Until recently, homeowners who took the home office deduction were subject to a special tax trap: If they took a home office deduction for more than three of the five years before they sold their house, they had to pay capital gains taxes on the profit from the home office portion of their home. For example, if you made a $50,000 profit on the sale of your house, but your home office took up 20% of the space, you would have had to pay a tax on $10,000 of your profit (20% x $50,000 = $10,000).

Fortunately, IRS rules no longer require this. As long as you live in your home for at least two out of the five years before you sell it, the profit you make on the sale—up to $250,000 for single taxpayers and $500,000 for married taxpayers filing jointly—is not taxable. (See IRS Publication 523, *Selling Your Home*.) If you sold your house after May 6, 1997 and paid capital gains tax on the home office portion, you may be entitled to amend your return for the year you sold the house and receive a tax refund from the IRS. (See Chapter 18.)

However, you will have to pay a capital gains tax on the depreciation deductions you took after May 6, 1997 for your home office. This is the deduction you are allowed for the yearly decline in value due to wear and tear of the portion of the building that contains your home office. (See Chapter 9 for more information on depreciation deductions.) These "recaptured" deductions are taxed at a 25% rate (unless your income tax bracket is lower than 25%).

> **EXAMPLE:** Sally bought a $200,000 home in the year 2000 and used one of her bedrooms as her home office. She sold her home in 2004 for $300,000, realizing a $100,000 gain (profit). Her depreciation deductions for her home office from 2000 through 2004 totaled $2,000. She must pay a tax of 25% of $2,000, or $500.

Having to pay a 25% tax on the depreciation deductions you took in the years before you sold your house is actually not a bad deal. This is probably no more—and is often less—tax than you would have had to pay if you didn't take the deductions in the first place and instead paid tax on your additional taxable income at ordinary income tax rates.

C. How to Deduct Home Office Expenses

How you deduct home office expenses depends on how you've legally organized your practice.

1. Sole Proprietors

If you are a sole proprietor or have a one-owner LLC taxed as a sole proprietorship (as most are), you deduct your business operating expenses by listing them on IRS Schedule C, *Profit or Loss From Business*. You also list your home office deduction on Schedule C. But, unlike any other operating expense deduction, you must file a special tax form to show how you calculated the home office deduction. This form, Form 8829, *Expenses for Business Use of Your Home*, tells the IRS that you're taking the deduction and shows how you calculated it. You should file this form even if you can't currently deduct your home office expenses because your business has no profits. By filing, you can apply the deduction to a future year in which you earn a profit. For detailed guidance on how to fill out Form 8829, see IRS Publication 587, *Business Use of Your Home.*

2. LLCs, LLPs, and Partnerships

If your practice is organized as a multimember LLC, LLP, or partnership and receives partnership tax treatment, there are two ways you can claim a home office deduction:

- you can deduct your home office expenses on your personal tax return, or
- the LLC, LLP, or partnership can reimburse you for your expenses and list them on its tax return (and the deduction is then passed through to, and shared by, all the business owners).

Personal Deduction

The preferred way for most LLC members or partners in LLPs and partnerships to deduct home office expenses is to claim them on their personal tax returns. In order to do this, however, you must be able to show that:

- you satisfy all the requirements for the home office deduction covered in Section A, above, and
- your partnership agreement or LLC operating agreement provides that the expense will *not* be reimbursed by the entity, or there must be an established routine practice of not reimbursing the expense.

If there is no written statement or practice prohibiting reimbursement for home office expenses, the IRS will assume that you have the right to be reimbursed for them by the entity. This means you get no personal deduction. Instead, you will have to seek reimbursement of the expenses from the partnership, LLP, or LLC.

If you meet the requirements for claiming the deduction, you can deduct your home office expenses on Part II of IRS Schedule E. They are not miscellaneous itemized deductions (and, therefore, are not subject to a 2% of AGI reduction). You don't have to file Form 8829.

Reimbursement

Instead of taking a personal deduction, an LLC member or partner in an LLP or partnership can seek reimbursement for his home office expenses from the business entity. In this event, the member or partner gets no separate deduction for the expenses on his personal return. The LLC or partnership lists the expenses on its return (IRS Form 1065, *U.S. Partnership Return of Income*), combines these expenses with all its other deductible expenses, and then subtracts all its expenses from its income to determine if the practice had a profit or loss for the year. The business's profits or losses then pass through the entity to the owners' individual tax returns. The owners pay individual tax on any profits. Thus, all reimbursed expenses are shared by all the LLC members or partners in a partnership or LLP.

To obtain reimbursement, you must:

- meet all the requirements for the home office deduction covered in Section A, above

- document your expenses with receipts and other necessary records, and
- be reimbursed under an "accountable plan," an agreement in which the LLC, LLP, or partnership promises to reimburse you only if you provide proper timely substantiation for your expenses. (See Chapter 17 for more on accountable plans.)

If reimbursement is not made under an accountable plan, the money the LLC member or partner receives is treated as a distribution from the LLC, LLP, or partnership and is subject to both income and self-employment taxes. (See Chapter 17 for a detailed discussion of the rules for reimbursing LLC members' or partners' expenses.)

3.   Corporations

If you have formed a corporation to own and operate your practice and work as its employee, there are two ways you can claim a home office deduction: You can take a personal deduction or you can have your corporation reimburse you and it takes the deduction.

Reimbursement

Your corporation can reimburse you directly for your home office expenses and then deduct this amount as an ordinary business expense on its tax return (Form 1120 or 1120S). You get no personal deduction, but you don't need one because your corporation has paid you directly for your home office expenses. Because of the limitations on employees' using the home office personal deduction (see below), this is often the best choice.

To do this you must meet all the requirements for a home office deduction described in Section A, above. Any reimbursement you receive will not be taxable to you personally if:

- you keep careful track of your home office expenses and can prove them with receipts or other records, and
- you have an accountable plan, an agreement in which the corporation promises to reimburse you only if you provide proper timely substantiation for your expenses. (See Chapter 17 for more on accountable plans.)

If you qualify for the deduction, but fail to comply with the accountable plan rules, your reimbursement will be treated by the IRS as additional employee compensation and will be subject to income and employment taxes. In this event, you can deduct your home office expenses, but only as a miscellaneous itemized deduction as described below.

Personal Deduction

Corporate employees, including professionals, who qualify for the home office deduction may deduct their home office expenses on their personal tax returns as an employee business expense.

However, this is not a good choice because employees must take the home office deduction as a miscellaneous itemized personal deduction on Schedule A of their personal tax returns. This means you may deduct home office expenses only if you itemize your deductions and only to the extent that your home office expenses, along with your other unreimbursed employee business expenses and other miscellaneous itemized deductions (if any), exceed 2% of your adjusted gross income (AGI).

For example, if your AGI is $100,000, you would get a tax benefit only on the amount of your home office and miscellaneous itemized deductions that exceed $2,000. A further reduction is made for taxpayers whose income exceeds a threshold amount—$145,950 in 2005. (See Chapter 17 for a detailed discussion.) This rule greatly reduces the value of the home office personal deduction for employees, and often eliminates it entirely for those who are highly compensated. For this reason, many employees don't take a personal deduction for their home offices and choose to get reimbursed by the corporation instead, or they rent their office to the corporation (see Section A3, above).

If your corporation reimburses you for some, but not all, of your home office expenses, you must file Form 2106, *Employee Business Expenses,* to deduct the unreimbursed amount.

D. Audit-Proofing Your Home Office Deduction

Some people believe that taking the home office deduction invites an IRS audit. The IRS denies this. But even if taking the deduction increases your audit chances, the risk of an audit is still low (see Chapter 19). Moreover, you have nothing to fear from an audit if you're entitled to take the deduction and you keep good records to prove it.

If you are audited by the IRS and your home office deduction is questioned, you want to be able to prove that you:

- qualify for the deduction, and
- have correctly reported the amount of your home office expenses.

If you can do both those things, you should be home free.

1.   Prove That You Are Following the Rules

Here are some ways to convince the IRS that you qualify for the home office deduction:

- Take a picture of your home office and draw up a diagram showing your home office as a portion of your home. Do not send the photo or diagram to the IRS. Just keep it in your files to use in case you're audited. The picture should have a date on it—this can be done with a digital camera, or you can have your film date-stamped by a developer.
- Have all of your business mail sent to your home office.
- Use your home office address on all of your business cards, stationery, and advertising.
- Obtain a separate phone line for your business and keep that phone in your home office.
- Encourage clients or customers to regularly visit your home office, and keep a log of their visits.
- To make the most of the time you spend in your home office, communicate with clients by phone, fax, or electronic mail instead of going to their offices. Use a mail or messenger service to deliver your work to customers.
- Keep a log of the time you spend working in your home office. This doesn't have to be fancy; notes on your calendar will do.

2.   Keep Good Expense Records

Be sure to keep copies of your bills and receipts for home office expenses, including:

- IRS Form 1098, *Mortgage Interest Statement* (sent by whoever holds your mortgage), showing the interest you paid on your mortgage for the year
- property tax bills and your canceled checks as proof of payment
- utility bills, insurance bills, and receipts for payments for repairs to your office area, along with your canceled checks paying for these items, and
- a copy of your lease and your canceled rent checks, if you're a renter.

■

Chapter 8

Deductions for Outside Offices

The great majority of professionals have outside offices in which they do their work. Most professionals rent their office space, but some own the building. Either way, an outside office presents many opportunities for tax deductions.

A. If You Rent Your Office

Virtually all the expenses you incur for an outside office that you rent for your practice are deductible, including:

- rent
- utilities
- insurance
- repairs
- improvements
- real estate broker fees and commissions to obtain the lease
- fees for option rights, such as an option to renew the lease
- burglar alarm expenses
- trash and waste removal
- security expenses
- parking expenses
- maintenance and janitorial expenses
- lease cancellation fees, and
- attorneys' fees to draft a lease.

If you sign a net lease, you'll have to pay part (or all) of the landlord's maintenance expenses, property taxes, insurance, and maybe even mortgage payments. These payments are treated the same as rent.

A rental deposit is not deductible in the year it is made if it is to be returned at the end of the lease. However, if the landlord applies the deposit to pay rent you owe, make repairs, or because you've breached the lease, you may deduct the amount in that year.

None of the rules applicable to the home office deduction covered in Chapter 7 apply to outside offices. Thus, unlike the home office deduction, there is no profit limit on deductions for outside rental expenses—you get your entire deduction even if it exceeds the profits from your practice. You report rental expenses for an outside office just like any other business expense. You don't have to file IRS Form 8829, which is required when sole proprietors take the home office deduction.

1.   Timing of Deductions

Because you will ordinarily be in your office for more than one year, some of the expenses you pay may benefit your practice for more than a single tax year. In this event, you may have to deduct the expense over more than one year instead of currently deducting it all in a single year. (This discussion assumes that you, like most professionals, are a cash basis taxpayer and use the calendar year as your tax year.)

Current vs. Multiyear Deductions

You may currently deduct any expense you pay for the use of your office during the current tax year.

> **EXAMPLE:** In 2006, Leona paid $800 rent each month for the outside office she uses for her psychotherapy practice. The $9,600 she paid in 2006 is fully deductible on Leona's 2006 taxes. The rental payments were a current expense because they benefited Leona for only a single tax year—2006.

But if an expense you pay applies beyond the current tax year, the general rule is that you can deduct only the amount that applies to your use of the rented property during the current tax year. You can deduct the rest of your payment only during the future tax year to which it applies.

> **EXAMPLE:** Last January, Steve leased an outside office for three years for $6,000 a year. He paid the entire $18,000 lease amount up front. Each year, Steve can deduct only $6,000—the part of the rent that applies to that tax year.

Subject to the exceptions noted below, these rules apply to office expenses, not just rent you pay in advance. For example, they apply to all expenses you pay to get a lease.

> **EXAMPLE:** Maxine pays $2,000 in attorney fees to draft her office lease. The lease has a five-year term, so the payment was for a benefit that lasts beyond the end of the following tax year. Thus, Maxine may not currently deduct the entire $2,000 in one year.

Instead, she must deduct the $2,000 in equal amounts over five years (60 months). This comes to $33.33 per month. Her lease began on March 1, 2006, so she can deduct $333.33 for 2006 (10 months x $33.33 = $333.33).

12-Month Rule

There is an important exception to the general rule about deducting in the current year. Under the "12-month rule," cash basis taxpayers may currently deduct any expense in the current year so long as it is for a right or benefit that extends no longer than the earlier of:

- 12 months, or
- until the end of the tax year after the tax year in which you made the payment.

EXAMPLE 1: Stephanie leased an office for five years beginning July 1, 2006. Her rent is $12,000 per year. She paid the first year's rent ($12,000) on June 30. Under the current year rule, Stephanie may deduct in 2006 only the part of her rent payment that applies to 2006. Her lease started July 1, 2006 (which is 50% of 2006), so she may deduct 50% of the $12,000, or $6,000. However, if Stephanie uses the 12-month rule, her entire $12,000 payment is deductible in 2006. The fact that 50% of her payment was for 2007 doesn't matter because the benefit she obtained—the use of her office—lasted for only 12 months: from July 1, 2006 to July 1, 2007.

EXAMPLE 2: Steve paid three years of rent in advance. He may not use the 12-month rule because the benefit he obtained from his payment lasted for three years, which is both more than 12 months and beyond the end of tax year after the tax year in which he made the payment.

EXAMPLE 3: Assume that Maxine (from the example in the previous section) paid $2,000 in attorney's fees to draft a lease that lasts for one year, starting March 1, 2006. She may currently deduct the whole amount under the 12-month rule.

To use the 12-month rule, you must apply it when you first start using the cash method for your practice. You must get IRS approval if you haven't been using the rule and want to start doing so. Such IRS approval is granted automatically. (See Chapter 20.)

Determining Your Lease Term

How long a lease lasts is important because it can determine whether you can currently deduct an expense or have to deduct it over the entire lease term. If you have to deduct an expense over the entire lease term, the length of the lease will determine the amount of your deduction each year. It might seem simple to tell how long a lease lasts—just look at the lease term in the lease agreement. However, things are not so simple if your lease includes an option to renew.

The IRS says that the term of the lease for rental expense deductions includes all renewal options plus any other period for which you and the lessor reasonably expect the lease to be renewed. For example, a one year lease with an option to renew for five years would be a six-year lease for deduction purposes.

However, this rule applies only if less than 75% of the cost of getting the lease is for the term remaining on the purchase date (not including any period for which you may choose to renew or extend the lease). Sound confusing? It is.

> **EXAMPLE 1:** You paid $10,000 to get a lease with 20 years remaining on it and two options to renew for five years each. Of this cost, you paid $7,000 for the original lease and $3,000 for the renewal options. Was 75% of the cost of the lease paid for the initial 20-year lease term? No. $7,000 is less than 75% of the total $10,000 cost of the lease. Thus, the IRS rule discussed above applies. The lease term for deduction purposes is the remaining life of your present lease plus the renewal periods—30 years in all. The $10,000 will have to be amortized (deducted in equal amounts) over 30 years.

> **EXAMPLE 2:** Assume the same facts as in Example 1, except that you paid $8,000 for the original lease and $2,000 for the renewal options. The $8,000 cost of getting the original lease was 80% of

the total cost of the lease, not less than 75%. Thus, the IRS rule doesn't apply and you can amortize the entire $10,000 over the 20-year remaining life of the original lease.

The crucial question is how you figure out how much of the cost of the lease was for the original lease term and how much was for the renewal term or terms. The IRS only says that the lease costs should be allocated between the original and renewal terms based on the facts and circumstances. The IRS also says that in some cases it may be appropriate to make the allocation using a present value computation. In such a computation a present value—a value in today's dollars—is assigned to an amount of money in the future, based on an estimated rate-of-return over the long term. You'll probably want an accountant to do this for you.

2. Improvements and Repairs

It's very common for professionals to have permanent improvements made to their offices—for example, they may install new carpeting or new walls. Landlords often give commercial tenants an allowance to make improvements before they move in. You get no deduction in this event. The landlord gets to depreciate improvements it paid for, not you.

However, if you pay for improvements with your own money, you. may deduct the cost as a business expense. You have multiple options:

- you can depreciate the improvements
- you can treat the money you spent for the improvements as rent, or
- the improvements may qualify for the Disabled Access Tax Credit or tax deduction for removal of barriers to the disabled (see Section B7).

Improvements may be depreciated over several years as described in Section B, below. They are depreciated over their recovery periods assigned by the IRS, not over the whole term of the lease. For example, the cost of installing new carpeting would be depreciated over five years, even if the lease term is ten years.

If you treat your expenses for improvements as rent, you deduct the cost the same as any other rent. Rent is deductible in a single year unless it is prepaid in advance (see Section 1, above.) This means you'll get your deduction much more quickly than if you depreciated the improvements over several years. However, if the cost of the improvement is substantial, part of the cost may have to be treated as prepaid rent and deducted over the whole lease term as described above.

Whether an improvement must be depreciated or treated as rent depends on what you and your landlord intended. Your intent should be written into your lease agreement.

In contrast to improvements, repairs may be currently deducted. How to tell the difference between improvements and repairs is discussed in Section B, below.

3.   Cost of Modifying a Lease

You may have to pay an additional "rent" amount over part of the lease period to change certain provisions in your lease. You must ordinarily deduct these payments over the remaining lease period. You cannot deduct the payments as additional rent, even if they are described as rent in the agreement.

> **EXAMPLE:** The ABC Medical Corporation signs a 20-year lease to rent part of a building starting on July 1. However, before it occupies the building, ABC decides it really needs less space. The lessor agrees to reduce ABC's rent from $60,000 to $50,000 per year and to release the excess space from the original lease. In exchange, ABC agrees to pay an additional rent amount of $25,000, payable in 60 monthly installments of $417 each. The extra payments must be deducted over the 20-year lease term. ABC's amortization deduction each year will be $1,250 ($25,000 ÷ 20 years), but it may deduct only half this amount the first year because the lease began on July 1. ABC cannot deduct the $5,004 (12 × $417) that it will pay during each of the first five years as rent.

The only exception to this rule is where the 12-month rule can be used. The lease will have to have a short term for the rule to apply.

> **EXAMPLE:** Assume that ABC Medical Corporation (from the example above) signed a nine-month lease starting on July 1, instead of a 20-year lease. It can currently deduct its lease modification expense under the 12-month rule because the benefit it obtains from the expense lasts less than 12 months and doesn't extend beyond the end of the following tax year.

4. Cost of Canceling a Lease

Unlike the cost of modifying a lease, you can ordinarily deduct as rent an amount you pay to cancel a business lease.

B. If You Own Your Office

If you own your outside office, you'll be entitled to most of the same deductions as a renter discussed above. You'll also get to depreciate the cost of your real estate.

1. Operating Expenses

Operating expenses are the day-to-day expenses you incur as result of owning your office. They are currently deductible unless you prepay them for more than one year. (See Section A1, above.) These expenses include:

- utilities
- insurance
- repairs
- burglar alarm expenses
- trash and waste removal
- security expenses
- parking garage expenses, and
- maintenance and janitorial expenses.

2.   Improvements and Repairs

Provided that they are ordinary, necessary, and reasonable in amount, repairs to your real property are operating expenses that are fully deductible the year in which they are incurred.

> **EXAMPLE:** Sally, a dentist, owns a small office building in which she carries on her practice. She discovers a leak in the building's foundation. She has John, a contractor, examine the 20-year-old foundation. He tells her he can fix the leak for $1,000. She agrees and pays John the money. Sally has paid for a repair. She's out $1,000, but at least she gets a tax deduction. The repair is a currently deductible operating expense that she may deduct in full from her taxes for the year.

However, not all upkeep constitutes a repair for tax purposes. Some changes made to real property are "capital improvements." Unlike repairs, improvements cannot be deducted in a single year. Instead, their cost must be depreciated over several years. Improvements to nonresidential real property must be depreciated over an especially long period—39 years.

> **EXAMPLE:** Assume that John, the contractor, told Sally she had two options with her foundation: She could have the leak patched for $1,000, or she could have an entirely new foundation put in at a cost of $10,000. Sally elects to have a new foundation installed and pays $10,000. This expense is an improvement that she will have to depreciate over 39 years. Assuming the work was done in January, she'd get to deduct $234 from her taxes that year, and $257 for the next 38 years.

Clearly, it is usually advantageous tax-wise to be able to characterize an expense as a repair instead of an improvement. This way, you can deduct the whole cost in a single year instead of having to deduct a little at a time over many years.

What Is a Repair

So, how do you tell the difference between a repair and an improvement? Here's the basic IRS rule: A repair keeps your real property in good operating condition; but, it does *not*:

- materially add to the value of your property
- substantially prolong its useful life, or
- make it more useful. (Reg. § 1.162-4.)

In contrast, an improvement adds to the value of your property, prolongs its life, or adapts it to new uses.

The problem with this definition is that virtually all repairs increase both the value and useful life of the property being repaired. The key difference between a repair and an improvement is that *a repair merely returns property to more or less the state it was in before it stopped working properly.* The property is not substantially more valuable, long-lived, or useful than it was before the need for the repair arose. In contrast, an improvement makes property *substantially* more valuable and/or long-lived or useful than it was before the improvement.

You need to compare the situation before and after you made the expenditure involved. Have you just returned your real property to the state it was in before the need for the repair arose? Or, have you made it much better? If the answer to the first question is "Yes," you've done a repair. If the answer to the second question is "Yes," you've paid for an improvement.

The cost of fixing the leaky 20-year-old foundation in the first example above is a repair because the foundation is in more or less the same condition as it was in before it began leaking. As a result of the patch, it may be stronger than it was before and last a little longer, and therefore be somewhat more valuable than in its original condition. But this increase in value and life is not substantial enough to make the expense an improvement.

If you install a new foundation in your office building, however, you've paid for an improvement. A building with a brand new foundation is obviously substantially more valuable and long lived than one with the original 20-year-old foundation.

Other good examples of repairs include repainting your property, fixing gutters or floors, fixing leaks, plastering, and replacing broken windows. Examples of improvements include installing a new heating system, or putting on a new roof.

The General Plan of Improvement Rule: A Trap for the Unwary

Under the "general plan of improvement" rule, an expense that is incurred as part of an overall plan of improvement, rehabilitation, or modernization must be depreciated; this is so even though the same expense, standing alone, would be currently deductible as a repair.

You have a general plan of improvement where you undertake a number of repairs and/or improvements at about the same time, or consecutively, to achieve an overall goal: improving, rehabilitating, or modernizing your property. A general plan of improvement can cover an entire building, or just part of it. Thus, to determine if an expense is a repair or improvement, you can't look at it in isolation. You must consider whether it is done alone or in conjunction with other items.

> **EXAMPLE:** The ABC Medical Corporation owns a medical building. It decides to fix up its public restrooms. It has the restrooms repainted, replaces a number of cracked tiles, replaces the hardware on the bathroom stall doors to make them work better, fixes several leaky faucets, and repairs toilets that weren't flushing properly. Singly, any one of these items is a currently deductible repair. But taken all together, they are all part of a general plan of improvement to upgrade the restrooms. Thus, the cost must be depreciated.

There are ways to get around the general plan of improvement rule:
- spread out your work over as much time as possible—preferably, do only one major repair project each year
- hire different contractors and repair people to do the work
- make sure you are separately billed for each repair or improvement, and
- never allow a contractor or repairperson to label the work, performed as an "improvement" in a contract or invoice.

3. Section 179 Expensing

Section 179 expensing allows you to deduct in a single year up to $105,000 of tangible personal property you buy for your practice. It may be used for personal property you purchase for your office, except for:

- buildings
- building components, or
- air conditioning and heating units.

> **EXAMPLE:** Donald, an architect who owns the building where he has his office, spends $5,000 for new office carpeting and $5,000 for new landscaping. A carpet is tangible personal property and is not a building component as long as it is not glued to the floor. He may deduct the entire $5,000 in one year using Section 179. Landscaping is not personal property, thus Donald may not deduct any of his landscaping costs using Section 179. He must depreciate the cost as described below.

Section 179 is covered in detail in Chapter 9.

4. Depreciation Deductions

You may deduct the cost of buying your outside office, and improving it, through depreciation. Depreciation is covered in detail in Chapter 9. The following discussion just covers the unique aspects of depreciation for nonresidential real property.

What You Depreciate

Typically, you don't have a single depreciation deduction. Instead, you have many separate depreciation deductions over time.

When your real property is first placed into service, you get to depreciate its tax basis (value for tax purposes). This includes the value of:

- the building and building components
- land improvements, such as landscaping, and
- any personal property items that are not physically part of the building but were included in the purchase price—for example, office furniture.

These items can all be depreciated together. However, you have the option of separately depreciating personal property inside your building, and certain land improvements. This is more complicated, but yields a larger total deduction the first years you own the property (see Subsection e, below).

How Much You Depreciate

You depreciate your property's tax basis—its value for tax purposes. If you've purchased your real property, your starting point in determining its basis is what you paid for the property. Logically enough, this is called cost basis. Your cost basis is the purchase price plus certain other expenses, less the cost of your land.

The following expenses are added to your property's basis:

- abstract fees
- charges for installing utility services
- legal fees
- mortgage commissions
- recording fees
- surveys
- transfer taxes
- title insurance, and
- any amounts the seller owes that you agree to pay, such as back taxes or interest, recording or mortgage fees, charges for improvements or repairs, and sales commissions.

Ordinarily, when you purchase a building with a structure or structures on it, you pay a single lump sum to the seller that includes both the cost of the building (along with its contents) and the land on which it sits. Because you can't depreciate land, you must deduct the value of the land from the purchase price to determine the basis for depreciation of the building. There are several ways to calculate how much your land is worth. Obviously, the less it's worth, the more depreciation you will have to deduct. Land valuation is the single most important factor within your control affecting the amount of your depreciation deductions.

If you construct your building yourself, your basis is the cost of construction. The cost includes the cost of materials and labor, as well as the cost of equipment (including rented equipment). However, you may not add the cost of your own labor to the property's basis. Interest you pay during the construction period must be added to basis; but interest paid before and after construction may be deducted as paid as an operating expense.

Depreciation Period and Method

Nonresidential real property has the longest depreciation period of any business property—39 years. But, in practice, it takes 40 years to fully depreciate a nonresidential building. You don't get a full year's worth of depreciation the first year, so you get some extra depreciation during the 40th year (if you own the building that long).

Older properties have a shorter depreciation period: 31.5 years for property placed in service before May 13, 1993 (or before January 1, 1994, if the purchase or its construction was under a binding contract in effect before May 13, 1993, or if construction began before May 13, 1993).

In addition to having the longest depreciation period, nonresidential real property must be depreciated using the slowest depreciation method: the straight-line method in which you receive equal deductions each year, except the first and last year. You may not use accelerated depreciation, which provides larger deductions in the first few years you own the property, and smaller deductions later on.

The following chart shows how much depreciation you get each year for a nonresidential building. From the second through the 39th year, you may deduct 2.564% of your property's tax basis—for example, if your basis is $200,000, you may deduct $5,128 each year (2.564% x $200,000 = $5,128). As the chart shows, the depreciation deductions for the first and 40th years differ depending on what month the property was placed in service.

Nonresidential Real Property
Midmonth Convention Straight Line—39 Years

Year	Month property placed in service											
	1	2	3	4	5	6	7	8	9	10	11	12
1	2.461%	2.247%	2.033%	1.819%	1.605%	1.391%	1.177%	0.963%	0.749%	0.535%	0.321%	0.107%
2–39	2.564	2.564	2.564	2.564	2.564	2.564	2.564	2.564	2.564	2.564	2.564	2.564
40	0.107	0.321	0.535	0.749	0.963	1.177	1.391	1.605	1.819	2.033	2.247	2.461

Depreciating Improvements

Typically, you'll make additions and improvements to your property after it has been placed into service These include:

- improvements to the building itself, or building components—for example, upgrading the heating or air conditioning system
- land improvements, such as planting new trees or shrubbery
- adding new personal property to the building—for example, new office furniture.

Such later additions and improvements are depreciated separately from the original property itself.

- **Recovery period.** The general rule is that building improvements are depreciated over 39 years. However, some building improvements made by a landlord or tenant during late 2004 and 2005 may be depreciated over 15 years. (See "15-Year Depreciation Period for Leasehold Improvements," below.)
- **Depreciation method.** Building improvements are depreciated using the straight-line method—the same method as used for the original building (described above). Land improvements are depreciated over 15 years using the 150% declining balance method.

Personal property inside your building is depreciated in the same way as any other personal business property. (See Chapter 9.)

Using Cost Segregation to Speed Up Your Depreciation Deductions

When you purchase real property, you ordinarily pay a single lump sum to the owner, but you are actually purchasing more than one asset. Your property consists of:

- the land the building sits on as well as any other surrounding land included with the purchase
- land improvements such as landscaping, walkways, exterior lighting, fencing, and parking lots
- the building itself, including all building components
- any personal property items that are not physically part of the building but were included in the purchase price—for example, office furniture, business equipment.

15-Year Depreciation Period for Leasehold Improvements

Some improvements to nonresidential buildings may be depreciated over 15 years, instead of the usual 39-year term. This gives you a substantially larger depreciation deduction each year. Improvements paid for either by the landlord or the tenant can qualify, but only if:

- The improvements were placed in service between October 22, 2004 and December 31, 2005.
- The building was in use for more than three years when the improvements were made.
- The improvements were made under a lease, a sublease, or commitment to enter into a lease not between related people.
- The building, or the portion of the building improved, is used exclusively by the tenant or subtenant.
- If paid for by the landlord, the improvements remain the landlord's property at the end of the lease term.
- The improvement was not a building enlargement, elevator, or escalator installation, or improvement to the building's common areas or internal structural framework.

EXAMPLE: The Acme Medical Corporation leased a building from AAA Investments, Ltd. Acme spent $250,000 to adapt the 20-year-old building to its needs and moved in on January 1, 2005. Acme may depreciate the $250,000 over 15 years instead of the normal 39-year term. In 2005, it gets a depreciation deduction of $15,972.22 and a $16,666.66 deduction for the next 15 years. If Acme had used the 39-year depreciation period, it would have been entitled to a depreciation deduction of only $6,143.16 in 2005 and $6,410.25 for the next 39 years.

Most people depreciate all these items together (excluding the land, which is not depreciable). However, you have the option of depreciating each asset separately. This process is called cost segregation.

Using cost segregation will result in a larger total depreciation deduction each year for the first several years you own the property. This is because personal property and land improvements have much shorter deprecation periods than does nonresidential real property—for example, land improvements may be depreciated over 15 years, some types of flooring and millwork over seven years, and most business equipment over five years. Moreover, you may use accelerated depreciation for improvements and personal property, instead of the slower straight-line method. You may also be able to deduct the entire cost of some personal property in a single year using the Section 179 deduction.

Your total depreciation deduction won't be any different, but you'll get it much more quickly. Because of the time value of money, you'll be better off than if you depreciate your entire property over 39 years using the straight-line method. For example, each $100,000 of personal property that you depreciate in five years instead of 39 years will result in about $16,000 in net-present-value savings, assuming a 5% discount rate and a 35% marginal tax rate.

To employ cost segregation, every element of your property must be classified as land, building, land improvement, or personal property and given a dollar value. This can be tricky, particularly determining which items can be classified as personal property. Many items you wouldn't ordinarily think of as personal property can fall within this classification—for example, carpeting, window treatments, and certain fixtures.

It's wise to hire an engineer to perform a cost segregation study to determine how to classify and value your property's various components. The engineer should inspect the property and, wherever possible, use construction-based documents such as blueprints and specifications to determine the value of the building components. When estimates are required, they should be based on costing data from contractors or reliable published sources. The engineer should prepare a detailed written report that you can show the IRS if you are audited and it questions your valuations. Such a study can be expensive—typically

$10,000 to $25,000—but the cost is a tax deductible business expense. Whether paying for such a study makes sense for you depends on how much your property is worth. The speedier depreciation you'll obtain will likely justify the expense if your property is worth $750,000 or more.

Cost segregation may be used for existing buildings or new construction. It may even be used by tenants who improve or remodel their leased space. If you've owned your property for several years and are now kicking yourself because you never used cost segregation, cheer up: you may be able to perform a cost segregation study now, recompute your depreciation deductions for previous years, and file amended returns for those years claiming the additional deductions. See your accountant about this.

The IRS has created a guide for its auditors called the *Cost Segregation Audit Techniques Guide*. It provides a detailed explanation of how cost segregation works. It can be downloaded from the IRS website at: www.irs.gov/pub/irs-utl/costsegatg.htm#Five10.

5. Interest Deductions

Most people, including professionals, borrow money from banks or other financial institutions to purchase real property. Mortgage interest you pay for your outside office is deductible as it is paid each year.

You deduct only the interest you pay on a loan to purchase or improve real property. You may not deduct payments of principal—that is, your repayments of the amount you borrowed. The principal is ordinarily added to the basis of your property and depreciated over 39 years.

In contrast, if you borrow money to repair your rental property, you may deduct the principle amount the year it is incurred as an operating expense.

Expenses you pay to obtain a mortgage on your real property cannot be deducted as interest. Instead, they are added to your basis in the property and depreciated along with the property itself. (See Section 4e, above.)

6.   Property Taxes

Regular property taxes you pay for your outside office are a deductible business expense. However, real estate taxes imposed to fund specific local benefits such as streets, sewer lines, and water mains, are not deductible as business expenses. Because these benefits increase the value of your property, you should add what you pay for them to the tax basis (cost for tax purposes) of your property. Water bills, sewer charges, and other service charges assessed against your business property are not real estate taxes, but they are deductible as business expenses.

7.   Tax Incentives for Improving Access for the Disabled

Two tax incentives are available to businesses to help cover the cost of making their offices more accessible to the disabled—for example, installing wheelchair ramps. Ordinarily, real property improvements such as these would have to be depreciated over as much as 39 years. These tax breaks permit small businesses to currently deduct, up to certain limits, their expenses for such improvements.

The first tax incentive is a tax *credit*. The second is a tax *deduction*. Both can be used at the same time, and they can be claimed each year you meet the requirements. These deductions may be used by professionals who own or lease their office.

Disabled Access Tax Credit

The Americans with Disabilities Act (ADA) prohibits private employers with 15 or more employees from discriminating against people with disabilities in the full and equal enjoyment of goods, services, and facilities offered by any "place of public accommodation." Professionals' offices are included in the definition of public accommodation.

The disabled access tax credit is designed to help small businesses defray the costs of complying with the ADA. The credit may be used by any business with either:

- $1 million or less in gross receipts for the preceding tax year; or
- 30 or fewer full-time employees during the preceding tax year.

The credit can be used to cover a variety of expenses, including the cost to remove barriers that prevent a business from being accessible to disabled people. However, the credit may be used only for buildings constructed before November 5, 1990. The credit may also be used for equipment acquisitions, and services such as sign language interpreters.

The disabled tax credit is a tax credit, not a tax deduction. Tax credits are better than tax deductions because, instead of just reducing your taxable income, they reduce the actual amount of tax you have to pay dollar for dollar.

The amount of the tax credit is equal to 50% of your disabled access expenses in a year that exceed $250 but are not more than $10,250. Thus, the maximum credit is $5,000. To claim the credit, you must file IRS Form 8826, *Disabled Access Credit*.

Disabled Access Tax Deduction

Businesses may deduct in a single year up to $15,000 of the cost of making their buildings or other facilities—such as roads, walks, and parking lots—accessible to the elderly or disabled.

The most you can deduct as a cost of removing barriers to the disabled and the elderly for any tax year is $15,000. However, you can add any costs over this limit to the basis of the property and depreciate these excess costs. The $15,000 deduction limit applies to a partnership as a whole and also to each individual partner in the partnership. This rule also applies to LLCs taxed as partnerships (as most are).

Your renovations must comply with applicable accessibility standards. Detailed standards are set forth in the ADA Accessibility Guidelines, which can be found on the Internet at www.access-board.gov/adaag/html/adaag.htm. IRS Publication 535, *Business Expenses*, also contains a summary of these standards.

You may claim the deduction on your income tax return for the tax year you paid for the work, or the year you incurred the expenses. Identify the deduction as a separate item. The choice applies to all of the qualifying costs you have during the year, up to the $15,000 limit. You must maintain adequate records to support your deduction—keep your receipts.

> **EXAMPLE:** Jason, a dentist, owns an old dental office building that is not wheelchair accessible. He installs four wheelchair ramps at a cost of $5,000. Ordinarily this would be an improvement that

Jason would have to depreciate. But due to the disabled access tax deduction, he may deduct the entire $5,000 in one year.

Using Both the Credit and Deduction

The two incentives can be used in combination during the same year if the requirements for each are met. In this event, the maximum tax deduction you may take during the year is equal to the difference between your total disabled access expenses and the amount of the tax credit you claim. You should take the maximum tax credit you can first, because it reduces your taxes dollar for dollar. Then, claim as much of the tax deduction as you can.

> **EXAMPLE:** During one recent year, the ABC Medical Corporation spent $25,000 to make its 20-year-old medical building more accessible to the disabled. It should first claim the maximum $5,000 tax credit, then deduct from its taxable income another $15,000 using the disabled access tax deduction. It can add the remaining $5,000 it spent to its property's basis and depreciate it.

8. Energy Efficiency Deduction

The Energy Tax Incentives Act, enacted by Congress in 2005, creates a brand-new deduction for expenses to make commercial buildings more energy efficient. It's intended to encourage building owners to upgrade their existing buildings and to design more energy-efficient new structures. The deduction may be used for both used and new buildings, but not for any building placed in service after December 31, 2007.

The deduction is rather complex and all the details have yet to be ironed out by the IRS. For example, it's unclear whether the deduction may be used by renters who make energy efficiency improvements or only by building owners.

In a nutshell, you may deduct in one year up to $1.80 per building square foot when, as part of a plan to reduce your total energy costs, you upgrade your:
- interior lighting system
- heating, cooling, ventilation, and hot water system, or
- building envelope.

For example, the owner of a 10,000-square-foot building who qualified for the deduction could deduct $18,000 ($1.80 x 10,000 = $18,000).

To obtain the full deduction, the upgrade must reduce the power costs for the system involved by at least 50%. If the reduction is less than 50%, a partial tax deduction may be available. There is no dollar limit on the deduction.

Detailed certification requirements have to be met to qualify for the deduction. The IRS is supposed to issue regulations explaining how to qualify.

C. If You Lease a Building to Your Practice

If your practice is organized as an LLC, LLP, partnership, or corporation, you can realize tax savings if you personally own an office building and lease it to the practice. You'll be the landlord and your practice your tenant. Your practice will pay you rent for the lease. This rent is a deductible expense for the practice as described in Section A above. You'll have to pay income tax on the rent you receive. However, you won't have to pay Social Security or Medicare taxes because income from real estate rentals is not subject to these taxes (except in the unlikely event that you are a real estate dealer).

This is a great way to take money out of your business without paying these taxes. Additionally, if your practice is a C corporation, such a lease arrangement helps you to avoid double taxation by reducing your corporation's profits. (See Chapter 16.)

This arrangement is perfectly legitimate so long as you have a real lease (it should be in writing) and charge your practice a reasonable rent. Don't charge more than market rates to obtain greater Social Security and Medicare tax savings.

> **EXAMPLE:** Edna is a doctor whose practice is organized as an LLC and taxed as a partnership. She personally buys a small building and leases it to her LLC for $5,000 per month, which is the going rate in the area. Edna must pay income tax on the $60,000 in rent she receives each year from her LLC, but not self-employment taxes (Social Security and Medicare taxes). Her LLC deducts the rent as a

business operating expense. This reduces by $60,000 the total profit that is passed through the LLC to Edna's personal return. Obviously, if the LLC owned the building instead of Edna, it wouldn't have to pay any rent to Edna and there would be an additional $60,000 to pass through the LLC to her personal return. But this money would be subject to both income and self-employment taxes.

Instead of personally owning the building, you can form another business entity, such as an LLC, to own it and in turn own the entity. This gives you a degree of limited liability if something goes wrong on the property. (See Chapter 2.) You still won't have to pay self-employment tax on any income your entity receives from renting real estate.

Moreover, you can have a family member or members own the building instead of you. This will result in a lower income tax burden if the family member is in a lower tax bracket than you. Family members can also own all or part of an LLC or other entity that owns the building.

■

Chapter 9

Deducting Long-Term Assets

This chapter explains how you can deduct long-term property you buy for your practice. You will need to be aware of, and follow, some tax rules that at times may seem complicated. But it's worth the effort. After all, by allowing these deductions, the government is effectively offering to help pay for your equipment and other business assets. All you have to do is take advantage of the offer.

A. Long-Term Assets

A long-term asset is business property that you reasonably expect to last for more than one year. Long-term assets are also called capital expenses—the terms are used interchangeably in this book. There are two methods for deducting long-term business property:

- Section 179, and
- regular depreciation.

Each is covered in the sections that follow.

Bonus Depreciation

Bonus depreciation was a temporary tax relief measure in effect from May 6, 2003 through December 31, 2005. It allowed businesses to increase their depreciation deduction by 30% or 50% for long-term property (other than real property) that was new and used over 50% of the time for business. Bonus depreciation was available in the first year that a business placed an eligible asset into service and was applied automatically to taxpayers who qualified for it. You could elect not to take the bonus depreciation by attaching a note to your tax return. If you opted out of bonus depreciation, but now wish you had taken it, you may be able to amend your tax return to get the bonus. (See Chapter 18.)

---

1. Long-Term Assets Versus Current Expenses

Whether an item is a long-term asset (a capital expense) or not depends on its useful life. The useful life of an asset is not its physical life, but rather the period during which it may reasonably be expected to be useful in your business—and the IRS, not you, makes this call. Anything you buy that will benefit your business for more than one year is a capital expense. For professionals, this typically includes items such as office furniture and equipment, computer equipment, medical and dental equipment, and other specialized equipment, buildings, automobiles, and books. These are all long-term assets. Anything you purchase that will benefit your practice for less than one year is a current expense, not a long-term asset.

> **EXAMPLE:** Reference books you purchase for your professional library that have a useful life of more than one year must be depreciated or expensed under Section 179. However, books and other publications with a useful life of less than one year may be currently deducted as a business operating expense. This includes, for example, publications that are purchased each year that are printed in a loose-leaf format and updated on a regular basis, continuously updated electronic databases, and publications on CD-ROM.

Are Paperclips Long-Term Assets?

Are paperclips and other inexpensive items that you buy for your business long-term assets for tax purposes? No. Although things like paperclips might be expected to last more than one year, you can treat these and other similar items as a current expense for tax purposes. Most businesses establish a minimum an asset must cost before they will treat it as a long-term asset. The IRS has no rules on the amount of the limit, except that it must be reasonable. For a small practice, a reasonable limit would be $100 to $250. Thus, for example, you would treat a $50 bookcase you buy for your practice as an operating expense, while a $500 bookcase would be a long-term asset. For larger practices, a $1,000 limit may be more appropriate. Talk to your tax professional about what limit to use.

2.   Deducting Capital Expenses

There are two basic ways to deduct capital expenses: You can depreciate them, deducting some of the cost each year over the asset's useful life, or you may be able to deduct all or most of the cost in one year under Section 179 of the Internal Revenue Code (IRC).

Because depreciation forces you to spread out your deduction over several years, many small business owners choose to deduct their capital expenses under Section 179 instead. Using Section 179, you can currently deduct up to $105,000 in long-term assets purchased each year. Because of the size of the Section 179 deduction (which was increased substantially in recent years), many small and medium-sized practices no longer need to depreciate long-term assets they purchase. This enormous change in the tax law could greatly benefit you.

3.   Repairs and Improvements

When you make repairs or improvements to long-term assets, it can be hard to tell if the cost is a capital or an operating expense. The rule is that ordinary repairs and maintenance for long-term assets are operating expenses that can be currently deducted. However, you must treat a repair or replacement as a capital expense if it:

- increases the value of your property
- makes it more useful, or
- lengthens its useful life.

EXAMPLE 1: Doug, an architect, spends $100 to repair the carburetor on his business car. This is a current expense because the repair doesn't increase the value of his car or lengthen its useful life. The repair merely allows the car to last for a normal time.

EXAMPLE 2: Doug spends $1,500 on a brand new engine for his car. This is a capital expense because the new engine increases the car's value and useful life.

This rule can be difficult to apply because virtually all repairs increase the value of the property being repaired. A repair becomes a capital improvement when it makes the property more valuable, long-lived, or useful than it was before the repair. Individual repairs made as part of a general plan of improvement are also capital expenses.

EXAMPLE: Doug buys an old house and fixes up one of the bedrooms to use as the office for his architecture practice. He pays to repaint and replaster the walls and ceilings, repair the floor, put in new wiring, and install an outside door. Ordinarily, plastering, painting, and floor work are repairs. However, because they are part of a general plan to alter the home for business use, they are capital expenses.

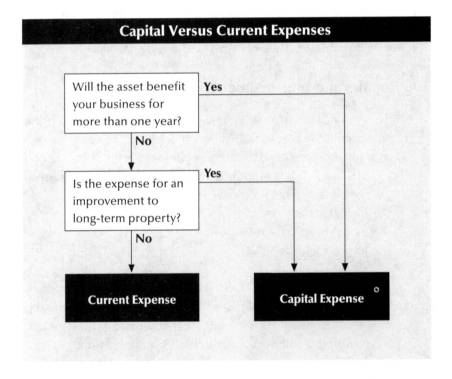

Capital Versus Current Expenses

Will the asset benefit your business for more than one year? — **Yes**

No

Is the expense for an improvement to long-term property? — **Yes**

No

Current Expense

Capital Expense

Inventory is not a business expense. This chapter covers the tax treatment of things you buy to use in your business. It does not cover the cost of items you buy or make to sell to others. Such items are called inventory. Inventory is neither a current nor capital expense. Rather, businesses deduct the cost of inventory as it is sold. (See Chapter 13 for more on inventory.)

B. Section 179 Deductions

If you learn only one section number in the tax code, it should be Section 179. This humble piece of the tax code is one of the greatest tax boons ever for small business owners, including professionals. Section 179 doesn't increase the total amount you can deduct, but it allows you to get your entire depreciation deduction in one year, rather than taking it a little at a time over the term of an asset's useful life—which can be up to 39 years. This is called first-year expensing or Section 179 expensing. (Expensing is an accounting term that means currently deducting a long-term asset.)

> **EXAMPLE:** In 2006, Ginger buys a $4,000 photocopy machine for her accounting practice. Under the regular depreciation rules (using the straight-line depreciation method—see Section C, below), Ginger would have to deduct a portion of the cost each year over its five-year useful life as follows:

Year	Depreciation Deduction
2006	$500
2007	$1,000
2008	$1,000
2009	$1,000
2010	$500

> By deducting the copier under Section 179 instead, Ginger can deduct the entire $4,000 expense from her income taxes in 2006. So she gets a $4,000 deduction in 2006 under Section 179, instead of the $500 deduction she gets using depreciation.

Should you take deductions now or later? Because of inflation and the time value of money, it is often better to use Section 179 if you can, to get the largest possible deduction for the current year. There are some circumstances, however, when it may be more advantageous to use depreciation instead. (See Section C1, below.)

1.   Property You Can Deduct

You qualify for the Section 179 deduction only if you buy long-term, tangible personal property that you use in your business more than 50% of the time. Let's look at these requirements in more detail.

Tangible Personal Property

Under Section 179, you can deduct the cost of tangible personal property (new or used) that you buy for your business, if the property will last more than one year. Examples of tangible personal property include computers, business equipment, and office furniture. Although it's not really tangible property, computer software can also be deducted under Section 179. (See Section C8, below, for more on deducting software.)

You can't use Section 179 to deduct the cost of:

- land
- permanent structures attached to land, including buildings and their structural components, fences, or paved parking areas
- inventory (see Chapter 13)
- intangible property such as patents, copyrights, and trademarks
- property used outside the United States, or
- air conditioning and heating units.

However, nonpermanent property attached to a nonresidential, commercial building is deductible. For example, refrigerators, testing equipment, and signs are all deductible under Section 179. Special rules apply to cars. (See Chapter 5 for more about deducting car expenses.)

Property Used Primarily (51%) for Business

To deduct the cost of property under Section 179, you must use the property primarily for business—that is, to provide your professional services. The deduction is not available for property you use solely for personal purposes or to manage personal investments or otherwise produce nonbusiness income.

> **EXAMPLE:** Jill, a family therapist, bought a computer for $3,000 in 2006. During that year, she used it to play games, manage her checkbook, and surf the Internet for fun. In other words, she used it only for personal purposes. The computer is not deductible under Section 179.

You can take a Section 179 deduction for property you use for both personal and business purposes, as long as you use it for your practice *more than half of the time*. The amount of your deduction is reduced by the percentage of your personal use. (See Section 2, below.) You'll need to keep records showing your business use of the property. If you use an item for business less than half the time, you will have to use regular depreciation instead and deduct the cost of the item over several years.

There is another important limitation regarding the business use of property. You must use the property over half the time for business in *the year in which you buy it*. You can't convert property you previously used for personal use to business use and claim a Section 179 deduction for the cost.

> **EXAMPLE:** Kim, an architect, bought a $2,000 digital camera in 2005 and used it to take family and other personal pictures. In 2007, Kim starts using her digital camera 75% of the time for her architecture practice. She may not deduct the cost under Section 179 because she didn't use the camera for business until two years after she bought it.

The Section 179 rules also require that you *actually be in business* to take the deduction. Property that you buy before you start your practice is not deductible under Section 179. This is one reason why it's a good idea to postpone large purchases until your business is up and running.

> **EXAMPLE:** Andre decides to quit his job as a salaried veterinarian at a local zoo and start his own practice. While still employed, and before he actually starts his own practice, he buys $10,000 worth of veterinary equipment. This amount is not deductible under Section 179 because he had not yet started his new practice.

There are other ways to deduct start-up costs. Business start-up expenses not deductible under Section 179 might be deductible under other tax law provisions. See Chapter 10 for information on deducting business start-up expenses.

Property That You Purchase

You can use Section 179 expensing only for property that you purchase—not for leased property or property you inherit or receive as a gift. You also can't use it for property that you buy from a relative or a corporation or an organization that you control. The property you purchase may be used or new.

2.   Calculating Your Deduction

There are several limitations on the amount you can deduct under Section 179 each year. The total you can deduct under Section 179 annually will depend on:

- what you paid for the property
- how much you use the property for business
- how much Section 179 property you buy during the year, and
- your annual business income.

Let's look at each of these factors more closely.

Cost of Property

The amount you can deduct for Section 179 property is initially based on the property's cost. The cost includes the amount you paid for the property, plus sales tax, delivery, and installation charges. It doesn't matter if you pay cash or finance the purchase with a credit card or bank loan. However, if you pay for property with both cash and a trade-in, the value of the trade-in is not deductible under Section 179. You must depreciate the amount of the trade-in.

> **EXAMPLE:** Stuart, a physician with his own practice, buys a $2,000 microscope. He pays $1,500 cash and is given a $500 trade-in for an older microscope that he owns. He may deduct $1,500 of the $2,000 purchase under Section 179; he must depreciate the remaining $500.

Percentage of Business Use

If you use Section 179 property solely for business, you can deduct 100% of the cost (subject to the other limitations discussed below). However, if you use property for both business and personal purposes, you must reduce your deduction by the percentage of the time that you use the property for personal purposes.

> **EXAMPLE:** Max buys a $4,000 computer in 2006. That year, he uses it for his consulting business 75% of the time and for personal purposes 25% of the time. He may currently deduct 75% of the computer's cost (or $3,000) under Section 179 for 2006. The remaining $1,000 is not deductible as a business expense.

You must continue to use property that you deduct under Section 179 for business at least 50% of the time for as many years as it would take to depreciate the item under the normal depreciation rules. For example, computers have a five-year depreciation period. If you deduct a computer's cost under Section 179, you must use the computer at least 50% of the time for business for five years.

If you don't meet these rules, you'll have to report as income part of the deduction you took under Section 179 in the prior year. This is called recapture, which is discussed in more detail in Section 4, below.

Annual Deduction Limit

There is a limit on the total amount of business property expenses that you can deduct each year under Section 179. In 2003, the limit was increased from $24,000 to $100,000. The limit was $102,000 in 2004 and increased to $105,000 in 2005 and 2006. These whopping increases were enacted by Congress on a temporary basis to jumpstart the faltering U.S. economy.

In 2008, the Section 179 limit is scheduled to go back down to $25,000. Congress could decide to make the higher limit permanent, but at this point no one knows what will happen. If you're planning on buying over $25,000 worth of property for your practice in one year and you want to deduct as much as possible under Section 179, your best bet is to make your purchases before 2008.

The annual deduction limit applies to all of your businesses combined, not to each business you own and run.

> **EXAMPLE:** Britney is a medical doctor in solo practice who also owns a medical laboratory. Because the Section 179 limit applies

to all her businesses together, in 2005 she may expense a total maximum of $105,000 in long-term asset purchases for both businesses.

You don't have to claim the full amount—it's up to you to decide how much to deduct under Section 179. Whatever amount you don't claim under Section 179 must be depreciated instead. (See Section D, below—depreciation is *not* optional.)

Because Section 179 is intended to help smaller businesses, there is also a limit on the total amount of Section 179 property you can purchase each year. You must reduce your Section 179 deduction by one dollar for every dollar your annual purchases exceed the applicable limit. For 2005 through 2008, the limit is $420,000, plus an amount to be added to account for inflation in 2006 and 2007. In 2008 and later, the limit is scheduled to go down to $200,000.

> **EXAMPLE:** The Acme Medical Corporation purchases $480,000 in medical equipment in 2006—$60,000 over the $420,000 total limit. As a result, Acme's $105,000 annual deduction limit is reduced by $60,000, which means that Acme can deduct only $45,000 of its asset purchases under Section 179. It must depreciate the remaining $435,000 over several years.

Year	Section 179 Deduction Limit	Property Value Limit
2002	$24,000	$200,000
2003	$100,000	$400,000
2004	$102,000	$410,000
2005	$105,000	$420,000
2006	$105,000	$420,000 + inflation adjustment
2007	$105,000 + inflation adjustment	$420,000 + inflation adjustment
2008 and later	$25,000	$200,000

The $105,000 Section 179 limit is so high that many professionals won't have to worry about ever reaching it. However, if you purchase enough business property in one year to exceed the limit, you can divide the deduction among the items you purchase in any way you want, as long as the total deduction is not more than the Section 179 limit. It's usually best to apply Section 179 to property that has the longest useful life and, therefore, the longest depreciation period. This reduces the total time you will have to wait to get your deductions, which usually works to your financial benefit.

> **EXAMPLE:** In 2006, the Acme Medical Corporation purchases a used MRI for $100,000, two $5,000 copiers, and a custom computer system for $25,000. This totals $135,000 in long-term asset purchases, which is $30,000 over the Section 179 limit for 2006. Acme can divide its Section 179 deduction among these items in any way that it wants. Under IRS depreciation rules, the copiers and computer system would have to be depreciated over five years and the MRI over seven years. Acme should use Section 179 for the MRI ($100,000), and then the remainder ($5,000) for the copiers or computer system. The portion of the cost of the copiers or computers that exceeds the Section 179 limit ($25,000) can be depreciated over five years. This way, Acme avoids having to wait seven years to get its full deduction for the MRI.

Business Profit Limitation

You can't use Section 179 to deduct more in one year than your total annual business income. Your business income is the total profit you earn from business during the year—whether you have one business or more than one. If you're a married sole proprietor (or owner of a one-person LLC taxed as a sole proprietorship) and file a joint tax return, you can include your spouse's salary and business income in this total as well. You can't count investment income—for example, interest you earn on your personal savings account—as business income. But you can include interest you earn on your business working capital—for example, interest you earn on your business bank account.

You can't use Section 179 to reduce your taxable income below zero. But you can carry to the next tax year (or any other year in the future) any amount you cannot currently take as a Section 179 deduction. You use the amount you carry over to determine your Section 179 deduction for the next year.

EXAMPLE: In 2006, James purchased $100,000 of equipment for his fledgling dental practice, but earned only $5,000. James's wife, however, earned $75,000 from her job as a college professor. Because James and his wife file a joint return, they may take a Section 179 deduction for up to $80,000 for 2006 ($5,000 + $75,000 = $80,000). Thus, James may deduct $80,000 of his equipment purchases in 2006 under Section 179 and deduct the remaining $20,000 in a future year.

If you're a partner in a partnership, LLP, member of a multiowner LLC, or shareholder in an S corporation, the Section 179 income limit applies both to the business entity and to each owner personally. The business determines its Section 179 deduction subject to the income limits. It then allocates the deduction among the partners or shareholders who each apply their own Section 179 income limit.

EXAMPLE: Alice, an optometrist, is a partner in the ABC Optometric Partnership. She is also a member of the Fancy Free LLC, a small company that makes specialty eyeglass frames. In 2006, ABC purchases $100,000 in equipment that it elects to expense under Section 179. Its business income for the year is $500,000, so it can deduct the full $100,000. ABC allocates $50,000 of the Section 179 deduction and $150,000 of its income to Alice. The Fancy Free LLC also purchases $100,000 of equipment that it elects to expense under Section 179 and allocates $50,000 of the deduction to Alice. But Fancy Free incurs a $100,000 loss for the year, $75,000 of which is allocated to Alice. Alice has $100,000 in equipment purchases allocated to her that could qualify for the Section 179 deduction. However, her total business income for the year is only $75,000 ($150,000 in income from ABC minus a $75,000 loss from Fancy Free). Thus, Alice may expense only $75,000 of the equipment purchases in 2006. She must carry over the remaining $25,000 to deduct in future years.

If your practice is organized as a C corporation, nothing is allocated to the shareholders. The corporation takes the Section 179 deduction on its own return, based on its own taxable income. This puts professionals who have C corporations in a bit of a quandary, because they ordinarily want their C corporations to have little or no taxable income for the year so as to avoid double taxation (see Chapter 16). If you have a C corporation and want to take a Section 179 deduction, you must make sure it has sufficient taxable income at the end of the year to cover the amount of your desired deduction.

Date of Purchase

As long as you meet the requirements, you can deduct the cost of Section 179 property up to the limits discussed above, no matter when you place the property in service during the year (that is, when you buy the property and make it available for use in your ongoing business). This differs from regular depreciation rules, by which property bought later in the year may be subject to a smaller deduction for the first year. (See Section C5 for more on regular depreciation rules about placing property in service.) This is yet another advantage of the Section 179 deduction over regular depreciation.

> **EXAMPLE:** John buys and places in service a $5,000 X-ray machine for his medical practice on January 1, 2006 and $5,000 of office furniture on December 31, 2006. Both purchases are fully deductible under Section 179 in 2006.

Use It or Lose It—Make Your Section 179 Claims

Section 179 deductions are not automatic. You must claim a Section 179 deduction on your tax return by completing IRS Form 4562, Part I, and checking a specific box. If you neglect to do this, you may lose your deduction. If you filed your return for the year without making the election, you can file an amended return within six months after your tax return was due for the year—April 15 plus any extensions you receive. Once this deadline passes, however, you lose your right to a Section 179 deduction forever—you can't file an amended return in a later year to claim the deduction. (See Section D, below, on tax reporting requirements.)

3. Listed Property

The IRS imposes special rules on certain items that can easily be used for personal as well as business purposes. These items, called listed property, include:

- cars and certain other vehicles
- motorcycles, boats, and airplanes
- computers
- cellular phones, and
- any other property generally used for entertainment, recreation, or amusement—for example, VCRs, cameras, stereos, and camcorders.

The IRS fears that taxpayers might use listed property for personal reasons, but claim a business deduction for it. For this reason, you're required to document your business use of listed property. You can satisfy this requirement by keeping a logbook showing when and how the property is used. (See Chapter 20 for more on record keeping.)

Exception for Computers

You generally have to document your use of listed property even if you use it 100% for business. However, there is an exception to this rule for computers: If you use a computer or computer peripheral (such as a printer) only for business and keep it at your business location, you need not comply with the record-keeping requirement. This includes computers that you keep at your home office if the office qualifies for the home office deduction. (See Chapter 7 for more on the home office deduction.)

> **EXAMPLE:** John, a sole proprietor consultant, works full time in his home office that he uses exclusively for business. The office is clearly his principal place of business and qualifies for the home office deduction. He buys a $4,000 computer for his office and uses it exclusively for his consulting practice. He does not have to keep records showing how and when he uses the computer.

This exception does not apply to items other than computers and computer peripheral equipment—for example, it doesn't apply to calculators, copiers, fax machines, or typewriters.

Deducting Listed Property

If you use listed property for business more than 50% of the time, you may deduct its cost just like any other long-term business property. For example, you may deduct the cost in one year using Section 179 or depreciate it over several years under the normal depreciation rules.

However, if you use listed property 50% or less of the time for business, you may not deduct the cost under Section 179 or use accelerated depreciation. Instead, you must use the slowest method of depreciation: straight-line depreciation. (See Section C7, below, for more on deducting listed property.)

4.   Recapture Under Section 179

Recapture is a nasty tax trap an unwary business owner can easily get caught in. It requires you to give back part of a tax deduction that you took in a previous year. You may have to recapture part of a Section 179 tax deduction if, during the property's recovery period, either:

- your business use of the property drops below 51%, or
- you sell the property.

The recovery period is the property's useful life as determined under IRS rules. The IRS has determined the useful life of all types of property that can be depreciated. The useful life of an asset is the time period over which you must depreciate the asset. For personal property that can be expensed under Section 179, the useful life ranges from three years for computer software to seven years for office furniture and business equipment. If you deduct property under Section 179, you must continue to use it in your business at least 51% of the time for its entire useful life—this is the IRS recovery period. For example, if you buy office furniture, you must use it over half of the time for business for at least seven years.

If your business use falls below 51% or you sell the property before the recovery period ends, you become subject to recapture. This means that you have to give back to the IRS all of the accelerated deductions you took under Section 179. You get to keep the amount you would have been entitled to under regular depreciation, but you must include the rest of your Section 179 deduction in your ordinary income for the year.

EXAMPLE: In 2006, Paul purchases office equipment worth $10,000 and deducts the entire amount under Section 179. He uses the property 100% for business during 2006 and 2007, but in 2008 he uses it only 40% for business. The equipment has a seven-year recovery period, so Paul is subject to recapture. He figures the recapture amount as follows:

First, he figures all the annual depreciation he would have been entitled to during 2006 through 2008 had he depreciated the property under the regular depreciation rules:

2006	$1,666
2007	2,222
2008	297 ($740.50 x 40% business use)
Total	$4,185

He then deducts this amount from the $10,000 Section 179 deduction he claimed in 2006: $10,000 – $4,185 = $5,815. Paul's 2008 recapture amount is $5,815. Paul must add $5,815 to his income for 2008. He can continue to depreciate the equipment for the next four years.

You eventually get back through depreciation any recapture amount you must pay. But recapture can spike your tax bill for the year, so it's best to avoid the problem by making sure that you use property you deduct under Section 179 at least 51% for business during its entire recovery period.

You can maximize your Section 179 deduction by keeping your percentage of business use of Section 179 property as high as possible during the year that you buy the property. After the first year, you can reduce your business use—as long as it stays above 50%—and avoid recapture.

EXAMPLE: Paul buys $10,000 of office equipment and uses it 90% for business in 2006. He may currently deduct $9,000 of the cost under Section 179 (90% business use x $10,000 cost = $9,000 deduction). In 2007 and 2008, he uses the equipment for business only 60% of the time. Nevertheless, he need not recapture any of his Section 179 deduction because his business use is still above 50%.

C. Depreciation

The traditional method of getting back the money you spend on long-term business assets is to deduct the cost a little at a time over several years (exactly how long is determined by the IRS). This process is called depreciation.

Depreciation is a complicated subject. The IRS instruction booklet on the subject (Publication 946, *How to Depreciate Property*) is over 100 pages long. For a comprehensive discussion of depreciation, read Publication 946. In this section, we cover the depreciation basics that all business owners should know.

Depreciation is not optional. Unlike the Section 179 deduction, depreciation is not optional. You must take a depreciation deduction if you qualify for it. If you fail to take it, the IRS will treat you as if you had taken it. This means that you could be subject to depreciation recapture when you sell the asset—even if you never took a depreciation deduction. This would increase your taxable income by the amount of the deduction you failed to take. (See Section 11, below.) So if you don't expense a depreciable asset under Section 179, be sure to take the proper depreciation deductions for it. If you realize later that you failed to take a depreciation deduction that you should have taken, you may file an amended tax return to claim any deductions that you should have taken in prior years. (See Chapter 18 for information about filing amended returns).

1.   When to Use Depreciation

Do you ever buy more than $105,000 worth of personal property for your practice in a year? For many professionals with small and medium-sized practices, the answer is "No." With the Section 179 deduction at $105,000 (at least through the end of 2007), you may never have to use depreciation.

However, you may need to use depreciation to write off the cost of long-term assets that don't qualify for Section 179 expensing. Also, under some circumstances, it may be better to use depreciation and draw out your deduction over several years instead of getting your deductions all at once under Section 179.

Assets That Don't Qualify Under Section 179

You must meet strict requirements to use Section 179 to currently deduct long-term business property. You will not be able to expense an item under Section 179 if any of the following are true:

- You use the item less than 51% of the time for business.
- It is personal property that you converted to business use.
- It is a structure, such as a building or building component.
- You financed the purchase with a trade-in (the value of the trade-in must be depreciated).
- It is an intangible asset such a patent, copyright, trademark, or business goodwill.
- You bought it from a relative.
- You inherited the property or received it as a gift.
- It is an air conditioning or heating unit.

For any items that fall within one or more of these categories, you will have to use regular depreciation instead of Section 179.

You will also have to use depreciation instead of Section 179 to the extent you exceed the Section 179 annual limit. This limit is $105,000 in 2005 through 2007, and $25,000 thereafter (unless Congress makes the higher limit permanent). In addition, Section 179 expensing is not available if you spend more than $500,000 on long-term assets in a year during 2005 through 2007, or more than $300,000 in 2008 or later.

Sometimes Depreciation Is Better

Section 179 expensing lets you take your total deduction up front and in one year, while depreciation requires you to deduct the cost of an asset a little at a time over several years. The slower depreciation method isn't always a bad thing. In some circumstances, you may be better off using depreciation instead of Section 179.

Remember: The value of a deduction depends on your income tax bracket. If you're in the 15% bracket, a $1,000 deduction is worth only $150 of federal income tax savings. If you're in the 28% bracket, it's worth $280. (See Chapter 1 for more on the value of a tax deduction.) If you expect to earn more in future years, it may make sense to spread out your deductions so you save some for later years when you expect to be in a higher tax bracket.

> **EXAMPLE:** Marie, a sole proprietor consultant, buys a $5,000 computer system for her business in 2006. She elects to depreciate the computer instead of using the Section 179 deduction. That way, she can deduct a portion of the cost from her gross income each year for the next six years. Marie is only in the 15% tax bracket in 2006 but expects to be in the 28% bracket by 2008.

The following chart shows how much more money Marie may deduct by using depreciation to deduct a portion of the computer's cost over six years, instead of taking a Section 179 deduction for the entire cost in the first year. Marie is using the straight-line depreciation method, under which she gets the same deduction every year, except for the first and last.

Of course, money grows in value over time because it earns interest or can otherwise be invested. So it's possible that Marie would be better off using Section 179 and getting $750 all at once, rather than waiting six years to collect a total of $1,305 through depreciation. However, $750 today will be worth more than $1,305 six years from now only if Marie earns at least 10% on her money each year—substantially more than she could get by putting it in the bank.

Comparison of Deductions: Section 179 and Depreciation			
Year	Marie's Marginal Federal Income Tax Rate	Federal Income Tax Saving Using Section 179 Deduction	Federal Income Tax Savings Using Depreciation Deduction
2006	15%	$750 (15% x $5,000 (total cost))	$ 75 (15% x $500 of total $5,000 cost)
2007	25%	0	250 (25% x $1,000)
2008	28%	0	280 (28% x $1,000)
2009	28%	0	280 (28% x $1,000)
2010	28%	0	280 (28% x $1,000)
2011	28%	0	140 (28% x $500)
Total		$750	$1,305

Your Income Is Too Low

The Section 179 deduction may not exceed your business income. If you're married and file a joint return, your spouse's income can be included. If your practice is making little or no money and you have little or no income from wages or your spouse, you may not be able take a Section 179 deduction for the current year.

In contrast, there is no income limitation on depreciation deductions. You can deduct depreciation from your business income; if this results in a net loss for a year, you can deduct the loss from income taxes you paid in prior years.

> **EXAMPLE:** Marvin made no money from his consulting business in 2006 but incurred $10,000 in expenses for depreciable property. He has no other income for the year, but he earned $100,000 in 2005 from a prior job, on which he paid $25,000 in federal taxes. By depreciating the $10,000 expense, he gets a $2,000 depreciation deduction for 2006 and his business ends up with a net loss of $2,000 for that year. He can file an amended tax return for 2005 and deduct this amount from his income for the year, resulting in a $500 tax refund. Had he deducted the $10,000 under Section 179 instead, he would have had to carry forward his $10,000 loss to the next year and use it then or in subsequent years.

2. Some Depreciation Basics

Depreciation is a tax deduction for the decline in value of long-term property over time due to wear and tear, deterioration, or obsolescence. Unless the Section 179 deduction applies, depreciation is the only way you can deduct the cost of long-term property—that is, property that lasts for more than one year, such as buildings, computers, equipment, patents, copyrights, and office furniture. You also depreciate the cost of major repairs or improvements that increase the value or extend the life of an asset—for example, the cost of a major upgrade to a computer system. (See Section A, above.)

Property You Cannot Depreciate:

You cannot depreciate:

- property that doesn't wear out, including land (whether undeveloped or with structures on it), stocks, securities, or gold
- property you use solely for personal purposes
- property purchased and disposed of in the same year
- inventory, or
- collectibles that appreciate in value over time, such as antiques and artwork.

If you use nondepreciable property in your business, you get no tax deduction while you own it. But if you sell it, you get to deduct its tax basis (see below) from the sales price to calculate your taxable profit. If the basis exceeds the sales price, you'll have a deductible loss on the property. If the price exceeds the basis, you'll have a taxable gain.

> **EXAMPLE:** A law partnership purchased an oil painting for its offices for $10,000 in 1990. Like all artwork, the painting could not be depreciated because it does not wear out or get used up over time. The firm sold the painting for $20,000 in 2006. Its $10,000 tax basis is subtracted from the sales price to determine the taxable gain on the sale—$10,000.

You also may not depreciate property that you do not own. For example, you get no depreciation deduction for property you lease. The person who owns the property—the lessor—gets to depreciate it. (However, you may deduct your lease payments as current business expenses.) Leasing may be preferable to buying and depreciating equipment that wears out or becomes obsolete quickly. (See Section E.)

When Depreciation Begins and Ends

You begin to depreciate your property when it is placed in service—that is, when it's ready and available for use in your practice. As long as it is available for use, you don't have to actually use the property for business during the year to take depreciation.

EXAMPLE: Tom, a general practitioner physician in a rural area, purchased a portable sonogram machine to take sonograms of unborn infants. He had the device ready for use in his office on November 1, 2006. However, he had no pregnant patients who needed a sonogram until 2007. Tom may take a depreciation deduction for the sonogram for 2006, even though he didn't actually use it that year, because it was ready and available for use in 2006.

You stop depreciating property either when you have fully recovered your cost or other basis or when you retire it from service, whichever occurs first. Property is retired from service when you stop using it for business, sell it, destroy it, or otherwise dispose of it.

EXAMPLE: Tom depreciates the $25,000 cost of his sonogram machine a portion at a time over seven years. At the end of that time, he has recovered his $25,000 basis and depreciation ends. He is free to continue using the machine, but he can't get any more depreciation deductions for it.

You must *actually be in business* to take depreciation deductions. In other words, you cannot start depreciating an asset until your practice is up and running. This is one important reason why it is a good idea to postpone large property purchases until your practice has begun. (See Chapter 10 for a detailed discussion of tax deductions for business start-up expenses.)

EXAMPLE: In 2006, Julia buys $10,000 worth of equipment for a new dental practice. However, the dental office does not open its doors for business until 2007. Julia may not take a depreciation deduction for the equipment in 2006, but she may in 2007 and later years.

Calculating Depreciation

How to calculate depreciation is one of the more confusing and tedious aspects of the tax law. In the past, most people had accountants perform the calculations for them. Today, you can use tax preparation software to calculate your depreciation deductions and complete the required IRS forms.

Although a tax preparation program can do the calculations for you, you still need to make some basic decisions about how you will depreciate your property. A computer can't do this for you. To make the best decisions, you'll need to have a basic understanding of how depreciation works.

In a nutshell, your depreciation deduction is determined by the following factors:

- your basis in the property (usually the asset's cost)
- the depreciation period, and
- the depreciation convention that determines how much depreciation you get in the first year.

Let's look at each of these factors.

3.   Figuring Out Your Tax Basis in the Property

Depreciation allows you to deduct your total investment in a long-term asset you buy for your business over its useful life. In tax lingo, your investment is called your basis or tax basis. Basis is a word you'll hear over and over again when the subject of depreciation comes up. Don't let it confuse you; it just means the amount of your total investment in the property.

Usually, your basis in depreciable property is whatever you paid for it. This includes not only the purchase price, but also sales tax, delivery charges, installation, and testing fees, if any. You may depreciate the entire cost, no matter how you paid for the property—in cash, on a credit card, or with a bank loan.

> **EXAMPLE:** The ABC Medical Corporation buys a laser to use for lasik eye surgery. It pays $90,000 cash, $5,400 in sales tax, and $4,600 for delivery and installation. Its basis in the property is $100,000.

Adjusted Basis

Your basis in property is not fixed. It changes over time to reflect the true amount of your investment. Each year, you must deduct from the property's basis the amount of depreciation allowed for the property—this is true regardless of whether you actually claimed any depreciation on your tax return. This new basis is called the adjusted basis, because it reflects adjustments from your starting basis. Eventually, your adjusted basis will be reduced to zero and you can no longer depreciate the property.

EXAMPLE: The ABC Medical Corporation, (from the above example) bought the laser in 2006. Its starting basis was $100,000. It depreciates the cost over the next eight years using the double declining balance method. (See Section 6, below.) The following chart shows its adjusted basis for each year.

Year	Depreciation Deduction	Adjusted Basis
2006	$14,290	$85,710
2007	$24,490	$61,220
2008	$17,490	$43,730
2009	$12,490	$31,240
2010	$8,930	$22,310
2011	$8,920	$13,390
2012	$8,930	$4,460
2013	$4,460	0

Your starting basis in property will also be reduced by:
• Section 179 deductions you take for the property
• casualty and theft losses, and
• manufacturer or seller rebates you receive.
If you sell depreciable property, your gain or loss on the sale is determined by subtracting its adjusted basis from the sales price.

EXAMPLE: If ABC sells its laser for $75,000 in 2008 when its adjusted basis is $43,730, its taxable gain on the sale will be $31,270 ($75,000 – $43,730 = $31,270). If it sells the device for $30,000 instead, it will incur a $13,730 loss that it can deduct from its taxable income.

If you abandon business property instead of selling it, you may deduct its adjusted basis as a business loss. You abandon property when you voluntarily and permanently give up possessing and using it with the intention of ending your ownership and without passing it on to anyone else. Loss from abandonment of business property is deductible as an ordinary loss, even if the property is a capital asset.

> **EXAMPLE:** ABC's laser breaks down five years after it bought it. It decides it's not worth the money to fix it and sends it to the scrap heap. It has abandoned it and may deduct the laser's adjusted basis—$22,310—as a business loss.

For more information on the tax implications of selling or otherwise disposing of business property, refer to IRS Publication 544, *Sales and Other Dispositions of Assets.*

Property Not Bought Entirely With Cash

Of course, not all business property is bought with cash. You may pay for it wholly or partly with a trade-in, inherit it, receive it as a gift, or convert personal property to property used for your business. In these cases, basis is not determined according to the property's cost.

If you buy property with a trade-in, your starting basis is equal to the adjusted basis in the trade-in property, plus any cash you pay for the property. Trading in old business property for new property can be a great tax strategy. When you sell business property, you have to pay taxes on any gain you receive. If you use old property for a trade-in, you defer any tax on the gain until you sell the newly acquired property.

> **EXAMPLE:** Assume that ABC from the examples above decides to buy a new laser in 2009. The laser it already owns has a basis of $43,730, and a fair market value of $70,000. If ABC sold the laser for its $70,000 fair market value, it would have to pay tax on its $22,270 profit ($70,000 − $43,730 = $26,270). Assuming a combined federal and state income tax rate of 40%, Acme would have to pay $10,508 in tax, leaving $59,492 from the sale. It would have to shell out another $40,508 to buy the $100,000 laser. Instead, Acme trades in the laser and pays $30,000 in cash for a new laser. Acme has no profit to pay tax on. Its starting basis in the new laser is $73,730. This is true even though the list price for the laser is $100,000.

If you convert personal property to business use, your starting basis is equal to the lesser of the property's fair market value or adjusted depreciable basis when you started using it for business. The fair market value will be lower than the property's adjusted basis unless it's gone up in value since you bought it.

> **EXAMPLE:** In 2006, Miranda decides to start her own architecture practice and converts a camera she bought two years earlier to business use. She bought the camera for $1,000 in 2004, which is its adjusted basis when she started using it for business. However, the fair market value of the camera in 2006 is $400, so this is her starting basis.

How do you determine your property's fair market value? By figuring out how much someone would be willing to pay for it. Look at classified ads and listings for similar property on eBay, or call dealers in the type of property involved. If you think the property is extremely valuable, get an appraisal from an expert. Keep records of how you figured out the property's value.

It's not likely that most personal property that you convert to business use will be worth much. You can't claim inflated values for old property just to take depreciation deductions.

> **EXAMPLE:** Kunz, the owner of a cement company, bought out a competitor for $60,000. Included in the purchase were 19 old trucks and cement mixers. Kunz claimed on his tax return that these were worth $32,900 and used this amount as his tax basis to figure out his depreciation deduction. The IRS found that the value Kunz assigned the equipment was "absurd" and "grossly excessive." In reality, the equipment was so old that it had no substantial value except as scrap or junk. This was shown by the fact that Kunz had resold one of the mixers for only $25. The IRS concluded that the items were worth only $2,700. (*Kunz v Comm'r*, 333 F.2d 556 (6th Cir. 1964), *aff'g* T.C. Memo 1962-276.)

Converting Your Reference Books to Business Use

Textbooks and other reference books you buy while doing your professional training are nondeductible personal property. However, once you enter practice, you may be able to convert them to business use and depreciate their fair market value over seven years. You must actually use the books in your practice to deduct them this way.

EXAMPLE: Dennis purchased $4,000 worth of medical reference books while in medical school. He starts his own practice and uses the books as part of his professional reference library. He may depreciate their fair market value over seven years. He determines they are worth $2,000 by looking for sales of similar used books on Amazon and eBay.

The starting basis of inherited property is its fair market value on the day the owner died. Your starting basis in gifted property is its fair market value at the time of the gift.

Mixed-Use Property

You may take a depreciation deduction for property you use for both business and personal purposes. However, your depreciable basis in the property will be reduced by the percentage of your personal use. This will, of course, reduce the amount of your depreciation deduction.

EXAMPLE: Miranda uses her $400 camera 75% of the time for business and 25% for personal use. Her depreciable basis in the camera is reduced by 25%, so her basis is only $300 instead of $400 (75% x $400 = $300). Miranda can depreciate only $300 over the asset's depreciation period.

You can take a depreciation deduction even if you use an asset only 1% of the time for business. This is one advantage of depreciation over the Section 179 deduction, which is available only for property you use more than 50% of the time for business.

If you use property for both business and personal purposes, you must keep a diary or log with the dates, times, and reasons the property was used to distinguish business from personal use. Moreover, special rules apply if you use cars and other types of listed property less than 50% of the time for business.

4. Depreciation Period

The depreciation period (also called the recovery period) is the time over which you must take your depreciation deductions for an asset. The tax code has assigned depreciation periods to all types of business assets, ranging from three to 39 years. These periods are somewhat arbitrary. However, property that can be expected to last a long time generally gets a longer recovery period than property that has a short life—for example, nonresidential real property has a 39-year recovery period, while software has only a three-year period. Most of the property that you buy for your practice will probably have a five- or seven-year depreciation period.

The major depreciation periods are listed below. These periods are also called recovery classes, and all property that comes within a period is said to belong to that class. For example, computers have a five-year depreciation period and thus fall within the five-year class, along with automobiles and office equipment.

5. First-Year Depreciation

Sid and Sam are identical twins who have competing law practices. Sid buys a $4,000 computer for his office and places it in service on January 2, 2006. In an effort to one-up him, Sam buys a $6,000 computer on December 30, 2006. How much depreciation should each be allowed for the first year they own their computers? Should Sid get a full year and Sam just a day?

The IRS has established certain rules (called "conventions") that govern how many months of depreciation you can take for the first year that you own an asset.

Depreciation Period	
Depreciation Period	**Type of Property**
3 years	Computer software
	Tractor units for over-the-road use
	Any racehorse over 2 years old when placed in service
	Any other horse over 12 years old when placed in service
5 years	Automobiles, taxis, buses, and trucks
	Computers and peripheral equipment
	Office machinery (such as typewriters, calculators, and copiers)
	Any property used in research and experimentation
	Breeding cattle and dairy cattle
	Appliances, carpets, furniture, and so on, used in a residential rental real estate activity
7 years	Office furniture and fixtures (such as desks, files, and safes)
	Agricultural machinery and equipment
	Any property that does not have a class life and has not been designated by law as being in any other class
10 years	Vessels, barges, tugs, and similar water transportation equipment
	Any single-purpose agricultural or horticultural structure
	Any tree or vine bearing fruits or nuts
15 years	Improvements made directly to land or added to it (such as shrubbery, fences, roads, and bridges)
	Any retail motor fuels outlet, such as a convenience store
20 years	Farm buildings (other than single-purpose agricultural or horticultural structures)
27.5 years	Residential rental property—for example, an apartment building
39 years	Nonresidential real property, such as a home office, office building, store, or warehouse

Half-Year Convention

The basic rule is that, no matter what month and day of the year an asset you purchase becomes available for use in your business, you treat it as being placed in service on July 1—the midpoint of the year. This means that you get one-half year of depreciation for the first year that you own an asset.

> **EXAMPLE:** If Sam buys one computer in January, one in March, and one in December, he treats them all as having been placed in service on July 1.

Midquarter Convention

You are not allowed to use the half-year convention if more than 40% of the long-term personal property that you buy during the year is placed in service during the last three months of the year. The 40% figure is determined by adding together the basis of all the depreciable property you bought during the year and comparing that with the basis of all of the property you bought during the fourth quarter only.

If you exceed the 40% ceiling, you must use the midquarter convention. You group all the property that you purchased during the year by the quarter it was bought and treat it as being placed in service at the midpoint of that quarter. (A quarter is a three-month period: The first quarter is January through March; the second quarter is April through June; the third quarter is July through September; and the fourth quarter is October through December.)

> **EXAMPLE:** Sam buys one computer in January, one in October, and one in December. Each computer costs $5,000, so the basis for all the computers he bought during the year is $15,000. He bought $10,000 of this amount during the fourth quarter, so more than 40% of his purchases were made in the fourth quarter of the year. Sam must use the midquarter convention. He must treat the first computer he bought as being placed in service on February 15— the midpoint of the first quarter. The second and last computers must be treated as being placed in service on November 15—the midpoint of the fourth quarter.

As a general rule, it's best to avoid having to use the midquarter convention. To do this, you need to buy more than 60% of your total depreciable assets before September 30 of the year. Assets you currently deduct using Section 179 do not count toward the 40% limitation, so you can avoid the midquarter convention by using Section 179 to deduct most or all of your purchases in the last three months of the year.

6. Depreciation Methods

There are several ways to calculate depreciation. However, most tangible property is depreciated using the Modified Accelerated Cost Recovery System, or MACRS. (A slightly different system, called Alternative Depreciation System or ADS, applies to certain listed property (see Section 7, below), property used outside the United States, and certain farm property and imported property.)

You can ordinarily use three different methods to calculate the depreciation deduction under MACRS: straight-line or one of two accelerated depreciation methods. Once you choose your method, you're stuck with it for the entire life of the asset.

In addition, you must use the same method for all property of the same class that you purchase during the year. For example, if you use the straight-line method to depreciate a computer, you must use that method to depreciate all other property in the same class as computers. Computers fall within the five-year class, so you must use the straight-line method for all other five-year property you buy during the year, such as office equipment.

Straight-Line Method

The straight-line method requires you to deduct an equal amount each year over the useful life of an asset. However, if the midyear convention applies, you deduct only a half-year's worth of depreciation in the first year. You make up for this by adding an extra one-half year of depreciation at the end. You can use the straight-line method to depreciate any type of depreciable property.

EXAMPLE: Sally buys a $1,000 printer-fax-copy machine for her accounting practice in 2006. It has a useful life of five years. (See the chart in Section 4, above). She bought more than 60% of her depreciable property for the year before September 30, so she can use the midyear convention. Using the straight-line method, she can depreciate the asset over six years. Her annual depreciation deductions are as follows:

2006	$ 100
2007	200
2008	200
2009	200
2010	200
2011	100
Total	$1,000

If the midquarter convention applies, you don't get one-half year's worth of depreciation the first year. Instead, your first year depreciation amount depends on the month of the year when you bought the property. For example, if Sally bought her machine in September, she would get only $75 deprecation in 2006, $200 in 2007 through 2010, and then $125 in 2011. If she bought it in December, she would get $25 in 2006 and $175 in 2011. If she bought it in January, she would get $175 in 2004 and $25 in 2011.

Accelerated Depreciation Methods

There is nothing wrong with straight-line depreciation, but the tax law provides an alternative that most businesses prefer: accelerated depreciation. As the name implies, this method provides faster depreciation than the straight-line method. It does not increase your total depreciation deduction, but it permits you to take larger deductions in the first few years after you buy an asset. You make up for this by taking smaller deductions in later years.

The fastest and most commonly used form of accelerated depreciation is the double declining balance method. This is a confusing name, but all it means is that you get double the deduction that you would get for the first full year under the straight-line method. You then get less in later years. However, in later years, you may switch to the straight-line method (which will give you a larger deduction). This is built into the IRS depreciation tables. This method may be used to depreciate all property within the three- , five- , seven- , and ten-year classes, excluding farm property. This covers virtually all the tangible personal property you buy for your business.

EXAMPLE: Sally decides to use the double declining balance method to depreciate her $1,000 printer-fax-copier machine. Her annual depreciation deductions are as follows:

2006	$ 200.00
2007	320.00
2008	192.00
2009	115.20
2010	115.20
2011	57.60
Total	$1,000.00

By using this method, she gets a $200 deduction in 2006, instead of the $100 deduction she'd get using straight-line depreciation. But starting in 2008, she'll get smaller deductions than she would using the straight-line method.

The following table prepared by the IRS shows you the percentage of the cost of an asset that you may deduct each year using the double declining balance method.

200% Declining Balance Depreciation Method					
Convention: Half-year					
	If the recovery period is:				
Year	3-year	5-year	7-year	10-year	15-year	20-year
1	33.33%	20.00%	14.29%	10.00%	5.00%	3.750%
2	44.45%	32.00%	24.49%	18.00%	9.50%	7.219%
3	14.81%	19.20%	17.49%	14.40%	8.55%	6.677%
4	7.41%	11.52%	12.49%	11.52%	7.70%	6.177%
5		11.52%	8.93%	9.22%	6.93%	5.713%
6		5.76%	8.92%	7.37%	6.23%	5.285%
7			8.93%	6.55%	5.90%	4.888%
8			4.46%	6.55%	5.90%	4.522%
9				6.56%	5.91%	4.462%
10				6.55%	5.90%	4.461%
11				3.28%	5.91%	4.462%
12					5.90%	4.461%
13					5.91%	4.462%
14					5.90%	4.461%
15					5.91%	4.462%
16					2.95%	4.461%
17						4.462%
18						4.461%
19						4.462%
20						4.461%
21						2.231%

An alternative to the double declining method is the 150% declining balance method. This method gives you one and one-half times the deduction in the first year than you would otherwise get using the straight-line method. The 150% method may be used for three- , five- , seven- , ten- , 15- , and 20-year personal property, including farm property.

EXAMPLE: Sally decides to use the 150% declining balance method to depreciate her printer-fax-copier. This gives her a smaller deduction in the first two years than the double declining balance method, but larger deductions in later years.

2006	$	150.00
2007		250.50
2008		178.50
2009		166.60
2010		166.60
2011		83.30
Total		$1,000.00

The following table prepared by the IRS shows you the percentage of the cost of an asset you may deduct each year using the 150% declining balance method.

150% Declining Balance Depreciation Method
Convention: Half-year

	If the recovery period is:						
Year	3-year	5-year	7-year	10-year	12-year	15-year	20-year
1	25.00%	15.00%	10.71%	7.50%	6.25%	5.00%	3.750%
2	37.50%	25.50%	19.13%	13.88%	11.72%	9.50%	7.219%
3	25.00%	17.85%	15.03%	11.79%	10.25%	8.55%	6.677%
4	12.50%	16.66%	12.25%	10.02%	8.97%	7.70%	6.177%
5		16.66%	12.25%	8.74%	7.85%	6.93%	5.713%
6		8.33%	12.25%	8.74%	7.33%	6.23%	5.285%
7			12.25%	8.74%	7.33%	5.90%	4.888%
8			6.13%	8.74%	7.33%	5.90%	4.522%
9				8.74%	7.33%	5.91%	4.462%
10				4.37%	7.32%	5.90%	4.461%
11					7.33%	5.91%	4.462%
12					3.66%	5.90%	4.461%
13						5.91%	4.462%
14						5.90%	4.461%
15						5.91%	4.462%
16						2.95%	4.461%
17							4.462%
18							4.461%

Using accelerated depreciation is not necessarily a good idea if you expect your income to go up in future years. There are also some restrictions on when you can use accelerated depreciation. For example, you can't use it for cars, computers, and certain other property that you use for business less than 50% of the time. (See Section 7, below.)

Depreciation Tables

Figuring out your annual depreciation deduction might seem to require some complicated math, but actually it's not that difficult. Of course, if you use a tax professional to do your taxes, he or she will do the math for you. Tax preparation software can also do this. However, if you want to do it yourself, you can use depreciation tables prepared by the IRS. These tables factor in the depreciation convention and method. They are all available in IRS Publication 946, *How to Depreciate Property*.

> **EXAMPLE:** In 2006, Joe buys a $9,600 computer system for his accounting practice. He wants to depreciate it using the double declining balance method so he can get the largest possible deduction during the first year. He uses the property 100% for business, and the half-year convention applies because he didn't buy more than 40% of his business property during the last three months of 2006. To figure his depreciation, he can use the applicable IRS depreciation table from Publication 946. Part of the table is reprinted below.

You can see from the table that for five-year property (like the computer system), you get 20% of your total depreciation deduction in the first year. To figure the deduction for the computer system, you multiply $9,600 by 20%, resulting in a $1,920 deduction in 2006. In 2007, the deduction will be $3,072 (32% x $9,600 = $3,072). For 2006, the deduction is smaller than for 2007 because of the midyear convention—that is, you get half only of the first year's depreciation because the property is assumed to have been purchased on July 1. This is factored into the table.

Publication 946 contains 18 different depreciation tables—one for each type of depreciation you can take. These are all included in Appendix A of Publication 946.

200% Declining Balance Depreciation Method Convention: Half-year				
Year	**If the recovery period is:**			
	3-year	**5-year**	**7-year**	**10-year**
1	33.33%	20.00%	14.29%	10.00%
2	44.45%	32.00%	24.49%	18.00%
3	14.81%	19.20%	17.49%	14.40%
4	7.41%	11.52%	12.49%	11.52%
5		11.52%	8.93%	9.22%
6		5.76%	8.92%	7.37%
7			8.93%	6.55%
8			4.46%	6.55%
9				6.55%
10				6.55%
11				3.28%

7. Listed Property

The IRS imposes special rules on listed property—items that can easily be used for personal as well as business purposes. (See Section B3, above, for a discussion of listed property.) If you use listed property for business more than 50% of the time, you may deduct its cost just like any other long-term business property (under Section 179 or normal depreciation rules).

However, if you use listed property 50% or less of the time for business, you may not deduct the cost under Section 179 or use accelerated depreciation. Instead, you must use the slowest method of depreciation: straight-line depreciation. In addition, you are not allowed to use the normal depreciation periods allowed under the MACRS depreciation system. Instead, you must use the depreciation periods provided for by the Alternative Depreciation System (ADS for short). These are generally longer than the ordinary MACRS periods. However, you may still depreciate cars, trucks, and computers over five years. The main ADS depreciation periods for listed property are provided in the following chart.

ADS Depreciation Periods	
Property	**Depreciation Period**
Cars and light trucks	5 years
Computers and peripheral equipment	5 years
Communication equipment	10 years
Personal property with no class life	12 years

If you start out using accelerated depreciation and in a later year your business use drops to 50% or less, you have to switch to the straight-line method and ADS period for that year and subsequent years. In addition, you are subject to depreciation recapture for the prior years—that is, you must calculate how much more depreciation you got in the prior years by using accelerated depreciation and count that amount as ordinary taxable income for the current year. This will, of course, increase your tax bill for the year.

8. Computer Software

Most professionals buy computer software; some also create it themselves. The tax law favors the latter group.

Software You Buy

The software you buy comes in two basic types for tax purposes: software that comes already installed on a computer that you buy and software you purchase separately and install yourself (often called "off-the-shelf" software).

Software that comes with a computer you buy and is included in the price—for example, your operating system—is depreciated as part of the computer, unless you're billed separately for the software.

Off-the-shelf software must be depreciated over three years using the straight-line method. You can also use bonus depreciation for off-the-shelf software.

In the past, Section 179 expensing was not available for computer software because it is intangible property. However, Congress temporarily changed the law in 2003 to permit off-the-shelf software to be currently deducted under Section 179. However, this exception applies only to software placed in service from January 1, 2003 through December 31, 2007. Starting in 2008, Section 179 will once again be prohibited for off-the-shelf software (unless, of course, the law is changed again).

If you acquire software that is not off-the-shelf software by buying another business or its assets, the rules discussed above don't apply. This software must be depreciated over 15 years using the straight-line method; this type of depreciation is called amortization. (IRC § 197.)

Software You Create

If, instead of buying off-the-shelf software, you create it yourself, you can currently deduct the cost under Section 174 of the Internal Revenue Code. This section allows deductions for research and experimentation expenses incurred in developing an invention, patent, process, prototype, formula, technique, or similar product.

You may currently deduct the costs under Section 174 whether the software is developed for your own use or to sell or license to others. (Rev. Proc. 2000-50.) For a detailed discussion of Section 174, see *What Every Inventor Needs to Know About Business & Taxes*, by Stephen Fishman (Nolo).

9.   Real Property

Land cannot be depreciated because it never wears out. However, this doesn't mean you don't get a tax deduction for land. When you sell it, you may deduct the cost of the land from the sale price to determine your taxable gain, if any. The cost of clearing, grading, landscaping, or demolishing buildings on land is not depreciable. It is added to the tax basis of the land—that is, to its cost—and subtracted from the money you get when you sell the land.

Unlike land, buildings do wear out over time and therefore may be depreciated. This means that when you buy property with buildings on it, you must separate out the cost of the buildings from the total cost of the property to calculate your depreciation.

As you might expect, the depreciation periods for buildings are quite long (after all, buildings usually last a long time). The depreciation period for nonresidential buildings placed in service after May 12, 1993 is 39 years. You must use the straight-line method to depreciate real property.

This means you'll be able to deduct only a small fraction of its value each year—1/39th of its value each year if the 39-year period applies.

Home Office Depreciation

If you have an office or other workplace you use solely for business in your home, you are entitled to depreciate the business portion of the home. For example, if you use 10% of your home for business, you may depreciate 10% of its cost (excluding the cost of the land). In the unlikely event your home has gone down in value since you bought it, you must use its fair market value on the date you began using your home office as your tax basis. You depreciate a home office over 39 years—the term used for nonresidential property. A home office is nonresidential property because you don't live in it.

Improvements to Leased Property

If you lease your office, as most professionals do, you may depreciate any improvements you make (and pay for)—for example, installing new carpeting. Ordinarily, such improvements must be depreciated over 39 years, but a new law permits many leasehold improvements to be depreciated over 15 years using the straight-line method (see Chapter 8, Section B4).

10. Intangible Assets

Long-term assets do not consist only of tangible things like office equipment and buildings. Intangible assets can also be deductible long-term assets. Intangible assets are things you can't see or touch. They include business goodwill, covenants not to compete, and intellectual property—patents, copyrights, trade secrets, and trademarks.

Buying Assets of an Existing Practice

Professionals who purchase the assets of an existing practice, ordinarily buy intangible property along with tangible property such as office equipment. This intangible property may consist of:

- business goodwill
- going concern value
- covenants not to compete

- business books and records, including patient or client files
- the value of having an existing workforce in place
- customer-based intangibles, such as the practice's existing client base
- patents, copyrights, trademarks, trade names, know-how, designs, and processes
- licenses, permits, and similar rights granted by government agencies, and
- supplier-based intangibles, such as a favorable arrangement with a supplier that will continue after the acquisition. (IRC § 197.)

You can deduct the cost of these intangible assets in equal amounts over 15 years. This process is called amortization. It is similar to straight-line depreciation. You deduct an equal amount of the cost of the asset each year over its useful life.

> **EXAMPLE:** Anita purchases all the assets of DDS, Inc., an incorporated dental practice wholly owned by Ralph, for $200,000. The purchase includes a small building and all of Ralph's dental equipment. All the tangible assets are worth $180,000. The remaining $20,000 of the purchase price is allocated to goodwill. Anita may amortize the $20,000 over 15 years—she deducts $1,333 per year.

However, you may amortize intangible assets only when you individually purchase the assets of an existing practice. You get no amortization if you acquire the assets of an incorporated practice by purchasing its stock; likewise if you purchase a partnership, LLP, or LLC rather than its assets. Corporate stock, and LLC, LLP, or partnership interests, are not considered to be amortizable intangible assets.

> **EXAMPLE:** Assume that Anita purchases 100% of the stock of DDS, Inc., for $200,000. She has control over all of DDS's assets, but gets no amortization deduction for goodwill or any other of its intangible assets.

Self-Created Intangible Assets

You may not amortize any of the intangible assets listed above if you created them yourself. For example, you can't amortize goodwill you create yourself by conducting your practice. It is not deductible at all.

However, if you create an invention, trademark, trade name, or copyrighted work of authorship like a book or film yourself, you may currently deduct the cost. Any costs that you can't currently deduct may be amortized as described above.

Amortization can be tricky, particularly determining how much intangible assets are worth. This is a complex area of taxation. Consult with a knowledgeable tax pro if you need to amortize intangible assets.

11. Depreciation Recapture

To currently deduct long-term property under Section 179 or depreciate listed property using accelerated depreciation, you must use the property for your business at least 51% of the time. If your business use falls under 51%, you'll have to give back part of the Section 179 or accelerated depreciation deductions you received. This is called "recapture" because the IRS is getting back—recapturing—part of your deduction. (See Section B4, above, for more on recapture.)

Recapture is required for listed property (personal use property) when your business use falls below 51% and for any property for which you took a Section 179 deduction. It is not required for nonlisted property for which you took no Section 179 deduction. For example, it is not required for a building or office equipment whose business use falls below 51%.

Recapture of all or part of the depreciation and/or Section 179 deduction previously allowed is also triggered when you sell any long-term, nonlisted asset for a gain—that is, for more than your adjusted basis.

EXAMPLE: Sam buys an X-ray machine for his dental practice for $5,000 in 2006. By 2008, he has taken $3,470 in depreciation deductions, leaving an adjusted basis of $1,530. He resells the machine in 2008 for $2,500. This gives Sam a gain of $970. This $970 gain is taxable as ordinary income.

You can't avoid recapture by not taking a Section 179 or depreciation deduction to which you were entitled. The IRS will treat you as though you took the deduction for recapture purposes, even if you really didn't.

EXAMPLE: If Sam fails to depreciate his X-ray machine and then sells it in 2008 for $2,500, the IRS will figure that his adjusted basis is $1,530, because he could have taken $3,470 in depreciation for it. So, he still has a taxable gain of $970.

D. Tax Reporting and Record Keeping for Section 179 and Depreciation

Depreciation and Section 179 deductions are reported on IRS Form 4562, *Depreciation and Amortization*. If you have more than one business for which you're claiming depreciation, you must use a separate Form 4562 for each business. You need to file Form 4562 only for the first year a deduction is claimed.

If you're a sole proprietor (or owner of an LLC taxed as a sole proprietorship), you carry over the amount of your depreciation and Section 179 deductions to your Schedule C and subtract them from your gross business income along with your other business expenses.

LLCs, LLPs, and partnerships report their depreciation deductions on IRS Form 1065. These deductions are subtracted from the entity's income, along with all other deductions. The resulting profits or losses are passed through to the owners' individual returns. S corporations use Form 1065S, but the principle is the same. If a Section 179 deduction is taken by an entity taxed as a partnership or S corporation, it must be separately stated on the Schedule K-1 forms given to each owner.

C corporations take all of their deductions, including deprecation, on their own tax returns, IRS Form 1120.

You need to keep accurate records for each asset you depreciate or expense under Section 179, showing:

- a description of the asset
- when and how you purchased the property
- the date it was placed in service
- its original cost
- the percentage of time you use it for business
- whether and how much you deducted under Section 179

- the amount of depreciation you took for the asset in prior years, if any
- its depreciable basis
- the depreciation method used
- the length of the depreciation period, and
- the amount of depreciation you deducted for the year.

If you have an accountant or bookkeeper, he or she should prepare these records for you.

If you do your taxes yourself, you can use tax preparation software to create a worksheet containing this information. You can also use an accounting program such as *QuickBooks* to keep track of your depreciating assets. Simple checkbook programs like *Quicken* and *MSMoney* are not designed to keep track of depreciation. You may also use a spreadsheet program to create your own depreciation worksheet. Spreadsheet templates are available for this purpose. Of course, you can also do the job by hand. The Instructions to IRS Form 4562 contain a worksheet you can use. Here's an example of a filled-out worksheet prepared by the IRS.

Depreciation Worksheet										
Description of Property	**Date Placed in Service**	**Cost or Other Basics**	**Business/Investment Use Percentage**	**Section 179 Deduction and Special Allowance**	**Depreciation in Prior Years**	**Basis for Depreciation**	**Method/Convention**	**Recovery Period**	**Rate or Table Percentage**	**Depreciation Deduction**
Used Equipment —Transmission Jack	1-3	3,000	100%	—	—	3,000	200 DB/HY	7	14.29%	$ 429
Used Pickup Truck	1-3	8,000	100%	—	—	8,000	200 DB/HY	5	20%	1,600
Used Heavy Duty Tow Truck	1-3	30,000	100%	—	—	30,000	200 DB/HY	5	20%	6,000
Used Equipment —Engine Hoist	1-3	4,000	100%	—	—	4,000	200 DB/HY	7	14.29%	572
										$8,601

For listed property, you'll also have to keep records showing how much of the time you use it for business and personal uses. (See Chapter 20.) You should also keep proof of the amount you paid for the asset—receipts, canceled checks, and purchase documents. You need not file these records with your tax return, but you must have them available to back up your deductions if you're audited.

E. Leasing Long-Term Assets

When you're acquiring a long-term asset for your practice, you should consider whether it makes more sense to lease the item rather than purchase it. Almost everything a professional needs can be leased—computers, office furniture, equipment. And leasing can be an attractive alternative to buying. However, it's important to understand the tax consequences of leasing when making your decision.

1. Leasing Versus Purchasing

So which is better, leasing or buying? It depends. Leasing equipment can be a better option for professionals who have limited capital or who need equipment that must be upgraded every few years. Purchasing equipment can be a better option for professionals with ample capital or who need equipment that has a long usable life. Each professional's situation is different and the decision to buy or lease must be made on a case-by-case basis.

The following chart summarizes the major tax and nontax differences between leasing and buying equipment.

Leasing Versus Buying		
	Leasing	**Buying**
Tax Treatment	Lease payments are a currently deductible business operating expense. No depreciation or Section 179 deductions.	Up to $105,000 in equipment purchases can be deducted in one year under Section 179 (if requirements satisfied). Otherwise, cost is depreciated over several years (usually 5 to 7 years). Interest on loans to buy equipment is currently deductible.
Initial Cash Outlay	Small. No down payment required. Deposit ordinarily required.	Large. At least a 20% down payment usually required. Bank loan may be required to finance the remaining cost.
Ownership	You own nothing at end of lease term.	You own the equipment.
Costs of Equipment Obsolescence	Borne by lessor because it owns equipment. Lessee may lease new equipment when lease expires.	Borne by buyer because buyer owns equipment, which may have little resale value.

Before deciding whether to purchase or lease an expensive item, it's a good idea to determine the total actual costs of each option. This depends on many factors, including:

- the cost of the lease
- the purchase price for the item
- the item's useful life
- the interest rate on a loan to purchase the item
- the item's "residual value"—how much it will be worth at the end of the lease term
- whether you will purchase the item at the end of the lease and how much this will cost

- how much it would cost to dispose of the item
- your income tax bracket
- whether the item qualifies for one-year Section 179 expensing or must be depreciated, and
- if the item must be depreciated, the length of the depreciation period.

There are several lease versus buy calculators on the Internet that you can use to compare the cost of leasing versus buying:

- www.lease-vs-buy.com
- http://partners.financenter.com/commercebusinesstools/calculate/ us-eng/business02.fcs
- www.chooseleasing.org.

Commercial software and computer spreadsheets can also be used for this purpose.

2.   Leases Versus Installment Purchases

An installment purchase (also called a conditional sales contract) is different from a lease—although the two can seem very similar. With an installment purchase, you end up owning all or part of the property, whereas with a lease you own nothing when the lease ends.

The distinction between a lease and an installment purchase is important because installment purchases are treated very differently for tax purposes. Installment purchase payments are not rent and cannot be deducted as a business operating expense. The purchaser may deduct installment purchase payments under Section 179 (if applicable) or depreciate the property's value over several years, except that any portion of the payments that represent interest may be currently deducted as an interest expense.

You can't simply label a transaction a lease or installment purchase depending on which is more advantageous. A lease must really be a lease (often called a "true lease" or "tax lease") to pass muster with the IRS. A lease that is really just a way of financing a purchase is a "financial lease," not a true lease, and will be treated as an installment purchase by the IRS.

Whether a transaction is a lease or installment purchase depends on the parties' intent. The IRS will conclude that a conditional sales contract exists if *any of the following* are true.

- The agreement applies part of each payment toward an ownership interest that you will receive.
- You get title to the property upon the payment of a stated amount required under the contract.
- The amount you pay to use the property for a short time is a large part of the amount you would pay to get title to the property.
- You pay much more than the current fair rental value for the property.
- You have an option to buy the property at a nominal price compared to the value of the property when you may exercise the option.
- You have an option to buy the property at a nominal price compared to the total amount you have to pay under the lease.
- The lease designates some part of the payments as interest, or part of the payments are easy to recognize as interest.

A transaction will also look like an installment purchase to the IRS (even if it's labeled a lease) if:

- the lease term is about equal to the functional or economic life of the property
- the lease may not be canceled, and
- the lessee is responsible for maintaining the property.

EXAMPLE: ABC Medical Corporation wants to obtain an MRI machine. If it purchased the device, it would cost $1 million and would have to be depreciated over seven years (it wouldn't qualify for Section 179 expensing because ABC would be way over the annual dollar limit on such expensing). Instead of buying the MRI, ABC leases it for four years at an annual rent of $250,000. At the end of four years, ABC has an option to purchase the MRI for $10,000. By characterizing the transaction as a lease, ABC gets to deduct its payments as rent, instead of having to depreciate the MRI. In effect, this allows ABC to deduct its cost over four years instead of seven and still end up owning the MRI. However, the IRS would likely recharacterize ABC's lease of the MRI as an installment purchase, not a true lease, because ABC has an option to buy the MRI for a nominal price ($10,000) compared to the total expense. Thus, the IRS would require ABC to depreciate the MRI, instead of deducting its payments as rent.

3.   Leasing Property You Own to Your Practice

Leasing equipment or real estate is a way a professional whose practice is taxed as a C corporation can take money out of the business without having it characterized as a dividend or salary. This is advantageous because (1) personal service corporations must pay a 35% corporate tax on dividends; and (2) employment taxes must be paid on salaries. (See Chapter 15.)

> **EXAMPLE:** Fred is a highly successful trial lawyer whose law practice is organized as a C corporation which he wholly owns. During profitable years, he is paid as much as $1 million per year in salary by his corporation. Fred personally purchases computers, video equipment, and office furniture and leases it to his C corporation for a term of three years. The original cost of the equipment is $750,000 and Fred receives rental payments from the law firm totaling $100,000 per year. His annual salary from his corporation is reduced by $100,000. The rental payments are deductible as a rent expense by the corporation. Fred has to pay personal income tax on the payments he receives from his corporation, but they are not subject to employment taxes. Since his salary is well over the Social Security tax ceiling, this saves him only the 2.9% Medicare tax. But he still saves $2,900 per year (2.9% x $100,000 = $2,900). Fred also gets to depreciate the cost of the equipment. He can't deduct any of the equipment under Section 179 (see "Limits on Section 179 Deduction for Leased Property," below).

Taking money out of a C corporation as lease payments instead of salary also helps keep a professional's salary at a reasonable level. The IRS can recharacterize unreasonably high salaries as constructive dividends, resulting in double taxation. (See Chapter 17.) In the example, above, Fred was able to reduce his annual salary by 10%, but still end up with the same amount of money in his pocket.

Because they are pass-through entities, LLCs, partnerships, LLPs, and S corporations don't have problems with dividends or unreasonable salaries, as do C corporations. (See Chapter 17.) But owners of such entities can avoid self-employment taxes by leasing property to their practice.

In addition, the lease payments must be reasonable—what would normally be charged for the property involved. Get a quote from an equipment leasing company for similar equipment. The IRS can disallow excessively high payments. Remember, a business operating expense such as rent must be reasonable in amount, as well as ordinary and necessary to be deductible. (See Chapter 3.)

Limits on Section 179 Deduction for Leased Property

A rental activity must qualify as a business for the owner of leased property to take a Section 179 deduction. Moreover, even if the rental activity is a business, such a deduction is allowed only if:

- the term of the lease (including options to renew) is less than 50% of the property's class life, and
- for the first 12 months after the property is transferred to the lessee, the total business deductions you are allowed on the property (other than rents and reimbursed amounts) are more than 15% of the rental income from the property.

Fred from the example above flunks the first test. His rental activity is too sporadic to be a business for tax purposes. It's an investment activity.

However, these rules do not apply to corporations.

---

4. Gift-Leaseback Arrangements

Another way to benefit from leasing assets to your practice is to use a gift-leaseback arrangement. Under this arrangement, you give property you personally own to someone (ordinarily a child, spouse, or other relative, or an irrevocable trust set up for such a relative) who then leases it back to your practice. The relative gets income from the lease payments and your practice gets a rent deduction.

Ideally, the leased property will already be fully depreciated or expensed under Section 179. This way, you effectively get to deduct the property twice—once when you owned it through depreciation or

Section 179, and a second time as a rental expense after you gifted it to a relative.

Only property that is individually owned qualifies for a gift-leaseback arrangement. Corporations may not make such gifts of business property. In addition, the rent must be reasonable—what you'd charge a nonrelative.

■

Chapter 10

Start-Up Expenses

E very professional knows that it costs money to get a new practice up and running or to buy an existing practice. What many professionals don't know is that these costs (called start-up expenses) are subject to special tax rules. This chapter explains what types of expenditures are start-up expenses and how you can deduct these costs as quickly as possible.

A. What Are Start-Up Expenses?

To have business deductions, you must actually be running a business. This commonsense rule can lead to problems if you want to start or buy a new practice. The money you spend to get your practice up and running is not a business operating expense because your business hasn't yet begun.

Instead, business start-up expenses are capital expenses because you incur them to acquire an asset (a business) that will benefit you for more than one year. Normally, you can't deduct these types of capital expenses until you sell or otherwise dispose of the business. However, a special tax rule allows you to deduct up to $5,000 in start-up expenses the first year you are in business, and then deduct the remainder in equal amounts over the next 15 years. (IRC § 195.) Without this special rule for business start-up expenses, these costs (capital expenses) would not be deductible until you sold or otherwise disposed of your practice.

Once your practice begins, the same expenses that were start-up expenses before it began become currently deductible business operating expenses. For example, rent you pay for office space *after* your practice starts is a currently deductible operating expense, but rent you pay *before* your practice begins is a start-up expense.

> **EXAMPLE:** Diana graduates from law school, passes the bar exam, and decides to open up her own law office. Her office opens for business on July 1. Before that date, however, Diana incurs various expenses, including travel expenses to obtain office space, office rent and utilities, lease expenses for office furniture and computer equipment, and advertising expenses. She spent $10,000 of her life savings to get her law practice up and running. Because these

are start-up expenses, she can't deduct them all in her first year of business. But, she can deduct up to $5,000 the first year she is in business and the remainder in equal amounts over the next 15 years. (IRC § 195.)

B. Starting a New Practice

Most of the money you spend investigating whether, where, and how to start a new practice, as well as the cost of actually creating it, are deductible business start-up expenses. The tax law is much more generous with deductions for start-up costs if you are creating a new practice than if you are buying an existing practice. (See Section C, below.)

1. Common Start-Up Expenses

Here are some common types of deductible start-up expenses:
- the cost of investigating what it will take to create a successful practice, including market research
- advertising costs, including advertising for your practice's opening
- costs for employee training before the practice begins
- travel expenses related to finding a suitable business location
- expenses related to obtaining financing, suppliers, and clients
- business licenses, permits, and other fees
- fees paid to lawyers, accountants, consultants, and others for professional services, and
- operating expenses incurred before the practice begins, such as rent, telephone, utilities, office supplies, and repairs.

2. Costs That Are Not Start-Up Expenses

There are some costs related to opening a business that are not considered start-up expenses. Many of these costs are still deductible, but different rules and restrictions apply to the way they are deducted.

Only Business Operating Expenses Qualify

You can deduct as start-up expenses only those costs that would be currently deductible as business operating expenses after your practice begins. This means the expenses must be ordinary, necessary, directly related to the business, and reasonable in amount. (See Chapter 3 for a discussion of business operating expenses.) For example, you can't deduct the cost of pleasure travel or entertainment *unrelated* to your practice. These expenses would not be deductible as operating expenses by an ongoing business, so you can't deduct them as start-up expenses either. (In fact, you can't deduct them at all.)

Inventory

Some professionals—for example, optometrists, veterinarians, and pharmacists—incur substantial costs for inventory before they start their practice. An optometrist starting a new practice would have to buy an inventory of eyeglass frames and lenses to provide to patients. The cost of purchasing this inventory is not treated as a start-up expense. Instead, you deduct inventory costs as you sell the inventory. (See Chapter 13 for more on deducting inventory costs.)

Long-Term Assets

Long-term assets are things you purchase for your practice that will last for more than one year, such as computers, office equipment, cars, and machinery. Long-term assets you buy before your practice begins are not considered part of your start-up costs. Instead, you treat these purchases like any other long-term asset you buy *after* your practice begins—you must either depreciate the item over several years or deduct the cost in one year under IRS Section 179. (Chapter 9 explains how to deduct long-term assets.) However, you can't take depreciation or Section 179 deductions until after your business begins.

Research and Development Costs

The tax law includes a special category for research and development expenses. These are costs a business incurs to discover something new (in the laboratory or experimental sense), such as a new invention, formula, prototype, or process. They include laboratory and computer supplies, salaries, rent, utilities, other overhead expenses, and equipment rental, but not the purchase of long-term assets. Research and development costs are currently deductible under Section 174 of the Internal Revenue Code, even if you incur them before the business begins operations.

Taxes and Interest

Any tax and interest that you pay before your practice begins is not a start-up expense. Instead, these costs are currently deductible as business operating expenses once your business begins. There are a few exceptions to this rule. Sales tax you pay for long-term assets for your practice is added to the cost of the asset for purposes of depreciation or the Section 179 deduction. (See Chapter 9.) And money you borrow to buy an interest in an S corporation, partnership, or LLC must be allocated among the company's assets. Interest on money you borrow to buy stock in a C corporation is treated as investment interest and may be currently deducted as a personal itemized deduction. (See Chapter 14.)

Organizational Costs

Costs you incur to form a partnership, limited liability company, or corporation are not part of your start-up costs. However, they are deductible in the same amounts as start-up expenses under a separate tax rule. (See Section H, below.)

You cannot deduct education expenses you incur to qualify for a new business or profession. For example, courts have held that IRS agents could not deduct the cost of going to law school, because a law degree would qualify them for a new business—being a lawyer. (*Jeffrey L. Weiler*, 54 T.C. 398 (1970).) (See Chapter 14.)

You also can't deduct fees you must pay to become accredited to initially practice a profession. For example, you may not deduct:

- bar exam fees and other expenses paid to obtain admission to the bar
- medical and dental license fees paid to get initial licensing, or
- accounting certificate fees paid for the initial right to practice accounting.

However, after you begin practicing your profession, you may currently deduct your annual licensing fees as an operating expense— for example, lawyers may deduct their annual bar association dues.

C. Buying an Existing Practice

Different rules apply if you buy an existing practice rather than create a new one. If you are buying a practice, you can deduct as start-up expenses only the costs you incur to decide *whether* to purchase a practice and *which* practice you should buy.

You don't have to make an offer, sign a letter of intent, or enter into a binding legal agreement to purchase an existing practice for your expenses to cease being start-up expenses. You just have to make up your mind to purchase a specific practice and focus on acquiring it. (Rev. Rul. 1999-23.)

> **EXAMPLE:** Sean, a dentist who works as an employee for a successful dental corporation, wants to purchase his own existing dental practice. He hires Duane, a professional practice broker, to help him. Duane evaluates several dental practices for sale, including the Acme DentalWorks. Sean decides he would like to buy Acme and hires accountant Al to conduct an in-depth review of its books and records to determine a fair acquisition price. Sean then enters into an acquisition agreement with Acme to purchase all its assets. The fees Sean paid to Duane are start-up expenses because they were paid to help Sean determine whether to purchase an existing business and which business to buy. The fees Sean paid to Al are not start-up expenses because they were incurred to help Sean purchase a specific existing business—the Acme DentalWorks.

The money you pay to actually purchase an existing practice is neither a start-up expense nor a currently deductible business operating expense. Instead, it is a capital expense. If you purchase an incorporated practice by buying its stock, or buy a professional LLC, LLP, or partnership by purchasing the LLC or partnership interests, the cost becomes part of the tax basis of your stock, or LLC or partnership interest. If and when you sell your stock or LLC or partnership interest, you will be able to deduct this amount from any profit you make on the sale before taxes are assessed. If, instead of buying the legal entity that owns a practice, you simply purchase its individual assets, you may depreciate the cost of tangible assets and amortize the cost of any intangible assets you purchase. (See Chapter 9.)

D. Expanding an Existing Practice

What if you already have an existing practice and decide to expand it? The cost of expanding an existing practice is considered a business operating expense, not a start-up expense. As long as these costs are ordinary and necessary, they are currently deductible.

> **EXAMPLE:** Sam, a highly successful sole practitioner dentist, decides to expand his practice. He rents larger office space in a new location and hires three new employees. The costs of renting and moving to the new office and training the new employees are currently deductible as ordinary and necessary operating expenses.

However, this rule applies only when the expansion involves a business that is the same as—or similar to—the existing business. The costs of expanding into a new business are start-up costs, not operating expenses.

> **EXAMPLE:** Assume that Sam, an avid golfer, decides to start a business to manufacture and sell a new type of golf putter he has invented. This business is unrelated to his dental practice. Therefore, the ordinary and necessary expenses he incurs before the business begins are start-up costs.

In addition, even though you perform the same services, you are not expanding an existing business when you create a new business entity for your practice.

> **EXAMPLE:** Art and Nicole, associates at a large law firm, decide to go out on their own and start their own law practice. They form an LLP, with themselves as the partners. Although Art and Nicole are performing the same legal services as they were when they were associates, the new law firm is a new business for tax purposes, not an expansion of an existing business. Thus, Art and Nicole's start-up costs would not be currently deductible operating expenses.

E.   When Does a Professional Practice Begin?

The date when your practice begins for tax purposes marks an important turning point. Operating expenses you incur once your practice starts are currently deductible, while expenses you incur before this crucial date may have to be deducted over many years.

The general rule is that a new business begins for tax purposes when it starts to function as a going concern and performs the activities for which it was organized. (*Richmond Television Corp. v. U.S.*, 345 F.2d 901 (4th Cir. 1965).) The IRS says that a venture becomes a going concern when it acquires all of the assets necessary to perform its intended functions and puts those assets to work. In other words, your practice begins when you start doing business, whether or not you are actually earning any money.

Applying this rule, a professional practice begins when you first offer your services to the public. No one has to hire you; you just have to be available for hire by clients or patients. For example, a dentist's practice begins when he or she opens a dental office and is ready to perform dental work on patients.

If you purchase an existing practice, your practice begins when the purchase is completed—that is, when you take over ownership.

Proving to the IRS That You're in Business

Because your business start date is so important for tax purposes, you should be able to prove to the IRS the exact date it began. There are many ways you can do this. Being able to show the IRS a copy of an advertisement for your practice is a great way to prove you were open for business. You can also mail out brochures or other promotional materials. But you don't have to advertise to show you are open—simply handing out business cards is sufficient. Give your first business cards to friends and associates who could testify for you if you're audited by the IRS. Establish your office to show you are ready to take on clients or customers. Take a photo of it with a digital camera (which will be date-stamped).

F. How to Deduct Start-Up Expenses

You can deduct $5,000 in start-up expenses the first year you're in business. Any expenses you have in excess of $5,000, you'll have to deduct in equal amounts over the first 180 months (15 years) you're in business. This process is called amortization. One hundred and eighty months is the minimum amortization period; you can choose a longer period if you wish (almost no one does).

If you have more than $50,000 in start-up expenses, however, you are not entitled to the full $5,000 deduction. You must reduce the $5,000 deduction by the amount that your start-up expenditures exceed $50,000. For example, if you have $53,000 in start-up expenses, you may deduct only $2,000 the first year, instead of $5,000. If you have $55,000 or more in start-up expenses, you get no current deduction for start-up expenses. Instead, the whole amount must be deducted over 180 months.

If Your Business Began in 2004

The start-up expense provision of the tax law (IRC § 195) was amended by Congress in 2004 to permit $5,000 of start-up expenses to be deducted in the first year a business is in operation. Before the change, all start-up expenses had to be deducted over the first 60 months a business was in operation. The amendment took effect on October 22, 2004. If your practice began before this date, the old rule applies to you. Deduct all your start-up expenses in equal monthly installments for the first 60 months you're in business.

EXAMPLE: Tom, an ophthalmologist, incurred $35,000 in start-up expenses to open his practice on November 1, 2006. He may deduct $5,000 of his expenses for 2006. He can deduct the remaining $30,000 over the first 15 years (180 months) he's in business—or $167 per month ($30,000 divided by 180 months equals $167). He was in business for only two months in 2006, so his total start-up expense deduction for 2006 is $5,334. He'll get a $2,000 deduction in 2007 and each year thereafter until he has deducted the entire $30,000.

1.   Who Gets Start-Up Deductions

If, like many professionals, you're a sole proprietor (or have a one-person LLC taxed as a sole proprietorship), you'll deduct your start-up expenses on your Schedule C along with your other business expenses. It makes no practical difference if you use personal funds or money from a separate business account for start-up expenses.

Things are different if you have a corporation, partnership, LLP, or LLC. Deductions for start-up expenses belong to the business entity, not to you personally. If you pay for them out of your personal funds, you should seek reimbursement from the entity. (See Chapter 17 for a detailed discussion.)

2.   Making a Section 195 Election

You must indicate that you want to deduct start-up costs on your tax return by making a Section 195 election. (Section 195 is the tax law governing start-up expenses). To do this, you attach a statement (called a Section 195 statement) to your tax return listing your start-up expenses, the dates you paid them, the date your business began, and a description of your business. If you have more than $5,000 in start-up expenses, you'll have to deduct the excess over 180 months. You must file IRS Form 4562, *Depreciation and Amortization*, with your return showing how much you're deducting. You must also list the number of months in the amortization period (180) in your Section 195 statement.

If you forget to list all of your start-up costs in your Section 195 statement, you can file an amended statement later listing any items you omitted. However, you may not list any expenses that you have already claimed were deductible under other tax laws—for example, as ordinary and necessary operating expenses.

> **EXAMPLE:** Tom failed to list a $1,000 legal fee as a start-up expense in his Section 195 statement. Instead, he deducted the fee as a currently deductible business operating expense. Three years later, he is audited. The auditor says Tom should have listed the fee as a start-up cost, not a currently deductible operating expense, and disallows the deduction. Tom cannot amend his Section 195

statement to add the fee as a start-up expense because he has already claimed, albeit mistakenly, that the fee was deductible under another tax rule. Even though Tom made an innocent mistake, he won't get any deduction for his accounting fee.

The moral is this: Be very careful when you prepare your first tax return after your business opens. Figure out how to categorize each of your expenses, and make sure to list every start-up expense in your Section 195 election.

⚠ **You must make a timely election to deduct start-up expenses.** If you want to deduct your start-up expenses, you must file your election (IRS Form 4562 and Section 195 statement) on or before the date your first tax return after you start your business is due. For example, if your business begins in 2006, you must file the election with your 2006 tax return, due April 15, 2007 (or later if you receive an extension). If you miss this deadline, you have one last chance to make your election: You may file an amended return making the election within six months after the date your original return was due. If you fail to do this, you will lose your right to deduct your start-up expenses and you'll have to treat them as capital expenses (as described in Section G2, below).

> **EXAMPLE:** Tom's ophthalmology practice began in 2006. He must file his election to deduct his start-up costs with his 2006 tax return, which is due April 15, 2007 (or later, if Tom gets an extension to file). If Tom fails to make the election to file by this deadline, he may file an amended tax return within six months—that is, by October 15, 2007 (or within six months after the end of any filing extension he obtains).

If you decide not to make a Section 195 election, your start-up costs become part of the tax basis of your business.

3. If Your Practice Doesn't Last 15 Years

Not all professional practices last for 15 years. If you had more than $5,000 in start-up expenses and are in the process of deducting the excess amount, you don't lose the value of your deductions if you sell or close your practice before you have had a chance to deduct all of your start-up expenses. You can deduct any leftover start-up expenses as ordinary business losses. (IRC § 195(b)(2).) This means that you may be able to deduct them from any income you have that year, deduct them in future years, or deduct them from previous years' taxes.

If you sell your practice or its assets, your leftover start-up costs will be added to your tax basis in the business. This is just as good as getting a tax deduction. If you sell your practice at a profit, the remaining start-up costs will be subtracted from your profits before taxes are assessed, which reduces your taxable gain. If you sell at a loss, the start-up costs will be added to the money you lost—because this shortfall is deductible, a larger loss means lower taxes.

Keep Good Expense Records

Whether you intend to start a new practice or buy an existing one, you should keep careful track of every expense you incur before the business begins. Obviously, you should keep receipts and canceled checks. You should also keep evidence that will help show that the money went to investigate a new business—for example, correspondence and emails with accountants, attorneys, business brokers, and consultants; marketing or financial reports; and copies of advertisements. You will need these records to calculate your deductions and to prove your expenses to the IRS if you face an audit.

G. Expenses for Practices That Never Begin

What if you investigate starting a new practice, but the venture never gets off the ground? While this is no doubt disappointing, you might be able to recoup some of your expenses in the form of tax deductions.

1.   General Start-Up Costs

General start-up costs are expenses you incur *before* you decide to start a new business or acquire a specific existing business. They include all of the costs of doing a general search for, or preliminary investigation of a new practice. If you never start the business, these costs are personal and not deductible—in other words, they are a dead loss.

One intended effect of this rule is that you can't deduct travel, entertainment, or other "fun" expenses by claiming that you incurred them to investigate a business unless you *actually start the business*. Otherwise, it would be pretty tough for the IRS to figure out whether you were really considering a new venture or just having a good time.

> **EXAMPLE:** Bruno, a Minnesota chiropractor employed by a chiropractic clinic, takes a vacation in Hawaii. While he's there, he investigates starting his own practice on Maui. He visits two locations where he could set up an office, and talks to other chiropractors in Hawaii. However, he decides not to make the move and goes back to Minnesota. His vacation expenses are not deductible as business start-up expenses.

Corporations can deduct general start-up costs. A corporation can deduct general start-up expenses as a business loss, even if the business never gets going.

2.   Costs to Start or Acquire a Specific Business

The expenses you incur to actually start or acquire a particular practice (that ultimately never begins operations) are start-up expenses. This includes any of the more common start-up expenses listed in Section B1, above—for example, legal or accounting fees you incur to start a new practice or acquire an existing practice.

These costs are deductible, but only as capital expenses. The cost of any property you acquire during your unsuccessful attempt to start a new practice becomes part of your basis in the asset. You get no direct tax deduction for these costs, but you may recover these costs when you dispose of the asset. Other costs may be deducted as investment expenses, which are generally deductible only as itemized miscellaneous deductions. (IRC § 165). (See Chapter 14.)

> **EXAMPLE:** Assume that Bruno takes concrete steps to start his chiropractic practice. He puts down a $2,000 nonrefundable deposit to lease an office and spends $2,000 for equipment. However, he decides at the last minute that he's not ready to take the plunge and work for himself. These expenses were made after Bruno decided to start a specific business, so they are deductible. He may deduct the $2,000 lost deposit as an investment expense. He must take it as a miscellaneous itemized deduction on his tax return, but the deduction is limited to the amount by which it (plus his other miscellaneous deductions) exceeds 2% of his adjusted gross income. He can deduct his $2,000 expense for the equipment as a capital expense. However, he can't simply deduct the $2,000 from his income for the year, or depreciate the equipment. Instead, the $2,000 is added to the tax basis of the equipment when he disposes of it. If he sells a refrigerator for $1,000, he has a $1,000 capital loss that he may deduct from his income for the year ($2,000 tax basis – $1,000 sales price = $1,000). If he sells the refrigerator for $3,000, he has a $1,000 capital gain on which he must pay tax.

H. Organizational Expenses

Many professionals form business entities, such as a corporation, partnership, LLP, or limited liability corporation. (See Chapter 2 for a discussion of different possible business structures.) The costs of forming an entity to run your practice are deductible. These organizational expenses are not considered start-up expenses, although they are deducted in much the same way.

If you form a corporation, you can deduct the cost of creating the corporation, including legal fees for drafting articles of incorporation, bylaws, minutes of organizational meetings and other organizational documents, and accounting fees for setting up the corporation and its books. You can also deduct state incorporation fees and other filing fees. However, you may not deduct the cost of transferring assets to the corporation or fees associated with issuing stock or securities—for example, commissions and printing costs. These are capital expenses.

If you form a partnership or LLC with two or more members, you may deduct the cost of negotiating and drafting a partnership or LLC agreement, accounting services to organize the partnership, and LLC filing fees.

Organizational expenses are deducted in the same way as start-up costs. You may deduct the first $5,000 the first year you are in business, and any excess over the first 180 months. However, your $5,000 deduction is reduced by the amount by which your organizational expenditures exceed $50,000. You must file IRS Form 4562 with your tax return (along with a statement listing the cost).

■

Chapter 11

Medical Expenses

As we all know, the cost of health insurance keeps going up. However, as business owners, professionals have an advantage that most others don't have with regard to these rising health care costs: They can deduct many of their health insurance costs from their taxes. In addition, you may be able to deduct a wide variety of uninsured medical expenses, including nonprescription medications, acupuncture, and eyeglasses. Finally, there is an entirely new way to pay for health care expenses that went into effect in 2004—the Health Savings Account (HSA). HSAs represent the most radical change in health care financing in the last 50 years and can be a real boon for many professionals looking for a cheaper way to pay for their medical expenses.

A. The Personal Deduction for Medical Expenses

All taxpayers—whether or not they own a business—are entitled to a personal income tax deduction for medical and dental expenses for themselves and their dependents. Eligible expenses include both health insurance premiums and out-of-pocket expenses not covered by insurance. However, there are two significant limitations on the deduction, which make it virtually useless (unusable) for most taxpayers.

In order to take the personal deduction, you must comply with both of the following requirements:

- You must itemize your deductions on IRS Schedule A. (You can itemize deductions only if all of your itemized deductions exceed the standard deduction for the year—$10,000 for joint returns and $5,000 for single returns in 2005.)
- You can deduct only the amount of your medical and dental expenses that is more than 7.5% of your adjusted gross income (AGI). (Your AGI is your net business income and other taxable income, minus deductions for retirement contributions and one-half of your self-employment taxes, plus a few other items (as shown at the bottom of your Form 1040).)

EXAMPLE: Al is a self-employed accountant whose adjusted gross income for 2005 is $100,000. He pays $450 per month for health insurance for himself and his wife. He spends another $2,200 in out-of-pocket medical and dental expenses for the year. Al may deduct his medical expenses only if all of his itemized deductions exceed the $10,000 standard deduction for the year. If they do exceed the standard deduction, his personal medical expense deduction is limited to the amount he paid that's more than $7,500 (7.5% x $100,000 = $7,500). Because he paid a total of $7,600 in medical expenses for the year, his deduction is limited to $100.

As you can see, unless your medical expenses are substantial, the 7.5% limitation eats up most or all of your deduction. The more money you make, the less you can deduct. For this reason, professionals need to look elsewhere for meaningful medical expense deductions.

B. Self-Employed Health Insurance Deduction

There is another health expense deduction that is more useful to professionals than the personal deduction: the self-employment health insurance income tax deduction. It allows self-employed people to deduct health insurance premiums (including dental and long-term care coverage) for themselves, their spouses, and their dependents.

Professionals who are sole proprietors, partners in partnerships, LLC members, or S corporation shareholders who own more than 2% of the company stock, can use this deduction. Basically, any business owner, other than a shareholder-employee of a regular C corporation, can take this deduction. It's important to understand, however, that this is not a business deduction. It is a special personal deduction for the self-employed. The deduction applies to your federal, state, and local income taxes, but not to self-employment taxes (Social Security and Medicare taxes).

> **EXAMPLE:** Kim is a sole proprietor lawyer who pays $10,000 each year for health insurance for herself, her husband, and her three children. Her practice earned a $100,000 profit for the year. She may deduct her $10,000 annual health insurance expense from her gross income for federal and state income tax purposes. Her combined federal and state income tax rate is 35%, so she saves

$3,500 in income taxes (35% x $10,000 = $3,500). She may not deduct her premiums from her income when she figures her self-employment taxes—in other words, she must pay the 15.3% self-employment tax on her full $100,000 business profit.

You get the deduction whether you purchase your health insurance policy as an individual or have your practice obtain it. If your practice obtains health insurance for you, it will add the amount of the premiums to your compensation (see Section C).

Self-Employment Tax Primer

Self-employment taxes are the Social Security and Medicare taxes that business owners must pay. They consist of a 12.4% Social Security tax and a 2.9% Medicare tax, for a total tax of 15.3%. The tax is paid on self-employment income, which is your net income from your business, not including deductions for retirement contributions. The Social Security tax is subject to an income ceiling that is adjusted each year for inflation. In 2006, the ceiling was $94,200 in self-employment income. Self-employed people who earn more than the ceiling amount pay only the 2.9% Medicare tax on the excess. If you earn more than the ceiling, being able to deduct your health insurance costs from your self-employment income will not give you a very significant tax savings, because you would have had to pay only a 2.9% tax on that income.

---

1.   Business Income Limitation

There is a significant limitation on the health insurance deduction for the self-employed: You may deduct only as much as you earn from your practice. If your practice earns no money or incurs a loss, you get no deduction. Thus, for example, if Kim from the above example earned only $3,000 in profit from her practice, her self-employed health insurance deduction would be limited to that amount; she wouldn't be able to deduct the remaining $7,000 in premiums she paid for the year.

If your practice is organized as an S corporation, your deduction is limited to the amount of wages you are paid by your corporation.

If you have more than one business, you cannot combine the income from all your businesses for purposes of the income limit. You may only use the income from a single business you designate to be the health insurance plan sponsor.

2.   Designating Your Plan Sponsor

If you purchase your health insurance plan in the name of one of your businesses, that business will be the sponsor. However, the IRS says you may purchase your health coverage in your own name and still get the self-employed health insurance deduction. (IRC Chief Counsel Memo 200524001.) This may be advantageous because it allows you to pick which of your businesses will be the sponsor at the start of each year. Obviously, you should pick the business you think will earn the most money that year.

Moreover, if you have more than one business, you can have one purchase medical insurance and the other purchase dental insurance and deduct 100% of the premiums for each policy subject to the income limits discussed above. This will be helpful if no single business earns enough income for you to deduct both policies through one business.

> **EXAMPLE:** Robert is a sole proprietor medical doctor who has a sideline business running a medical lab. He purchases a medical insurance policy for himself and his family with his medical practice as the sponsor. He also purchases a dental insurance plan with his lab business as the sponsor. He may deduct 100% of the premiums for each policy, subject to the income limits.

3.   No Other Health Insurance Coverage

You may not take the self-employed health insurance deduction if you are eligible to participate in a health insurance plan maintained by your employer or your spouse's employer. This rule applies separately to plans that provide long-term care insurance and those that do not. Thus, for example, if your spouse has employer-provided health insurance that does not include long-term care, you may purchase your own long-term care policy and deduct the premiums.

4. Tax Reporting

Because the self-employed health insurance deduction is a personal deduction, you take this deduction directly on your Form 1040 (it does not go on your Schedule C if you're a sole proprietor). If you itemize your deductions and do not claim 100% of your self-employed health insurance costs on your Form 1040, you may include the rest with all other medical expenses on Schedule A, subject to the 7.5% limit. You would have to do this, for example, if your health insurance premiums exceed your business income.

C. Deducting Health Insurance as an Employee Fringe Benefit

You can deduct health insurance costs as a currently deductible business expense if your business pays them on behalf of an employee. The benefit to treating these costs as a business expense is that you can deduct them from your business income for tax purposes. The premiums are an employee fringe benefit and are not taxable income for the employee. Unfortunately, if (like many professionals) you are a sole proprietor, partner in a partnership, LLC member, or S corporation shareholder with more than 2% of the company stock, you can't deduct these costs as a business expense because you cannot be an employee of your own business for these purposes.

1. Deducting Health Insurance Costs Paid on Behalf of Employees

There is no law that says a business has to provide health insurance for its employees. But the tax code encourages businesses to do so by allowing health insurance costs paid for employees, their spouses, and dependents to be deducted as a business expense. The premiums are an employee fringe benefit and are not taxable income for the employee.

EXAMPLE: Mona, a sole proprietor optometrist, hires Milt to work as an employee in her practice. She pays $250 per month to provide Milt with health insurance. The payments are a business expense that she can deduct from her business income. Milt need not count the value of the insurance as income or pay any tax on it. Mona deducts her $3,000 annual payments for Milt's insurance from her business income for both income tax and self-employment tax purposes.

No written plan is required to deduct health insurance costs. Moreover, you have great flexibility on how you provide health insurance benefits to your employees. You can purchase a group policy to cover them, or have each employee purchase his or her own policy and reimburse all or part of the cost. (See Section C.) You can also fully or partly fund a Health Savings Account (HSA) instead of providing traditional health insurance. Moreover, you can require employees to pay part of the premiums instead of paying them all yourself—for example, you could require employees to pay for the cost of covering their spouses.

Unlike the case with most employee fringe benefits, health insurance can be provided on a discriminatory basis, as long as you don't discriminate based on health factors such as an employee's medical history. (IRC § 9802.) Thus, you can give some employees better coverage than others, provided the selection criteria has nothing to do with health factors. For example, you could provide key employees with better health coverage then less vital employees.

2. Sole Proprietors, LLCs, S Corporations, Partnerships, and LLPs

If (like the majority of professionals) you are a sole proprietor, partner in a partnership, LLC member, LLP partner, or S corporation shareholder with over 2% of the company stock, you cannot be an employee of your own practice for health insurance purposes. If your partnership, LLC, LLP, or S corporation buys health insurance on your behalf, it may deduct the cost as a business expense, but it must also add the amount to your taxable income.

If your practice is organized as a partnership, LLC, or LLP, the premiums are ordinarily treated as a guaranteed payment. The practice lists the payment on the Schedule K-1 it provides the IRS and you showing your income from the practice. You'll then have to pay income and self-employment tax on the amount.

You can still take the self-employed health insurance tax deduction discussed in Section B above, which will effectively wipe out the extra income tax you had to pay. But the self-employed health insurance deduction is a personal deduction, not a business deduction, and thus does not reduce your business income for self-employment tax purposes.

> **EXAMPLE:** Jim is a co-owner of a five-lawyer law firm organized as an LLC. The firm spends $10,000 for health insurance for Jim. It treats the money as a guaranteed payment and lists it as income to Jim on the K-1 form it provides the IRS. The LLC gets to deduct the payment as a business expense. Jim must pay income and self-employment tax on the $10,000. However, he may also deduct the $10,000 from his income tax as a personal deduction using the self-employed health insurance deduction. The net result is that Jim pays self-employment tax only on the $10,000. The same result would have been achieved if Jim had purchased his health insurance himself.

Partnerships, LLC, and LLPs can avoid having to report health insurance payments as income if they don't take a tax deduction for them. This will have the same tax result and make things simpler.

If your practice is an S corporation, the insurance costs are added to your employee compensation and are deducted as such by the corporation. However, you have to pay income tax only on the amount, not employment taxes. Again, you can take the self-employed health insurance deduction and wipe out the extra income tax you had to pay.

3. C Corporations

If your practice is organized as a C corporation, you ordinarily will work as its employee and will be entitled to the full menu of tax-free employee fringe benefits, including health insurance. This means the corporation can purchase health insurance for you, deduct the cost as a business expense, and not have to include the cost in your employee compensation. Your health insurance is completely tax-free.

If you want to convert your health insurance premiums to a tax-free fringe benefit and you don't have a C corporation, you must form one to run your practice and work as its employee. You can do this even if you're running a one-person practice.

However, because your health insurance is 100% deductible from your income taxes if you use the self-employed health insurance tax deduction, it may not be worthwhile to incorporate just to save on Social Security and Medicare taxes. This is particularly true if your employee income would substantially exceed the 12.4% Social Security tax ceiling—$94,200 in 2006—with the result that you'd only save having to pay the 2.9% Medicare tax.

On the other hand, it may be worthwhile to convert to a C corporation if you want to use a medical reimbursement plan. (See Section D, below.)

4.   Employing Your Spouse

There's another way to make your health insurance costs a completely tax-free employee fringe benefit: Hire your spouse to work in your practice as an employee and provide him or her with health insurance. The insurance should be purchased in the name of the spouse/employee, not in the employer's name. The policy can cover your spouse, you, your children, and other dependents as well. You (or your practice if it is a business entity) can deduct the cost of the health insurance as a business expense, but your spouse will not have to pay tax on it—neither income nor Social Security or Medicare tax.

> **EXAMPLE:** Joe is a self-employed consultant. He hires his wife, Martha, to work as his employee assistant. He pays her $25,000 per year and provides her with a health insurance policy covering both of them and their two children. The annual policy premiums are $5,000. Joe may deduct the $5,000 as a business expense for his consulting practice, listing it as an expense on his Schedule C.

He gets to deduct the $5,000 not only from his $80,000 income for income tax purposes, but also from his self-employment income. His federal and state income tax rate is 40%, so he saves $2,000 in income tax. The self-employment tax is a 15.3% tax (up to the Social Security tax ceiling—$94,200 in 2006), so Joe saves $765 in self-employment taxes.

If you do this and you're self-employed, do *not* take the health insurance deduction for self-employed people discussed in Section B, above.

There are a couple of catches to this deduction. First, this method ordinarily doesn't work if you have an S corporation because your spouse is deemed to be a shareholder of the corporation along with you and can't also be a corporate employee. In addition, your spouse must be a bona fide employee. In other words, he or she must do real work in your business, you must pay applicable payroll taxes, and you must otherwise treat your spouse like any other employee. (See Chapter 15 for a detailed discussion.)

You'll probably want to pay your spouse as low a salary as possible, because both of you will have to pay Social Security and Medicare taxes on that salary (but not on employee benefits like health insurance and medical expense reimbursements). You should, however, regularly pay your spouse at least some cash wages, or the IRS could claim your spouse is not a real employee. You can make the cash wages a relatively small part of your spouse's total compensation—wages plus fringe benefits like your medical reimbursement plan.

No matter how you pay your spouse, his or her total compensation must be reasonable—that is, you can't pay more than your spouse's services are worth. For example, you can't pay your spouse at a rate of $100 per hour for simple clerical work. Total compensation means the sum of the salary, plus all the fringe benefits you pay your spouse, including health insurance and medical expense reimbursements.

EXAMPLE: Tina's husband, Tim, works part time doing collections for her dental practice. Tina calls a few employment agencies and learns that other dentists in the area pay helpers like Tim about

$10 per hour. She decides to pay him at this rate for 500 hours of work per year (ten hours per week, 50 weeks per year). His total compensation should be about $5,000 (500 hours x $10/hr. = $5,000). Tina wants to provide Tim with a health insurance policy covering him and his family (including Tina) and a medical reimbursement plan. She would like to purchase a health insurance policy for $7,500 per year, but she knows she can't justify this expense since Tim's total annual compensation can't be more than about $5,000. Instead, Tina has her practice provide Tim with $3,500 worth of health insurance, $500 of medical reimbursements, and $1,000 in salary. Tina and Tim must pay a 15.3% tax on his $1,000 in wages. But Tina gets to deduct the wages and the $4,000 in health insurance and medical reimbursement costs as a business expense. This saves her (and Tim) $1,500 in federal and state taxes for the year.

Your Spouse May Not Be Your Partner

A marriage may be a partnership, but you can't be partners with your spouse in your practice and also claim he or she is your employee for purposes of health insurance deductions. If your spouse co-owns the practice with you, he or she is treated as self-employed—not an employee—for purposes of health insurance. You and your spouse are co-owners if you file partnership returns for your practice (IRS Form 1065) listing him or her as a partner, or if your spouse has made a substantial financial investment in your practice with the spouse's own money.

Of course, if you're single, you won't be able to hire a spouse to take advantage of this method for turning health insurance costs into a business expense. However, if you're a single parent, you could hire your child and deduct the cost of your child's health insurance as a business expense. But your child's policy cannot also cover you or other family members.

D. Adopting a Medical Reimbursement Plan

Health insurance usually doesn't cover all your medical expenses. For example, it doesn't cover preexisting conditions, or deductibles or copayments—that is, amounts you must pay yourself before your insurance coverage kicks in. Many costs aren't covered at all, including ongoing physical therapy, fertility treatment, and optometric care. As a result, the average American pays about $900 a year in out-of-pocket health-related expenses. One way to deduct these expenses is to establish a medical reimbursement plan. Another way is to use a Health Savings Account. (See Section E, below.)

1. What Is a Medical Reimbursement Plan?

A medical reimbursement plan is an arrangement under which an employer reimburses its employees for health or dental expenses. These plans are usually self-funded—that is, the employer pays the expenses out of its own pocket, not through insurance.

Why would an employer do this? One good reason is that the reimbursements are tax deductible business expenses for the employer. Also, the employee doesn't have to include the reimbursements as taxable income (as long as the employee has not taken a deduction for these amounts as a personal medical expense).

If your practice is organized as a C corporation, you'll be its employee and will qualify for a medical reimbursement plan as described below. However, if you don't have a C corporation, you won't be an employee and can't have such a plan.

But all is not necessarily lost. Again, your spouse (if you have one) can come to the rescue. You can hire your spouse as your employee and provide him or her with a medical reimbursement plan. The plan may cover not only your spouse, but also you, your children, and other dependents. This allows your business to reimburse your and your family's out-of-pocket medical expenses and deduct the amounts as a business expense. And you need not include the reimbursements in your own taxable income. The IRS has ruled that this is perfectly legal. (Tax Advice Memo 9409006.)

EXAMPLE: Jennifer has her own public relations firm. She hires her husband Paul to work as her part-time employee assistant. She establishes a medical reimbursement plan covering Paul, herself, and their young child. Paul spends $6,000 on medical expenses. Jennifer reimburses Paul for the $6,000 as provided by their plan. Jennifer may deduct the $6,000 from her business income for the year, meaning she pays neither income nor self-employment tax on that amount. Paul need not include the $6,000 in his income—it's tax free to him. The deduction saves Jennifer and Paul $2,000 in taxes for the year.

Your spouse must be a legitimate employee. Your spouse must be a legitimate employee for your medical reimbursement plan to pass muster with the IRS. You can't simply hire your spouse on paper—he or she must do real work in your business. If you can't prove your wife or husband is a legitimate employee, the IRS will disallow your deductions. The IRS will be particularly suspicious if your spouse is your only employee.

EXAMPLE: Mr. Haeder, a sole proprietor attorney who practiced law in his home, claimed that he hired his wife as his employee to answer the telephone, greet visitors, type legal papers, and clean his office. Mrs. Haeder had no employment contract or work schedule, did not maintain any time records, and did not directly or regularly receive a salary. Instead, Mr. Haeder paid her the maximum amount she could deduct as an IRA contribution. Annually, he transferred money in his brokerage account to an IRA in his wife's name. For all but one of the years audited by the IRS, no W-2 was issued to Mrs. Haeder. Mr. Haeder sponsored a medical reimbursement plan that covered out-of-pocket expenses for his wife, her children, and her spouse—that is, himself. Mrs. Haeder submitted bills for out-of-pocket medical expenses to her husband, which he reimbursed and attempted to deduct as business expenses. The IRS determined Mr. Haeder was not entitled to deduct the reimbursements under the medical reimbursement plan because Mrs. Haeder was not a bona fide employee. The tax court agreed, finding that there was no credible evidence that Mrs. Haeder performed any services other than those reasonably expected of a family member. (*Haeder v. Comm'r*, T.C. Memo 2001-7 (2001).)

Again, the medical expense reimbursement plan deduction is available only to your employees, not to you (the business owner). The only way you can qualify as an employee is if your business is a C corporation. (See Section C, above.) However, if you don't have a spouse to employ, you could employ your child and provide him or her with a reimbursement plan. But the plan may not cover you or any other family members.

2.   What Expenses May Be Reimbursed?

One of the great things about medical reimbursement plans is that they can be used to reimburse employees for a wide variety of health-related expenses. Indeed, deductible medical expenses include any expense for the diagnosis, cure, mitigation, treatment, or prevention of disease, or any expense paid to affect the structure or function of the human body. (IRS Reg. 1.213.1(e).)

This includes, of course, premiums in health and accident insurance, and health insurance deductibles and copayments. But it also includes expenses for acupuncture, chiropractors, eyeglasses and contact lenses, dental treatment, laser eye surgery, psychiatric care, and treatment for learning disabilities. (See Section E5, below, for more information on the expenses that can and cannot be deducted.) You can draft your plan to include only those expenses you wish to reimburse. Presumably, though, you'd want to include as many expenses as possible if the plan covers only your spouse, yourself, and your family.

In addition, the IRS ruled in 2003 that a medical expense reimbursement plan may include reimbursements for employee expenses for nonprescription medicines and drugs. (Rev. Rul. 2003-102.) Any over-the-counter drug or medicine is covered except for dietary supplements and other items that are used only for general health, not for specific medical problems. Thus, for example, reimbursements may be provided for nonprescription antacids, allergy medicines, pain relievers, and cold medicines. So, if you have a medical reimbursement plan, you can even get a tax deduction for aspirin! (You can't deduct nonprescription drugs under the personal medical expense deduction discussed in Section A, above.)

3. Plan Requirements

If you decide to adopt a medical expense reimbursement plan, the plan must be in writing, it may not discriminate in favor of highly compensated employees, and it must reimburse employees only for medical expenses that are not paid for by insurance.

The nondiscrimination rule will affect you only if you have many employees other than your spouse or children. If you do, a medical reimbursement plan may be too expensive for you, because you'll have to provide coverage to nonfamily members as well. A plan is nondiscriminatory under IRS rules if it:

- covers at least 70% of all employees
- covers at least 80% of all employees eligible to benefit from the plan, provided that 70% or more of all employees are eligible, or
- is found to be nondiscriminatory by the IRS based on the facts and circumstances.

However, the plan may exclude employees who:

- work less than 25 hours a week
- are not yet 25 years old
- work for you less than seven months in a year, or
- have worked for you less than three years.

> **EXAMPLE:** Jim employs 12 people in his medical practice. Two work only 20 hours per week. To be nondiscriminatory, Jim's medical expense reimbursement plan must cover 80% of his ten employees eligible to participate—in other words, he must cover eight of his ten full-time employees.

If a plan is found to be discriminatory by the IRS, all or part of the medical benefits paid to highly compensated employees under the plan will be taxable to the employee. Highly compensated employees include:

- anyone among the top 25% highest-paid employees
- the five highest paid corporate officers (if your business is incorporated), and
- shareholders who own more than 10% of the corporation stock.

12 Steps to Audit-Proof Your Medical Reimbursement Plan

Your medical reimbursement plan is subject to attack by the IRS if it doesn't look like a legitimate business expense. Your spouse must be a real employee, you must treat him or her as such, and you must manage your plan in a business-like manner.

1. Have your spouse sign a written employment agreement specifying his or her duties and work hours.

2. Adopt a written medical reimbursement plan for your practice.

3. Keep track of the hours your spouse works with timesheets.

4. Make sure your spouse's total compensation is reasonable.

5. Have your spouse open a separate bank account he or she uses to pay medical expenses or receive reimbursements from your business.

6. Comply with all payroll tax, unemployment insurance, and workers' compensation requirements for your spouse-employee.

7. Reimburse your spouse for covered expenses by check from a separate business bank account or pay the health care provider directly from your business account. Make a notation on the check that the payment is made under your medical reimbursement plan.

8. Never pay your spouse in cash.

9. Your spouse should submit all bills to be reimbursed or paid by your business at least twice a year, or monthly or quarterly if you prefer. Keep all documentation showing the nature and amounts of the medical expenses paid for by your plan—receipts, cancelled checks, and so on, to show that you didn't reimburse your spouse too much and that the payments were for legitimate business expenses.

10. Don't pay for expenses incurred before the date you adopted your plan.

11. If you have employees other than your spouse, make sure you meet the nondiscrimination requirements.

12. Claim your deduction on the correct tax form:
    - sole proprietors—Schedule C, line 14, "Employee benefit programs"
    - LLCs and partnerships—Form 1065, line 19, "Employee benefit programs"
    - C Corporations—Form 1120, Line 25, "Employee Benefit Programs."

4.   How to Establish a Plan

If a medical expense reimbursement plan sounds attractive to you, you should act to establish one as early in the year as possible because it applies only to medical expenses incurred after the date the plan is adopted. (Rev. Rul. 2002-58.) Forget about using a plan to reimburse your spouse or yourself for expenses you have already incurred. If you do, the reimbursement must be added to your spouse's income for tax purposes and you must pay employment tax on it.

A written medical reimbursement plan must be drawn up and adopted by your practice. If your practice is incorporated, the plan should be adopted by a corporate resolution approved by the corporation's board of directors. You can find a form for this purpose in *The Corporate Records Handbook*, by Anthony Mancuso (Nolo).

5.   Sample Plan

A sample medical expense reimbursement plan is provided below. It's self-explanatory, with the following exceptions:

Eligibility. If you have employees other than your spouse (or think you may have them in the future), you must decide whether to place limitations on which employees may be covered by your plan. You may cover all your employees or exclude certain classes of employees as described in Section C3, above. It's up to you to decide. But, be careful about who you exclude from your plan—make sure you don't eliminate your spouse. For example, if your plan excludes all employees who work less than 25 hours per week, your spouse will have to work at least 25 hours to qualify for your plan. If your spouse will only work 15 hours per week, your plan should exclude only those employees who work less than 15 hours.

Dollar Limits. You have the option of placing an annual dollar limit on the reimbursements you'll make. If your spouse is your only employee, you probably won't want a limit. But, if you have other employees—or may have them in the future—a limit may be advisable.

Claims Submission. Finally, you must decide how often the employee must submit claims for reimbursement. Twice a year is fine, but you can make it more often if you wish.

Medical Expense Reimbursement Plan

Effective _____ [date], _____

[*your business name*] ("Employer") will reimburse all eligible employees for medical expenses incurred by themselves and their dependents, subject to the conditions and limitations set forth below.

1. Uninsured Expenses

Employer will reimburse eligible employees and their dependents only for medical expenses that are not covered by health or accident insurance.

2. Medical Expenses Defined

Medical expenses are those expenses defined by Internal Revenue Code Sec. 213(d). They consist of any expense for the diagnosis, cure, mitigation, treatment, or prevention of disease; or any expense paid to affect the structure or function of the human body. Medical expenses include both prescription and nonprescription drugs and medicines.

3. Dependent Defined

Dependent is defined by IRC Sec. 152. It includes any member of an eligible employee's family for whom the employee and his or her spouse provides more than half of the financial support.

4. Eligibility

[*Choose Alternative A or B.*]

Alternative A:

The plan shall be open to all employees.

Alternative B:

The plan shall be open to all employees who:

[*Check applicable boxes—you may check any number*]

☐ work more than _____ [*specify—25 hrs/week is maximum*] hours per week

☐ are at least _____ [*specify—25 years old is maximum*] years of age

☐ have completed _____ [*specify—3 years is maximum*] years of service with Employer

☐ work _____ [*specify—7 months is maximum*] months per year.

5. Limitation (*Optional*)

Employer shall reimburse any eligible employee no more than _____ [*dollar amount*] in any calendar year for medical expenses.

6. Submission of Claims

Any eligible employee seeking reimbursement under this Plan shall submit to Employer, [*choose one*] ☐ monthly, ☐ quarterly ☐ at least twice a year on _____ [date] and _____ [date], all bills for medical care, including those for accident or health insurance. Such bills and other claims for reimbursement shall be verified by Employer prior to reimbursement. Employer, in its sole discretion, may terminate the employee's right to reimbursement if the employee fails to comply.

7. Direct Payments

At its option, Employer may pay all or part of a covered employee's medical expenses directly, instead of making reimbursements to the employee. Such a direct payment shall relieve Employer of all further liability for the expense.

8. Termination

Employer may terminate this Plan at any time. Medical expenses incurred prior to the date of termination shall be reimbursed by Employer. Employer is under no obligation to provide advance notice of termination.

9. Benefits Not Taxable

Employer intends that the benefits under this Plan shall qualify under IRC Sec. 105 so as to be excludable from the gross income of the employees covered by the Plan.

_____   _____
Employer's Signature   Date

_____   _____
Employee's Signature   Date

E.   Health Savings Accounts

Another tax-advantaged method of buying health insurance has been available since 2004: Health Savings Accounts (HSAs). Although HSAs have only been around a short time, they are becoming quite popular. Experts predict that they will grow in number from 391,000 in 2005 to more than 6.3 million in 2008 (Forrester Research Inc.).

1.   What Are Health Savings Accounts?

The HSA concept is very simple: Instead of relying on health insurance to pay small or routine medical expenses, you pay them yourself. To help you do this, you establish a Health Savings Account with a health insurance company, bank, or other financial institution. Contributions to the account are tax deductible, and you don't have to pay tax on the interest or other money you earn on the money in your account. You can withdraw the money in your HSA to pay almost any kind of health-related expense, and you don't have to pay any tax on these withdrawals.

In case you or a family member gets really sick, you must also obtain a health insurance policy with a high deductible—at least $1,000 for individuals, and $2,100 for families. The money in your HSA can be used to pay this large deductible and any copayments you're required to make.

Using an HSA can save you money in two ways:

- You'll get a tax deduction for the money you deposit in your account.
- The premiums for your high-deductible health insurance policy should be lower than those for traditional comprehensive coverage policies or HMO coverage.

2.   Establishing an HSA

You may individually establish an HSA for yourself and your family and pay for your health insurance with personal funds. Alternatively, if your practice is a corporation, LLC, partnership, or LLP, you can have it establish an HSA for you and make contributions to your HSA on your behalf with business funds. In either event, the rules discussed below apply.

To participate in the HSA program, you need two things:

- a high-deductible health plan that qualifies under the HSA rules, and
- an HSA account.

HSA-Qualified Plans

You can't have an HSA if you're covered by health insurance other than a high-deductible HSA plan—for example, if your spouse has family coverage for you from his or her job. So you may have to change your existing coverage. However, you may get your own HSA if you are not covered by your spouse's health insurance. In addition, people eligible to receive Medicare may not participate in the HSA program.

You need to obtain a bare-bones high-deductible health plan that meets the HSA criteria (is "HSA-qualified"). You may obtain coverage from an HMO, PPO, or traditional plan. If the coverage is only for you, your plan must have a $1,000 minimum annual deductible. If the coverage is for you and your family, your plan must have a $2,100 minimum deductible.

In the case of families, the deductible must apply to the entire family, not each family member separately. With such a per family deductible, expenses incurred by each family member accumulate and are credited toward the one family deductible—for example, a family of four would meet the $2,100 deductible if $525 in medical expenses were paid for each family member during the year (4 x $525 = $2,100). This is a unique feature of the HSA program.

You can have a deductible that is larger than the minimum amount if you wish. However, keep in mind that there are limits on how much money you can contribute to your HSA account each year. To be on the safe side, you don't want your deductible to exceed these limits or your account may not have enough money in it to cover the deductible if you become seriously ill—particularly if you develop a chronic illness that will require payments year after year. In 2006, the maximum annual contribution to an HSA is $2,700 for individuals and $5,450 for families. These amounts are adjusted each year for inflation.

Special Rule for Preventive Care

A special rule permits high deductible health plans to provide coverage for Preventive health care without the insured first satisfying the minimum annual deductible. Preventive care means care that doesn't treat a preexisting condition. It includes, but is not limited to:

- periodic health evaluations, including tests and diagnostic procedures ordered in connection with routine examinations, such as annual physicals
- routine prenatal and well-child care
- child and adult immunizations
- tobacco cessation programs
- obesity weight-loss programs, and
- health screening services. (IRS Notice 2004-23.)

For example, your plan can pay for your annual physical even though you have not met the annual deductible.

Your plan must also have a cap on the annual out-of-pocket payments you must make each year. Out-of-pocket payments include deductibles, copayments, and other amounts (other than insurance premiums) you must pay for covered benefits under your health plan. As you can see from the following chart, the maximum annual out-of-pocket payments that your insurer can require are $5,250 for individuals and $10,200 for families.

2006 HSA Deductibles and Out-of-Pocket Caps		
Type of Coverage	Minimum Annual Deductible	Maximum Annual Out-of-Pocket Payments
Self only	$1,000	$5,250
Family	$2,000	$10,200

In addition, your health insurance plan must be "HSA-qualified." To become qualified, the insurer must agree to participate in the HSA program and give the roster of enrolled participants to the IRS. If your insurer fails to report to the IRS that you are enrolled in an HSA-qualified insurance plan, the IRS will not permit you to deduct your HSA contributions.

HSA-qualified health insurance policies should be clearly labeled as such on the cover page or declaration page of the policy. It might be possible to convert a high-deductible health insurance policy you already have to an HSA-qualified health insurance policy; ask your health insurer for details.

You can obtain an HSA qualifying health plan from health insurers that participate in the program. The following websites contain directories and contact information for insurers providing HSAs: www.hsainsider.com and www.hsafinder.com. The U.S. Treasury has an informative website on HSAs at www.treas.gov/offices/public-affairs/hsa. You can also contact your current health insurer.

The premiums you pay for an HSA-qualified health plan are deductible to the same extent as any other health insurance premiums. This means that if you're a sole proprietor, you may deduct your entire premium from your federal income tax as a special personal deduction. (See Section A, above.)

HSA Account

Once you have an HSA-qualified health insurance policy, you may open your HSA account. An HSA must be established with a trustee. The HSA trustee keeps track of your deposits and withdrawals, produces annual statements, and reports your HSA deposits to the IRS.

Any person, insurance company, bank, or financial institution already approved by the IRS to be a trustee or custodian of an IRA is approved automatically to serve as an HSA trustee. Others may apply for approval under IRS procedures for HSAs.

Health insurers can administer both the health plan and the HSA. However, you don't have to have your HSA administered by your insurer. You can establish an HSA with banks, insurance companies, mutual funds, or other financial institutions offering HSA products.

Whoever administers your account will usually give you a checkbook or debit card to use to withdraw funds from the account. You can also make withdrawals by mail or in person.

Look at the plans offered by several companies to see which offers the best deal. Compare the fees charged to set up the account, as well as any other charges (some companies may charge an annual service fee, for example). Ask about special promotions and discounts. And find out how the account is invested.

3. Making Contributions to Your HSA

When you have your HSA-qualified health plan and HSA account, you can start making contributions to your account. There is no minimum amount you are required to contribute each year; you may contribute nothing if you wish.

If your practice is a corporation, partnership, LLC, or LLP, you don't have to make all the contributions to your HSA from your personal funds. All or part of your annual contribution can be paid for by your practice from its funds. But, as described in the following section, this changes how the contributions are deducted.

There are maximum limits on how much may be contributed to an HSA each year:

- If you have individual coverage, the maximum annual contribution is the amount of your annual deductible or $2,700, whichever is less.
- If you have family coverage, the maximum annual contribution is the amount of your annual deductible or $5,450, whichever is less.

These figures are for 2006. They will be adjusted for inflation each year.

EXAMPLE 1: Elvira has an individual HSA-qualified policy with a $1,500 deductible. The maximum that can be contributed to her HSA account each year is $1,500.

EXAMPLE 2: Jim has a family health policy with a $6,000 deductible. The maximum that may be contributed to his HSA account each year is $5,450.

Catch-Up Contributions

Optional tax-free catch-up contributions can be made to HSAs for individuals who are 55 to 65 years old. The amounts are shown in the following chart. This rule is intended to compensate for the fact that older folks won't have as many years to fund their accounts as younger taxpayers. If you're in this age group, it's wise to make these contributions if you can afford them so your HSA account will have enough money to pay for future health expenses.

Year	Maximum Annual Catch-Up Contribution
2005	$600
2006	$700
2007	$800
2008	$900
2009 and later	$1,000

Where to Invest HSA Contributions

HSA contributions may be invested just like IRA contributions. You can invest in almost anything: money market accounts, bank certificates of deposit, stocks, bonds, mutual funds, Treasury bills, and notes. However, you can't invest in collectibles such as art, antiques, postage stamps, or other personal property. Most HSA funds are invested in money market accounts, and certificates of deposit.

Every year, you may roll over up to $500 of unused funds in your HSA into an Individual Retirement Account (IRA) without paying tax on the money.

4. Deducting HSA Contributions

The amounts contributed each year to HSA accounts, up to the annual limit, are deductible from federal income taxes.

Individual Contributions

You can deduct HSA contributions made with your personal funds as a personal deduction on the first page of your IRS Form 1040. You deduct the amount from your gross income, just like a business deduction. This means you get the full deduction whether or not you itemize your personal deductions.

> **EXAMPLE:** Martin, an actuary, establishes an HSA for himself and his family with a $2,100 deductible. Every year, he contributes the maximum amount to his HSA account: $2,100. Because he is in the 25% federal income tax bracket, this saves him $525 in federal income tax each year.

Contributions by Your Practice

If your practice is a partnership, LLP, or LLC and it makes an HSA contribution for you as a distribution of partnership or LLC funds, it is reported as a cash distribution to you on your Schedule K-1 (Form 1065). You may take a personal deduction for the HSA contribution on your tax return (IRS Form 1040) and the contribution is not subject to income or self-employment taxes.

However, the tax result is very different if the contribution is made as a guaranteed payment to the partner or LLC member. A guaranteed payment is like a salary paid to a partner or LLC member for services performed for the partnership or LLC. The amount of a guaranteed payment is determined without reference to the partnership's or LLC's income. The partnership or LLC deducts the guaranteed payment on its return and lists it as a guaranteed payment to you on your Schedule K-1 (Form 1065). You must pay income and self-employment tax on the amount. You may take a personal income tax deduction on your Form 1040 for the HSA contribution.

Contributions by an S corporation to a shareholder-employee's HSA are treated as wages subject to income tax, but they normally are not subject to employment taxes. The shareholder can deduct the contribution on his or her personal tax return (IRS Form 1040) as an HSA contribution.

If you've formed a C corporation and work as its employee, your corporation can make a contribution to your HSA and deduct the amount as employee compensation. The contribution is not taxable to you. However, if you have other employees, similar contributions must be made to their HSAs. You may also make contributions from your own funds. (See Section 3, above.)

5. Withdrawing HSA Funds

If you or a family member needs health care, you can withdraw money from your HSA to pay your deductible or any other medical expenses. You pay no federal tax on HSA withdrawals used to pay qualified medical expenses. Qualified medical expenses are broadly defined to include many types of expenses ordinarily not covered by health insurance—for example, dental or optometric care. This is one of the great advantages of the HSA program over traditional health insurance.

No Approval Required

HSA participants need not obtain advance approval from their HSA trustee (whether their insurer or someone else) that an expense is a qualified medical expense before they withdraw funds from their accounts. You make that determination yourself. You should keep records of your medical expenses to show that your withdrawals were for qualified medical expenses and are therefore excludable from your gross income.

> **EXAMPLE:** Jane, a self-employed consultant and single mother, obtains family health insurance coverage with a $2,500 deductible. She sets up an HSA at her bank and deposits $2,500 every year for three years. She deducts each contribution from her gross income for the year for income tax purposes. Jane pays no taxes on the interest she earns on the money in her account, which is invested in a money market fund. By the end of three years, she has $7,500 in the account. Jane becomes ill after the third year and is hospitalized. She withdraws $2,000 from her HSA to pay her deductible. She also withdraws $3,000 to pay for speech therapy for her son, which is not covered by her health insurance. She pays no federal tax on these withdrawals.

However, you may not use HSA funds to purchase nonprescription medications. The only way to deduct these is to hire your spouse and establish a medical reimbursement plan.

Tax-Free Withdrawals

If you withdraw funds from your HSA to use for something other than qualified medical expenses, you must pay the regular income tax on the withdrawal plus a 10% penalty. For example, if you were in the 25% federal income tax bracket, you'd have to pay a 35% tax on your nonqualified withdrawals.

Once you reach the age of 65 or become disabled, you can withdraw your HSA funds for any reason without penalty. If you use the money for nonmedical expenses, you will have to pay regular income tax on the withdrawals. When you die, the money in your HSA account is transferred to the beneficiary you've named for the account. The transfer is tax-free if the beneficiary is your surviving spouse. Other transfers are taxable.

If you elect to leave the HSA program, you can continue to keep your HSA account and withdraw money from it tax-free for health care expenses. However, you won't be able to make any additional contributions to the account.

What HSA Funds Can Be Used For

Health insurance ordinarily may not be purchased with HSA funds. However, there are three exceptions to this general rule. HSA funds can be used to pay for:

- a health plan during any period of continuation coverage required under any federal law—for example, when you are terminated from your job and purchase continuing health insurance coverage from your employer's health insurer, which the insurer is legally required to make available to you under COBRA
- long-term health care insurance, or
- health insurance premiums you pay while you are receiving unemployment compensation.

You can use HSA funds to pay for a broad array of medical expenses, including many that ordinarily are not covered by health insurance. This includes all your standard physician, dental, eye care, and mental health costs, as well as alcoholism and fertility treatment, nursing home expenses, and many other health-related costs.

For a complete list of what is and is not covered, refer to IRS Publication 502, *Medical and Dental Expenses*. Copies may be obtained from the IRS website at www.irs.gov or by calling 1-800-TAX-FORM.

Comparing HSAs and Medical Reimbursement Plans

HSAs and medical reimbursement plans (see Section D, above) both allow you to deduct the costs for most types of health care. However, there are some significant differences and each arrangement has certain advantages.

Advantages of an HSA

As a business owner, you can obtain your own HSA to cover you and your family. This is so whether you're a sole proprietor, partner in a partnership, LLC owner, or S corporation shareholder. This is not true for medical reimbursement plans. Medical reimbursement plans are only for employees. To get your family covered under a medical reimbursement plan, you must be married, hire your spouse as a legitimate employee, and provide him or her with the plan. (Or you must form a C corporation to own your business and work as its employee).

You can deduct whatever you contribute to an HSA—up to the annual limit—regardless of whether it is actually spent on medical expenses. This can allow you to put tax-deductible savings aside for the future. With medical reimbursement plans, you can only deduct and get reimbursed for actual out-of-pocket medical expenses each year.

Advantages of a Medical Reimbursement Plan

There is no annual limit on how much you can reimburse a spouse-employee for medical expenses. This is true for any expenses incurred by the spouse, you, or your children each year under a medical reimbursement plan. HSAs, on the other hand, are subject to an annual contribution limit—$5,250 in 2005 if you have family coverage. Once that limit is reached, you get no more tax deduction for the year. This can be a crucial difference if you have substantial health insurance premiums and/or uninsured medical expenses. (You can, however, establish an annual limit in your medical reimbursement plan if you want one.)

Money an employer spends on a medical reimbursement plan is a business tax deduction. Thus, it lowers your business income for self-employment taxes—Social Security and Medicare taxes—and income taxes. The combined Social Security and Medicare tax is 12.4% on net self-employment income up to $94,200 in 2006. With HSAs, on the other hand, you get no self-employment tax deduction when you make a contribution to the HSA. You get only an income tax deduction.

6.   Are HSAs a Good Deal?

Should you get an HSA? It depends. HSAs appear to be a very good deal if you're young or in good health and don't go to the doctor often or take many expensive medications. You can purchase a health plan with a high deductible, pay lower premiums, and have the security of knowing you can dip into your HSA if you get sick and have to pay the deductible or other uncovered medical expenses.

If you don't tap into the money, it will keep accumulating free of taxes. You also get the benefit of deducting your HSA contributions from your income taxes. And you can use your HSA funds to pay for many health-related expenses that aren't covered by traditional health insurance.

If you enjoy good health while you have your HSA and don't have to make many withdrawals, you may end up with a substantial amount in your account that you can withdraw without penalty for any purpose once you turn 65. Unlike all other existing tax-advantaged savings or retirement accounts, HSAs provide a tax break when funds are deposited and when they are withdrawn. No other account provides both a "front end" and "back end" tax break. With IRAs, for example, you must pay tax either when you deposit or when you withdraw your money. This feature can make your HSA an extremely lucrative tax shelter—a kind of super IRA.

On the other hand, HSAs are not for everybody. You could be better off with traditional comprehensive health insurance if you or a member of your family has substantial medical expenses. When you're in this situation, you'll likely end up spending all or most of your HSA contributions each year and earn little or no interest on your account (but you'll still get a deduction for your contributions). Of course, whether traditional health insurance is better than an HSA depends on its cost, including the deductibles and copayments you must make.

In addition, depending on your medical history and where you live, the cost of an HSA-qualified health insurance plan may be too great to make the program cost-effective for you. However, if your choice is an HSA or nothing, get an HSA.

7. HSAs for Employees

Employers may provide HSAs to their employees. If you have employees, this may be an attractive option for you because it could cost less than providing your employees with traditional health insurance.

Any business, no matter how small, may participate in the HSA program. The employer purchases an HSA-qualified health plan for its employees, and they establish their own individual HSA accounts. The employer may pay all or part of its employees' insurance premiums and make contributions to their HSA accounts. Employees may also make their own contributions to their individual accounts. The combined annual contributions of the employer and employee may not exceed the limits listed in Section 2, above.

HSAs are portable when an employee changes employers. Contributions and earnings belong to the account holder, not the employer. Employers are required to report amounts contributed to an HSA on the employee's Form W-2.

Health insurance payments and HSA contributions made by businesses on behalf of its employees are currently deductible business expenses. The employees do not have to report employer contributions to their HSA accounts as income. You deduct them on the "Employee benefit programs" line of your business income tax return.

Are You an Employee?

A professional in private practice is an employee for HSA purposes only if the practice is legally organized as a C corporation (or it is a partnership, LLP, or LLC and it has elected to be taxed as a C corporation). You are not an employee for these purposes if your practice is an S corporation, LLC, LLP, or partnership.

Your C corporation employer may establish an HSA on your behalf and deduct its contributions on its own tax return. The contributions are not taxable to you, but you get no personal deduction for them. You do get a deduction, however, if you make contributions to your HSA account from your personal funds.

Hiring Your Spouse

If you're a sole proprietor or have formed any business entity other than an S corporation, you may hire your spouse as your employee and have your business pay for an HSA-qualified family health plan for your spouse, you, and your children and other dependents. Your spouse then establishes an HSA, which your business may fully fund each year. The money your business spends for your spouse's health insurance premiums and to fund the HSA is a fully deductible business expense. This allows you to reduce both your income and self-employment taxes. (See Section B, above.)

Nondiscrimination Rules

If your practice is a C corporation and you have employees other than yourself, your spouse, or other family members, you'll need to comply with nondiscrimination rules—that is, you'll have to make comparable HSA contributions for all employees with HSA-qualified health coverage during the year. Contributions are considered comparable if they are either of the same amount or the same percentage of the deductible under the plan. The rule is applied separately to employees who work less than 30 hours per week. Employers who do not comply with these rules are subject to a 35% excise tax.

Archer Medical Savings Accounts

Starting in 1997, Congress began a pilot program that allowed self-employed people and companies with 50 or fewer employees to establish Archer Medical Savings Accounts (MSAs). Archer MSAs were very similar to HSAs; they were a way for Congress to try out the health savings account concept. However, very few self-employed people and businesses have elected to establish MSAs. If you are one of the few with an Archer MSA, you may roll it over into an HSA without paying taxes on the money. Ask your insurer or Archer MSA trustee about this.

8. Tax Reporting for HSAs

You must report to the IRS each year how much you deposit to and withdraw from your HSA. You make the report using IRS Form 8889, *Health Savings Accounts*. You'll also be required to keep a record of the name and address of each person or company whom you pay with funds from your HSA

■

Chapter 12

Retirement Deductions

When you have your own practice it's up to you to establish and fund your own pension plan to supplement the Social Security benefits you'll receive when you retire. The tax law helps you do this by providing tax deductions and other income tax benefits for your retirement account contributions and earnings.

This chapter provides a general overview of the retirement plan choices you have as a business owner. Choosing what type of account to establish is just as important as deciding what to invest in once you open your account—if not more so. Once you set up your retirement account, you can always change your investments within the account with little or no difficulty. But changing the type of retirement account you have may prove difficult and costly. So it's best to spend some time up front learning about your choices and deciding which plan will best meet your needs.

For additional information on the tax aspects of retirement, see:
- IRS Publication 560, *Retirement Plans for the Small Business*, and
- IRS Publication 590, *Individual Retirement Accounts*.

Both are available from the IRS website, at www.irs.gov.

Two easy-to-understand guides on retirement investing are:
- *Get a Life: You Don't Need a Million to Retire Well*, by Ralph Warner (Nolo), and
- *Investing for Dummies*, by Eric Tyson (IDG Books).

You should get professional help with your plan if you have employees (other than a spouse). Having employees makes it much more complicated to set up a retirement plan. (See "Having Employees Complicates Matters Tremendously" in Section A , below.) Because of the many complex issues raised by having employees, any professional with employees should turn to a professional consultant for help in choosing, establishing, and administering a retirement plan.

In late 2005, Congress enacted special tax relief legislation for Hurricane Katrina victims. This legislation included waivers of penalties for early withdrawals from retirement accounts. For more information, check the IRS website at www.irs.gov.

A. Why You Need a Retirement Plan (or Plans)

In all likelihood, you will receive Social Security benefits when you retire. However, Social Security will probably cover only half of your needs when you retire—possibly less, depending upon your retirement lifestyle. You'll need to make up this shortfall with your own retirement investments.

When it comes to saving for retirement, small business owners are better off than employees of most companies. This is because the federal government allows small businesses to set up retirement accounts specifically designed for small business owners. These accounts provide enormous tax benefits that are intended to maximize the amount of money you can save during your working years for your retirement years. The amount you are allowed to contribute each year to your retirement account depends upon the type of account you establish and how much money you earn.

The two biggest benefits that most of these plans provide—tax deductions for plan contributions and tax deferral on investment earnings—are discussed in more detail below.

How Much Money Will You Need When You Retire?

How much money you'll need when you retire depends on many factors, including your lifestyle. You could need anywhere from 50% to 100% of the amount you were earning while you were employed. On average, retirees need about 70% to 80% of their pre-retirement earnings.

---

1. Tax Deduction

If you satisfy the requirements discussed below, you can deduct the amount you contribute to a retirement account from your income taxes (except for Roth IRAs and Roth 401(k)s). If you are a sole proprietor, partner in a partnership or LLP, or LLC member, you can deduct your contributions from your personal income tax. If you have incorporated your practice, the corporation can deduct as a business expense contributions that it makes on your behalf. Either way, you or your corporation get a substantial income tax savings.

> **EXAMPLE:** Art, a sole proprietor, contributes $10,000 this year to a qualified retirement account. He can deduct the entire amount from his personal income taxes. Because Art is in the 28% tax bracket, he saves $2,800 in income taxes for the year (28% x $10,000), and he has also saved $10,000 toward his retirement.

2. Tax Deferral

In addition to the tax deduction you receive for putting money into a retirement account, there is another tremendous tax benefit to retirement accounts: tax deferral. When you earn money on an investment, you usually must pay taxes on those earnings in the same year that you earn the money. For example, you must pay taxes on the interest you earn on a savings account or certificate of deposit in the year when the interest accrues. And when you sell an investment at a profit, you must pay income tax in that year on the gain you receive. For example, you must pay tax on the profit you earn from selling stock in the year that you sell it.

   A different rule applies, however, for earnings you receive from a retirement account. You do not pay taxes on investment earnings from retirement accounts until you withdraw the funds. Because most people withdraw these funds at retirement, they are usually in a lower income tax bracket when they pay tax on these earnings. This results in tax savings for most people, who would have had to pay higher taxes on these earnings if they paid as the earnings accumulated.

> **EXAMPLE:** Bill and Brian both invest in municipal bonds and Treasury bills. Bill has a taxable individual account, while Brian invests through a tax-deferred retirement account. They each invest $5,000 per year. They earn 8% on their investments each year and pay income tax at the 28% rate. At the end of 30 years, Brian has

$566,416. Bill has only $272,869. Reason: Bill had to pay income taxes on the interest his investments earned each year, while Brian's interest accrued tax-free because he invested through a retirement account. Brian must pay tax on his earnings only when he withdraws the money (but he'll have to pay a penalty tax if he makes withdrawals before age 59½, subject to certain exceptions).

The following chart compares the annual growth of a tax-deferred account and a taxable account.

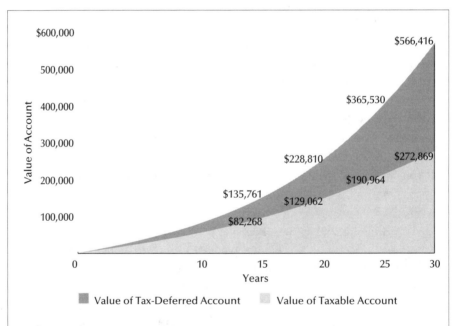

Assumptions:
- Investments earn 8% annually.
- $5,000 is invested annually in the tax-deferred account.
- $3,600 (what's left after $5,000 is taxed at 28%) is invested annually in the non-tax-deferred account.
- Income on the non-tax-deferred account is taxed annually at 28%, and recipient does not pay state income tax.)

Having Employees Complicates Matters Tremendously

If your practice is not incorporated and you have no employees (other than your spouse), you can probably choose, establish, and administer your own retirement plan with little or no assistance. The instant you add employees to the mix, however, virtually every aspect of your plan becomes more complex. This is primarily due to something called nondiscrimination rules. These rules are designed to ensure that your retirement plan benefits all employees, not just you. In general, the laws prohibit you from doing the following:

- making disproportionately large contributions for some plan participants (like yourself) and not for others,
- unfairly excluding certain employees from participating in the plan, and
- unfairly withholding benefits from former employees or their beneficiaries.

If the IRS finds the plan to be discriminatory at any time (usually during an audit), the plan could be disqualified—that is, determined not to satisfy IRS rules. If this happens, you and your employees will owe income tax and probably penalties, as well.

Having employees also increases the plan's reporting requirements. You must provide employees with a summary of the terms of the plan, notification of any changes you make, and an annual report of contributions. And you must file an annual tax return. Because of all the complex issues raised by having employees, any business owner with employees (other than a spouse) should seek professional help when creating a retirement plan.

Beware of retirement account deadlines. If you want to establish any of the retirement accounts discussed in this chapter and take a tax deduction for the year, you must meet specific deadlines. The deadlines vary according to the type of account you set up, as shown in the following chart. Once you establish your account, you have until the due date of your tax return for the year (April 15 of the following year, plus any filing extensions) to contribute to your account and take a deduction.

Retirement Account Deadlines	
Plan Type	**Deadline for Establishing Plan**
Traditional IRA	Due date of tax return (April 15 plus extensions)
Roth IRA	Due date of tax return (April 15 plus extensions)
SEP-IRA	Due date of tax return (April 15 plus extensions)
Simple IRA	October 1
Keogh Profit-Sharing Plan	December 31
Keogh Money Purchase Plan	December 31
Keogh Defined Benefit Plan	December 31
401(k) Plan	December 31

B.   Types of Retirement Plans

There is a bewildering array of retirement plans. Some can be used only
if you are self-employed, others are only for employees, and still others
are for everybody. All these plans can be grouped into the following
categories:

- Individual IRAs
- Employer IRAs
- Qualified Plans, and
- Nonqualified Plans.

1.   Individual IRAs

An IRA is a tax-favored retirement account you establish on your
own as an individual. Your practice does not contribute to it. The
annual contributions you can make to IRAs are relatively modest.
The accounts are very simple to set-up and use, so you don't need
to hire a professional to help you. There are two types of individual
IRAs: traditional IRAs and Roth IRAs. (See Section C, below, for more
information on these plans.)

2. Employer IRAs

Employer IRAs are established by businesses on behalf of their employees. However, business owners are considered employees for these purposes. Thus, even if you're self-employed and have no employees working for you, you can still have an employer IRA. There are two types of employer IRAs: SEP IRAs and SIMPLE IRAs. Both allow substantially greater annual contributions than individual IRAs. (See Section D, below, for more information on these plans.)

3. Tax Qualified Plans

Tax qualified plans are the heavy-duty retirement plans. These plans include 401(k) plans and Keogh plans. They are more complicated than IRAs, and, if you have employees, you'll want to hire a pension consultant to help you choose a tax qualified plan. (See Section E, below, for more information on these plans.)

4. Nonqualified Plans

Nonqualified pension plans do not meet the requirements for tax qualification under the tax code. These plans do not receive the beneficial tax treatment accorded to qualified plans. In return for giving up these tax benefits, you are not subject to the many restrictions on qualified plans—for example, rules that prohibit you from discriminating against your employees when you fund the plan. Nonqualified plans are designed for people who make a lot of money. You'll need to consult a pension expert to set up a nonqualified plan.

C. Individual Retirement Accounts—IRAs

The simplest type of tax-deferred retirement account is the individual retirement account, or IRA. An IRA is a retirement account established by an individual, not a business. There are two different types of IRAs: traditional IRAs and Roth IRAs.

You can have an IRA whether you're a business owner or an employee in someone else's practice. Moreover, you can establish an IRA for yourself as an individual and also set up one or more of the other types of retirement plans discussed in Sections D and E, below, which are just for businesses. However, there are limitations on your deductions for, or contributions to, IRAs if you have other retirement plans and your income exceeds certain limits.

An IRA is a trust or custodial account set up for the benefit of an individual or his or her beneficiaries. The trustee or custodian administers the account. The trustee can be a bank, mutual fund, brokerage firm, or other financial institution (such as an insurance company).

IRAs are extremely easy to set up and administer. You need a written IRA agreement but don't need to file any tax forms with the IRS. The financial institution you use to set up your account will usually ask you to complete IRS Form 5305, *Individual Retirement Trust Account*, which serves as an IRA agreement and meets all of the IRS requirements. Keep the form in your records—you don't file it with the IRS.

Most financial institutions offer an array of IRA accounts that provide for different types of investments. You can invest your IRA money in just about anything: stocks, bonds, mutual funds, Treasury bills and notes, and bank certificates of deposit. However, you can't invest in collectibles such as art, antiques, stamps, or other personal property.

You can establish as many IRA accounts as you want, but there is a maximum combined amount of money you can contribute to all of your IRA accounts each year. This amount goes up every year through 2008 as shown in the chart below. After 2008, the limit will be adjusted each year for inflation in $500 increments.

There are different limits for workers who are at least 50 years old. Anyone at least 50 years old at the end of the year can make increased annual contributions of $500 per year in 2005, and $1,000 per year thereafter. This rule is intended to allow older people to catch up with younger folks, who will have more years to make contributions at the higher levels.

Annual IRA Contribution Limits		
Tax Year	**Under Age 50**	**Aged 50 or Over**
2005	$4,000	$4,500
2006-2007	$4,000	$5,000
2008 and later	$5,000	$6,000

If you are married, you can double the contribution limits. For example, a married couple in 2005 can contribute up to $4,000 per spouse into their IRAs, or a total of $8,000. This is true even if one spouse isn't working. To take advantage of doubling, you must file a joint tax return, and the working spouse must earn at least as much as the combined IRA contribution.

1. Traditional IRAs

Traditional IRAs have been around since 1974. The principal feature of these IRAs is that you receive an income tax deduction for the amount you contribute each year to your account. Once you've made a contribution, your earnings accumulate in the account tax-free until you withdraw them.

Combining Traditional IRAs With Other Plans

You can have a traditional IRA and other retirement plans. But, if you or your spouse are covered by one of the other plans covered in this chapter, your ability to deduct your contributions is limited. Your deduction starts to phase out when your modified adjusted gross income exceeds certain levels. You will get no deduction at all if your modified adjusted gross income exceeds $50,000 if you're single, or $85,000 if you're married and file a joint return (in 2007 and later, the amount for married people filing jointly will be increased to $100,000). Your modified adjusted income is your adjusted gross income before it is reduced by your IRA contribution and certain other more unusual items.

Withdrawals

There are time restrictions on when you can (and when you must) withdraw money from your IRA. You are not supposed to withdraw any money from your IRA until you reach age 59½, unless you die or become disabled. And you must begin to withdraw your money by April 1 of the year after the year you turn 70. Once you start withdrawing money from your IRA, the amount you withdraw will be included in your regular income for income tax purposes.

As a general rule, if you make early withdrawals, you must pay regular income tax on the amount you take out, plus a 10% federal tax penalty. There are some exceptions to this early withdrawal penalty (for example, if you withdraw money to purchase a first home or pay educational expenses, the penalty doesn't apply—subject to dollar limits). To learn about these and other exceptions in detail, see *IRAs, 401(k)s, & Other Retirement Plans: Taking Your Money Out*, by Twila Slesnick and John Suttle (Nolo).

2. Roth IRAs

Like traditional IRAs, Roth IRAs are tax-deferred and allow your retirement savings to grow without any tax burden. Unlike traditional IRAs, however, your contributions to Roth IRAs are not tax deductible. Instead, you get to withdraw your money from the account tax-free when you retire.

You can combine a Roth IRA with other retirement plans. But, once your income reaches a certain level you won't be allowed to make any more contributions. If you are single and your modified adjusted gross income reaches $95,000, your ability to contribute to your Roth IRA will begin to phase out. Once your income reaches $110,000, you will no longer be able to make contributions. If you are married and filing a joint return with your spouse, your ability to contribute to your account will start to phase out when your modified adjusted gross income reaches $150,000, and you will be prohibited from making any contributions at all when your income reaches $160,000.

Roth IRAs have the same restrictions on early withdrawals as traditional IRAs. You are not, however, required to make withdrawals when you reach age 70½. Because Roth IRA withdrawals are tax-free, the government doesn't care if you leave your money in your account indefinitely. However, your money will be tax-free on withdrawal only if you leave it in your Roth IRA for at least five years.

If the Roth IRA sounds attractive to you, and you already have a traditional IRA, you may convert it to a Roth IRA. This is called a "rollover."

D. IRAs for Businesses

The individual IRAs described above are established by individuals on their own behalf and funded from their personal funds. You don't have to be a business owner to have one. However, when you are a business owner, you have the option of establishing a business IRA—also called employer IRAs. These IRAs are established by your business on behalf of its employees, not by you personally. For these purposes, business owners are considered to be employees.

You can establish an employer IRA as long as you are in business and earn a profit. Although these IRAs are called employer IRAs, you don't have to have employees working for you to have one. And it doesn't matter how your practice is organized: You can be a sole proprietor, partner in a partnership or LLP, member of a limited liability company, or owner of a C or S corporation.

The great advantage of employer IRAs is that you can contribute more than you can with traditional IRAs and Roth IRAs, both of which have much lower annual contribution limits. And as long as you meet the requirements for establishing an employer IRA, you can have this type of IRA in addition to one or more individual IRAs. However, if your income exceeds certain limits, your individual IRA contributions won't be deductible.

Like regular IRAs, employer IRAs are very easy to set up and administer. You complete a simple application and the bank or other financial institution that administers the account handles most of the paperwork. Nothing has to be filed with the IRS to establish the IRA.

There are two kinds of employer IRAs to choose from: SEP-IRAs and SIMPLE IRAs.

1. SEP-IRAs

A SEP-IRA is a simplified employee pension. They are specifically designed for the self-employed. Any person who receives self-employment income from providing a service can establish a SEP-IRA. SEP-IRAs are very popular with professionals because they are easy to set up and run and have large contribution limits.

A SEP-IRA is very similar to an IRA—each participant has his or her own SEP-IRA account that he owns and controls. However, contributions to the account are made by your business, not by you personally.

The interest on your SEP-IRA investments accrues tax-free until you withdraw the money. Withdrawals from SEP-IRAs are subject to the same rules that apply to traditional IRAs. This means that if you withdraw your money from your SEP-IRA before you reach age 59½, you'll have to pay a 10% tax penalty plus regular income taxes on your withdrawal, unless an exception applies. And you must begin to withdraw your money by April 1 of the year after the year you turn 70.

Contribution Limits

Far more money can be contributed each year to a SEP-IRA than to an individual IRA. Instead of being limited to a $4,000 to $5,000 annual contribution (see the chart in Section C, above), you can contribute as much as $44,000 each year as of 2006 (this amount is adjusted for inflation annually). If you are a sole proprietor, or your practice is organized as a partnership, LLP, or LLC, you may contribute 20% of your net profit from self-employment up to the annual limit ($44,000 in 2006). If your practice is incorporated and you work as its employee, you may invest up to 25% of your compensation every year, up to the annual limit. This limit also applies to employees who work for you.

You don't have to make contributions every year, and your contributions can vary from year to year. As with IRAs, you can invest your money in almost anything (stocks, bonds, notes, mutual funds).

Tax Deductions

Because employer SEP-IRAs are funded by a business for its employees (including the business owners), the business gets to deduct the contributions from its income taxes, not the employees. This is a distinction without a difference if you're a sole proprietor because you and your business are one and the same. But if your practice is organized as a corporation, LLC, partnership, or LLP, the entity will deduct the contributions it makes on its tax return; you won't directly deduct them on your personal return. Of course, if you have a pass-through entity—anything other than a C corporation—the deduction will reduce the taxable profits that pass through the entity to your personal return.

Employees Must Be Included

If you have employees, establishing a SEP-IRA can be expensive because you must establish a SEP-IRA account for all employees who are at least 21 years old and have been employed by you for three of the last five years. Any year you decide to make a contribution to your own SEP-IRA, you must also contribute to your employees' SEP-IRAs. However, you can elect to use a contribution formula that permits you to make higher contributions for highly compensated employees than for the rank-and-file. Consult with a professional before setting up a SEP-IRA if you have employees.

2.   SIMPLE IRAs

Self-employed people and companies with fewer than 100 employees can set up SIMPLE IRAs. If you establish a SIMPLE IRA, you are not allowed to have any other retirement plans for your practice (although you may still have an individual IRA).

SIMPLE IRAs may be established only by an employer on behalf of its employees. If you are a sole proprietor, you are deemed to employ yourself for these purposes and may establish a SIMPLE IRA in your own name as the employer. If you are a partner in a partnership, LLC member, or owner of an incorporated practice, you are also an employee for SIMPLE IRA purposes, but the SIMPLE IRA must be established by your practice, not you personally.

The money in a SIMPLE IRA can be invested like any other IRA. Withdrawals from SIMPLE IRAs are subject to the same rules as traditional IRAs with one big exception: Early withdrawals from SIMPLE IRAs are subject to a 25% tax penalty if the withdrawal is made within two years after the date you first contributed to your account. Other early withdrawals are subject to a 10% penalty, the same as traditional IRAs, unless an exception applies.

Contribution Limits

You don't have to contribute to your SIMPLE IRA every year, or contribute the same amount every year. Contributions to SIMPLE IRAs are divided into two parts:

- a "salary reduction contribution" which is based on your net business income if you are a business owner, and on your employee salary if you are an employee of an incorporated practice, and
- an "employer contribution."

The salary reduction contribution can be up to $10,000 each year ($12,500 if you're over 50), so long as this amount is not more than 100% of your compensation. The employer contribution can match the salary reduction contribution so long as it doesn't exceed 3% of your net business income (or 3% of salary for employees).

Tax Treatment of Contributions

Sole proprietors, and owners of entities taxed as partnerships (general partnerships, LLPs, and most LLCs) may deduct their contributions to their own SIMPLE IRAs on their personal Form 1040. If you are a partner, contributions on your behalf are shown on the Schedule K-1 (Form 1065) you get from the partnership.

You can also deduct contributions you make on behalf of your employees to their own SIMPLE IRAs and the employees need not pay income tax on them.

SIMPLE IRA contributions are not subject to federal income tax with-holding. However, salary reduction contributions made by employees are subject to Social Security, Medicare, and federal unemployment (FUTA) taxes.

Nondiscrimination Rules

As with SEP-IRAs, if you have employees, you'll have to include them in your SIMPLE IRA. SIMPLE IRAs must be offered to all employees who have earned income of at least $5,000 in any two years prior to the current year and are reasonably expected to earn at least $5,000 in the current year. As an employer, you'll have to match the contributions your participating employees elect to make to their SIMPLE IRAs each year. Alternatively, you can elect to make an employer contribution each year to all participating employees regardless of whether they make their own contributions to their SIMPLE IRAs. The contribution must equal 2% of the employee's compensation, but can't be more than $4,200 (in 2005).

E. Qualified Retirement Plans

Qualified retirement plans are what we normally think of as traditional pension plans. They are not IRAs. To be "qualified," a retirement plan must satisfy a number of complex rules. Among other things, these rules limit how much can be contributed each year and bar a company's owners or highly compensated employees from denying coverage to, or otherwise discriminating against, ordinary "rank-and-file" employees.

In return for meeting these requirements, a qualified plan's participants receive some great tax benefits:

- The amount the employer contributes to the plan is tax deductible (within certain limits) in the year contributions are made.
- The earnings on the investment of plan assets are tax-exempt.
- Participants do not have to pay income tax on the employer's contribution to the plan on their behalf or on the earnings to those contributions until benefits are received.
- Income taxes on certain distributions may be deferred by rolling over the distribution into an IRA or to another qualified plan.
- Installment or annuity payments provided by qualified plans are taxed only when the participant receives them.

As is the case with IRAs, the money from a qualified plan is not supposed to be distributed to plan participants until they reach age 59½. Early distributions are subject to a 10% tax penalty, but there are exceptions like those provided for IRAs.

Regular qualified plans are designed to be used by businesses for their employees. The employer contributes to the plan on its employees' behalf (but employees make their own contributions to 401(k) plans). If your practice is incorporated, you will qualify as an employee for these purposes and be covered by a plan you establish for your employees. If you want to do this, see a pension professional to help you set up your plan.

If you are a sole proprietor, or your practice is an LLC, LLP, or partnership, you can't participate in a regular qualified plan because you are not an employee. (However, you may set one up for your employees.) Instead of a regular qualified plan you must use a Keogh plan or solo 401(k) plan. These are qualified plans designed for self-employed people.

Whether they are used by employees or business owners, qualified retirement plans are broadly classified into two categories based on the nature of the benefits provided: defined benefit pension plans and defined contribution plans.

1.   Defined Benefit Plans

With a defined benefit plan, you decide how much you want to receive from the plan each year when you retire—for example, you can decide you want to receive an amount equal to 100% of your final year's salary. You then hire an actuary to determine how much you need to contribute each year to obtain this defined benefit amount when you retire. Obviously, the older you are and the more you want to have upon retirement, the larger your contribution must be. The annual contribution limits for such a plan are much higher than for any other retirement plan. In fact, you may contribute 100% of the average compensation you received for your highest three consecutive calendar years. But, you may not contribute more than $175,000 (for 2006).

Defined benefit plans can be very attractive for high income professionals, particularly those who are older and don't have much time left to fund their retirements. You must hire a pension professional to help you set up such a plan and administer it.

2.   Defined Contribution Plans

By far the most popular pension plans are defined contributions plans. These are the opposite of defined benefit plans. Instead of deciding how much you want to receive in benefits when you retire and then contributing the amount necessary to attain that goal, you simply decide how much you want to contribute each year. However much money that turns out to be when you retire is how much you'll have.

Examples of defined contribution plans include:

- profit-sharing plans where contributions are based on the business's profits and don't have to be made every year
- 401(k) plans, a type of profit-sharing plan in which a business's employees make plan contributions from their salaries and the business makes a matching contribution, and
- money purchase plans in which the annual contributions are fixed, mandatory, and not based on your business's profits.

You can have as many defined contribution plans as you want, but annual contributions to all of them together cannot exceed the lesser of:

- 100% of the participant's annual compensation, or
- $44,000 in 2006 (this amount is adjusted each year for inflation).

For participants over 50, an additional $5,000 can be added each year.

F.   Keogh Plans

Keogh plans—named after the Congressman who sponsored the legislation that created them—are qualified plans designed for business owners who are sole proprietors, partners in partnerships, or LLC members. A Keogh plan may be a defined benefit plan (see Section E1, above), or a defined contribution plan. These plans can be used separately or in tandem with one other.

1.   Setting Up a Keogh Plan

As with individual IRAs and employer IRAs, you can set up a Keogh plan at most banks, brokerage houses, mutual funds, and other financial institutions, as well as trade or professional organizations. You can also choose among a huge array of investments for your money.

If you don't have employees you can set up a Keogh plan yourself. If you have employees, consult a pension professional.

To set up your plan, you must adopt a written Keogh plan and set up a trust or custodial account with your plan provider to invest your funds. Your plan provider will ordinarily have an IRS-approved master or prototype Keogh plan for you to sign. You can also have a special plan drawn up for you, but this is expensive and unnecessary for most small business owners.

2.   Profit-Sharing Plans

If your Keogh is a profit-sharing plan, you can contribute up to 20% of your net self-employment income to a profit-sharing Keogh plan, up to a maximum of $44,000 per year in 2006. You can contribute any amount up to the limit each year, or not contribute at all.

3.   Money Purchase Plans

In a money purchase plan, you contribute a fixed percentage of your net self-employment earnings every year. You decide how much to contribute each year. Make sure you will be able to afford the contributions each year because you can't skip them, even if your business earns no profit for the year. You can contribute the same amount as you can for profit-sharing plans.

4.   Withdrawing Your Money

You may begin to withdraw your money from your Keogh plan after you reach age 59½. If you have a profit-sharing plan, early withdrawals are permitted without penalty in cases of financial hardship, if you become disabled, or if you have to pay health expenses in excess of 7.5% of your adjusted gross income. If you have a money purchase plan, early withdrawals are permitted if you become disabled, leave your business after you turn 55, or make child support or alimony payments from the plan under a court order. Otherwise, early withdrawals from profit-sharing and money purchase Keogh plans are subject to a 10% penalty.

G. Solo 401(k) Plans

Until recently, self-employed people and businesses without employees rarely used 401(k) plans because they offered no benefit over other profit-sharing plans, which are much easier to set up and run. However, things have changed. Now, any business owner who has no employees (other than a spouse) can establish a solo self-employed 401(k) plan (also called a one-person or individual 401(k)). Solo 401(k) plans are designed specifically for business owners without employees. They can also be used by professionals with one-person corporations.

Like all 401(k)s, solo 401(k) contributions consist of two separate elements:

- a profit sharing contribution of up to 20% of your net profit from self-employment , plus
- a salary deferral contribution of up to $15,000 (in 2006).

The maximum total contribution per year is $44,000 in 2006 (the same maximum amount as for profit-sharing and money purchase plans discussed in Section F, above). Business owners over 50 may make additional catch-up elective deferral contributions of up to $5,000 per year that are not counted towards the $44,000 limit.

If your practice is incorporated, you may contribute 25% of your employee compensation plus the elective deferral.

As with other plans, you must pay a 10% penalty tax on withdrawals you make before age 59½, but you may make penalty-free early withdrawals for reasons of personal hardship (defined as an "immediate financial need" that can't be met any other way). However, if you need money, you can borrow up to $50,000 from your solo 401(k) plan, as long as you repay the loan within five years. In contrast, you cannot borrow any money from a traditional IRA, Roth IRA, SEP-IRA, or SIMPLE IRA.

You can set up a solo 401(k) plan at most banks, brokerage houses, mutual funds, and other financial institutions and invest the money in a variety of ways. You must adopt a written plan and set up a trust or custodial account with your plan provider to invest your funds. Financial institutions that offer solo 401(k) plans have preapproved ready-made plans that you can use.

H. Roth 401(k) Plans

In 2006, a brand new type of 401(k) plan became available: the Roth 401(k). Roth 401(k)s are much the same as regular 401(k)s with one big difference: The money contributed to the plan is not tax deductible. In return, withdrawals made upon retirement are tax-free.

This is the same type of tax treatment you get with a Roth IRA. But, one big advantage the Roth 401(k) has over the Roth IRA is that anyone can have one, no matter how high his or her income. In contrast, you can't contribute to a Roth IRA if your income exceeds $110,000 if you're single, or $160,000 if you're married and file a joint tax return.

Only the elective deferral portion of your annual 401(k) contribution receives the Roth treatment. This limits your contribution to $15,000 per year, or $20,000 if you're over 50.

■

Chapter 13

Inventory

Many professionals must carry inventories even though their primary business is providing professional services. This chapter provides an overview of how to determine which of your purchases, if any, constitute inventory, how to value your inventory, and how to calculate your deduction for inventory costs.

 If you only provide services to clients or customers, you don't need to worry about inventories. You can skip ahead to the next chapter.

A. What Is Inventory?

Inventory is made up of merchandise—the goods and products that a business keeps on hand to sell to customers in the ordinary course of business. It includes almost any tangible personal property that a business offers for sale. It does not include real estate or intangible personal property, like patents or copyrights. It makes no difference whether a business manufactures the goods itself or buys finished goods to resell to customers. Merchandise includes not only finished products, but also unfinished work in progress, as well as the raw materials and supplies that will become part of the finished merchandise. (IRS Reg. 1.471-1.)

> **EXAMPLE:** Gloria, a sole proprietor optometrist, provides her patients with eye exams. However, in addition to providing this service, she sells eyeglasses and contact lenses to her patients. The eyeglasses and lenses are inventory. This is so whether she purchases finished lenses from a commercial supplier or grinds her own lenses. (G.C.M. 37699, 1978 IRS GCM LEXIS 378.)

Separately billing patients or clients for an item tends to show it is merchandise. For example, Gloria, like most optometrists, gives her patients separate bills for eyeglasses and for her optometric services. However, this factor is not determinative in and of itself.

Long-term assets that you purchase to use in your business—for example, equipment, office furniture, and vehicles—are not a part of your inventory. These items are deductible capital expenses that you may depreciate over several years or, in many cases, deduct in a single year under Section 179. (See Chapter 9 for more on deducting long-term assets.)

> **EXAMPLE:** Gloria, from the example above, buys a new computer to help keep track of her patient records. The computer is not part of Gloria's inventory because she bought it to use in her practice, not to resell to patients. Because it will last for more than one year, it's a long-term asset, which she must either depreciate or expense under Section 179.

Only things to which you hold title—that is, things you own—constitute merchandise that must be inventoried. This includes items you haven't yet received or paid for, as long as you own them. For example, an item you buy with a credit card counts as inventory, even if you haven't paid the bill yet. However, if you buy merchandise that is sent C.O.D., you acquire ownership only after the goods are delivered and paid for.

1.   Supplies Are Not Inventory

Supplies are materials and property consumed or used up during the production of merchandise or provision of services. Good examples are rubber gloves and disposable syringes used by doctors and nurses to provide medical services. These items do not physically become part of merchandise a business sells so they are not included in inventory.

Unless they are incidental supplies, the cost of the supplies must be deducted *in the year in which they are used or consumed*, which is not necessarily the year when you purchase them. This means that you must keep track of how much material you use each year.

The same item can constitute supplies for one business and inventory for another. It all depends on whether the item is furnished to the patient or client or consumed in performing a service. For example, the paper and ink used to prepare blueprints are inventory in the hands of a paper and ink manufacturer, but supplies in the hands of an architect.

With professionals, it is not always as clear when a product is merchandise and when it should be classified as supplies. For example, are drugs a doctor provides to a patient merchandise or supplies consumed while performing medical services? In one case, the tax court held that drugs were supplies, not merchandise, because they were an "indispensable and inseparable part" of the rendering of medical services to patients. The case involved a medical corporation treating cancer patients with chemotherapy drugs. The drugs were expensive and billed separately to Medicare. In reaching its conclusion, the court noted that the drugs could be obtained only by cancer patients undergoing treatment, and that the doctors kept only a small amount on hand and did not maintain a formal written record of the supply. (*Osteopathic Medical Oncology and Hematology, PC v. Comm'r,* 113 T.C. 26.)

On the other hand, the IRS ruled that crowns, bridges, and dentures used by a dentist were merchandise, even though they were sold only to patients who obtained dental services from the dentist. (LTR 9848001.) Similarly, the IRS said that artificial limbs and orthopedic braces were merchandise, not supplies used to perform a service, even though the company that manufactured and sold them performed considerable services fitting them to handicapped patients and instructing them in their use. (Rev. Rul. 73-485.)

The standards are far from clear in this area. If you are unsure whether you sell merchandise to your patients or clients, talk to a tax professional for advice on dealing with inventory.

2. Incidental Supplies

There is an important exception to the rule that the cost of materials and supplies may be deducted only as they are used or consumed. You may deduct the entire cost of supplies that are *incidental* to your business in the year when you purchase them. Supplies are incidental if:

- they are of minor or secondary importance to your business (see Section C, below). If you treat the cost of supplies on hand as an asset for financial reporting purposes they are not incidental (you do *not* keep a record of when you use the supplies)
- you do not take a physical inventory of the supplies at the beginning and end of the tax year, and

- deducting the cost of supplies in the year you purchase them does not distort your taxable income (IRS Reg § 1.162-3; Private Letter Ruling 9209007).

(See IRS Private Letter Rulings 8630003 and 9209007 and IRS Reg. § 1.162-3.)

> **EXAMPLE:** Last year, Gloria purchased $100 worth of lens cleaning fluid she used to clean her patients' eyeglasses. She did not keep a record of how much cleaning fluid she used during the year or take a physical inventory of how much she had on hand at year's end. The cleaning fluid constitutes incidental supplies. Gloria may deduct the entire $100 in that year, regardless of how much of the fluid she actually used that year.

B. Do You Have to Carry an Inventory?

A business is said to maintain or carry an inventory when it must include unsold inventory items as assets on its books, to be deducted only when the items are sold or become worthless. If you are required to carry an inventory, you may currently deduct only the value of the inventory you sell during the year, not your entire inventory.

> **EXAMPLE:** Gloria purchased $20,000 worth of eyeglasses to sell to her patients last year. However, she sold only $10,000 worth of them during the year. If Gloria is required to carry an inventory, she'll be able to deduct only the cost of the eyeglasses she sold. The $10,000 worth of unsold eyeglasses is inventory, which she must include as a business asset on her books. She will have to wait until she sells the glasses (or they become worthless) to deduct their cost.

A business—even one that provides professional services—is required to carry an inventory if the production or sale of merchandise is an "income producing factor" for the business—that is, it accounts for a substantial portion of the business's revenues. When do sales become substantial enough to be considered an "income producing factor"?

There's no exact figure, but many tax experts believe that a business that derives 8% or less of its total gross revenue from the sale or production of merchandise need not maintain an inventory. A business that makes at least 15% of its money from selling or producing merchandise has to maintain an inventory, and a business that earns 9% to 14% of its money from merchandise is in a gray area.

Thus, for example, the IRS held that a veterinarian had to maintain inventories because the sale of drugs, pet foods, and livestock antibiotic food additives constituted approximately 50% of his gross receipts each year. (IRS Private Letter Ruling 9218008.) However, even though a dentist's crowns, bridges, and dentures were merchandise, the IRS ruled he didn't have to carry an inventory because he didn't earn enough money from those items. (IRS Private Letter Ruling 9848001.)

C. Deducting Inventory Costs

If you are required to carry an inventory, you may deduct only the cost of the goods you sold during the year (or the cost of goods that became worthless). To do this, you must calculate the cost (to you) of the merchandise you sold during the year. You then deduct this amount from your gross income.

1. Computing the Cost of Goods Sold

To figure out the cost of goods sold, start with the cost of any inventory on hand at the beginning of your tax year. Add the cost of inventory that you purchased or manufactured during the year. Subtract the cost of any merchandise you withdrew for personal use. The sum of all this is the cost of all goods available for sale during the tax year. Subtract from this amount the value of your inventory at the end of your tax year. (See Section 2, below, for information on how to calculate this value.) The cost of all goods sold during the year (and therefore, the amount you can deduct for inventory expenses on your taxes) is the remainder. This can be stated by the following equation:

	Inventory at beginning of year
Plus:	Purchases or additions during the year
Minus:	Goods withdrawn from sale for personal use
Equals:	Cost of goods available for sale
Minus:	Inventory at end of year
Equals:	Cost of goods sold

EXAMPLE: Gloria, the optometrist from the above examples, had $50,000 in inventory at the beginning of the year and purchased another $20,000 of inventory during the year. She removed $500 of inventory for her own personal use. The cost of the inventory she had left at the end of the year is $40,500. She would calculate her cost of goods sold as follows:

Inventory at beginning of year	$ 50,000
Purchases or additions during the year	+ 20,000
Goods withdrawn from sale for personal use	– 500
Cost of goods available for sale	= 69,500
Inventory at end of year	– 40,500
Cost of goods sold	= $ 29,000

Note that all of these costs are based on what Gloria paid for her inventory, not what she sold it for (which was substantially greater).

2.   Determining the Value of Inventory

To use the equation in Section 1, above, you must be able to calculate the value of the inventory you have left at the end of the year. There is no single way to do this—standard methods for tracking inventory vary according to the type and size of business involved. As long as your inventory methods are consistent from year to year, the IRS doesn't care which method you use.

Need more information on how to value your inventory? This section provides only a small overview of a large subject. For more information on valuing inventory, refer to:

- *The Accounting Game,* by Darrell Mullis and Judith Orloff (Sourcebooks, Inc.)
- *Small Time Operator,* by Bernard B. Kamoroff (Bell Springs Publishing)
- IRS Publication 334, *Tax Guide for Small Businesses* (Chapter 7), and
- IRS Publication 538, *Accounting Periods and Methods.*

Taking Physical Inventory

You need to know how much inventory you have at the beginning and end of each tax year to figure your cost of goods sold. If, like most businesses, you use the calendar year as your tax year, this means that you need to figure out your inventory each December 31. Unless you hold a New Year's Eve sale, your inventory on January 1 will usually be the same as the prior year's ending inventory—your inventory on December 31. Any differences must be explained in a schedule attached to your tax return.

Until recently, the IRS required all businesses that sold or manufactured goods to make a physical inventory of the merchandise they owned—that is, to actually count it. This process, often called "taking inventory," is usually done at the end of the year, although it doesn't have to be. Nor is it necessary to count every single item in stock. Businesses can make a physical inventory of a portion of their total merchandise, then extrapolate their total inventory from the sample.

The IRS no longer requires small businesses to take physical inventories. (Small businesses are those that earn less than $1 million in gross receipts per year, and service businesses that earn up to $10 million per year.) But even small businesses must keep track of how much inventory they buy and sell to determine their cost of goods sold for the year. With modern inventory software, it is possible for a business to keep a continuous record of the goods on hand during the year. Keep copies of your invoices and receipts to prove to the IRS that you correctly accounted for your inventory, in case you are audited.

Identifying Inventory Items Sold During the Year

The second step in figuring out your cost of goods sold is to identify which inventory items were sold during the year. There are several ways to do this. You can specifically track each item that is sold during the year. This is generally done only by businesses that sell a relatively small number of high-cost items each year, such as automobile dealers or jewelers.

If you don't want to identify specific items by their invoices, you must make an assumption about which items were sold during the year and which items remain in stock. Small businesses ordinarily use the first-in, first-out (FIFO) method. The FIFO method assumes that the first items you purchased or produced are the first items that you sold, consumed, or otherwise disposed of.

Another method of identifying inventory makes the opposite assumption. Under the last-in, first-out (LIFO) method, you assume that the last items purchased or produced were the first to sell. This method is not favored by the IRS. You may use it only if you use the accrual method of accounting (see Chapter 20) and take physical inventory. To use the LIFO method, you must file IRS Form 970, *Application to Use LIFO Inventory Method*, and follow some very complex tax rules.

Valuing Your Inventory

You must also determine the value of the inventory you sold during the year. The value of your inventory is a major factor in figuring out your taxable income, so the method that you use is very important. The two most common methods are the cost method and the lower of cost or market method. A new business that doesn't use LIFO to determine which goods were sold (see above) may choose either method to value its inventory. You must use the same method to value your entire inventory, and you cannot change the method from year to year without first obtaining IRS approval.

Cost Method

As the name indicates, when you use the cost method, your inventory cost is the amount that you paid for the merchandise. Note that this is not the same as what you sold it for, which will (hopefully!) be higher.

Using the cost method is relatively easy when you purchase goods to resell. To calculate the value of each item, start with the invoice price. Add the cost of transportation, shipping, and other money you had to spend to acquire the items. Subtract any discounts you received.

Things get much more complicated if you manufacture goods to sell. In this situation, you must include all direct and indirect costs associated with the goods. This includes:

- the cost of products or raw materials, including the cost of having them shipped to you
- the cost of storing the products you sell, and
- direct labor costs (including contributions to pension or annuity plans) for workers who produce the products; this does not include your own salary unless you are a corporate employee.

In addition, larger businesses (those with more than $10 million in gross receipts) must include an amount for depreciation on machinery used to produce the products and factory overhead expenses.

Lower of Cost or Market Method

What if the retail value of your inventory goes down during the year? This could happen, for example, if your inventory becomes obsolete or falls out of fashion. In this event, you may use the lower of cost or market method to value your inventory. Under this method, you compare the market (retail) value of each item on hand on the inventory date with its cost, and use the lower value as its inventory value. By using the lower of these two numbers, your inventory will be worth less and your deductible expenses will be greater, thereby reducing your taxable income.

> **EXAMPLE:** This year Gloria, the optometrist, purchased several Armani eyeglass frames for $2,000. Due to a change in fashion, Gloria finds they are no longer popular with customers and she can sell the frames for only $1,000. Using the lower of cost or market method, she may value the frames at $1,000.

However, you can't simply make up an inventory item's market value. You must establish the market value of your inventory through objective evidence, such as actual sales price for similar items.

Consider donating excess inventory to charity. One way to get rid of inventory you can't sell is to donate it to charity. You'll benefit a worthwhile charity and, by removing the items from your shelves, generate a tax deduction as well.

D. IRS Reporting

You must report the cost of goods sold on your tax return. If you're a sole proprietor, the amount goes directly on your Schedule C. Part III of Schedule C tracks the cost of goods equation provided in Section C, above. LLCs and partnerships report their cost of goods sold on Schedule A of IRS Form 1065, *U.S. Partnership Return of Income.* S corporations report cost of goods sold on Schedule A of Form 1120, *U.S. Income Tax Return for an S Corporation.* C corporations report this information on Schedule A of Form 1020, *U.S. Corporation Income Tax Return.*

Technically speaking, the cost of goods sold is not a business expense. Rather, it is subtracted from a business's gross income to determine its gross profit for the year. Business expenses are then subtracted from the gross profit to determine the business's taxable net profit, as shown by the following formula:

	Gross income
Minus:	Cost of goods sold
Equals:	Gross profit
Minus:	Deductible business expenses
Equals:	**Net profit**

As a practical matter, this is a distinction without a difference—both the cost of goods sold and business expenses are subtracted from your business income to calculate your taxable profit. However, you cannot deduct the cost of goods sold to determine your gross profit and then deduct it again as a business expense—this would result in a double deduction.

EXAMPLE: Gloria subtracts her $29,000 cost of goods sold from her gross income (all the money she earned from her optometry practice) to determine her gross profit. She earned $250,000 in total income for the year and had $100,000 in business expenses, including rent and employee salaries. She calculates her net profit as follows:

Gross income		$ 250,000
Cost of goods sold	–	29,000
Gross profit	=	221,000
Business expenses	–	100,000
Net profit	=	$ 121,000

Gloria has to pay tax only on her $121,000 in net profit.

Obviously, the larger the cost of goods sold, the smaller your taxable income will be and the less tax you'll have to pay.

■

Chapter 14

More Deductions

Thomas chapter looks at some of the most common deductible business expenses that professionals incur. You can deduct these costs as business operating expenses as long as they are ordinary, necessary, and reasonable in amount and meet the additional requirements discussed below.

A. Advertising

Almost any type of business-related advertising is a currently deductible business operating expense. You can deduct advertising undertaken to help obtain new clients, establish goodwill for your practice, or just to get your practice known. Advertising includes expenses for:

- business cards
- brochures
- client newsletters
- advertisements in the local Yellow Pages
- newspaper and magazine advertisements
- professional publication advertisements
- radio and television advertisements
- advertisements on the Internet
- fees you pay to advertising and public relations agencies
- billboards, and
- signs.

However, advertising to influence government legislation is never deductible. And help-wanted ads you place to recruit workers are not advertising costs, but you can deduct them as ordinary and necessary business operating expenses.

1. Goodwill Advertising

If it relates to business you reasonably expect to gain in the future, you can usually deduct the cost of institutional or "goodwill" advertising meant to keep your name before the public. Examples of goodwill advertising include:

- advertisements that encourage people to contribute to charities, such as the Red Cross or similar causes

- sponsoring a little league baseball team, bowling team, or golf tournament
- giving away product samples, and
- holding contests and giving away prizes.

However, you can't deduct time and labor that you give away as an advertising expense, even though doing so promotes goodwill. You must actually spend money to have an advertising expense. For example, a lawyer who does pro bono work for indigent clients to advertise his law practice may not deduct the cost of his services as an advertising expense.

2.   Giveaway Items

Giveaway items that you use to publicize your practice (such as pens, coffee cups, T-shirts, refrigerator magnets, calendars, tote bags, and key chains) are deductible. However, you are not allowed to deduct more than $25 in business gifts to any one person each year. (See Section I, below.) This limitation applies to advertising giveaway items unless they:

- cost $4 or less
- have your name clearly and permanently imprinted on them, and
- are one of a number of identical items you distribute widely.

EXAMPLE 1: David, a dentist, orders 1,000 toothbrushes with his name and office address printed on them and gives them to his patients. Each toothbrush costs $1. The toothbrushes do not count toward the $25 gift limit. David may deduct the entire $1,000 expense for the toothbrushes.

EXAMPLE 2: The Abel and Baker law firm buys a $200 fountain pen and gives it to its most valuable client as a Christmas gift. The pen is a business gift to an individual, so Abel and Baker can deduct only $25 of the cost.

Signs, display racks, and other promotional materials that you give away to other businesses to use on their premises do not count as gifts.

3. Business Websites

The cost of a business website you use to publicize your services is a deductible business expense. You can deduct the cost of designing the site and maintaining it—for example, the monthly charge you pay to an Internet access provider.

4. Permanent Signs

Signs that have a useful life of less than one year—for example, paper or cardboard signs—are currently deductible as business operating expenses. However, a permanent metal or plastic sign that has a useful life of more than one year is a long-term business asset, which you cannot currently deduct as a business operating expense. Instead, you must either depreciate the cost over several years or deduct it in one year under Section 179. (See Chapter 9 for more on deducting long-term assets.)

B. Business Bad Debts

Business bad debts are debts that arise from your business activities, such as:
- lending money for a business purpose
- selling inventory on credit, or
- guaranteeing business-related loans.

Strict requirements must be met to deduct a business debt.

1. Three Requirements for Deduction

The following three requirements must be satisfied to deduct a business bad debt as a business operating expense:
- You must have a bona fide business debt.
- The debt must be wholly or partly worthless.
- You must have suffered an economic loss from the debt.

Most debts owed to professionals do not satisfy all these requirements, thus they cannot be deducted. If the requirements are satisfied, however, you can currently deduct business bad debts as a business operating expense when they become wholly or partly worthless.

A Bona Fide Business Debt

A bona fide debt exists when someone has a legal obligation to pay you a sum of money—for example, you provide your services on credit. A bona fide debt also exists if there is written evidence to support it—for example, a signed promissory note or other writing stating the amount of the debt, when it is due, and the interest rate (if any). An oral promise to pay may also be legally enforceable, but would be looked upon with suspicion by the IRS.

A business debt is a debt that is created or acquired in the course of your practice or becomes worthless as part of your practice. Your primary motive for incurring the debt must be business-related. Debts taken on for personal or investment purposes are not business debts. (Remember, investing is not a business.)

> **EXAMPLE 1:** Mark, an attorney, lends $10,000 to his brother-in-law, Scott, to invest in his bird diaper invention. Mark will get 25% of the profits if the invention proves successful. This is an investment, not a business debt.

> **EXAMPLE 2:** Mark lends $10,000 to one of his best business clients to help keep the client's business running. Because the main reason for the loan was business-related (to keep his client in business so he will continue as a client), the debt is a business debt.

A Worthless Debt

A debt must be wholly or partly worthless to be deductible. A debt becomes worthless when there is no longer any chance that the amount owed will be paid back to you. You don't have to wait until a debt is due to determine that it is worthless, and you don't have to go to court to try to collect it. You just have to be able to show that you have taken reasonable steps to try to collect the debt or that collection efforts would be futile. For example:

- You've made repeated collection efforts that have proven unsuccessful.
- The debtor has filed for bankruptcy or already been through bankruptcy and had all or part of the debt discharged (forgiven) by the bankruptcy court.
- You've learned that the debtor has gone out of business, gone broke, died, or disappeared.

Keep all documentation that shows a debt is worthless, such as copies of unpaid invoices, collection letters you've sent the debtor, logs of collection calls you've made, bankruptcy notices, and credit reports.

You must deduct the entire amount of a bad debt in the year it becomes totally worthless. If only part of a business debt becomes worthless—for example, you received a partial payment before the debt became uncollectible—you can deduct the unpaid portion that year, or you can wait until the following year to deduct it. For example, if you think you might get paid more the next year, you can wait and see what your final bad debt amount is before you deduct it.

An Economic Loss

You are not automatically entitled to deduct a debt because the obligation has become worthless. To get a deduction, you must have suffered an economic loss. According to the IRS, you have a loss only when you:

- have already reported as business income the amount you were supposed to be paid
- paid out cash, or
- made credit sales of inventory that were not paid for.

This requirement makes it impossible for professionals to deduct most of their business debts.

2. Applying the Rules

Let's apply the rules to the various types of debts professionals are commonly owed.

Nonpaying Clients or Patients

Unfortunately, if, like most professionals, you're a cash-basis taxpayer, you can't claim a bad debt deduction if a client fails to pay you. As a cash-basis taxpayer, you don't report income until you actually receive it. As a result, you don't have an economic loss (in the eyes of the IRS) when a client fails to pay.

> **EXAMPLE:** Bill, a self-employed consultant, works 50 hours for a client and bills the client $2,500. The client never pays. Bill is a cash-basis taxpayer, so he doesn't report the $2,500 as income because he never received it. As far as the IRS is concerned, Bill has no economic loss and cannot deduct the $2,500 the client failed to pay.

The IRS strictly enforces this rule (harsh as it may seem). Absent the rule, the IRS fears that businesses will inflate the value of their services in order to get a larger deduction.

Accrual basis taxpayers, on the other hand, report sales as income in the year the sales are made—not the year payment is received. These taxpayers can take a bad debt deduction if a client fails to pay for services rendered, because they have already reported the money due as income. Therefore, accrual taxpayers have an economic loss when their services are not paid for.

> **EXAMPLE:** Acme Consulting Co. bills a client $10,000 for consulting services it performed during the year. Because Acme is an accrual basis taxpayer, it characterizes the $10,000 as income on its books and includes this amount in its gross income in the year in which it billed for the services, even though Acme hasn't actually received payment. The client later files for bankruptcy, and the debt becomes worthless. Acme may take a business bad debt deduction to wipe out the $10,000 in income it previously charged on its books.

There's no point in trying to switch from cash basis to the accrual method to deduct bad debts. The accrual method doesn't result in lower taxes—the bad debt deduction merely wipes out a sale that was previously reported as income.

Refer to Chapter 20 for a detailed discussion of the cash basis and accrual accounting methods.

Credit Sales of Inventory

Most deductible business bad debts result from credit sales of inventory by professionals to their patients. If you sell merchandise on credit to a patient or customer and are not paid, you get a deduction whether you are an accrual or cash-basis taxpayer. You deduct the cost of the inventory at the end of the year to determine the cost of goods sold for the year. (See Chapter 13 for more about deducting inventory.)

Cash Loans

When you lend out cash, and it is not repaid, you have an economic loss whether you are a cash-basis or accrual taxpayer. Thus, cash loans you make for a business purpose are deductible as bad debts in the year they become worthless.

> **EXAMPLE:** John, a veterinarian, lends $10,000 to Al, a racehorse trainer and one of John's best clients. John makes the loan for a business reason: To help keep Al's struggling business running. Al later goes bankrupt and cannot repay John. John may deduct the $10,000 as a business bad debt.

Business Loan Guarantees

If you guarantee a debt that becomes worthless, it qualifies as a business bad debt only if you:
- made the guarantee in the course of your business
- have a legal duty to pay the debt
- made the guarantee before the debt became worthless, and
- received reasonable consideration (compensation) for the guarantee—you meet this requirement if the guarantee is for a good faith business purpose or according to normal business practices.

> **EXAMPLE:** The Acme Medical Corporation is the owner of a subsidiary corporation called the Reliable Medical Lab, Inc. Reliable needs to borrow money to expand its operation, but has poor

credit. To help it obtain the money, Acme guarantees a $100,000 loan for Reliable. Reliable later filed for bankruptcy and defaulted on the loan. Acme had to make full payment to the bank. It can take a business bad debt deduction because its guarantee was made for a good faith business purpose—its desire to help the lab expand.

Loans or Guarantees to Your Corporation

If your practice is incorporated, you cannot take a bad debt deduction for a loan to your corporation if the loan is actually a contribution to capital—that is, part of your investment in the practice. You must be careful to treat a loan to your corporation in the same way that you treat a loan made to a business in which you have no ownership interest. You should have a signed promissory note from your corporation setting forth:

- the loan amount
- the interest rate—which should be a reasonable rate
- the due date, and
- a repayment schedule.

When you are a principal shareholder in a small corporation, you'll often be asked to personally guarantee corporate loans and other extensions of credit. Creditors do this because they want to be able to go after your personal assets if they can't collect from your corporation. If you end up having to make good on your guarantee and can't get repaid from your corporation, you will have a bad debt. You can deduct this bad debt as a business debt if your dominant motive for making the loan or guarantee was to protect your employment status and ensure your continuing receipt of a salary. If your primary motive was to protect your investment in the corporation, the debt is a personal debt. The IRS is more likely to think you are protecting your investment if you receive little or no salary from the corporation or your salary is not a major source of your overall income.

EXAMPLE: Andre, a chiropractor, is employed by, and the sole shareholder of, ABC Chiropractic, Inc. The corporation pays Andre a $75,000 annual salary, which is his sole source of income. ABC applies for a $50,000 bank loan. Before approving the loan, the bank requires Andre to personally guarantee payment of the loan.

ABC defaults on the loan and Andre has to make full payment to the bank from his personal funds. Andre is entitled to a business bad debt deduction because his primary motive for guaranteeing the loan was to protect his job with his corporation, not to protect his investment in the corporation.

Personal Debts

The fact that a debt doesn't arise from your business doesn't mean it's not deductible. Bona fide personal debts that become worthless are deductible as *short-term capital losses*. This means they can be deducted only to offset any capital gains you received from the sale of capital assets during the year. (Capital assets include items such as real estate, stocks, and bonds.) Your total deduction for personal debts is limited to $3,000 per year. Any loss in excess of this limit may be carried over to future years to offset future capital gains. Unlike business bad debts, personal debts are deductible only if they become wholly worthless.

Client Costs Advanced by Attorneys

Lawyers often pay for various costs themselves while they are working on a case with the expectation that they will later be reimbursed by the client. Such advances are particularly common by personal injury lawyers who take cases on a contingency fee basis, and who expect to obtain reimbursement from any recovery that is made when the case is settled or a court award obtained. Advances typically include attorney travel expenses, medical record costs, costs of reports, witness fees, deposition costs, filing fees, investigation costs, costs of photographs, laboratory test fees, and process server fees.

You might think attorneys could deduct these costs as business operating expenses—you'd be wrong. Client costs advanced by attorneys are not deductible because they are viewed as loans made by attorneys to their clients. Loans are not a deductible business expense because they are made on the condition that they be repaid by the borrower. (*Canelo v. Comm'r*, 53 T.C. 217 (1969).)

Because advances are loans, they are deductible only if they become uncollectible. And the bad debt rules discussed above apply. If an advance is repaid, it is not taxable income for the law firm.

There is one exception that allows attorneys to deduct client costs: when an attorney enters into a "gross fee contingency" agreement with a client. Under such a fee agreement, the attorney pays all the litigation costs and does not obtain reimbursement from any recovery made for the client. Because the attorney has no expectation of having the advanced costs repaid by the client, they are not loans. They may be deducted as a business operating expense in the year they are incurred. (*Boccardo v. Comm'r,* 56 F.3d 1016 (9th Cir. 1995).)

C. Casualty Losses

Casualty losses are damage to property caused by fire, theft, vandalism, earthquake, storm, floods, terrorism, or some other "sudden, unexpected or unusual event." There must be some external force involved for a loss to be a casualty loss. Thus, you get no deduction if you simply lose or misplace property or it breaks or wears out over time.

You may take a deduction for casualty losses to business property if, and only to the extent that, the loss is not covered by insurance. Thus, if the loss is fully covered, you'll get no deduction.

1. Amount of Deduction

How much you may deduct depends on whether the property involved was stolen or completely destroyed or only partially destroyed. However, you must always reduce your casualty losses by the amount of any insurance proceeds you actually receive or reasonably expect to receive. If more than one item was stolen or wholly or partly destroyed, you must figure your deduction separately for each and then add them all together.

Total Loss

If the property is stolen or completely destroyed, your deduction is figured as follows:

$$
\begin{array}{r}
\text{Adjusted Basis} \\
-\ \text{Salvage Value} \\
-\ \underline{\text{Insurance Proceeds}} \\
=\ \underline{\text{Casualty Loss}\qquad}
\end{array}
$$

Your adjusted basis is the property's original cost, plus the value of any improvements, minus any deductions you took for depreciation or Section 179 expensing (see Chapter 9). Obviously, if an item is stolen, there will be no salvage value.

> **EXAMPLE:** Sean's business computer is stolen from his apartment by a burglar. The computer cost $2,000. Sean has taken no tax deductions for it because he purchased it only two months ago, so his adjusted basis is $2,000. Sean is a renter and has no insurance covering the loss. Sean's casualty loss is $2,000. ($2,000 Adjusted Basis – $0 Salvage Value – $0 Insurance Proceeds = $2,000.)

Partial Loss

If the property is only partly destroyed, your casualty loss deduction is the lesser of the decrease in the property's fair market value or its adjusted basis, reduced by any insurance you receive or expect to receive.

> **EXAMPLE:** Assume that Sean's computer (from the example above) is partly destroyed due to a small fire in his home. Its fair market value in its partly damaged state is $500. Since he spent $2,000 for it, the decrease in its fair market value is $1,500. The computer's adjusted basis is $2,000. He received no insurance proceeds. Thus, his casualty loss is $1,500.

Inventory

You don't have to treat damage to or loss of inventory as a casualty loss. Instead you may deduct it as part of the cost of your goods sold. (See Chapter 13 for a detailed discussion of inventory.) However, if you do this, you must include any insurance proceeds you receive for the inventory loss in your practice's gross income for the year.

Personal Property

You can deduct casualty losses to personal property—that is, property you don't use for your practice—from your income tax as an itemized personal deduction, but the deduction is severely limited: You can deduct only the amount of the loss that exceeds 10% of your adjusted gross income for the year. This greatly limits or eliminates many casualty loss deductions. To add insult to injury, you must also subtract $100 from each casualty or theft you suffered during the year.

> **EXAMPLE:** Ken suffers $5,000 in losses to his personal property when a fire strikes his home. His adjusted gross income for the year is $75,000. He can deduct only that portion of his loss that exceeds $7,500 (10% x $75,000 = $7,500). He lost $5,000, so he gets no deduction.

Casualty Gains

In some cases, the insurance reimbursement you receive will exceed the value of the property that is stolen or destroyed. In this event, you have a casualty gain, not a deductible loss.

> **EXAMPLE:** Jeanette's laptop computer is stolen from her car. She has computer insurance covering the loss. Her insurer pays her $1,500. Jeanette paid $2,500 for the computer but deducted the entire amount in one year under Section 179; thus, her adjusted basis is 0. As a result, she has a $1,500 gain ($0 Adjusted Basis – $1,500 Insurance Proceeds = $1,500 casualty gain).

If you have a gain, you might have to pay tax on it. If you owned the property one year or more, the gain is a capital gain taxed at capital gains rates. Gains on property owned less than one year are taxed at ordinary income tax rates. However, you can defer any taxes you owe to a later year (or even indefinitely) by buying property to replace your loss within certain time limits.

Special Rules for Hurricane Katrina Victims

The limits on deductions for casualty losses to personal property do not apply to Hurricane Katrina victims—that is, they may deduct their entire uninsured loss. The $100 per casualty or theft floor and the 10% of AGI floor don't apply. For purposes of applying the 10%-of-AGI threshold to other personal casualty or theft losses, losses attributable to Hurricane Katrina are disregarded. For more details on this and other tax relief for Katrina victims, see the IRS website at www.irs.gov.

2. Damage to Your Home Office

If you take the home office deduction, you may deduct losses due to damage to or destruction of your home office as part of your deduction. However, your loss is reduced by any insurance proceeds you receive or expect to receive.

You can deduct casualty losses that affect your entire house as an indirect home office expense. The amount of your deduction is based on your home office use percentage.

> **EXAMPLE:** Dana's home is completely destroyed by a fire. Her fire insurance covered only 80% of her loss. Her home office took up 20% of her home. She can deduct 20% of her total casualty loss as an indirect home office deduction.

You can fully deduct casualty losses that affect only your home office—for example, if only your home office is burned in a fire—as direct home office expenses. However, you can't deduct as a business expense casualty losses that don't affect your home office at all—for example, if your kitchen is destroyed by fire.

If the loss involves business property that is in your home office but is not part of your home—for example, a burglar steals your home office computer—it's not part of the home office deduction.

See Chapter 7 for a detailed discussion of the home office deduction.

3.   Tax Reporting

Professionals who are sole proprietors report casualty losses to business property on Part B of IRS Form 4684, *Casualties and Thefts*, and then transfer the deductible casualty loss to Form 4797, *Sales of Business Property*, and the first page of their Form 1040. The amount of the deductible casualty loss is subtracted from the adjusted gross income for the year. However, casualty losses are not deducted from self-employment income for Social Security and Medicare tax purposes. These reporting requirements are different from the reporting for other deductions covered in this chapter, which are reported on IRS Schedule C, Form 1040.

Partnerships, S corporations, and LLCs must also fill out Form 4797. The amount of the loss is taken into account when calculating the entity's total business income for the year. This amount is reported on the entity's information tax return (Form 1065 for partnerships and LLCs; Form 1120S for S corporations). C corporations deduct their casualty losses on their own tax returns (Form 1120).

If you take a casualty loss as part of your home office deduction, you must include it on Form 8829, *Expenses for Business Use of Your Home*.

D.   Charitable Contributions

Tax deductions can be taken for charitable contributions to qualified organizations. To become a qualified organization, most organizations, other than churches and governments, must apply to the IRS. You can ask any organization whether it is a qualified organization, and most will be able to tell you. Or you can check IRS Publication 78, which lists most qualified organizations.

1.   Contributions of Money

If you are a sole proprietor, partner in a partnership, LLC member, or S corporation shareholder, the IRS treats any charitable contributions of money your practice makes as a personal contribution by you and any co-owners. As such, the contributions are not business expenses—you can deduct them only as a personal charitable contribution. You may deduct these contributions only if you itemize deductions on your personal tax return; they are subject to certain income limitations. See IRS Publication 526, *Charitable Contributions.*

Charitable contributions are treated very differently for C corporations. C corporations can deduct charitable contributions as a business expense on their own corporate tax returns.

2.   Contributions of Property

If you contribute business property to a qualified charitable organization, you may deduct its fair market value on the date of the contribution.

> **EXAMPLE:** Barry, a sole proprietor engineer, wants to buy a new computer and get rid of his old one. He decides to donate the old computer to a local charity. By looking at sales data for similar computers on eBay, he determines that the computer's fair market value is $1,000. The actual amount of his deduction will be limited to the amount that all his itemized deductions exceed 2% of his adjusted gross income.

He may deduct this amount as an itemized deduction on Schedule A of his tax return. He may not deduct it as a business expense on Schedule C.

The rules differ somewhat if the property you contribute is inventory (merchandise you sell to patients or customers; see Chapter 13). You may deduct the smaller of:

- its fair market value on the day you contributed it, or
- its tax basis.

If a C corporation contributes inventory to a public charity or operating foundation that uses the items to care for the needy or infants, it may add 50% of the difference between the inventory's tax basis (cost) and fair market value (up to twice the basis) to the deduction amount. This makes inventory contributions particularly attractive for C corporations.

You must remove the amount of your deduction from your opening inventory. It is not part of the cost of goods sold.

There are several organizations that specialize in facilitating charitable donations of unsold inventory by corporations, including the National Association for Exchange of Industrial Resources (NAEIR) at www.naeir .org.

3.   Contributions of Services

If you contribute your personal services to a charity, you get no deduction for the value of your time or services. However, you may take a personal deduction for your out-of-pocket expenses, such as travel expenses. To be deductible, such expenses must be:

- unreimbursed
- directly connected with the charitable services
- expenses you had only because of the services you gave, and
- not personal, living, or family expenses.

For example, you can deduct unreimbursed out-of-pocket expenses, such as the cost of gas and oil, that are directly related to the use of your car in giving services to a charitable organization. If you do not want to bother keeping track of your actual expenses, you can use a standard mileage rate equal to 70% of the standard mileage rate for business driving to figure your contribution.

> **EXAMPLE:** Dr. Smith, a radiologist, volunteers ten hours of his time every week to a nonprofit hospital in his community. He may deduct the cost of his gas and parking, but not the value of his time or medical services.

E.   Clothing

You can deduct the cost of clothing only if:

- it is essential for your practice
- it is not suitable for ordinary street wear, and
- you don't wear the clothing outside of business.

Thus, for example, a doctor may deduct the cost of scrubs or lab coats, because they are not suitable for street wear. But an attorney may not deduct the cost of a business suit because it is suitable for ordinary street wear. Likewise a doctor can't deduct the cost of comfortable shoes he wears with his scrubs because the shoes can be worn on the street.

If your clothing is deductible, you may also deduct the cost of dry cleaning and other care.

F.   Disabled Access Tax Credit

The Americans with Disabilities Act (ADA) prohibits private employers with 15 or more employees from discriminating against people with disabilities in the full and equal enjoyment of goods, services, and facilities offered by any "place of public accommodation." Professionals' offices are included in the definition of public accommodation.

The tax law provides a tax credit to help small businesses defray the costs of complying with the ADA. Among other things, the credit may be used help offset amounts paid to acquire or modify equipment or devices for the disabled. The credit may be used by any business with either:

- $1 million or less in gross receipts for the preceding tax year; or
- 30 or fewer full-time employees during the preceding tax year.

1.   Use of Credit by Health Care Providers

The disabled access credit can be used by health care professionals who purchase or modify equipment to satisfy the ADA's prohibition on discrimination against the disabled. For example, the credit may be used when a health care provider purchases equipment to allow him to treat disabled patients he couldn't treat previously.

> **EXAMPLE:** Dr. David Hubbard, a Nevada optometrist, was unable to treat deaf, retarded, or wheelchair-bound patients because he used a manual refractor that required that they sit in an examination chair and answer questions while viewing an eye chart. Deaf people couldn't hear the questions, retarded people couldn't understand them, and wheelchair-bound people couldn't fit behind the refractor. To eliminate this problem, Dr. Hubbard purchased

an automatic refractor/keratometer for $18,000. This instrument enabled him to measure patients' vision without using eye charts. Dr. Hubbard took the maximum $5,000 disabled tax credit for his purchase. The IRS claimed that Dr. Hubbard was not entitled to the credit because he used the refractor for all his patients, not just the disabled. The tax court disagreed; it held that Dr. Hubbard was entitled to the credit because it enabled him to treat disabled patients he couldn't treat previously. (*Hubbard v. Comm'r*, T.C. Memo 2003-245.)

However, the disabled access credit may not be used by health care providers who are already in compliance with the ADA.

> **EXAMPLE:** Dr. Fan, a dentist, purchased an intraoral camera system that included a wand-shaped oral camera that could be inserted inside patients' mouths, a monitor, and educational videotapes, all of which enabled patients to watch Fan perform dental work and watch videos that explained various diagnoses and treatments. Fan claimed that the system enabled him to treat deaf patients, so he was entitled to the disabled tax credit. The IRS and tax court denied him the credit because he had previously been treating deaf patients by using handwritten notes for communication. Thus, he had never discriminated against the deaf and was already in compliance with the ADA when he purchased the camera system. (*Fan v. Comm'r*, 117 T.C. 132).

2.   Amount of Credit

The disabled tax credit is a tax credit, not a tax deduction. Tax credits are better than tax deductions because, instead of just reducing your taxable income, they reduce the amount of tax you have to pay dollar for dollar. The amount of the credit is equal to 50% of "eligible access expenditures" of at least $250 but not more than $10,250 for a tax year. Thus, the maximum credit is $5,000. A business may take the credit each year that it makes an eligible access expenditure. To claim the credit, you must file IRS Form 8826, *Disabled Access Credit.*

G. License Fees, Dues, and Subscriptions

License fees and other dues you pay to professional, business, and civic organizations are deductible business expenses, as long as the organization's main purpose is not to provide entertainment facilities to members. This includes dues paid to:

- bar associations, medical associations, and other professional organizations
- trade associations, local chambers of commerce, real estate boards, business leagues, and
- civic or public service organizations, such as a Rotary or Lions club.

You may also deduct dues to join professional societies, even if such membership is not required to practice your profession. For example, an architect could deduct the dues to be a member of the American Institute of Architects.

You get no deduction for dues you pay to belong to other types of social, business, or recreational clubs—for example, country clubs or athletic clubs. (See Chapter 4.) For this reason, it's best not to use the word "dues" on your tax return, because the IRS may question the expense. Use other words to describe the deduction—for example, if you're deducting membership dues for a trade organization, list the expense as "professional association membership fees."

You may deduct subscriptions to professional, technical, and trade journals as a business expense.

H. Education Expenses

You can deduct your expenses for business-related education—for example, a continuing professional education course or seminar. You can also deduct the cost of attending a convention or professional meeting as an education expense. To qualify for an education deduction, you must be able to show that the education:

- maintains or improves skills required in your profession, or
- is required by law or regulation to maintain your professional status.

EXAMPLE 1: Sue is an attorney. Every year, she is required by law to attend 12 hours of continuing education to keep her status as an active member of the state bar. The legal seminars she attends to satisfy this requirement are deductible education expenses.

EXAMPLE 2: Jerry, a general practitioner doctor, takes a two-week course reviewing new developments in several specialized fields of medicine. The cost is a deductible education expense because the course maintains or improves Jerry's skills as a doctor.

Deductible education expenses include tuition, fees, books, and other learning materials. They also include transportation and travel (see below). You may also deduct expenses you pay to educate or train your employees.

1.   Entering a New Profession

You cannot currently deduct education expenses you incur to qualify for a *new* profession. For example, courts have held that IRS agents could not deduct the cost of going to law school, because a law degree would qualify them for a new profession—being a lawyer. (*Jeffrey L. Weiler*, 54 T.C. 398 (1970).) On the other hand, a practicing dentist was allowed to deduct the cost of being educated in orthodontia, because becoming an orthodontist did not constitute the practice of a new business or profession for a dentist. (Rev. Rul. 74-78.)

2.   Minimum Educational Requirements

You cannot deduct the cost required to meet the minimum or basic level educational requirements for a profession. Thus, for example, you can't deduct the expense of going to law school, medical school, or dental school.

3.   Traveling for Education

Local transportation expenses paid to get to and from a deductible educational activity are deductible. This includes transportation between either your home or business and the educational activity. Going to or from home to an educational activity does not constitute nondeductible commuting. If you drive, you may deduct your actual expenses or use the standard mileage rate. (See Chapter 5 for more on deducting car expenses.)

There's no law that says you must take your education courses as close to home as possible. You may travel outside your geographic area for education, even if the same or a similar educational activity is available near your home or place of business. Companies and groups that sponsor educational events are well aware of this rule and take advantage of it by offering courses and seminars at resorts and other enjoyable vacation spots such as Hawaii and California. Deductible travel expenses may include airfare or other transportation, lodging, and meals. However, if you don't spend the majority of your time on educational activities, your deduction will be greatly limited. (See Chapter 6 for more about travel expenses.)

You cannot claim travel itself as an education deduction. You must travel to some sort of educational activity. For example, an architect could not deduct the cost of a trip to Paris because he studied the local architecture while he was there—but he could deduct a trip to Paris to attend a seminar on French architecture.

I.   Gifts

If you give someone a gift for business purposes, your business expense deduction is limited to $25 per person per year. Any amount over the $25 limit is not deductible. If this amount seems awfully low, that's because it was established in 1954!

> **EXAMPLE:** Lisa, a marketing consultant, gives a $200 Christmas gift to her best client. She may deduct $25 of the cost.

A gift to a member of a customer's family is treated as a gift to the customer, unless you have a legitimate nonbusiness connection to the family member. If you and your spouse both give gifts, you are treated as one taxpayer—it doesn't matter if you work together or have separate businesses.

The $25 limit applies only to gifts to individuals. It doesn't apply
if you give a gift to an entire company, unless the gift is intended
for a particular person or group of people within the company. Such
company-wide gifts are deductible in any amount, as long as they are
reasonable.

> **EXAMPLE:** The Acme Company is one of accountant Bob's best
> clients. Just before Christmas, he drops off a $100 cheese basket at
> the company's reception area for all of Acme's employees. He also
> delivers an identical basket to Acme's president. The first basket
> left in the reception area is a company-wide gift, not subject to the
> $25 limit. The basket for Acme's president is a personal gift and
> therefore is subject to the limit.

J. Insurance for Your Practice

You can deduct the premiums you pay for any insurance you buy for
your practice as a business operating expense. This includes:
- medical insurance for your employees (see Chapter 11)
- fire, theft, and flood insurance for business property
- credit insurance that covers losses from business debts
- liability insurance
- professional malpractice insurance—for example, medical or legal
  malpractice insurance
- workers' compensation insurance you are required by state
  law to provide your employees (if you are an employee of an S
  corporation, the corporation can deduct workers' comp payments
  made on your behalf, but they must be included in your employee
  wages)
- business interruption insurance
- life insurance covering a corporation's officers and directors if you
  are not a direct beneficiary under the policy, and
- unemployment insurance contributions (either as insurance costs
  or business taxes, depending on how they are characterized by
  your state's laws).

1. Homeowner's Insurance for Your Home Office

If you have a home office and qualify for the home office deduction, you may deduct the home office percentage of your homeowner's or renter's insurance premiums. For example, if your home office takes up 20% of your home, you may deduct 20% of the premiums. You can deduct 100% of any special coverage that you add to your homeowner's or renter's policy for your home office and/or business property. For example, if you add an endorsement to your policy to cover business property, you can deduct 100% of the cost.

2. Car Insurance

If you use the actual expense method to deduct your car expenses, you can deduct the cost of insurance that covers liability, damages, and other losses for vehicles used in your practice as a business expense. If you use a vehicle only for business, you can deduct 100% of your insurance costs. If you operate a vehicle for both business and personal use, you can deduct only the part of the insurance premiums that applies to the business use of your vehicle. For example, if you use a car 60% for business and 40% for personal reasons, you can deduct 60% of your insurance costs. (See Chapter 5.)

If you use the standard mileage rate to deduct your car expenses, you get no separate deduction for insurance. Your insurance costs are included in the standard rate. (See Chapter 5).

K. Interest on Business Loans

Interest you pay on business loans is usually a currently deductible business expense. It makes no difference whether you pay the interest on a bank loan, personal loan, credit card, line of credit, car loan, or real estate mortgage. Nor does it matter whether the collateral you used to get the loan was business or personal property. If you use the money for business purposes, the interest you pay to get that money is a deductible business expense. It's how you use the money that counts, not how you get it. Borrowed money is used for business when you buy something with the money that's deductible as a business expense.

> **EXAMPLE:** Dr. Smith borrows $50,000 from the bank to buy new medical equipment. He pays 6% interest on the loan. His annual interest expense is deductible as a business expense because the loan is a business loan.

Your deduction begins only when you spend the borrowed funds for business purposes. You get no business deduction for interest you pay on money that you keep in the bank. Money in the bank is considered an investment—at best, you might be able to deduct the interest you pay on the money as an investment expense. (See Section 6, below.)

1.   Home Offices

If you are a homeowner and take the home office deduction, you can deduct the home office percentage of your home mortgage interest as a business expense. (See Chapter 7 for a detailed discussion of the home office deduction.)

2.   Car Loans

If you use your car for business, you can deduct the interest that you pay on your car loan as an interest expense. You can take this deduction whether you deduct your car expenses using the actual expense method or the standard mileage rate, because the standard mileage rate does not include interest on a car loan.

If you use your car only for business, you can deduct all of the interest you pay. If you use it for both business and personal reasons, you can deduct the business percentage of the interest. For example, if you use your car 60% of the time for your practice, you can deduct 60% of the interest you pay on your car loan.

There is one important exception to this rule: Employees may not deduct car loan interest, even if they use the car for business.

3. Loans to Buy a Practice

If you borrow money to buy an interest in an S corporation, partnership, or LLC, it's wise to seek an accountant's help to figure out how to deduct the interest on your loan. It must be allocated among the company's assets and, depending on what assets the business owns, the interest might be deductible as a business expense or an investment expense, which is more limited. (See Section 6, below.)

Interest on money you borrow to buy stock in a C corporation is always treated as investment interest. This is true even if the corporation is small (also called "closely held") and its stock is not publicly traded.

4. Loans From Relatives and Friends

If you borrow money from a relative or friend and use it for business purposes, you may deduct the interest you pay on the loan as a business expense. However, the IRS is very suspicious of loans between family members and friends. You need to carefully document these transactions. Treat the loan like any other business loan: sign a promissory note, pay a reasonable rate of interest, and follow a repayment schedule. Keep your cancelled loan payment checks to prove you really paid the interest.

5. Interest You Can't Deduct

You can't deduct interest:
- on loans used for personal purposes
- on debts you or your practice don't owe
- on overdue taxes (only C corporations can deduct this interest)
- that you pay with funds borrowed from the original lender through a second loan (but you can deduct the interest once you start making payments on the new loan)
- that you prepay if you're a cash basis taxpayer (but you may deduct it the next year)
- on money borrowed to pay taxes or fund retirement plans, or
- on loans of more than $50,000 that are borrowed on a life insurance policy on yourself or another owner or employee of your business.

Points and other loan origination fees that you pay to get a mortgage on business property are not deductible business expenses. You must add these costs to the cost of the building and deduct them over time using depreciation.

6.   Deducting Investment Interest

Investing is not a business, so you get no business expense deduction for interest that you pay on money borrowed to make personal investments. You may take a personal deduction for investment interest, but you may not deduct more than your net annual income from your investments. Any amount that you can't deduct in the current year can be carried over to the next year and deducted then.

> **EXAMPLE:** Donald borrows $10,000 on his credit card to invest in the stock market. The interest he pays on the debt is deductible as an itemized personal deduction he lists on his Schedule A, Form 1040. He cannot deduct more than he earned during the year from his investments.

7.   Keeping Track of Borrowed Money

When you borrow money for your practice, you should not deposit it in a personal bank account. Deposit it in a separate account for your practice.

If you deposit a business loan in a personal account, you'll have to be able to prove that the money was actually spent on business. Complex IRS allocation rules may have to be followed.

However, if you buy something for your practice within 30 days of borrowing money, the IRS presumes that the payment was made from those loan proceeds (up to the amount of the loan proceeds). This is true regardless of the method or bank account you use to pay the business expense. If you receive the loan proceeds in cash, you can treat the payment as made on the date you receive the cash instead of the date you actually make the payment.

L. Legal and Professional Services

You can deduct fees that you pay to attorneys, accountants, consultants, and other professionals as business expenses if the fees are paid for work related to your practice.

> **EXAMPLE:** Ira, a doctor, hires attorney Jake to represent him in a malpractice suit. The legal fees Ira pays Jake are a deductible business expense.

Legal and professional fees that you pay for personal purposes generally are not deductible. For example, you can't deduct the legal fees you incur if you get divorced or you sue someone for a traffic accident injury. Nor are the fees that you pay to write your will deductible, even if the will covers business property that you own.

1. Buying Long-Term Property

If you pay legal or other fees in the course of buying long-term business property, you must add the amount of the fee to the tax basis (cost) of the property. You may deduct this cost over several years through depreciation or deduct it in one year under Section 179. (See Chapter 9 for more on depreciation.)

2. Starting a Practice

Legal and accounting fees that you pay to start your practice are deductible only as business start-up expenses. You can deduct $5,000 of start-up expenses the first year you're in business and any amounts over $5,000 over 180 months. The same holds true for incorporation fees or fees that you pay to form a partnership or LLC. (See Chapter 10 for more or start-up expenses.)

3. Accounting Fees

You can deduct any accounting fees that you pay for your practice as a deductible business expense—for example, fees you pay an accountant to set up or keep your tax return, or give you tax advice for your practice.

Sole proprietor professionals may deduct the cost of having an accountant or other tax professional complete the business portion of their tax returns—Schedule C and other business tax forms—but they cannot deduct the time the preparer spends on the personal part of their returns. If you are a sole proprietor and pay a tax professional to complete your Form 1040 income tax return, make sure that you get an itemized bill showing the portion of the tax preparation fee allocated to preparing your Schedule C (and any other business tax forms attached to your Form 1040).

M. Taxes

Most taxes that you pay in the course of your practice are deductible.

1. Income Taxes

Federal income taxes that you pay on your business income are not deductible. However, a corporation or partnership can deduct state or local income taxes it pays. Individuals may deduct state and local income taxes only as an itemized deduction on Schedule A, Form 1040. This is a personal, not a business, deduction. However, an individual can deduct state tax on gross business income as a business expense—for example, Michigan has a Single Business Tax of 2% on business gross receipts over $250,000. This tax is a federally deductible business operating expense. Of course, you can't deduct state taxes from your income for state income tax purposes.

2. Self-Employment Taxes

If you are a sole proprietor, partner in a partnership, or LLC member, you may deduct one-half of your self-employment taxes from your total net business income. This deduction reduces the amount of income on which you must pay personal income tax. It's an adjustment to gross income, not a business deduction. You don't list it on your Schedule C; instead, you take it on page one of your Form 1040.

The self-employment tax is a 15.3% tax, so your deduction is equal to 7.65% of your income. To figure out your income after taking this deduction, multiply your net business income by 92.35% or .9235.

> **EXAMPLE:** Billie, a self-employed consultant, earned $70,000 from her business and had $20,000 in business expenses. Her net business income was $50,000. She multiplies this amount by .9235 to determine her net self-employment income, which is $46,175. This is the amount on which Billie must pay federal income tax.

This deduction is intended to help ease the tax burden on the self-employed.

3. Employment Taxes

If you have employees, you must pay half of their Social Security and Medicare taxes from your own funds and withhold the other half from their pay. These taxes consist of a 12.4% Social Security tax, up to an annual salary cap ($94,200 in 2006), and a 2.9% Medicare tax on all employees' pay. You may deduct half of this amount as a business expense. You should treat the taxes you withhold from your employees' pay as wages paid to your employees on your tax return.

> **EXAMPLE:** You pay your employee $18,000 a year. However, after you withhold employment taxes, your employee receives $14,500. You also pay an additional $1,500 in employment taxes from your own funds. You should deduct the full $18,000 salary as employee wages and deduct the $1,500 as employment taxes paid.

4. Sales Taxes

Some states impose sales taxes on various types of services. You may not deduct state and local sales taxes on your goods and services that you are required to collect from a client or patient and turn over to your state or local government. Do not include these taxes in gross receipts or sales.

However, you may deduct sales taxes that you pay when you purchase goods or services for your practice. The amount of the tax is added to the cost of the goods or services for purposes of your deduction for the item.

> **EXAMPLE:** Jean, a sole proprietor lawyer, buys a $200 briefcase to use for her practice. She had to pay $15 in state and local sales taxes on the purchase. She may take a $215 deduction for the briefcase. She claims the deduction on her Schedule C as a purchase of supplies.

If you buy a long-term business asset, the sales taxes must be added to its basis (cost) for purposes of depreciation or expensing under IRC Section 179.

> **EXAMPLE:** Jean buys a $2,000 computer for her law office. She pays $150 in state and local sales tax. The computer has a useful life of more than one year and is therefore a long-term business asset for tax purposes. She can't currently deduct the cost as a business operating expense. Instead, Jean must depreciate the cost over several years or expense the cost (deduct the full cost in one year) under Section 179. The total cost to be depreciated or expensed is $2,150.

5.   Real Property Taxes

You can deduct your current year's state and local property taxes on business real property as business expenses.

Home Offices

If you are a homeowner and take the home office deduction, you may deduct the home office percentage of your property taxes. However, as a homeowner, you are entitled to deduct all of your mortgage interest and property taxes, regardless of whether you have a home office. Taking the home office deduction won't increase your income tax deductions for your property taxes, but it will allow you to deduct them from your income for the purpose of calculating your self-employment taxes. You'll save $153 in self-employment taxes for every $1,000 in property taxes you deduct (15.3% self-employment tax x $1,000 = $153).

> **EXAMPLE:** Suzy uses 20% of her three-bedroom Tulsa home as a home office. She pays $10,000 per year in mortgage interest and property taxes. By taking the home office deduction, she gets to deduct this amount from her income for self-employment tax purposes, which saves her $1,530.

Charges for Services

Water bills, sewer charges, and other service charges assessed against your business property are not real estate taxes, but they are deductible as business expenses. If you have a home office, you can deduct your home office percentage of these items.

However, real estate taxes imposed to fund specific local benefits such as streets, sewer lines, and water mains, are not deductible as business expenses. Because these benefits increase the value of your property, you should add what you pay for them to the tax basis (cost for tax purposes) of your property.

Buying and Selling Real Estate

When real estate is sold, the real estate taxes must be divided between the buyer and seller according to how many days of the tax year each held ownership of the property. You'll usually find information on this in the settlement statement you receive at the property closing.

6.   Other Taxes

Other deductible taxes include:

- excise taxes—for example, Hawaii imposes a general excise tax on businesses ranging from 0.5% to 4% of gross receipts
- state unemployment compensation taxes or state disability contributions
- corporate franchise taxes

- occupational taxes charged at a flat rate by your city or county for the privilege of doing business, and
- state and local taxes on personal property—for example, equipment that you use in your practice.

N. Domestic Production Activities

A brand-new business tax deduction came into effect in 2005—the domestic production activities deduction. (IRC § 199.) This deduction is intended to give a tax break to businesses that hire employees to produce goods or engage in certain other manufacturing or production activities within the United States, rather than farming out the work overseas. The deduction can be used by some professionals, particularly engineers and architects. It's very complicated so we give only a brief overview of how the deduction works.

1. Activities That Qualify for the Deduction

Domestic production activities include:
- engineering or architectural services performed in the United States for construction projects in the United States
- any sale, lease, rental, license, exchange, or other disposition of tangible personal property, computer software, or sound recordings that you manufactured, produced, grew, or extracted, in whole or in significant part, within the United States
- construction performed in the United States—including both new buildings and substantial renovations of existing buildings.

However, rental income from real property isn't eligible for the deduction.

The second category mentioned above—the tangible personal property category—is by far the broadest and most inclusive category, and could include many types of professionals.

Tangible personal property is any tangible property other than land, buildings, and structural components of buildings. If you produce any tangible personal property "in significant part" in the United States and later dispose of it by sale or otherwise in the course of your practice, you may be entitled to the deduction. According to the IRS, "significant part" means that the labor and overhead incurred in the United States was at least 20% of the total cost of the property. (IRS Notice 2005-14.)

Almost any activity relating to manufacturing, producing, growing, extracting, installing, developing, improving, or creating tangible personal property qualifies for the deduction. This includes making tangible property from new or raw material, or by combining or assembling two or more articles.

> **EXAMPLE:** Barbie, an optometrist, has two employees who grind lenses and assemble them into eyeglasses for sale. The lenses and eyeglasses qualify as tangible personal property produced in significant part in the United States. Barbie's activity qualifies for the domestic production deduction.

2. Tangible Personal Property Mixed With Services

If you produce tangible personal property as a part of the services you provide patients or clients, you can still obtain the deduction. But you must separately allocate the income you earn from your service and from your production activities. Only the production activity income qualifies for the deduction. However, an exception applies if you earn less than 5% of your gross receipts from providing a service.

> **EXAMPLE:** Marcus is a doctor with his own practice, but he also runs a medical lab that performs medical tests. The work his lab does qualifies as a domestic production activity, but the medical services he provides his patients do not. If his income from the lab is more than 5% of his total gross income, Marcus must separately allocate the income he receives from the lab and from his medical practice. Only the lab income can qualify for the domestic production activities deduction.

3. Amount of Deduction

For 2005, the deduction is 3% of the income you earn from your domestic production activities. Income means your gross receipts from a production activity reduced by the cost of goods sold and related expenses, including the cost of production and a portion of your indirect expenses such as rent. The deduction will increase in later years as shown in the following chart:

Year	Deduction for Domestic Production Activities
2005-2006	3%
2007-2009	6%
2010 and later	9%

The IRS has proposed various ways to make it easier for small businesses to use the deduction, including simplified formulas for determining income from domestic production activities and W-2 wages. (See IRS Notice 2005-14.)

4.   Limits on the Deduction

The domestic production activities deduction is intended to encourage businesses to hire more employees in the United States, and thereby benefit the American public. Thus, a business can qualify for the deduction only if it has employees.

If you have employees, you can get the deduction if you meet all the other requirements. However, it cannot exceed 50% of the total wages you paid all your employees during the calendar year and listed on their IRS W-2 forms. For example, if your total annual payroll is $100,000, your total domestic production activities deduction is limited to $50,000. Obviously, you can increase your deduction limit if you hire more employees instead of doing work yourself or hiring independent contractors. However, the value of the deduction may not justify the increased expense of having employees.

There is one more significant limitation on the deduction: It may not exceed your adjusted gross income if you're a sole proprietor, or the owner of an LLC, partnership, or S corporation. If your practice is a C corporation, the deduction may not exceed the corporation's taxable income. Thus, businesses that don't earn a profit and pay no taxes get no domestic production activities deduction

If you want to take this deduction, seek guidance from a tax professional. It may increase your bookkeeping and accounting burdens. It could also subject you to the uniform capitalization rules (IRC § 263A). These rules prevent you from taking a current business deduction for the direct, and some indirect, costs incurred in production activities. Thus, for example, you could be prohibited from currently deducting all or part of your labor and overhead costs. Instead, you recover the costs through depreciation, amortization, or deducting the cost of goods sold when you sell or otherwise dispose of the property. This can take much longer than obtaining a current deduction.

■

Chapter 15

Hiring Employees and Independent Contractors

T his chapter is about the host of tax rules that apply to professionals who hire other people to help them, whether as employees or independent contractors. These rules apply whether you hire strangers, friends, or family members.

If you are an employee of your own practice, however, different rules apply that are not covered in this chapter. This is usually the situation if you have incorporated your practice (or chosen corporate tax treatment for an unincorporated practice). Chapter 16 covers the rules for when professionals are employees of their own business.

A. Employees Versus Independent Contractors

As far as the IRS is concerned, there are only two types of people you can hire to help in your practice: employees and independent contractors. It's very important to understand the difference between the two because the tax rules are very different for each. If you hire an employee, you become subject to a wide array of state and federal tax requirements. You must withhold taxes from your employee's pay, and you must pay other taxes yourself. You must also comply with complex and burdensome bookkeeping and reporting requirements. If you hire an independent contractor, none of these requirements apply. Tax deductions for businesses that hire employees and independent contractors differ as well.

Independent contractors (ICs) go by a variety of names: self-employed, freelancers, free agents, consultants, entrepreneurs, or business owners. What they all have in common is that they are people who are in business for themselves. Employees work for someone else's business.

Initially, it's up to you to determine whether any person you hire is an employee or an IC. However, your decision about how to classify a worker is subject to review by various government agencies, including:
- the IRS
- your state's tax department
- your state's unemployment compensation insurance agency, and
- your state's workers' compensation insurance agency.

These agencies are mostly interested in whether you have classified workers as independent contractors when you should have classified them as employees. The reason is that you must pay money to each of these agencies for employees, but not for independent contractors. The more workers who are classified as employees, the more money flows into the agencies' coffers. In the case of taxing agencies, employers must withhold tax from employees' paychecks and hand it over to the government; ICs pay their own taxes, which means the government must wait longer to get its money and faces the possibility that ICs won't declare their income or will otherwise cheat on their taxes. An agency that determines that you misclassified an employee as an IC may impose back taxes, fines, and penalties.

Scrutinizing agencies use various tests to determine whether a worker is an IC or an employee. The determining factor is usually whether you have the right to control the worker. If you have the right to direct and control the way a worker performs—both as to the final results and the details of when, where, and how the work is done—then the worker is your employee. On the other hand, if your control is limited to accepting or rejecting the final results the worker achieves, then that person is an IC.

An employer may not always exercise its right of control. For example, if an employee is experienced and well trained, the employer may not feel the need to closely supervise him or her. But the employer still maintains the right to do so at any time.

> **EXAMPLE:** Mary, a lawyer in solo practice, hires Barry as her legal secretary. When Barry starts work, Mary closely supervises how he does his job. Virtually every aspect of Barry's behavior on the job is under Mary's control, including what time he arrives at and leaves work, when he takes his lunch break, and the sequence of tasks he must perform. If Barry proves to be an able and conscientious worker, Mary may choose not to look over his shoulder very often. But she has the right to do so at any time. Barry is an employee.

In contrast, a worker is an independent contractor if the hiring firm does not have the right to control the person on the job. Because the worker is an independent businessperson not solely dependent on you (the hiring party) for a living, your control is limited to accepting or rejecting the final results the IC achieves.

EXAMPLE: Mary files a lawsuit and needs to serve the complaint on a hard-to-find defendant. She hires Jackie, a process server, to track down the defendant and serve him. Mary is just one of Jackie's many clients. Mary does not tell Jackie how to find the defendant or otherwise supervise her in any way. If Jackie is successful in serving the paper, Mary will pay her the agreed-upon fee. If Mary doesn't like the results Jackie achieves, she can refuse to pay her. Mary has no other control over Jackie. Jackie is an independent contractor.

The difficulty in applying the right-of-control test is determining whether you have the right to control a worker you hire. Government auditors can't look into your mind to see if you are controlling a worker. They rely instead on indirect or circumstantial evidence indicating control or lack of it—for example, whether you provide a worker with equipment, where the work is performed, how the worker is paid, and whether you can fire the worker. The following chart shows the primary factors used by the IRS and most other government agencies to determine if you have the right to control a worker.

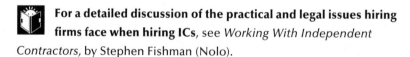 **Part-time workers and temps can be employees.** Don't assume that a person you hire to work part time or for a short period automatically qualifies as an IC. People who work for you only temporarily or part time are your employees if you have the right to control the way they work.

For a detailed discussion of the practical and legal issues hiring firms face when hiring ICs, see *Working With Independent Contractors*, by Stephen Fishman (Nolo).

IRS Test for Worker Status		
Behavioral Control	Workers will more likely be considered ICs if you: • do not give them instructions • do not provide them with training	Workers will more likely be considered employees if you: • give them instructions they must follow about how to do the work • give them detailed training
Financial Control	Workers will more likely be considered ICs if they: • have a significant investment in equipment and facilities • pay business or travel expenses themselves • make their services available to the public • are paid by the job • have opportunity for profit or loss	Workers will more likely be considered employees if: • you provide them with equipment and facilities free of charge • you reimburse their business or travel expenses • they make no effort to market their services to the public • you pay them by the hour or other unit of time • they have no opportunity for profit or loss—for example, because they're paid by the hour and have all expenses reimbursed
Relationship Between You and the Worker	Workers will more likely be considered ICs if they: • don't receive employee benefits such as health insurance • sign a client agreement with the hiring firm • can't quit or be fired at will • perform services that are not part of your regular business activities	Workers will more likely be considered employees if they: • receive employee benefits • have no written client agreement • can quit at any time without incurring any liability to you • can be fired at any time • perform services that are part of your core business

B.   Tax Deductions for Employee Pay and Benefits

Hiring employees costs you money, but you may deduct most or all of what you pay them as a business expense. Thus, for example, if you pay an employee $50,000 per year in salary and benefits, you'll ordinarily get a $50,000 tax deduction. You should factor this into your calculations whenever you're thinking about hiring an employee or deciding how much to pay him.

1.   Employee Pay

Employee pay may be in the form of salaries, bonuses, vacation allowances, sick pay (as long as it's not covered by insurance), or fringe benefits. For tax deduction purposes, it doesn't really matter how you measure or make the payments. Ordinarily, amounts you pay employees to work in your practice will be business operating expenses. These expenses are currently deductible as long as they are:

- ordinary and necessary
- reasonable in amount
- paid for services actually performed, and
- actually paid or incurred in the year the deduction is claimed (as shown by your payroll records).

An employee's services are ordinary and necessary if they are common, accepted, helpful, and appropriate for your business; they don't have to be indispensable. An employee's pay is reasonable if the amount is in the range of what other businesses would pay for similar services. These requirements usually won't pose a problem when you hire an employee to perform any legitimate business function.

> **EXAMPLE:** Ken, an architect, hires Kim to work as his personal assistant and pays her $5,000 per month—a typical salary for this kind of work. Ken can deduct Kim's $5,000 monthly salary as a business operating expense. If Kim works a full year, Ken will get a $60,000 deduction.

Payments to employees for personal services are not deductible as business expenses.

EXAMPLE: Ken hires Samantha to work as a live-in nanny for his three children. Samantha is Ken's employee, but her services are personal, not related to his business. Thus, Ken may not deduct her pay as a business expense.

Special rules apply if you hire family members to work in your business. (See Section D, below.)

However, employee compensation for services performed during the start-up phase of your practice is a business start-up expense. It is not currently deductible, but you may deduct up to $5,000 in start-up expenses the first year you're in business, provided your expenses don't exceed $50,000. Any excess can be deducted over 180 months. (See Chapter 10 for more on deducting start-up expenses.)

2.   Payroll Taxes

Whenever you hire an employee, you become an unpaid tax collector for the government. You are required to withhold and pay both federal and state taxes for the worker. These taxes are called payroll taxes or employment taxes. Federal payroll taxes consist of:

- Social Security and Medicare taxes—also known as FICA
- unemployment taxes—also known as FUTA, and
- federal income taxes—also known as FITW.

You must periodically pay FICA, FUTA, and FITW to the IRS, either electronically or by making federal tax deposits at specified banks which then transmit the money to the IRS. You are entitled to deduct as a business expense payroll taxes that you pay yourself. You get no deductions for taxes you withhold from employees' pay.

Every year, employers must file IRS Form W-2, *Wage and Tax Statement*, for each of their workers. The form shows the IRS how much the worker was paid and how much tax was withheld.

IRS Circular E, *Employer's Tax Guide,* **provides detailed information on these requirements.** You can a get free copy by calling the IRS at 800-TAX-FORM, by calling or visiting your local IRS office, or by downloading it from the IRS website at www.irs.gov.

Employer's FICA Contributions

FICA is an acronym for Federal Income Contributions Act, the law requiring employers and employees to pay Social Security and Medicare taxes. FICA consists of:

- a 12.4% Social Security tax on an employee's wages up to an annual ceiling or cap—in 2006, the cap was $94,20 per year, and
- a 2.9% Medicare tax on all employee wages paid.

This adds up to a 15.3% tax, up to the Social Security tax ceiling. Employers must pay half of this—7.65%—out of their own pockets. They must withhold the other half from their employees' pay. You are entitled to deduct as a business expense the portion of the tax that you pay yourself.

The ceiling for the Social Security tax changes annually. You can find out what the Social Security tax ceiling is for the current year from IRS Circular E, *Employer's Tax Guide*; the amount is printed right on the first page.

FUTA

FUTA is an acronym for the Federal Unemployment Tax Act, the law that establishes federal unemployment taxes. Most employers must pay both state and federal unemployment taxes. Even if you're exempt from the state tax, you may still have to pay the federal tax. Employers alone are responsible for FUTA—you may not collect or deduct it from employees' wages.

You must pay FUTA taxes if either of the following is true:

- You pay $1,500 or more to employees during any calendar quarter—that is, any three-month period beginning with January, April, July, or October.
- You had one or more employees for at least some part of a day in any 20 or more different weeks during the year. The weeks don't have to be consecutive, nor does it have to be the same employee each week.

Technically, the FUTA tax rate is 6.2%, but, in practice, you rarely pay this much. You are given a credit of 5.4% if you pay the applicable state unemployment tax in full and on time. This means that the actual FUTA tax rate is usually 0.8%. In 2005, the FUTA tax was assessed on the first $7,000 of an employee's annual wages. The FUTA tax, then, is usually $56 per year per employee. This amount is a deductible business expense.

FITW

FITW is an acronym for federal income tax withholding. You must calculate and withhold federal income taxes from your employees' paychecks. Employees are solely responsible for paying federal income taxes. Your only responsibility is to withhold the funds and remit them to the government. You get no deductions for FITW.

State Payroll Taxes

Employers in every state are required to pay and withhold state payroll taxes. These taxes include:

- state unemployment compensation taxes in all states
- state income tax withholding in most states, and
- state disability taxes in a few states.

Employers in every state are required to contribute to a state unemployment insurance fund. Employees make no contributions, except in Alaska, New Jersey, Pennsylvania, and Rhode Island, where employers must withhold small employee contributions from employees' paychecks. The employer contributions are a deductible business expense.

If your payroll is very small—below $1,500 per calendar quarter—you probably won't have to pay unemployment compensation taxes. In most states, you must pay state unemployment taxes for employees if you're paying federal FUTA taxes. However, some states have more strict requirements. Contact your state labor department for the exact rules and payroll amounts.

All states except Alaska, Florida, Nevada, South Dakota, Texas, Washington, and Wyoming have income taxation. If your state has income taxes, you must withhold the applicable tax from your employees' paychecks and pay it to the state taxing authority. Each state has its own income tax withholding forms and procedures. Contact your state tax department for information. Of course, employers get no deductions for withholding their employees' state income taxes.

California, Hawaii, New Jersey, New York, and Rhode Island have state disability insurance that provides employees with coverage for injuries or illnesses that are not related to work. Employers in these states must withhold their employees' disability insurance contributions from their pay. Employers must also make their own contributions in Hawaii, New Jersey, and New York—these employer contributions are deductible.

In addition, subject to some important exceptions, employers in all states must provide their employees with workers' compensation insurance to cover work-related injuries. Workers' compensation is not a payroll tax. Employers must purchase a workers' compensation policy from a private insurer or state workers' compensation fund. Your worker's compensation insurance premiums are deductible as a business insurance expense. (See Chapter 14 for more on deducting business insurance.)

⚠️ **Employers in California must withhold for parental leave.** Employers in California are also required to withhold (as part of their disability program) for parental leave.

Bookkeeping Expenses Are Deductible

Figuring out how much to withhold, doing the necessary record keeping, and filling out the required forms can be complicated. Professionals often hire a bookkeeper or payroll tax service to do the work. Amounts you pay a bookkeeper or payroll tax service are deductible business operating expenses. You can find these services in the phone book or on the Internet under payroll tax services. You can also find a list of payroll service providers on the IRS website at www.irs.gov. Payroll tax services charge about $30 to $50 a month for a small company. However, if you wish, you may do the work yourself and save the money. If you have a computer, computer accounting programs (such as *QuickBooks* or *QuickPay*) can help with all the calculations and print out your employees' checks and IRS forms.

EXAMPLE: Isaac hires Vendela to work as a part-time nurse in his Seattle-based medical practice at a salary of $2,000 per month. Isaac may deduct this amount as a business operating expense. In addition, he may deduct his payroll tax contributions on her behalf. These consist of a monthly $153 FICA contribution (7.65% x $2,000 = $153), $56 annual FUTA contribution, and $1,200 annual Washington state unemployment contribution. Isaac must withhold

$300 from Vendela's pay each month to cover her FICA and FITW taxes and send it to the IRS. He need not withhold state income taxes because Washington has no income tax. He gets no deduction for these withheld amounts. So Isaac's annual tax deduction for Vendela is $27,092 ($24,000 salary + $1,836 FICA contribution + $1,200 state unemployment insurance + $56 FUTA = $27,092).

3.   Employee Fringe Benefits

There is no law that says you must provide your employees with any fringe benefits—not even health insurance, sick pay, or vacation. However, the tax law encourages you to provide employee benefits by allowing you to deduct the cost as a business expense. (These expenses should be deducted as employee benefit expenses, not employee compensation.) Moreover, your employees do not have to treat the value of qualified fringe benefits as income on which they must pay tax. So you get a deduction, and your employees get tax-free goodies. Tax-free employee fringe benefits include:

- health insurance (see Chapter 11)
- accident insurance
- Health Savings Accounts (see Chapter 11)
- dependent care assistance
- educational assistance
- group term-life insurance coverage—limits apply based on the policy value
- qualified employee benefit plans, including profit-sharing plans, stock bonus plans, and money purchase plans
- employee stock options
- lodging on your business premises
- moving expense reimbursements
- achievement awards
- commuting benefits
- employee discounts on the goods or services you sell
- supplemental unemployment benefits
- de minimis (low-cost) fringe benefits such as low-value birthday or holiday gifts, event tickets, traditional awards (such as a retirement gift), other special occasion gifts, and coffee and soft drinks, and

- cafeteria plans that allow employees to choose among two or more benefits consisting of cash and qualified benefits.

Employee fringe benefits are covered in detail in Chapter 16.

C. Reimbursing Employees

There may be times when your employees must pay for a work-related expense. Most commonly, this occurs when an employee is driving, traveling, or entertaining while on the job. However, depending on the circumstances, an employee could end up paying for almost any work-related expense—for example, an employee might pay for office supplies or parking at a client's office.

All these employee payments have important tax consequences, whatever form they take. The rules discussed below apply whether the expenses are incurred by an employee who is not related to you or by an employee who is your spouse or child.

1. Reimbursement Under an Accountable Plan

The best way to reimburse or otherwise pay your employees for any work-related expenses is to use an accountable plan. Basically, this means the employee must submit all his or her documentation to the practice in a timely manner and return any excess payments. An accountable plan need not be in writing (although it's not a bad idea). All you need to do is set up procedures for your employees to follow that meet the requirements for accountable plans. (See Chapter 17 for more on accountable plans.)

When you pay employees for their expenses under an accountable plan, two great things happen:

- you don't have to pay payroll taxes on the payments, and
- the employees won't have to include the payments in their taxable income.

Moreover, the amounts you pay will be deductible by you, just like your other business expenses, subject to the same rules.

EXAMPLE: The ABC Medical Corporation decides that Manny, its senior nurse, should attend a nursing convention in Las Vegas. Manny pays his expenses himself. When he gets back, he fully documents his expenses as required by Acme's accountable plan. These amount to $2,000 for transportation and hotel and $1,000 in meal and entertainment expenses. Acme reimburses Manny $3,000. Acme may deduct as a business expense the entire $2,000 cost of Manny's flight and hotel and deduct 50% of the cost of the meals and entertainment. Manny need not count the $3,000 reimbursement as income (or pay taxes on it), and Acme need not include the amount on the W-2 form it files with the IRS reporting how much Manny was paid for the year. Moreover, Acme need not withhold income tax or pay any Social Security or Medicare taxes on the $3,000.

The reimbursements can be made through advances, direct reimbursements, charges to a company credit card, or direct billings to the employer.

The accountable plan rules are intended to prevent employees from seeking payment for personal expenses (or nonexistent phony expenses) under the guise that they are business expenses. Employees used to do this all the time to avoid paying income tax on the reimbursed amounts (employees must count employer reimbursements for their personal expenses as income, but not reimbursements for the employer's business expenses).

2. Unreimbursed Employee Expenses

Unless you've agreed to do so or your state's labor laws require it (see the warning below), you have no legal obligation to reimburse or pay employees for job-related expenses they incur. Employees are entitled to deduct from their own income any ordinary and necessary expenses arising from their employment that are not reimbursed by their employers. In this event, you (the employer) get no deduction, because you haven't paid for the expense.

> ⚠️ **Some states require reimbursement.** Check with your state's labor department to find out the rules for reimbursing employee expenses. You might find that you are legally required to repay employees, rather than letting your employees deduct the expenses on their own tax returns. In California, for example, employers must reimburse employees for all expenses or losses they incur as a direct consequence of carrying out their job duties. (Cal. Labor Code § 2802.)

Employees may deduct essentially the same expenses as business owners, subject to some special rules. For example, there are special deduction rules for employee home office expenses (see Chapter 7), and employees who use the actual expense method for car expenses may not deduct car loan interest.

However, it's much better for the employees to be reimbursed by the employer under an accountable plan and let the employer take the deduction. Why? Because employees can deduct unreimbursed employee expenses only if the employee itemizes his or her deductions and only to the extent these deductions, along with the employee's other miscellaneous itemized deductions, exceed 2% of his adjusted gross income. Adjusted gross income (AGI) is the employee's total income, minus deductions for IRA and pension contributions and a few other deductions (shown on Form 1040, line 35). Moreover, if an employee's AGI exceeds $149,950, the deductible amount is reduced by 3% of the excess (this figure is adjusted each year for inflation).

D. Employing Your Family

Whoever said "never hire your relatives" must never have read the tax code. The tax law promotes family togetherness by making it highly advantageous for small business owners, including professionals, to hire their spouses or children. If you're single and have no children, you're out of luck.

1.   Employing Your Children

Believe it or not, your children can be a great tax savings device. If you hire your children as employees to do legitimate work in your practice, you may deduct their salaries from your business income as a business expense. Your child will have to pay tax on the salary only to the extent it exceeds the standard deduction amount for the year—$5,000 in 2005. Moreover, if your child is under 18, you won't have to withhold or pay any FICA (Social Security or Medicare) tax on the salary (subject to a couple of exceptions).

These rules allow you to shift part of your business income from your own tax bracket to your child's bracket, which should be much lower than yours (unless you earn little or no income). This can result in substantial tax savings.

The following chart shows the federal income tax brackets for 2005. A child need only pay a 10% tax on taxable income up to $7,300—taxable income means total income minus the standard deduction. Thus, a child could earn up to $12,000 and pay only a 10% income tax. In contrast, if you were married and earned just $59,401, you'd have to pay a 25% federal income tax on that money. You'd also have to pay a 15.3% Social Security and Medicare tax (up to an annual ceiling), which your child under the age of 18 need not pay.

2005 Federal Personal Income Tax Brackets		
Tax Bracket	**Income If Single**	**Income If Married Filing Jointly**
10%	Up to $7,300	Up to $14,600
15%	$7,301 to $29,700	$14,601 to $59,400
25%	$29,701 to $71,950	$59,401 to $119,950
28%	$71,951 to $150,150	$119,951 to $182,800
33%	$150,151 to $326,450	$182,801 to $326,450
35%	All over $326,450	All over $326,450

EXAMPLE: Carol hires Mark, her 16-year-old son, to perform computer inputting services for her medical practice, which she owns as a sole proprietor. He works ten hours per week and she pays him $20 per hour (the going rate for such work). Over the course of a year, she pays him a total of $9,000. She need not pay FICA tax for Mark because he's under 18. When she does her taxes for the year, she may deduct his $9,000 salary from her business income as a business expense. Mark pays tax only on the portion of his income that exceeds the $5,000 standard deduction—so he pays federal income tax only on $4,000 of his $9,000 salary. With such a small amount of income, he is in the lowest federal income tax bracket—10%. He pays $400 in federal income tax for the year.

What About Child Labor Laws?

You're probably aware that certain types of child labor are illegal under federal and state law. However, these laws generally don't apply to children under 16 who are employed by their parents, unless the child is employed in mining, manufacturing, or a hazardous occupation. Hazardous occupations include driving a motor vehicle; being an outside helper on a motor vehicle; and operating various power-driven machines.

A child who is at least 16 may be employed in any nonhazardous occupation. Children at least 17 years of age may spend up to 20% of their time driving cars and trucks weighing less than 6,000 pounds as part of their job if they have licenses and no tickets, drive only in daylight hours, and go no more than 30 miles from home. They may not perform dangerous driving maneuvers (such as towing) or do regular route deliveries. For detailed information, see the Department of Labor Website (www.dol.gov).

No Payroll Taxes

As mentioned above, one of the advantages of hiring your child is that you need not pay FICA taxes for your child under the age of 18 who works in your trade or business, or your partnership if it's owned solely by you and your spouse.

EXAMPLE: Lisa, a 16-year-old, does filing and other office chores for her mother's accounting practice, which is operated as a sole proprietorship. Although Lisa is her mother's employee, her mother need not pay FICA taxes on her salary until she turns 18.

Moreover, you need not pay federal unemployment (FUTA) taxes for services performed by your child who is under 21 years old.

However, these rules do not apply—and you must pay both FICA and FUTA—if you hire your child to work for:

• your corporation, or

• your partnership, unless all the partners are parents of the child.

EXAMPLE: Ron, a 15-year-old, works for his father's law firm, cleaning the office and answering the phone. The law firm is a partnership involving Ron's father and three other lawyers unrelated to Ron. FICA and FUTA taxes must be paid for Ron because he is working for a partnership and not all of the partners are his parents.

No Withholding

In addition, if your child has no unearned income (for example, interest or dividend income), you must withhold income taxes from your child's pay only if it exceeds the standard deduction for the year. The standard deduction was $5,000 in 2005 and is adjusted every year for inflation. Children who are paid less than this amount need not pay any income taxes on their earnings.

EXAMPLE: Connie, a 17-year-old girl, is paid $4,000 a year to help out in her mother's chiropractic practice. She has no income from interest or any other unearned income. Her parents need not withhold income taxes from Connie's salary because she has no unearned income and her salary was less than the standard deduction amount for the year.

However, you must withhold income taxes if your child has more than $250 in unearned income for the year and her total income exceeds $800 (in 2005).

EXAMPLE: If Connie (from the above example) is paid $4,000 in salary and has $500 in interest income, her parents must withhold income taxes from her salary because she has more than $250 in unearned income and her total income for the year was more than $800.

2. Employing Your Spouse

You don't get the benefits of income shifting when you employ your spouse in your business, because your income is combined when you file a joint tax return. You'll also have to pay FICA taxes on your spouse's wages, so you get no savings there either. However, you need not pay FUTA tax if you employ your spouse in your unincorporated business. This tax is usually only $56 per year, so this is not much of a savings.

The real advantage of hiring your spouse is in the realm of employee benefits. You can provide your spouse with any or all of the employee benefits discussed in Section B, above. You'll get a tax deduction for the cost of the benefit, and your spouse doesn't have to declare the benefit as income, provided the IRS requirements are satisfied. This is a particularly valuable tool for health coverage—you can give your spouse health insurance coverage and reimbursements for uninsured expenses as a tax-free employee benefit. (See Chapter 11 for a detailed discussion.)

Another benefit of hiring your spouse is that you can both go on business trips and deduct the cost as a business expense, as long as your spouse's presence was necessary (for your business, not for you personally). In addition, you can establish a tax deferred retirement account for your spouse, such as a SIMPLE IRA or defined benefit pension plan. (See Chapter 12.)

Have Your Spouse Work at Home

Having your spouse spend all day with you at your office might sound like too much togetherness, and could even cause problems with your other staff members. Fortunately, there is no law that says your spouse must work in your office. He or she can work at home. Professionals' spouses typically do accounting, collections, or marketing work for the family practice. All these activities can easily be conducted from a home office.

Having your spouse work at home has tax benefits as well. If you set up a home office for your spouse that is used exclusively for business purposes, you'll get a home office deduction. Your spouse has no outside office, so the home office will easily pass the convenience of the employer test. (See Chapter 7.) Moreover, you can depreciate or deduct under Section 179 the cost of office furniture, computers, additional phone lines, copiers, fax machines, and other business equipment you buy for your spouse's use on the job.

3. Rules to Follow When Employing Your Family

The IRS is well aware of the tax benefits of hiring a child or spouse, so it's on the lookout for taxpayers who claim the benefit without really having their family members work in their businesses. If the IRS concludes that your children or spouse aren't really employees, you'll lose your tax deductions for their salary and benefits. And they'll have to pay tax on their benefits. To avoid this, you should follow these simple rules.

Rule 1: Your Child or Spouse Must Be a Real Employee

First of all, your children or spouse must be a bona fide employee. Their work must be ordinary and necessary for your business, and their pay must be for services actually performed. Their services don't have to be indispensable, only common, accepted, helpful, and appropriate for your business. Any real work for your business can qualify—for example, you could employ your child or spouse to clean your office, answer the phone, perform word processing, do photocopying, stuff envelopes, input data, or do filing. You get no business deductions when you pay your child for personal services, such as babysitting or mowing your lawn at home. On the other hand, money you pay for yard work performed on business property could be deductible as a business expense.

The IRS won't believe that an extremely young child is a legitimate employee. How young is too young? The IRS has accepted that a seven-year-old child may be an employee (*Eller v. Comm'r*, 77 T.C. 934 (1981)), but probably won't believe that children younger than seven are performing any useful work for your practice.

You should keep track of the work and hours your children or spouse perform by having them fill out time sheets or timecards. You can find these in stationery stores or make a timesheet yourself. It should list the date, the services performed, and the time spent performing the services. Although not legally required, it's also a good idea to have your spouse or child sign a written employment agreement specifying his or her job duties and hours. These duties should be related only to your practice.

Junior's Timesheet

Date	Time In	Time Out	Total Work Time	Services Performed
1/9/04	3:30 pm	5:30 pm	2 hours	copying, some filing
1/14/04	3:30 pm	5:00 pm	1 1/2 hours	printed out bills and prepared for them for mailing
1/15/04	3:45 pm	5:15 pm	1 1/2 hours	copying and filing
1/24/04	10:00 am	3:00 pm	5 hours	answered phones
1/30/04	3:30 pm	5:30 pm	2 hours	copying, filing
ʔ1/04	10:00 am	2:00 pm	4 hours	cleaned office

Rule 2: Compensation Must Be Reasonable

When you hire your children, it is advantageous (tax-wise) to pay them as much as possible. That way, you can shift as much of your income as possible to your children, who are probably in a much lower income tax bracket. Conversely, you want to pay your spouse as little as possible since you get no benefits from income shifting. This is because you and your spouse are in the same income tax bracket (assuming you file a joint return, as the vast majority of married people do). Moreover, your spouse will have to pay a 7.65% Social Security tax on his or her salary—an amount that is not tax deductible. (As your spouse's employer, you'll have to pay employment taxes on your spouse's salary as well, but these taxes are deductible business expenses.) The absolute minimum you can pay your spouse is the minimum wage in your area.

However, you can't just pay any amount you choose: Your spouse's or child's wages must be reasonable. This is determined by comparing the amount paid with the value of the services performed. You should have no problem as long as you pay no more than what you'd pay a stranger for the same work—don't try paying your child $100 per hour for office cleaning just to get a big tax deduction. Find out what workers performing similar services in your area are being paid. For example, if you plan to hire your teenager to do word processing, call an employment agency or temp agency in your area to see what these workers are being paid.

To prove how much you paid (and that you actually paid it), you should pay your child or spouse by check, not cash. Do this once or twice a month as you would for any other employee. The funds should be deposited in a bank account in your child's or spouse's name. Your child's bank account may be a trust account.

Rule 3: Comply With Legal Requirements for Employers

You must comply with most of the same legal requirements when you hire a child or spouse as you do when you hire a stranger.

- **At the time you hire:** When you first hire your child or spouse, you must fill out IRS Form W-4. You, the employer, use it to determine how much tax you must withhold from the employee's salary. A child who is exempt from withholding should write "exempt" in the space provided and complete and sign the rest of the form. You must also complete U.S. Citizenship and Immigration Services (USCIS) Form I-9, *Employment Eligibility Verification*, verifying that the employee is a U.S. citizen or is otherwise eligible to work in the U.S. Keep both forms. You must also record your employee's Social Security number. If your child doesn't have a number, you must apply for one. In addition, you, the employer, must have an

Employment Identification Number (EIN). If you don't have one, you may obtain it by filing IRS Form SS-4.

- **Every payday:** You'll need to withhold income tax from your child's pay only if exceeds a specified amount. (See Section 1, above.) You don't need to withhold FICA taxes for children younger than 18. You must withhold income tax and FICA for your spouse, but not FUTA tax. If the amounts withheld, plus the employer's share of payroll taxes, exceed $2,500 during a calendar quarter, you must deposit the amounts monthly by making federal tax deposits at specified banks or electronically depositing them with the IRS.

- **Every calendar quarter:** If you withhold tax from your child's or spouse's pay, you must deposit it with the IRS or a specified bank. If you deposit more than $1,000 a year, you must file Form 941, *Employer's Quarterly Federal Tax Return,* with the IRS showing how much the employee was paid during the quarter and how much tax you withheld and deposited. If you need to deposit less than $2,500 during a calendar quarter, you can make your payment along with the Form 941 instead of paying monthly. Starting in 2006, employers with total employment tax liability of $1,000 or less may file employment tax returns once a year instead of quarterly. The IRS is developing a new Form 944 for annual filers.

- **Each year:** By January 31 of each year, you must complete and give to your employee a copy of IRS Form W-2, showing how much you paid the employee and how much tax was withheld. You must also file copies with the IRS and Social Security Administration by February 28. You must include IRS Form W-3 with the copy you file with the Social Security Administration. If your child is exempt from withholding, a new W-4 form must be completed each year.

You must also file Form 940 or Form 940-EZ, *Employer's Annual Federal Unemployment (FUTA) Tax Return.* The due date is January 31; however, if you deposited all of the FUTA tax when due, you have ten additional days to file. You must file a Form 940 for your child even though you are not required to withhold any unemployment taxes from his or her pay. If your child is your only employee, enter his or her wages as "exempt" from unemployment tax. If all this sounds like too much work to do yourself, and you have no one on your staff who can do it for you, you can hire a payroll tax service to perform these functions for you for a moderate monthly fee.

IRS Circular E, *Employer's Tax Guide*, and Publication 929, *Tax Rules for Children and Dependents,* **provide detailed information on these requirements.** You can get free copies by calling the IRS at 800-TAX-FORM, by calling or visiting your local IRS office, or by downloading them from the IRS website at www.irs.gov.

E. Tax Deductions When You Hire Independent Contractors

As far as tax deductions are concerned, hiring independent contractors is very simple. Most of the time, the amounts you pay an IC to perform services for your practice will be deductible as business operating expenses. These expenses are deductible as long as they are ordinary, necessary, and reasonable in amount.

> **EXAMPLE:** Emily, an architect, hires Don, an attorney, to sue a client who failed to pay her. He collects $5,000, and she pays him $1,500 of this amount. The $1,500 is an ordinary and necessary business operating expense—Emily may deduct it from her business income for the year.

Of course, you get no business deduction if you hire an IC to perform personal services.

> **EXAMPLE:** Emily pays lawyer Don $2,000 to write her personal will. This is a personal expense. Emily cannot deduct the $2,000 from her business income.

If you hire an IC to perform services on your behalf in the start-up phase of your business, to manufacture inventory, or as part of a long-term asset purchase, the rules for deducting those types of expenses must be followed.

> **EXAMPLE:** Don hires Ralph, a business broker, to help him find a good dental practice to buy. After a long search, Ralph finds the right practice and Don buys it for $200,000. He pays Ralph a

$12,000 broker's fee. This fee is a business start-up expense, which Don may deduct $5,000 of during the first year he's in practice and the remaining $7,000 over the first 180 months he's in business.

1.   No Deductions for IC's Taxes

When you hire an independent contractor, you don't have to withhold or pay any state or federal payroll taxes on the IC's behalf. Therefore, you get no deductions for the IC's taxes; the IC is responsible for paying them.

However, if you pay an unincorporated IC $600 or more during the year for business-related services, you must:

- file IRS Form 1099-MISC telling the IRS how much you paid the IC, and
- obtain the IC's taxpayer identification number.

The IRS may impose a $100 fine if you fail to file a Form 1099 when required. But, far more serious, you'll be subject to severe penalties if the IRS later audits you and determines that you misclassified the worker.

If you're not sure whether you must file a Form 1099-MISC for a worker, go ahead and file one. You lose nothing by doing so and will save yourself the consequences of not filing if you were legally required to do so.

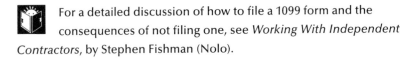 For a detailed discussion of how to file a 1099 form and the consequences of not filing one, see *Working With Independent Contractors*, by Stephen Fishman (Nolo).

2.   Paying Independent Contractor's Expenses

Independent contractors often incur expenses while performing services for their clients—for example, for travel, photocopying, phone calls, or materials. Many ICs want their clients to separately reimburse them for such expenses. The best practice is not to do this. It's better to pay ICs enough so they can cover their own expenses, rather than paying them less and having them bill you separately for expenses. This is because ICs who pay their own expenses are less likely to be viewed as your employee by the IRS or other government agencies.

However, it's customary in some businesses and professions for the client to reimburse the IC for expenses. For example, a lawyer who handles a business lawsuit will usually seek reimbursement for expenses such as photocopying, court reporters, and travel. If this is the case, you may pay these reimbursements.

When you reimburse an IC for a business-related expense, you, not the IC, get the deduction for the expense. Unless the IC fails to follow the adequate accounting rules discussed below, you should not include the amount of the reimbursement on the 1099 form you must file with the IRS reporting how much you paid the IC. The reimbursement is not considered income for the IC. Make sure to require ICs to document expenses with receipts and save them in case the IRS questions the payments.

The rules differ depending on whether the IC provides you with an "adequate accounting."

Adequate Accounting for Travel and Entertainment Expenses

To make an adequate accounting of travel and entertainment expenses, an IC must comply with all the record-keeping rules applicable to business owners and employees. The IRS is particularly suspicious of travel, meal, and entertainment expenses, so there are special documentation requirements for these. (See Chapter 20 for more on record keeping.) You are not required to save the IC's expense records except for records for entertainment expenses.

You may deduct the IC's travel, entertainment, and meal expenses as your own business expenses; but remember that meal and entertainment expenses are only 50% deductible. You do not include the amount of the reimbursement you pay the IC on the Form 1099 you file with the IRS reporting how much you paid the IC.

> **EXAMPLE:** Tim hires Mary, a self-employed marketing consultant, to help him increase his business's sales. In the course of her work, Mary incurs $1,000 in meal and entertainment expenses while meeting potential customers. She makes an adequate accounting of these expenses and Tim reimburses her the $1,000. Tim may deduct 50% of the $1,000 as a meal and entertainment expense for his business; Mary gets no deduction. When Tim fills out the 1099 form

reporting to the IRS how much he paid Mary, he does not include the $1,000. Tim should save all the documentation Mary gave him showing her entertainment expenses.

No Adequate Accounting for Travel and Entertainment Expenses

If an IC doesn't properly document travel, meal, or entertainment expenses, you do not have to keep records of these items. You may reimburse the IC for the expenses and deduct the full amount as IC payments, provided they are ordinary, necessary, and reasonable in amount. You are deducting these expenses as IC compensation, not as travel, meal, or entertainment expenses, so the 50% limit on deducting meal and entertainment costs does not apply. You must include the amount of the reimbursement as income paid to the IC on the IC's 1099 form. Clearly, you are better off if the IC doesn't adequately account for travel, meal, and entertainment expenses—but the IC is worse off because he'll have to pay tax on the reimbursements.

EXAMPLE: Assume that Mary (from the example above) incurs $1,000 in meal and entertainment expenses but fails to adequately account to Tim. Tim reimburses her the $1,000 anyway. Tim may deduct the full $1,000 as a payment to Mary for her IC services. Tim must include the $1,000 as a payment to Mary when he fills out her 1099 form, and Mary must pay tax on the money. She may deduct the expenses as business expenses on her own tax return, but her meal and entertainment expenses will be subject to the 50% limit. Moreover, she'll need to have adequate documentation to back up the deductions if she is audited by the IRS.

■

Chapter 16

Professionals Who Incorporate

I f you've incorporated your practice, or are thinking about it, this chapter is for you. When you form a professional corporation, you will ordinarily work as its employee, and be a shareholder as well. Your employee status presents some unique tax problems and opportunities.

If your practice is an LLC, LLP, or partnership, you can elect to be taxed as a corporation, so you also may be interested in learning about corporate tax treatment.

A. Automatic Employee Status

If you form a professional corporation to own and operate your practice and you continue to actively work in the practice, you automatically become an employee of your corporation. So even though you own the corporation (alone or with others in a group practice), you are also an employee of your corporation. In effect, you wear two hats: corporate shareholder and employee. Typically, you also serve as an officer of your corporation—president, vice president, secretary, or treasurer. In a one-shareholder corporation, one person holds all these officer positions and is an employee as well.

You're not an employee if your practice is organized in any other way—as a sole proprietorship, LLC, partnership, or LLP. Even though you actively work in your unincorporated practice, you remain a self-employed business owner. It's only when you form a corporation that your status changes to that of an employee.

The tax rules that apply to you as an employee of a business that you own or co-own are the same as those that apply to any corporation with employees. The tax consequences of being an employee instead of a self-employed business owner are significant—with a mix of good and bad.

First, let's look at some of the disadvantages of being an employee.

- Your corporation must pay half of your employment taxes from its funds, withhold the other half from your pay, and send the entire amount to the IRS.
- Your corporation must send a W-2 form to the IRS each year showing how much you were paid.

- Your corporation must pay unemployment taxes on your behalf (see Chapter 15).
- Your corporation will probably have to provide you with workers' compensation coverage.
- Business expenses that are not reimbursed by your corporation must be deducted on your personal return as miscellaneous itemized deductions or characterized as shareholder loans (see Chapter 17).
- You'll qualify for the home office tax deduction only if your use of your home office is for the "convenience of your employer" (see Chapter 7).
- You can't deduct interest on a car loan for a car you use for business driving (see Chapter 5).

However, there are certain tax benefits that you get by incorporating and becoming an employee. If your corporation is taxed as a C corporation, you qualify for various tax-free employee fringe benefits. If your corporation is taxed as an S corporation, you don't get tax-free fringe benefits but you may be able to reduce your employment taxes by paying part of your compensation as a corporate distribution.

In the rest of this chapter, we focus on how incorporated professionals can fine tune their compensation—with a mix of salary, employee benefits, dividends, and loans—to minimize the taxes they must pay and take advantage of their employee status. And we go over the differences in how to do this with a C corporation and an S corporation.

Forget About Being a Nonemployee Shareholder

To avoid paying employment taxes, many incorporated professionals who actively work in their practices have tried to claim that they were not employees of their corporation and that the money they received from their corporation was a dividend—not employee compensation. All have lost.

The courts have consistently held that corporation officer/shareholders who provide more than minor services to their corporation and receive remuneration are employees.

In one case, an accountant who was the president and owner of an S corporation claimed he was not an employee of his corporation, even though he did all of the accounting for the corporation and signed all of its tax returns. The accountant characterized the money he took out of his corporation as corporate dividends. The court found that the accountant provided substantial services that were essential to the corporation and that he was an employee (not an independent contractor), so the dividends were actually wages subject to employment taxes. (*Spicer Accounting, Inc. v. United States*, 1988 U.S. Dist. LEXIS 16891 (D. Idaho 1988), *aff'd* 918 F. 2d 90 (9th Cir. 1990).)

Even if you avoid serving as a corporate officer, you will still be an employee of your corporation if you spend all your time working for it.

B. Paying Yourself

When you have an incorporated practice, one of your most important decisions is how much to pay yourself and what form the payments should take. Your decision will have important tax consequences. This is not the case when your practice is a sole proprietorship, LLC, LLP, or partnership. The owners of these entities pay personal income taxes on all their business profits each year, so it doesn't matter how they take the money out of their business.

If, like most shareholders of professional corporations, you work as your corporation's employee, you can make payments to yourself in any of the following ways:

- employee compensation—salary, bonus, and fringe benefits such as health insurance and pension benefits
- corporate distributions, and/or
- loans from your corporation to you.

(Of course, corporation shareholders can also liquidate (bring an end to) their corporation and distribute its assets to themselves. But this can only be done once, and can have substantial tax costs.)

Most of your payments will likely be as employee salary, bonuses, benefits, and distributions. It is very important to get the mix between distributions and employee compensation right. Depending on whether your professional corporation is a C or S corporation, too much of one or the other can result in extra taxes.

1.   The Tax Treatment of Compensation Versus Distributions

Compensation that an incorporated business, including a professional practice, pays its employee is a deductible business expense provided the compensation is:

- ordinary and necessary
- paid for services actually performed, and
- reasonable in amount.

If your corporation is a C corporation, it deducts employee compensation on its own corporate tax return. You get no personal deduction for it. If your corporation is an S corporation, the deduction decreases the S corporation's profits that pass through the corporation to the shareholders' personal tax returns. (See Chapter 2.)

Corporate dividends are not tax deductible but they are taxable income to the shareholder who receives them. A dividend is not a payment for a shareholder/employee's services to the corporation as its employee. Rather, it represents a return on the capital the person has invested in the corporation as a shareholder.

On the other hand, employee wages are not only subject to income tax, but also to employment tax—this is a 12.4% Social Security tax up to an annual ceiling ($90,000 in 2005), and a 2.9% Medicare tax on all employee earnings. Corporate distributions are not subject to any employment tax because they constitute payments to shareholder/employees as shareholders, not for their services as employees.

So, which is better to receive when you are a shareholder/employee of a professional corporation—employee compensation or shareholder distributions? It all depends on whether your corporation is a C corporation or S corporation.

LLCs, LLPs, and Partnerships Can Also Be Taxed Like C Corporations

You don't necessarily have to have a corporation to obtain C corporation tax treatment for your practice. Although they are normally taxed as pass-through entities, LLCs, LLPs, and partnerships can obtain C corporation tax treatment by filing an election with the IRS. However, sole proprietors may not do this; they must form a C corporation to obtain such tax treatment. (See Chapter 2.)

---

2. C Corporations and the Advantages of Employee Compensation

If your professional corporation is a C corporation—that is, a taxpaying entity (see Chapter 2)—it is usually advantageous to take money out of the corporation in the form of employee compensation. This is because C corporations are subject to double taxation. The corporation must pay corporate income tax on its annual profit, and then the shareholders pay personal income tax on the same profits if they are distributed to them as dividends by the corporation.

Small C corporations, including most professional corporations, avoid double taxation by making sure their corporation has little or no profit at the end of the tax year. To accomplish this, the corporation's tax deductions must offset ("zero out") all or most of its income, leaving it with no taxable profit. (See Chapter 2.) Employee compensation is usually the largest single tax deduction professional corporations have. Because they are not deductible, paying out dividends will not avoid double taxation—indeed it will promote it.

EXAMPLE 1: DDS, Inc., is a professional corporation owned by Mark, a dentist, who is its sole shareholder and employee. DDS had a net income of $100,000 during the year ($300,000 revenue minus $100,000 operating expenses, including a $100,000 employee salary for Mark). DDS distributes its profits by giving Mark a $100,000 dividend. DDS, Inc., gets no tax deduction for the distribution. Thus, it's left with the $100,000 profit at the end of the year on which it must pay corporate income tax. It pays this tax at a 35% flat rate because it is a personal services corporation. Mark must then pay a 15% personal income tax on the distribution he receives. The distribution is not subject to employment taxes. DDS must pay $35,000 in corporate income tax on the $100,000 dividend (35% x $100,000 = $35,000). That leaves $65,000 to distribute to Mark, and on which he must pay personal income tax. Mark is in the 33% income tax bracket, so he pays $21,450 (33% x $65,000 = $21,450). The total tax paid on the $100,000 dividend is $56,450.

EXAMPLE 2: Assume that DDS does not pay any dividends to Mark. Instead, it pays the $100,000 profit to him as an employee bonus. Because employee salaries and bonuses are a deductible business expense, DDS now has no profits for the year on which it must pay corporate income tax ($100,000 profit – $100,000 bonus = 0 net profit). Mark must pay personal income tax on his $100,000 bonus, and DDS and Mark must each pay one-half of the applicable employment tax (Social Security and Medicare) on the salary. The total employment tax is $2,900. Only the 2.9% Medicare tax need be paid because Mark's total salary and bonus are above the Social Security tax ceiling. Mark is in the 33% personal income tax bracket, so his income tax on the $98,550 actually distributed to him after DDS withheld his one/half share of his employment tax is $32,522. The total tax on the $100,000 employee bonus is $35,422. Mark and his corporation save over $22,000 in taxes by characterizing the $100,000 as a bonus instead of a dividend.

These examples illustrate that a C corporation's shareholder/employees have a strong incentive to pay themselves as much employee compensation as possible to avoid double taxation. Paying large salaries to C corporation employees has another advantage—it increases the amount you can contribute to tax-advantaged retirement accounts each year. (See Chapter 12.)

The IRS, however, is well aware of all this. Unfortunately, it likes double taxation and has a powerful weapon to help maintain it: If the IRS determines that a corporation has paid a shareholder/employee an unreasonably high salary for the services actually performed, the IRS can treat the excess part of the salary as a dividend. Such a pretend dividend is called a constructive dividend. The C corporation will lose its deduction for that amount and will have to pay income tax on it. For most professional corporations, this means a 35% income tax because they are personal service corporations. The shareholder/employee who receives the payment will have to pay personal income tax on the amount. Currently, the top income tax on distributions is 15% (see Chapter 2). However, in some cases, the IRS will not permit salary disallowed as unreasonable to be treated as a constructive dividend to the shareholder (although it is treated that way for the corporation). Instead, the payment remains as compensation in the hands of the employee-shareholder who must pay income tax on it at ordinary personal income tax rates, usually far above 15%. Employment tax must be paid on the amount as well. (*Stemo Sales Corp.*, 345 F.2d 552 (Ct. Cl. 1965).)

Thus, if you're the shareholder/employee of a C corporation, it is crucial for you to know how much the corporation can pay you as employee compensation without bringing down the IRS's wrath. You must be able to prove to the IRS that your pay is reasonable.

> ⚠️ **You can't use Section 179 if you "zero out" your corporation's profits.** This could be a big drawback taxwise for your business. Section 179 allows businesses to deduction up to $105,000 of the cost of equipment and other tangible personal property bought for the business. However, the deduction is limited to the business's annual profits. No profit, no deduction. Thus, if you want to use the Section 179 deduction, you need to make sure that your C corporation has enough profit left at the end of the tax year. (See Chapter 9 for a detailed discussion of Section 179.)

What Is Reasonable Compensation?

There is no mathematical formula for determining whether compensation is reasonable. Rather, the IRS looks as all the facts and circumstances. The general rule is that reasonable pay is the amount that like enterprises would pay for the same, or similar, services. Among the factors the IRS and courts consider are:

- the duties performed by the employee
- the volume of business handled
- the type of work and amount of responsibility
- the complexity of the business
- the amount of time required
- the cost of living in the locality
- the ability and achievements of the individual employee performing the service
- the pay compared with the gross and net income of the business, as well as with distributions to shareholders
- the company's policy regarding pay for all employees, and
- the payment history for each employee.

These factors are judged based on the circumstances that exist when you contract for the services, not those that exist when reasonableness is questioned by the IRS. No single factor is determinative, and not all are considered in every case. Indeed, some courts consider only one factor: whether an independent financial investor (a person with no interest in the company, other than stock ownership) would be willing to pay the compensation involved.

One-Person Corporations

If you have a one-person professional corporation for which you perform all the professional services, it's often easy to figure out how much you should be paid. Usually, it's the corporation's entire profit (that is, an amount equal to its gross income minus its operating expenses, not counting your compensation). The reasoning behind this is simple: A professional corporation earns its income from providing a service; thus, if you're the only one providing that service for the corporation, your services must be worth all that the corporation earns, less operating expenses.

EXAMPLE: Richard Ashare, a Michigan attorney, formed a professional corporation of which is he was sole shareholder and professional employee. For several years, Ashare's firm devoted itself to a single class action lawsuit which it won, obtaining a $70 million judgment. The firm was awarded a $12.6 million fee. Ashare had his corporation pay him $12.24 million of the fee over five years as employee salary. The tax court held that the compensation was reasonable because Ashare's personal services had earned the fee. (*Ashare v. Comm'r*, T.C. Memo. 1999-282.)

Corporations With Multiple Shareholder/Employees

What if a professional corporation is owned by two or more professionals who provide employee services? You should not have a problem with the IRS if each shareholder/employee's compensation is based on the amount of money he or she brings into the practice. Compensation may also be added for the value of work a shareholder/employee does that does not directly lead to collections, such as administrative and management duties, business development, and community relations. (*Richlands Medical Association v. Comm'r*, T.C. Memo 1990-660.)

However, the IRS will become suspicious if the shareholder/employees' compensation is based on the proportion of their stock ownership of the corporation, rather than the actual value of their work as employees. For example, if a three-person professional corporation where each person owns one-third of the stock always pays each shareholder/employee one-third of the profits, the IRS will likely raise the issue of unreasonable compensation in an audit.

Corporations With Nonshareholder Employees

Where professional corporations can really run into problems with unreasonable compensation is when they have nonshareholder employees who provide professional services for the corporation, as well as shareholder/employees. The shareholder/employees' compensation cannot include amounts derived from the nonshareholders' work. A shareholder/employee can be paid only for the reasonable value of the services he or she actually performs, not those performed by others.

EXAMPLE: Pediatric Surgical Associates, a professional corporation taxed as a C corporation, had shareholder surgeons who received monthly salaries and cash bonuses based on the corporation's net profit, and nonshareholder surgeons who received only monthly salaries. The corporation deducted the entire amount paid to the shareholder surgeons as employee compensation. Both the IRS and tax court found that part of the salaries paid to the shareholder surgeons was unreasonable because it exceeded the value of their services to the corporation based on their collections. Rather, the excessive amounts represented the profits the corporation earned through the services of the nonshareholder surgeons. These profits could not be distributed to the shareholder surgeons as employee compensation because they were not for work actually performed by them. (*Pediatric Surgical Associates, P.C. v. Comm'r,* T.C. Memo 2001-81.)

Strategies to Avoid Unreasonable Compensation Problems

It's up to you to prove that your salary is reasonable if you are audited by the IRS. The time to think about how you will do this is long before you hear from the IRS. Here are some things you can do to prove you're worth what your corporation pays you.

Keep records of your work. Keep detailed records showing why you are worth what you're being paid. These should show the number of hours you worked, your contributions to the practice that may not directly result in collections (such as management and administrative tasks), and any other factors which could affect how much you're paid.

Keep records of your training and accomplishments. Employees with specialized training and/or experience can justify higher salaries than those without it. Professionals ordinarily have substantial training and other accomplishments they can brag about to the IRS. Maintain a file of all education credits, seminars, degrees, certificates, notable accomplishments, honors, and achievements that relate to your practice. Also keep records of what you earned as a professional before you established your corporation. These can provide strong evidence of what your services are worth. In one case, a court held that an incorporated dentist was entitled to a salary equal to what he had earned as a sole proprietor. (*Bianchi v. Comm'r,* 66 T.C. 324 (1976).)

Document your employment relationship. Draw up a written employment agreement and corporate resolution detailing your abilities, qualifications, and responsibilities. These should show why you're worth what your corporation is paying you. If your pay is more than your professional services are worth, the agreement should detail all the administrative duties you must perform and how much pay they merit above and beyond compensation for your professional services.

A corporate resolution should also be drafted whenever you receive a raise or a salary that documents the reasons for the increase in pay—for example, the substantial income your efforts bring in to the corporation. (For examples of such a corporate resolution, see *The Corporate Records Handbook*, by Anthony Mancuso (Nolo)).

Avoid large year-end bonuses. Try to avoid paying yourself large discretionary bonuses at the end of the year after your corporation's annual profits have been calculated. Such bonuses look like an effort to avoid corporate income tax, not pay you for your employee services to the corporation. If possible, the amount of any bonuses should be established in your employment agreement and based on a quantifiable figure, such as your annual billings. Bonuses should never be a percentage of the corporation's net profit or based on your stock ownership.

Establish annual salary in advance. One way to establish your annual salary is for a specific amount to be provided in your employment agreement. This will have to be redone at the beginning of each year. Another approach is to use a formula to set shareholder/employee salaries. If this is done, the formula should not be based on the corporation's net profits—this makes it look like a distribution. Instead, base the formula on the monetary value of the shareholder/employee's actual services. For example, you could base it on a percentage of collections the shareholder/employee brings in, plus the value of other administrative or managerial services.

Pay some distributions. It's best for a professional corporation to pay its shareholder/employees at least some distributions, some years. These should be more than a token amount or they won't impress the IRS. However, professional corporation distributions are ordinarily smaller than those issued by most other business corporations because they have less capital invested. Talk to your tax pro about how much your corporation should distribute as a dividend.

Consider all your compensation. All your compensation should be considered when determining whether it will pass muster with the IRS as reasonable. This includes not just your salary and bonus, but employee benefits, retirement plan contributions, and fringe benefits like company cars.

3. S Corporations and the Advantages of Corporate Distributions

If you are the shareholder/employee of a professional corporation that is an S corporation, you want to pay yourself as little employee wages and as much in S corporation distributions as possible. This, of course, is the exact opposite of a C corporation. The reason distributions are good when you have an S corporation is that distributions are not subject to employment taxes. Employee wages, on the other hand, are subject to such taxes. The fact that distributions are not deductible is meaningless for an S corporation because it is a pass-through entity—it pays no taxes. (See Chapter 2.)

> **EXAMPLE:** Senator John Edwards ran as the Democratic Party vice presidential candidate in 2004. Prior to his political career, he was one of the most successful medical malpractice lawyers in the United States. In 1995, he converted his law firm to an S corporation of which he was the sole shareholder. He paid himself an employee salary of $600,000 in 1996 and $540,000 in 1997, on which he and his firm paid employment taxes. As the sole stockholder, Edwards received distributions from his S corporation of $5 million for each of those two years, or $10 million total. He only had to pay income tax, not employment taxes, on the $10 million in distributions. How much did this save him? Had the $10 million been paid out as employee compensation, he would have had to pay 2.9% Medicare tax on this amount. (He wouldn't owe Social Security tax because his annual salary was well above the Social Security tax ceiling.) The Medicare tax really adds up, though, when you earn $5 million per year. In this case, Edwards saved a total of $290,000 ($10,000,000 x

$2.9\% = \$290,000$). Even though Edwards was subjected to criticism in the press during the 2004 campaign for his S corporation, his tax strategy was perfectly legal.

It's up to the people who run an S corporation—its officers and directors—to decide how much salary to pay the corporation's employees. When you are employed by an S corporation that you own (alone or with others), you'll be the one making this decision. In fact, 70% of all S corporations are owned by just one person, so the owner has complete discretion to decide on his salary.

However, an S corporation must pay reasonable employee compensation (subject to employment taxes) to a shareholder/employee in return for the services the employee provides before a distribution (not subject to employment taxes) may be given to the shareholder/employee. Whether compensation paid to an S corporation is reasonable is determined according to the same standards as those used for C corporations. (See Section 2 above).

If you don't pay yourself enough employee compensation, the IRS can reclassify all or part of the distribution as employee salary. This is particularly likely to occur if you pay yourself no employee compensation at all. For example, an attorney who incorporated his practice and was its only full-time employee took no salary and, instead, received only distributions from his corporation. The IRS and courts found that the distributions were disguised employee compensation and were, therefore, subject to employee taxes. (*Joseph Radtke v. U.S.*, 712 F. Supp. 143 (E.D, Wisc. 1989).)

How low can you go and still pay yourself a reasonable salary? There are no precise guidelines. IRS officials have stated that they make the determination on a case-by-case basis. After examining all the circumstances, they establish a range of reasonable salaries, from low to high. In one case, the IRS concluded that a reasonable salary for an Arkansas certified public accountant was $45,000 to $49,000. The accountant in that case had paid himself no salary and received $83,000 in corporate distributions. The IRS used salary information from a large financial services recruiting firm to determine what was reasonable. (*Barron v. Comm'r*, T.C. Summ. 2001-10.) Some IRS offices have software that provides salary information for a variety of occupations throughout the country.

Paying yourself the minimum wage likely won't be considered reasonable by the IRS. Some tax professionals believe that you'll have no problems as long as you pay yourself an amount at least equal to the Social Security tax ceiling—$90,000 in 2005. However, it is unclear if this is really true. A good approach is to find out what professionals performing similar services as employees are being paid in your area, and pay yourself on the low side of the salary range.

Also, keep in mind that there is a downside to paying yourself a small employee salary: You may end up reducing the amount you can contribute each year to a tax-advantaged retirement plan. This is because your annual tax deductible contribution limit is based on your employee salary. The smaller your salary, the less you may contribute and the smaller your deduction will be. (See Chapter 12.) To maximize their retirement plan contributions, some S corporation shareholder-employees elect to pay themselves the highest level salary that is used to determine the maximum annual contribution amount. This amount changes each year. In 2005, it was $210,000. The shareholders take the rest of their compensation, if any, as an S corporation distribution. It seems highly unlikely that the IRS would claim that an S corporation shareholder/employee who is paid $210,000 is not receiving a reasonable salary.

S corporation employee compensation is an IRS hot button area. The IRS recently announced that payment of unreasonably low employee compensation to S corporation shareholder/employees was an area of widespread taxpayer noncompliance that would receive greater scrutiny in the future. A 2005 report by the United States Treasury Inspector General shows why the IRS is concerned: The Inspector found that unreasonably low S corporation salaries cost the federal government $5.7 billion in employment taxes in 2000 alone. In that year, the owners of 36,000 one-shareholder S corporations with incomes of $100,000 or more paid themselves no employee wages at all. They passed $13.2 billion in profits to themselves without paying any employment taxes. The first sign of this increased scrutiny came in late 2005, when the IRS announced that it would audit 5,000 randomly selected S corporation tax returns from 2003 and 2004 as part of a national research program study to assess the reporting compliance of S corporations.

C. Employee Fringe Benefits

The most significant tax advantage that C corporations have over pass-through entities (sole proprietorships, partnerships, LLCs, LLPs, and S corporations) is in the area of employee fringe benefits. The main reason some professionals continue to form C corporations (or obtain C corporation tax treatment for an LLC, LLP, or partnership) is to obtain these benefits.

An employee fringe benefit is a form of payment for the employee's services. However, instead of paying the employee money, the employer provides the employee with property or services—for example, health insurance, retirement benefits, and company cars.

1. Qualified Fringe Benefits

Ordinarily, employee fringe benefits are treated the same as employee salary or bonus: They are tax deductible by the C corporation employer as a business expense, but their cost or value must be added to the recipient employee's taxable wages. This means that both income and employment taxes must be paid on the benefit's costs.

However, certain types of fringe benefits are tax-free—that is, the corporate-employer may deduct them as a business operating expense, and the employees don't need to include their cost in their income. The tax law lists the benefits that can be tax-free and establishes requirements that must be met to obtain this coveted status. Benefits that meet the requirements are said to be "qualified." Nonqualified benefits are taxable to the employee.

The rules are different for retirement benefits. They are not tax-free to the employee, but tax on them is deferred until the employee collects the benefits, which can be many years in the future.

If your professional practice is taxed as a C corporation and you work as its employee (which incorporated professionals ordinarily do), you can have your company provide employee benefits to you in your capacity as an employee which can result in tax savings.

> **EXAMPLE:** Marvin is a dentist who has formed a professional corporation taxed as a C corporation. He is the sole shareholder and

the only employee. Marvin has his corporation pay the premiums for a generous disability insurance policy for him. He also establishes a medical reimbursement plan to have his corporation reimburse him for health-related expenses not covered by insurance. The total cost of these benefits is $10,000 per year. His corporation gets to deduct the cost of the insurance, and he doesn't have to include the cost in his employee income. He's in the 33% federal income tax bracket, so this saves him $3,300 in income tax that he would have had to pay had he taken $10,000 in employee salary and purchased the insurance with his personal funds. He and his corporation also avoid paying employment taxes on the amount.

Professionals whose practices are taxed as sole proprietorships, partnerships, LLCs, LLPs, or S corporations must include in their incomes, and pay tax on, the value of any fringe benefits they receive from their company. For example, if Marvin in the above example had his practice organized as an LLC and taxed like a partnership, the LLC could have deducted the insurance premiums and medical reimbursements, but Marvin would have had to include them in his taxable income—thus, he would have $10,000 more in self-employment income to pay both income and self-employment tax on.

However, when it comes to the most important benefits—health insurance and retirement plans—things aren't nearly as bad for owners of pass-through entities as they used to be. Pass-through entity owners may deduct 100% of their health insurance expenses as a special personal income tax deduction (see Chapter 11). They can also establish their own retirement plans that are just as good as those for employees. (See Chapter 12.)

Pass-through entity owners, however, may not obtain tax-free medical reimbursement plans for themselves. This is a huge advantage for C corporations. But there is one way professionals who have pass-through entities can obtain tax-free treatment for medical reimbursement plans and all the other employee fringe benefits: The professional can hire his or her spouse as an employee and provide the spouse with the benefits. The spouse must be a legitimate employee, however. (See Chapter 11.)

Also, S corporation shareholder/employees who own less than 2% of the corporate stock receive the same treatment as C corporation shareholder/employees. However, few professionals own so little stock in their corporations (an S corporation shareholder can't stay under the less than 2% ownership ceiling by transferring stock to a spouse or other family member).

The IRS scrutinizes employee fringe benefits. Some companies try to avoid paying any taxes on profits by distributing them to employees in the form of money or reimbursements for bogus tax-free fringe benefits. In one case, an employer paid its employees $180 per month for nonexistent parking expenses. Because employee parking expenses are a tax-free employee fringe benefit (within certain limits), they didn't pay any income or employment tax on the payments. The IRS discovered the subterfuge and recharacterized the payments as taxable employee wages. (IRS Rev. Rul. 2004-98.) If you pay yourself for an employee benefit, make sure it's a legitimate benefit and keep proper records.

2. Types of Fringe Benefits

The most important employee fringe benefits are:
- health insurance and other health benefits (see Chapter 11)
- retirement benefits (see Chapter 12), and
- working condition fringe benefits (see Chapter 17).

Health and retirement benefits are so important that each has its own chapter. Working condition fringes are covered in the chapter on paying expenses.

Other fringe benefits are discussed below. Most have dollar limits. If the limit is exceeded, the employee must pay tax on the excess. In addition, to qualify for tax-free treatment, many of these fringe benefits must be offered to C corporation employees on a nondiscriminatory basis—that is, the corporation cannot provide the benefits just to highly compensated employees. These are employees who:
- own 5% or more of the corporation stock, or
- whose compensation exceeds a threshold amount.

If the nondiscrimination rules are violated, the cost or value of the benefit must be included in the highly compensated employee's income for tax purposes. What this means is that providing a tax-free fringe benefit could get very expensive if a C corporation has many nonshareholder employees. As a result, many small professional corporations do not provide employee fringe benefits that are subject to nondiscrimination rules. The benefits subject to these rules are noted below.

For more information on these fringe benefits, refer to IRS Publication 15-B, *Employer's Tax Guide to Fringe Benefits*. It can be found on the IRS website at www.irs.gov; or you can obtain a copy by calling 800-TAX-FORM.

Group Term Life Insurance

A corporation may provide up to $50,000 in group term life insurance to each employee tax-free. If an employee is given more than $50,000 in coverage, the corporation still gets to deduct the full premium, but the employee must pay tax on the excess amount. However, this tax is paid at very favorable rates.

For a group term life insurance plan to qualify for tax-free treatment, it must cover at least ten full-time employees. If the corporation has fewer than ten employees, all insurable employees must be covered. In addition, the plan must not discriminate in favor of key employees. An employee life insurance plan does not discriminate if any of the following are true:

- the plan benefits at least 70% of all employees
- at least 85% of all participating employees are not key employees, or
- the plan benefits employees who qualify under a classification that is set up by the employer and found by the IRS not to discriminate in favor of key employees.

Disability Insurance

If a professional corporation pays disability insurance premiums for an employee (and the employee is the beneficiary), the premiums are excluded from the employee's income. However, the employee must pay income tax on any disability benefits received under the policy. There is an important exception, however: Disability payments for the loss of a bodily function or limb are tax-free.

An employee can obtain disability benefits tax-free by paying for the premiums. If an employee pays for disability insurance himself, any disability benefits paid to the employee under the policy are not taxable to the employee. The IRS has ruled that an employee need only pay the disability premiums in the policy year the disability occurred to obtain tax-free treatment; the employer can pay the premiums for the preceding years. (IRS Private Letter Ruling 8027088.) The company can withhold the premiums from the employee's salary, or the employee can pay the premiums directly.

Educational Assistance

Employers may pay employees up to $5,250 tax-free each year for educational expenses such as tuition, fees, and books. However, there is a strict nondiscrimination requirement: No more than 5% of the benefits may be paid to shareholder/employees who are highly compensated employees. This eliminates this benefit for most professional corporations.

No Additional Cost Services

You may provide your employees (or their spouses or dependent children) with a service that you regularly provide to your clients. However, this benefit is tax-free only as long as it does not cause the company to incur any substantial additional costs. Additional costs usually include the cost of labor, materials, and supplies. If substantial additional costs are incurred, the cost of the *entire* service is taxable income to the employee, not just the added costs. Thus, for example, a medical corporation can't perform an operation on an employee and treat it as a tax-free benefit. The entire cost of the operation would have to be added to the employee's income.

This benefit is also subject to nondiscrimination rules. A highly compensated employee must include this cost in his income unless it's offered to all employees, or a group of employees defined under a reasonable classification you set up that does not favor highly compensated employees.

Employee Discounts

Employees may be given discounts of up to 20% for an employer's services or products. For example, a professional medical corporation can give employees a 20% discount for medical services. This benefit is subject to nondiscrimination rules.

Dependent Care Assistance

Up to $5,000 in dependent care assistance may be provided to an employee tax-free. For example, the company could help pay for day care for an employee's child. This benefit is subject to nondiscrimination rules. Unlike all the other benefits covered in this chapter, this benefit may be provided to owners of pass-through entities.

Moving Expense Reimbursements

Employees may also be paid or reimbursed for moving expenses. However, this benefit is tax-free to the employee only if the employee could deduct the expense if he paid it himself. The move must meet both a distance test and time test. The distance test requires that the new job location be at least 50 miles farther from the employee's old home than the old job location. The time test is met if the employee works at least 39 weeks during the first 12 months after arriving in the general area of the new job location.

Meals

Any meal or meal money you provide to an employee is tax-free if it has so little value (taking into account how frequently you provide such meals) that separately accounting for it makes no sense. This includes, for example:

- coffee, doughnuts, or soft drinks
- occasional meals or meal money provided to enable an employee to work overtime, and
- occasional parties or picnics for employees and their guests.

Meals you provide your employees on your business premises are also tax-free if they are furnished for your convenience—that is, for a substantial business reason. Boosting employee morale is not a good reason.

Athletic Facilities

If a corporation has an on-premises gym or other athletic facility, it can allow its employees to use it tax-free if substantially all use of the facility during the year is by corporation employees, their spouses, and their dependent children.

De Minimis (Minimal) Benefits

De minimis (minimal) employee benefits are also tax-free. A de minimis benefit is property or services you provide to an employee that have so little value that accounting for it would be unreasonable. Cash, no matter how little, is never excludable as a de minimis benefit, except for occasional meal money or transportation fare.

Examples of de minimis benefits include:
- holiday gifts, other than cash, with a low fair market value
- group-term life insurance payable on the death of an employee's spouse or dependent if the face amount is not more than $2,000
- occasional parties or picnics for employees and their guests, and
- occasional tickets for entertainment or sporting events.

Transportation Benefits

De minimis (minimal) transportation benefits may be provided to employees tax-free. These cost so little that it makes no sense to keep track of them—for example, occasional transportation fare given to an employee because the employee is working overtime. Employers may also pay up to $200 per month for employee parking or up to $105 per month for mass transit passes for those employees who don't drive to work.

Cafeteria Plans

A cafeteria plan (also called a flexible spending account) allows employees to choose benefits from a range of choices such as health insurance, dental plans, short-term disability coverage, and life insurance. They are called "cafeteria plans" because it's similar to choosing a meal in a cafeteria. Typically, these plans also allow employees to lower their income and employment taxes by making their own contributions and deducting them from their salaries.

Unfortunately, cafeteria plans are subject to nondiscrimination rules. Highly compensated employees must include benefits from such plans in their taxable income if they receive more than 25% of plan benefits. For this reason, professional corporations often don't use such plans.

3. Benefits That Are Not Tax Deductible

Some types of fringe benefits are not tax deductible at all—the corporate employer may not deduct them, and the recipient employee must include their cost or value in his income. Any benefit provided by a corporation to an employee is nondeductible if the employee couldn't deduct it as a business expense if he bought it himself. This includes, for example:

- paying for an employee's membership in country clubs
- paying for meals and entertainment that are not de minimis (see Section 2, above) and do not meet the requirements for deductibility set forth in Chapter 4,
- paying for an employee's personal vacations or other nonbusiness travel
- permitting an employee to use corporate property for personal purposes free of charge—for example, using a company car for a personal vacation
- allowing an employee to rent corporate property at below market rates
- allowing an employee to purchase corporate property at below market rates, and
- giving an employee any other property or service used solely for personal purposes.

The cost or fair market value of all such nondeductible benefits must be added to the employee's taxable income.

> **EXAMPLE:** Phil, the shareholder/employee of an engineering firm, has his company purchase a cell phone which he takes home and gives to his daughter. The cost of the phone would not be deductible as a business expense by Phil if he bought it himself because the phone is used only for personal purposes. Therefore, the cost of the phone must be added to Phil's employee income by his professional corporation/employer.

D. Shareholder Loans

Borrowing money from your corporation can appear to be a very attractive option because a loan is tax-free: It is not taxable income to you and the company need not pay employment taxes on the amount. In the past, small business owners avoided taxes by making cash advances to shareholders and treating them as loans, even though there was no intention that the money would ever be paid back. Today, there are strict IRS rules to prevent such abuses.

Loans are not a deductible expense. A loan is not a deductible expense for the lender. Thus, a C corporation that makes a loan to a shareholder from its corporate earnings must pay corporate income tax on the amount of the loan, even though the money is no longer in the corporation's bank account. Professional corporations normally pay income tax at the 35% personal service corporation rate. This result can be avoided only if the shareholder/borrower pays back the money before the corporation files its tax return; or if the corporation has losses that can be used to offset the loan. If a loan is made to a shareholder of an S corporation, no corporate income tax will be due because S corporations don't pay income tax. The money will pass through the corporation to the shareholder's personal returns, however, and he'll have to pay personal income tax on it. Again, this can be avoided only through timely repayment or offsetting losses.

1.   Only Bona Fide Loans Are Recognized by the IRS

A corporate loan to a shareholder/employee must be a bona fide (real) loan or the IRS will recharacterize it as employee compensation or a corporate distribution. A bona fide loan is made with the intention that it be repaid by the borrower.

The loan should have all the characteristics of a loan made by a bank: There should be a signed promissory note with a stated interest rate requiring repayment on a specific date or in installments. Banks ordinarily don't make unsecured personal loans, so the loans should also be secured by the shareholder/employee's personal property, such as the employee's corporate stock, or a house or car. The loan should be listed on the company's balance sheet as a receivable, and the corporation's minutes should reflect approval of the loan. And, most important, the terms of the loan must be followed—that is, the shareholder/employee must repay the loan on time.

If an IRS auditor concludes that a shareholder/employee loan is not bona fide, it will be recharacterized as something else for tax purposes. If the corporation is an S corporation, IRS auditors will usually try to reclassify a bogus loan as employee compensation, with the consequences described above—income and employment taxes will be due on the money, as well as penalty taxes for underpayment of taxes. If the corporation is a C corporation, the IRS auditor will likely reclassify the loan as a taxable constructive dividend.

2. Below Market Loans

Even if a shareholder/employee loan is bona fide, there will still be tax problems if it is a below-market loan—a loan for no interest or interest below the applicable federal rate. The applicable federal rate is based on the rate the federal government pays on new borrowings and is adjusted monthly. The rate can be found on the IRS website (www.irs.gov). There are three different rates: short-term (for loans not over three years), mid-term (for four- to nine- year loans), and long-term (for loans over nine years). In July 2005, the annual short-term rate was 3.45%, the midterm rate was 3.86%, and the long-term rate was 4.35%. If the corporation charges at least this much interest, the IRS will not complain.

However, if no interest is charged, or the rate is below the applicable federal rate, interest will be imputed by the IRS. That is, the IRS will pretend that interest equal to the applicable federal rate was charged on the loan. The corporation is treated as transferring the imputed interest to the shareholder/employee as additional compensation and the employee must pay tax on it. However, this interest might be deductible as a personal deduction by the shareholder if the loan proceeds are used for investment purposes.

EXAMPLE: Arnold, the sole shareholder of the Arnold Professional Corporation, a C corporation, takes a $100,000 no-interest loan from the corporation. The applicable federal rate is 3.42%, compounded semiannually. The IRS imputes $3,452 in interest: The IRS pretends for tax purposes that Arnold paid $3,452 in interest to the Arnold Corporation, and that the corporation returned the money to Arnold as a constructive dividend. Arnold now has $3,452 in dividend income he must pay personal income tax on at the 15% dividends rate. The Arnold Corporation has interest income of $3,452 it must pay corporate income tax on at the 35% personal service corporation tax rate. The corporation gets no deduction for the constructive dividends. However, Arnold might get a personal deduction for part of the pretend interest he paid the corporation if he used the loan proceeds for investment purposes.

There is one important exception to the below-market loan rules: A shareholder can borrow up to $10,000 from the corporation interest-free, and the IRS will not impute any interest. However, this exception does not apply if one of the principal purposes of the loan is tax avoidance.

∎

Chapter 17

How You Pay Business Expenses

Does it make any difference how you pay for a business expense? In other words, is an expense's deductibility affected by whether you pay the expense out of your own pocket or from business funds? The short answer is Yes!

Consider this example: Clarence, an attorney and partner in a ten-lawyer law firm organized as an LLC, receives a $500 bill for his state bar association dues. He pays the bill with his personal funds and then has his firm reimburse him. Sounds simple. But how is this transaction treated for tax purposes? Is the $500 reimbursement income that Clarence must pay taxes on? Can Clarence's practice deduct the expense? Would it make any difference if Clarence's firm paid the bill directly?

This chapter discusses the different ways you can pay business expenses and how it affects their deductibility.

> **Sole proprietors can skip to Section C.** The material in Sections A and B do not apply to professionals who are sole proprietors or owners of one-person LLCs taxed as sole proprietorships. It makes no difference if you pay an expense from your personal funds or business funds because your practice and personal finances are one and the same.

A. Your Practice Pays

The best way to pay for business expenses you incur is to have your practice pay for them. This can be done in several ways:

- The practice can pay the expense directly—that is, the practice pays the bill with money from its own bank account.
- The practice can give you a cash allowance that you use to pay for the expense.
- The practice can give you a company credit card to pay for the expense.

1. Tax Treatment

Your practice will be entitled to deduct the cost of anything it pays for that you use for your work. Such expenses fall under a broad category of deductible business expenses called working condition fringe benefits—property and services a business provides to its workers so that they can perform their jobs. Anything can be a working condition fringe benefit as long as it is used, at least part of the time, by the worker for his or her job. This includes many of the more common business expenses, such as:

- local and long-distance travel for business
- business-related meals and entertainment
- professional association dues
- professional liability insurance
- professional publications
- business equipment, such as computers and telephones, and
- company cars.

The worker can be an employee of an incorporated practice or the owner of a practice taxed as a partnership (which includes most LLCs, LLPs, and partnerships), or even an independent contractor. For purposes of working condition fringe benefits all such people are treated alike—we'll refer to them as workers.

A working condition fringe benefit is tax-free to a worker to the extent that the worker would be able to deduct the cost of the property or services as a business or depreciation expense if he paid for it himself. If the worker uses the benefit 100% for work, it is 100% tax-free. But the value of any personal use of a working condition fringe benefit must be included in the worker's compensation and he must pay tax on it.

> **EXAMPLE:** Lloyd, the employee/shareholder of a small incorporated engineering firm, has his company purchase a cell phone which he uses to keep in touch with his office and clients when he's in the field. If Lloyd uses the cell phone 100% for his work, it is tax free to him. But if he uses it only 50% of the time for work and 50% of the time for personal purposes, he would have to pay income tax on 50% of its value. Either way, Lloyd's corporation gets to deduct 100% of its payment for the cell phone.

The value of the personal use is determined according to its fair market value.

EXAMPLE: It costs Lloyd, Inc. $100 a month to pay for the cell phone used by Lloyd, the employee. If Lloyd uses the cell phone 50% of the time for work and 50% of the time for nondeductible personal uses, he would have to add $50 per month to his taxable compensation.

2. Documentation Requirements

For a working condition fringe benefit to be tax free, all applicable documentation requirements must be satisfied. There must be documentation showing that the expense was business-related, which the company should keep. At a minimum, this means that there must be a receipt (except for travel, meal, or entertainment expenses of less than $75) and proof of payment, such as a canceled check or credit card statement. Additional documentation is required for meal, entertainment, and travel expenses. If the property is listed property—for example, cars, computers, cell phones—the amount of business and personal use must be documented. (See Chapter 20 for a detailed discussion of all these documentation requirements.)

In addition, if instead of paying the bill directly, the practice gives you a cash allowance, or a credit card or other cash equivalent, you must follow the accountable plan rules covered in Section D.

B. Using Personal Funds to Pay for Business Expenses

It's better not to pay for a business expense from your personal funds; however, this may not always be possible. If you do pay for something yourself, you need to understand and follow the rules. Failure to follow the rules could result in the complete loss of the deduction—and even extra taxes for you. The rules differ depending on how your practice is legally organized.

1. LLCs, Partnerships, and LLPs

If you're involved in a group practice organized as an LLC, partnership, or LLP, your practice will ordinarily receive partnership tax treatment (although you can elect to be taxed as a corporation; see Chapter 2). Your practice and your personal finances are separate, and your LLC, LLP, or partnership must have a separate bank account. There are two ways to deal with business expenses you pay from your own pocket:

- obtain reimbursement from the practice, or
- deduct the expense on your personal return.

Obtaining Reimbursement

Unless your partnership, LLP, or LLC makes clear in writing, or by an established unwritten policy, that it will *not* reimburse you for the type of expense you've paid yourself while performing services for the partnership, you must obtain reimbursement from the LLC, LLP, or partnership. If the accountable plan rules discussed in Section D are followed, the reimbursement will not be taxable income to you, and the practice may deduct the amount as an operating expense.

It is very important to understand that if a partner or LLC member has the right to be reimbursed for an expense, he or she is *not entitled to any tax deduction for the expense.* The reasoning behind this rule is that if a partner or LLC member has the right to be reimbursed for an expense, it is not a "necessary" expense for that LLC member or partner, and only necessary business expenses are deductible. Obviously, it is a necessary expense for the LLC, LLP, or partnership. (IRS Private Letter Ruling 931600.)

For a reimbursed expense to be deductible by your LLC, LLP, or partnership, and not taxable income to you, the reimbursement must be made under an accountable plan. An accountable plan is a set of procedures intended to ensure that your practice doesn't reimburse you for personal expenses and then take a deduction for it.

In brief, you must:

- make an "adequate accounting" of the expense—that is, follow all the applicable record-keeping and other substantiation rules for the expense

- timely submit your expense report and receipts to your LLC, partnership, or LLP, and
- timely return any payments that exceed what you actually spent for business expenses.

These rules apply not only when you are reimbursed for an expense, but also to cash advances and allowances. They also apply when you use a company credit card. See Section D, below, for a detailed discussion of accountable plan rules.

If the accountable plan rules are followed, your LLC, LLP, or partnership lists the reimbursed expense on its own tax return (IRS Form 1120) as an operating expense deduction. You don't list it on your personal return. It is combined with all the other deductions for the business, and then subtracted from its income to determine if the practice had a profit or loss for the year. The profits or losses then pass through the business entity to the owners' individual tax returns. The owners pay individual tax on their share of the profits. Thus, in effect, the LLC member or partners share all the tax deductions for expenses reimbursed by the practice.

> **EXAMPLE:** Louis is a surgeon who is a member of a group practice organized as an LLC and taxed as a partnership. He takes a trip to Paris to attend a medical convention that costs $5,000. He charges the whole amount on his personal credit card. When he gets back home, he quickly submits an expense report, along with all required receipts, to the LLC which then reimburses him for the expense. Because he has followed the accountable plan rules, the $5,000 is not taxable income to Louis. The reimbursement is an LLC tax deduction that is listed on the LLC's tax return, not Louis's. It is deducted from all the income the LLC earned during the year to determine the LLC's annual profit. The $5,000 deduction reduces the LLC's annual profit from $305,000 to $300,000. Louis and his two partners each pay personal tax on their one-third share of these profits.

If reimbursement of a working condition fringe benefit is not made under an accountable plan, the money you receive is treated as compensation to you from your LLC, LLP, or partnership and subject to both income and self-employment taxes. Your LLC, partnership, or LLP may be able to deduct the payment as a guaranteed payment to you. But you get no deduction for the expense on your personal tax return—as explained above, a partner or LLC owner may not take a personal deduction for an expense that the partnership or LLC will reimburse him for.

> **EXAMPLE:** Assume that Louis from the above example fails to follow the accountable plan rules for his $5,000 reimbursement. His LLC doesn't get to deduct the $5,000 and must report it as taxable compensation to Louis, who will have to pay income and self-employment tax on it. Louis may not deduct the $5,000 as a business expense on his own tax return.

Deducting the Expense on Your Personal Tax Return

Another approach is for a partner or LLC member to deduct as a business expense on his own personal tax return the expenses he pays while providing services to the practice. This way, you get the total deduction instead of having to share it with the other LLC members or partners. The deduction not only reduces your taxable income for income tax purposes, but reduces self-employment income as well, so you pay less Social Security and Medicare tax.

However, a personal deduction is allowed only if:

- a written partnership agreement or LLC operating agreement provides that the expense will not be reimbursed by the partnership or LLC, or
- the business has an established routine practice of not reimbursing the expense.

Absent such a written statement or practice, no personal deduction may be taken. Instead, you must seek reimbursement from the partnership, LLP, or LLC.

> **EXAMPLE:** Dr. Magruder, a pathologist, was a member of a South Carolina group medical practice organized as a partnership. He regularly invited medical technologists employed by various hospitals he dealt with to join him for lunch and paid the cost out of his own pocket. Dr. Magruder did not seek to have the lunch

expenses reimbursed by his partnership; instead, he tried to deduct them as business expenses on his personal tax return. The IRS and tax court disallowed the expenses because Magruder failed to show that his partnership had a written policy, or unwritten practice, denying reimbursement for such expenses. (*Magruder v. Comm'r*, T.C.Memo 1989-169.)

The moral is clear: Unless your LLC, LLP, or partnership has a written policy, or well-established unwritten policy, of *not* reimbursing an expense, you should always seek reimbursement. Otherwise, the expense may not be deductible at all.

If you want to take a personal deduction for an expense but your partnership, LLP, or LLC agreement doesn't require that you pay it personally, you'll have to amend the agreement to make clear that partners or LLC members will not be reimbursed for specified expenses. A partnership agreement can be amended as late as the due date for the partnership return for the tax year (excluding extensions) and still be effective for the entire partnership year. For example, a partnership agreement may be amended as late as April 15, 2006 and the change will be effective for all of 2005. (IRC § 761(c).)

In addition, you must comply with all applicable record-keeping and documentation requirements for the expense—for example, you should use a mileage log to document car expenses. (See Chapter 5.) Keep these records and receipts with your personal tax records. You don't need to provide them to the LLC, LLP, or partnership because it isn't taking the deduction.

To deduct business expenses on your personal return, list them on Schedule E (Form 1040), Part II. Check the "yes" box on line 27 to indicate that you're claiming unreimbursed partnership expenses. List the unreimbursed partnership expenses themselves on a separate line in column (h) of line 28. Write "UPE" or "Unreimbursed Partnership Expenses" in column (a) of line 28.

If you deduct a business expense on your personal tax return, you may not also obtain reimbursement from your LLC, LLP, or partnership—no "double dipping" is allowed.

2.   Corporations

If your practice is incorporated (whether it's taxed as a C or S corporation), you'll ordinarily be its employee for tax purposes. You have three options for dealing with expenses you incur while performing services for your corporation:

- seek reimbursement from the corporation
- deduct the expense on your personal tax return, or
- make a shareholder loan to the corporation.

These rules apply to all employees, including family members who work as your employees.

Obtaining Reimbursement

From a tax standpoint, the best option is to have your corporation reimburse you for your expenses. You must comply with all the documentation rules for the expense and your reimbursement should be made under an accountable plan. As described below in Section D, an accountable plan is a set of procedures that ensures that employees don't get reimbursed for personal expenses.

If you comply with the requirements for an accountable plan, your corporation gets to deduct the expense and you don't have to count the reimbursement as income. The reimbursement should not be included in the W-2 form the corporation files with the IRS showing how much you were paid for the year.

If you fail to follow the rules, any reimbursements must be treated as employee income subject to tax. Thus, the corporation must include them on your W-2. You'll then have to deduct the expense on your personal tax return as described below.

Deducting the Expense on Your Personal Tax Return

Another option is simply to pay the expense yourself, forgo reimbursement from your corporation, and deduct it on your personal tax return. However, a corporate employee is entitled to a personal deduction for an unreimbursed employee expense only if he does not have the right to be reimbursed for the expense by the corporation. If an employee has a right to reimbursement, but fails to claim it, a personal deduction for the employee's expenses is not allowed because the employee's expenditures are not "necessary." (*Heidi v. Comm'r*, 274 F.2d 25 (7th Cir. 1959).)

> **EXAMPLE:** Burten Schaeffer, a medical doctor employed by a Cleveland hospital, traveled to Chicago to attend a presentation on antibiotics and to look into purchasing laboratory equipment for the hospital's pathology laboratory. Dr. Schaeffer never sought reimbursement for his expenses from the hospital. Instead, he deducted the cost of the trip on his personal tax return. The IRS and tax court disallowed the deduction because Schaeffer failed to show that the hospital would not have reimbursed him for the expense had he asked for it. (*Schaeffer v. Comm'r*, T.C. Memo. 1994-227.)

How do you prove to the IRS that you don't have the right to be reimbursed for an expense from your corporation? The best way is for the corporation's directors to adopt a corporate resolution that the corporation's employees will not be reimbursed for the type of expense involved. Alternatively, a written policy may be drafted. Another method is to ask the corporation for reimbursement and be refused in writing.

If you fail to show that you would not have been reimbursed for an employee expense you paid yourself, your payment will be treated by the IRS either as a contribution to your corporation's capital, or as a loan from you to the corporation (see below). If it's characterized as a loan, it may be deductible by the corporation. (*Deputy v. Du Pont*, 308 U.S. 488 (1940).)

If you are able to deduct the unreimbursed expense on your personal return, it must be listed on IRS Schedule A, Form 1040, as a miscellaneous itemized deduction. You must also file IRS Form 2106, reporting the amount of the expense.

However, it's much better for you to be reimbursed by your employer (your corporation) under an accountable plan and let the corporation take the deduction. Why? Because employees can deduct unreimbursed employee expenses only as miscellaneous itemized deductions. Thus, they are deductible only if they itemize their deductions and only to the extent that these deductions, along with any other miscellaneous itemized deductions, exceed 2% of the employee's adjusted gross income. Adjusted gross income (AGI) is an employee's total income, minus deductions for IRA and pension contributions and a few other deductions (shown on Form 1040, line 35).

> **EXAMPLE:** Eric has formed a regular C corporation for his dental practice. He is its president and employee. He travels to Boston to attend an educational seminar for his practice, incurring $3,500 in expenses. He pays these expenses out of his own pocket and does not seek reimbursement from his corporation. $1,000 of his expenses were for meals and entertainment, so they are only 50% deductible. He may deduct the remaining $2,500 as an unreimbursed business expense, but only to the extent that this amount, along with his other miscellaneous itemized deductions, exceeds 2% of his adjusted gross income. Eric's AGI for the year was $100,000, and he had no other miscellaneous deductions, so he may deduct his $2,500 expense only to the extent it exceeds $2,000 (2% x $100,000 = $2,000). He therefore may deduct only $500 of his $3,500 convention expenses.

But wait, it gets worse. There is an additional overall limit on itemized deductions for higher-income taxpayers, which includes many professionals. All itemized deductions—except for deductions for medical expenses, investment interest, casualty and theft losses, and some gambling losses—must be reduced by 3% of the amount that a taxpayer's AGI exceeds a threshold amount. In 2005, the threshold was $145,950 (this figure is adjusted each year for inflation). For example, a taxpayer with a 2005 AGI of $245,950 would be $100,000 above the threshold. Thus, the taxpayer's itemized deductions would be reduced by $3,000 (3% x $100,000 = $3,000). This reduction is made after the 2% limitation and any other limits are applied. However, a taxpayer's total itemized deductions cannot be reduced by more than 80%.

> **EXAMPLE:** Jessica is a doctor with an incorporated practice, for which she works as an employee. Her 2005 AGI was $245,950. She had $50,000 in itemized deductions, including $20,000 in unreimbursed employee expenses. Her employee expenses are first reduced by 2% of her AGI (2% x $245,950 = $4,919). Her total itemized deductions are now $45,081. Her AGI is $100,000

above the $145,950 threshold for the 3% phase-out. Thus, her total itemized deductions must be reduced by $3,000 (3% x $100,000 = $3,000). This leaves her with only $42,081 in itemized deductions. If Jessica had had her corporation reimburse her for the $20,000 of business expenses under an accountable plan, the corporation could have deducted the entire amount, and Jessica would not have had to include the reimbursement in her income. Jessica would also have fewer itemized deductions to be affected by the 3% itemized deduction phase-out.

The 3% itemized deduction phase-out (also called a cutback adjustment) is scheduled to be reduced over the next several years and then eliminated, at least temporarily. It will be cut by one-third for tax years 2006 and 2007, by two-thirds for 2008 and 2009, and then eliminated entirely in 2010. However, the phase-out will be reinstated starting in 2011, unless Congress acts to eliminate it permanently—something President Bush has requested.

Shareholder Loan to the Corporation

Instead of obtaining reimbursement or personally deducting an expense you pay yourself, you may be able to treat the payment as a loan from you, a shareholder, to your corporation. However, the payment must be handled like a real loan—that is, it should be properly documented as a loan on your corporation's books and the corporation must pay it back. If more than a nominal amount is involved, the loan should be documented with a signed promissory note and corporation resolution approving the loan and repayment. If you fail to treat your payment as a true loan, the IRS may recharacterize it as a contribution by you to your corporation's capital, and any loan repayments you receive as taxable dividends.

It's best to charge your corporation interest for any payments you treat as loans. However, your corporation may borrow up to $10,000 from you interest-free, so long as it is not done to avoid taxes. (IRC § 7872(c)(3).) The $10,000 limit is an aggregate figure—that is, your corporation cannot owe you more than a total of $10,000 at any one time. If you lend more than $10,000 to your corporation, you must charge interest at market rates or the IRS may impute interest—that is, it will pretend that interest equal to the applicable federal rate was charged on the loan. (See Chapter 16.) Repayment of the loan is not taxable income to you, the lender; but any interest you receive from your corporation, or that the IRS imputes, is taxable income.

C. Your Client Reimburses You

Many professionals—for example, attorneys and accountants—typically have all or some of the expenses they incur while working for a client reimbursed by the client. This is particularly common for local and long-distance travel expenses. These types of expenses are working condition fringe benefits.

Obviously, if you incur a deductible expense while performing services for the client, and the client does not reimburse you, you may deduct the expense on your own return. (If your practice is a partnership, LLP, LLC, or corporation, "you" means the business entity, not you personally.) Your client gets no deduction for the expense, because it didn't pay it.

But, if your client reimburses you for an expense, your client gets the deduction, not you. However, you need not include the reimbursement in your income if you provide an adequate accounting of the expenses to your client—you should follow the accountable plan rules discussed in Section D, below. If the reimbursement is for entertainment expenses, the client must keep your records documenting each element of the expense. The reimbursement should not be included in any 1099-MISC form the client files with the IRS reporting how much you were paid for the year.

> **EXAMPLE:** Jason, an attorney based in Chicago, is hired by Acme Corp. to handle a trial in Albuquerque, New Mexico. He incurs $5,000 in travel expenses, which he fully documents. Acme reimburses Jason for the $5,000 expense. Jason need not include this amount in his income for the year. Acme may deduct it as a business expense.

If you do not adequately account to your client for these expenses, the client still gets to deduct the expense, but *you must pay tax on the reimbursement*. Moreover, the client must include the amount of the reimbursement in any 1099-MISC it files with the IRS reporting how much it paid you for your services.

> **EXAMPLE:** Assume that Jason doesn't keep proper records of his travel expenses, but is still reimbursed $5,000 by Acme. Acme must include the $5,000 payment in the 1099-MISC form it files with the IRS reporting how much it paid Jason. Jason will have to pay tax on the $5,000.

Clients Often Improperly Include Reimbursements in 1099s

Clients should not include expense reimbursements in the 1099-MISC forms they file with the IRS (reporting how much they paid you) if you provided an adequate accounting for the expense. However, some clients do it anyway. If this happens, you should report the entire amount on the 1099-MISC as income and deduct the amount of the reimbursement as a business expense. That way, everything will even out.

> **EXAMPLE:** Annie, a sole proprietor accountant, is reimbursed $5,000 by ABC, Inc., for expenses she incurred performing accounting work. Annie provided an adequate accounting to ABC, but ABC included the $5,000 in the 1099-MISC it filed with the IRS. Thus, the 1099 shows Annie receiving $10,000 in income from ABC, instead of $5,000. Annie should include the whole $10,000 in her income on her tax return, and deduct the $5,000 in expenses on her Schedule C.

For simplicity in bookkeeping, some professionals routinely deduct all expenses they incur, even those that were reimbursed by clients. But, they also include the amount of all the reimbursements they receive from their clients in their income and pay tax on them. This is fine with the IRS. What you cannot do is deduct an expense and not report as income a reimbursement you received for it.

Deducting all your expenses yourself does not lessen the IRS's record-keeping requirements. If you lack proper documentation for an expense, your deduction will be disallowed by the IRS in the event of an audit.

D. Accountable Plans

The accountable plan rules are a set of procedures intended to prevent workers from avoiding paying tax on money their company gives them that they use for personal, nondeductible expenses. You need to understand and follow the accountable plan rules if:

- your practice gives you cash or a credit card (or other cash equivalent) to pay a business-related expense
- your practice reimburses you for an expense you pay for yourself, or
- a client reimburses you for expenses.

If you follow the rules, any reimbursement or allowance you receive will not be taxable income to you. But, if you fail to follow the rules, you'll have to pay tax on the amount.

1. What Is an Accountable Plan?

An accountable plan is an arrangement in which a company agrees to reimburse or advance worker expenses only if the worker:

- pays or incurs expenses that qualify as deductible business expenses while performing services for the company
- adequately accounts to the company for the expenses within a reasonable period of time, and
- returns to the company within a reasonable time any amounts received in excess of the actual business expenses incurred.

An accountable plan need not be in writing (although it's not a bad idea). What you need to do is set up procedures for you and other company workers to follow that meet the following three requirements:

Requirement #1. The expense must be for business. The expense must have a business connection—that is, the worker must have paid it while performing services for the company. The expense must have been deductible as a business expense had the worker paid for it with his or her own money.

Requirement #2. The worker must make an adequate accounting. The worker must provide the company with an "adequate accounting" for the expense within a reasonable time after it was paid or incurred. This means the worker must document and follow all the applicable recordkeeping and other substantiation rules for the expense. For example, the worker must keep receipts for all expenditures (except for travel, meal, and entertainment expenses below $75; or travel and meal expenses paid on a per diem basis).

Requirement #3. Excess payments must be timely returned. Workers who are advanced or reimbursed more than they actually spent for business expenses must return the excess payments to the company within a reasonable time.

Payments a company makes under an accountable plan should be deducted on the company's tax return in the category of the expense paid. For example, reimbursements for business travel should be deducted as travel expenses.

2.   Time Limit to Make Adequate Accounting

A worker can't wait forever to meet the accountable plan requirements. An adequate accounting must be provided to the company within a reasonable time. If this is not done, the entire amount the company paid the worker must be added to the worker's income for tax purposes. Likewise, any excess payments must be returned within a reasonable time. Any amounts not so returned are treated as taxable compensation for the worker.

There are three ways to meet the reasonable time requirement:

- **Fixed date method.** Under this method, the expense must be substantiated by the worker within 60 days after it is paid or incurred. If the worker received more money from the company than he actually spent on business expenses, the excess amount must be returned to the company within 120 days after the expenses were paid or incurred. If the company gives the worker an advance to cover expenses, it may be paid no more than 30 days before the expense is incurred.

- **Periodic statement method.** Under this method, the company provides the worker with a periodic statement (at least quarterly) listing any excess amounts that the worker must return to the company. The worker must substantiate all his expenses and return any excess payments within 120 days after receiving the statement. This gives the worker as much as 210 days to meet the requirements.

- **Other reasonable method.** You use any other time periods that are reasonable under the circumstances—for example, a worker on an extended business trip might be given a longer period to substantiate expenses and return any excess allowance than a worker on a single overnight trip.

EXAMPLE: Tom is the sole shareholder and employee of his engineering consulting firm, which is a C corporation. He has his corporation give him a $5,000 cash advance to cover his expenses for a business trip—in other words, he takes $5,000 out of the corporation's bank account and puts it in his pocket. While on the trip, he spends $4,000 on his travel and meal expenses, which he fully documents. He files his expense diary and receipts with his corporation tax records within 60 days after he paid his expenses. He returns the excess $1,000 payment to his corporate bank account within 120 days after he paid his expenses. Tom has complied with the accountable plan rules. If he had failed to return the extra $1,000 within 120 days, it would have had to have been characterized as worker wages for tax purposes, and added to Tom's W-2 showing his annual wages.

3.   Payments Not Made Under an Accountable Plan

Any payments to workers for business-related expenses that do not comply with the accountable plan rule are deemed to be made under an "unaccountable plan." The result is that the payments are considered to be taxable compensation to the worker.

If your practice is a corporation and you work as its employee, this means that:

- you must report the payments as income on your tax return and pay tax on them
- you may deduct the expenses—but only as an itemized deduction (unreimbursed employee expenses) on your Schedule A—and you must have the documentation to back up the deduction if you're audited
- your corporation may deduct the payments as employee wages paid to you
- the corporation must withhold your income taxes and share of Social Security and Medicare taxes from the payments, and
- the corporation must pay its 7.65% share of your Social Security and Medicare taxes on the payments.

If your practice is an LLC, partnership, or LLP, you will not be its employee, thus the payments will not be characterized as employee wages and there will be no withholding. Instead, they will be taxable distributions to you from your business entity. You must report the payments as income on your personal tax return and pay both income and self-employment taxes on them. Your LLC, partnership, or LLP may be able to deduct the payments as a guaranteed payment to you. You may deduct them as business expenses on your personal return; but, again, you must have the documentation to back them up if you're audited by the IRS.

■

Chapter 18

Amending Tax Returns

Sam, a doctor with his own practice, used his car 60% for business driving last year. He paid $5,000 in interest on a loan for the vehicle. However, he failed to deduct any portion of the payments because he didn't realize that the business portion of car loan interest was deductible as a business expense. After reading this book, he realizes that he should have claimed the deduction on his last two tax returns. Had he done so, he would have saved thousands of dollars on his taxes. But what can he do now?

Fortunately, tax returns are not engraved in stone. If, like Sam, you realize that you failed to claim tax deductions which you were entitled to take, you may be able to amend your tax returns for those years and get the IRS to send you a refund check.

A. Reasons for Amending Your Tax Return

It's very common for taxpayers to file amended tax returns. Here are some reasons why you might want to amend a tax return:

- You forgot to take a deduction.
- You have a net operating loss for the year and want to apply it to prior years.
- You claimed a deduction which you were not entitled to take.
- You entered incorrect information on your return.
- A retroactive change in the tax laws makes you eligible for an additional deduction.

You need not amend your return if you discover that you made a simple math error. These will be corrected by the IRS computers, and you'll be notified of the change by mail.

However, if you made a mistake in your favor, failed to report income, or took deductions which you were not entitled to take, amending your return may avoid all or some fines, interest, and penalties if you're later audited by the IRS.

Filing an amended return makes an audit more likely. You don't have to file an amended return if you don't want to. Filing an amended tax return increases the chances that your tax return for the year involved will be audited by the IRS. Thus, it may not be worth doing unless you are entitled to a substantial refund. If you're not sure whether to amend, consult a tax professional for advice.

1. Net Operating Losses

Some professionals pay out more for expenses than they take in as income. This is most likely to occur when they are just starting out. When a business's expenses for a tax year exceed its income, it has a "net operating loss" (NOL for short). Although it may not be pleasant to lose money over an entire year, an NOL has some important tax benefits: You can apply the NOL to reduce your taxable income from other sources for the same tax year—for example, your spouse's income or investment income. If you still have all or part of your NOL left over, you have the option of applying it to future tax years. This is called carrying a loss forward. You can carry the NOL forward for up to 20 years and use it to reduce your taxable income in the future.

Alternatively, you may apply the loss to past tax years by filing an amended return for those years. Ordinarily, you may elect to carry back the loss for the two years before the year you incurred the loss. However, if you had an NOL for 2001 or 2002, you may carry back the loss to five years before the NOL year. The loss is used to offset the taxable income for the earliest year first, and then applied to the next year(s). This will reduce the tax you had to pay for those years and result in a tax refund. This is called carrying a loss back.

As a general rule, it's advisable to carry a loss back, so you can get a quick refund from the IRS on your prior years' taxes. However, you may elect not to carry an NOL back if you paid no income tax in prior years, or if you expect your income to rise substantially in future years and you want to use your NOL in the future when you'll be subject to a higher tax rate.

Need to know more about NOLs? Refer to IRS Publication 536, *Net Operating Losses*, for more information. You can download it from the IRS website at www.irs.gov, or obtain a paper copy by calling the IRS at 800-TAX-FORM.

2.   Retroactive Tax Laws

Sometimes, Congress or the IRS changes the tax laws or regulations and makes the change retroactive—that is, the change applies to returns filed some time before the change was made. If a retroactive change is more favorable to you than the laws that were in effect when you filed your return, you might be entitled to a refund for prior years.

House Sales After May 6, 1997

One important retroactive tax change involves the home office deduction. Under the tax law in effect before 2003, business owners who took the home office deduction often had to pay extra tax when they sold their homes. If they took a home office deduction for more than three of the five years before they sold their house, they had to pay capital gains tax on the profit from the home office portion of their home.

Fortunately, effective December 24, 2002, the IRS changed its regulations to eliminate this requirement. As long as you live in your home for at least two of the five years before you sell it, the profit you make on the sale—up to $250,000 for single taxpayers and $500,000 for married taxpayers filing jointly—is not taxable. (See Chapter 7 for more information on the home office deduction.) Moreover, the change was made retroactive to May 6, 1997. If you sold your house after this date and paid capital gains tax on the home office portion, and you meet the two-out-of-five-year requirement, you are entitled to a refund of the tax. You obtain your refund by filing an amended tax return for the year.

> **EXAMPLE:** Greta sold her house in July 2002 for a $50,000 profit. She used 20% of the space in her house as a home office for her business, and took a home office deduction every year. When she did her taxes for 2002, she mistakenly paid a $2,000 capital gains tax on her profit from the house sale (20% x $50,000 = $10,000 x 20% = $2,000). Greta made the error because she didn't know the change in the tax law was retroactive. In 2006, she discovers her error, amends her 2002 tax return to eliminate the capital gains tax, and receives a refund from the IRS of the $2,000.

However, it may be too late for you to claim this refund, because there are limits on how far back you can go to amend your returns. See Section B, below, for information on these time limits.

Bonus Depreciation

Another instance of a retroactive change in the tax laws involves bonus depreciation. In March 2002, Congress enacted a law allowing business owners to take an additional 30% (later increased to 50%) first-year depreciation deduction for business assets purchased after 9/11/01, the date of the attack on the World Trade Center. Not every taxpayer wanted to take bonus depreciation—it might not have been advantageous if you expected your income to go up substantially in future years, which would have placed you in a higher tax bracket and made the deductions you took in the future more valuable.

However, bonus depreciation applied automatically for tax years 2002 through 2004, unless you filed a statement with your tax return that you wished to opt out of the deduction. If you didn't take bonus depreciation, but failed to file the statement opting out, you should file an amended tax return including such a statement. If you don't file the statement, the IRS will act as if you took a bonus depreciation deduction, even though you really didn't. This could result in your having to pay extra taxes if you sell long-term assets you purchased during 2002 to 2004. You must file your amendment within the six-month period described above. (Write "Filed pursuant to Section 301.9100-2" on the amended return.) Bonus depreciation ended on Dec. 31, 2004, so it won't be automatically applied to tax years 2005 and later.

3.   Casualty Losses

There is a special rule for certain types of casualty losses—losses to business property caused by things like fire, floods, or earthquakes. If you suffer a loss to your business property due to a disaster that occurs in an area the president declares to be a disaster area, you have the option of deducting the loss from your previous year's taxes. You do this by filing an amended tax return for the year and deducting the amount of the loss from your taxable income for that year. This will reduce the taxes you had to pay for the year, and the IRS will send you a refund check for the difference. Alternatively, you can wait and deduct your loss from the current year's taxes. But if you want to get some money from the IRS quickly, you should file an amended return (unless you paid no tax the prior year). (See Chapter 14 for a detailed discussion of casualty losses.)

John Kerry Amends His Tax Return
In the midst of the 2004 presidential campaign, Senator John Kerry released his 2003 tax return to the public. A Texas CPA who analyzed the return discovered an error. Kerry and his wife had sold a rare Dutch painting they co-owned for $1,350,000. Kerry's share of the profit on the sale was $175,000. For some reason, his accountant thought this gain should be taxed at the 20% capital gains rate then in effect. However, this was clearly wrong. Kerry's profit should have been taxed at his 28% income tax rate, because the painting was not a capital asset. Soon after this was brought to his attention, Kerry filed an amended tax return for 2003 and paid an extra $11, 577 in income tax for the year.

B. Time Limits for Filing Amended Returns

Unfortunately, you can't wait forever to amend a tax return for a prior year. If you wait too long, you'll forever lose your right to file an amended return for the year, even if it means you'll be forced to give up a deduction for the year in which you were legally entitled to the deduction.

1. Three-Year Amendment Period

The general rule is that you can file an amended return until the later of:

- three years after the date you filed the original return (April 15 or later if you obtained an extension to file), or
- two years after the date you paid the tax, whichever is later.

Even if you filed your return for the year before April 15, it is deemed to be filed on that date for amendment purposes. For example, you have until April 15, 2008 to file an amended return for your 2004 taxes, which are deemed to have been filed on April 15, 2005 (even if you filed them earlier). The three-year period applies in most cases.

> **EXAMPLE:** Sam failed to claim a deduction for the interest he paid on a loan for a car he used in his business during 2005. He filed his 2005 taxes on April 1, 2006. How long does Sam have to amend his 2005 tax return to claim the deduction? Until April 15, 2009, three years after he is deemed to have filed his original tax return for 2005 (April 15, 2006). If he fails to meet the deadline, he loses his right to claim the deduction and obtain a tax refund.

However, if you obtain an extension of time to file your original return for the year involved, you may add that time to the three-year period. You can get an automatic extension of time to file your return until August 15, and a further extension until October 15 if the IRS agrees, which it usually does.

> **EXAMPLE:** Assume that Sam (from the above example) obtained an extension of time to file his 2005 tax return to August 15, 2006. He would have until August 15, 2009 to amend his tax return for 2005.

2.   Section 179 Deductions

There are two different rules for amending tax returns to claim or disclaim a Section 179 deduction. For the years 2002 through 2005, you may amend your return for Section 179 deductions in the same manner as other amendments (as described above). (IRS Reg. 1.179-5T.)

For tax years before 2002 and after 2005, amendments are much more difficult. You must file your amended return within six months after the due date for the return for the tax year involved, including any extensions of time you received. Because tax returns are ordinarily due on April 15, you must file your amended return by October 15 to claim a Section 179 deduction for the prior year, unless you received an extension of time to file your return.

EXAMPLE: Jill bought a $3,000 computer for her optometry practice during 2006. When she did her taxes for the year in early 2007, she thought she had to depreciate the computer's cost over five years. She took a depreciation deduction for the computer on her 2006 tax return. However, she learned later that she could have deducted the entire cost in one year using Section 179. She has until October 15, 2007 to file an amended 2006 return to claim the deduction. If she fails to do so, she loses the right to claim a Section 179 deduction for the property and must use depreciation instead.

3. Net Operating Losses

There are two ways to claim a refund of a prior year's taxes due to a later net operating loss: You can file IRS Form 1040X, *Amended U.S. Individual Income Tax Return* (see Section C, below) within the usual three-year limitation period, or you can seek a quick refund by filing IRS Form 1045, *Application for Tentative Refund*. If you file Form 1045, the IRS is required to send your refund within 90 days. However, you must file Form 1045 within one year after the end of the year in which the NOL arose.

4. Bad Debts

In some instances, you may be able to deduct a business bad debt as a business operating expense. A debt doesn't become "bad" until it is clearly worthless. This may occur years after the loan was originally made. (See Chapter 14 for more on the requirements for deducting bad debts.) If you failed to claim a bad debt deduction on your original tax return for the year the debt became totally worthless, you have up to seven years to file an amended return listing the bad debt. However, the seven-year term applies only to debts that are completely worthless. If a debt is only partially worthless, you must amend your return within the usual three-year period.

5. Business Start-Up Expenses

If you want to deduct your business start-up expenses, you must file an election with the IRS on or before the date your first tax return is due after you start your business. For example, if your business begins in 2006, you must file the election with your 2006 tax return, due April 15, 2007 (or later if you receive an extension). If you miss this deadline, you have one last chance to make your election: You may file an amended return making the election within six months after the date your original return was due (April 15, or later if you got an extension). If you fail to do this, you will lose your right to deduct your start-up expenses and you'll have to treat them as capital expenses. (See Chapter 10 for a detailed discussion of deducting business start-up expenses.)

Should You File Your Amendment as Late as Possible?

The IRS ordinarily has only three years after a return is filed to audit the return. Filing a Form 1040X does not extend this period. Thus, if you file your Form 1040X near the end of the three-year period, the IRS will have very little time to audit your return for the year involved. As a result, it might accept your claim without auditing your return. However, it might also refuse to accept your 1040X unless you agree to extend the time it has to audit your return for the year.

C. How to Amend Your Return

If, like most small business owners, you are a sole proprietor, you amend your income tax return by filing IRS form 1040X, *Amended U.S. Individual Income Tax Return*. When you file Form 1040X to obtain a refund of taxes you've already paid, it is called a "claim for refund."

Filing an amended tax return is not terribly difficult. You can usually do it yourself, with or without the aid of a computer tax-preparation program. The heart of the form consists of three columns: A, B, and C. You record the relevant figures from your original tax return in Column A; the corrected information is listed in Column C; and the difference between the two is listed in Column B. You must also provide a brief explanation for the changes. For example, Senator Kerry included the following explanation when he filed a Form 1040X to amend his 2003 taxes: "The tax on the one-half interest in the Adam Willerts painting was inadvertently calculated at the 20% rather than the 28% rate."

If you're amending your previous year's tax return and are entitled to an additional refund for that year, tax experts suggest that you wait until you receive your original refund check for that year. You can go ahead and cash the first refund check as soon as you receive it. Of course, you can file your amended return immediately if you were not entitled to a refund on your original return.

You must mail or hand deliver Form 1040X to the IRS. You can't file it electronically. If you mail it, send it by certified mail, with postal return receipt requested. This will let you know when the IRS received it. If you amend your returns for more than one year, mail each 1040X in a separate envelope. The 1040X instructions show where to mail the form.

You may also hand deliver the form to the IRS service center where you file your tax returns. If you do this, be sure to get a stamped copy as your filing receipt.

To obtain a refund due to an NOL, you may file either IRS Form 1045 alone, or along with Form 1040X. You can often get your refund faster by using Form 1045 alone. The calculations required to figure out how much you can deduct from your income in prior years can be complicated, so it's a good idea to get some help from a tax professional. Refer to IRS Publication 536, *Net Operating Losses*, for more information.

Don't forget your state tax returns. The IRS routinely shares information with states that impose income taxes (every state except Alaska, Florida, Nevada, South Dakota, Texas, Washington, and Wyoming). Thus, your state tax department will probably learn that you amended your federal tax return. For this reason, tax experts advise that you also amend your state tax returns for the years affected.

D. How the IRS Processes Refund Claims

The IRS doesn't like paying back money to taxpayers. When you file a Form 1040X, your tax return for that year will receive extra special attention. An IRS employee will pull your return and examine it and your 1040X to decide whether you're really entitled to a refund; and if so, how much. Your claim may be denied or accepted as filed, or the amended items may be audited. If a claim is audited, the procedures are almost the same as in the audit of a regular tax return. Moreover, the IRS has the option of extending the audit to your entire tax return, not just the amended items. Thus, *filing an amended tax return increases your chances of an audit.*

You should receive your refund, if you're entitled to one, in about 12 weeks. However, your refund may be reduced by amounts you owe for past-due child support, debts you owe to another federal agency, or past-due state income tax obligations. You will be notified if this happens.

If the IRS denies your claim, it must explain why—for example, because you filed it late. You have the right to appeal such a denial. For a detailed discussion of IRS appeals, refer to *Stand Up to the IRS*, by Frederick W. Daily (Nolo).

■

Chapter 19

Staying Out of Trouble With the IRS

his chapter explains IRS audits and provides tips and strategies that will help you avoid attracting the attention of the IRS—or come out of an audit unscathed, if you find yourself in the government's crosshairs.

Need more information on dealing with the IRS? For a detailed discussion of audits and other IRS procedures, see *Stand Up to the IRS*, by Frederick Daily (Nolo).

A. Anatomy of an Audit

You can claim any deductions you want to take on your tax return—after all, your tax preparer (or you) fills it out, not the government. However, all the deductions you claim are subject to review by the IRS. This review is called a tax audit. There are three types of audits: correspondence audits, office audits, and field audits.

- **Correspondence audits.** As the name indicates, correspondence audits are handled entirely by mail. These are the simplest, shortest, and most common type of IRS audit, usually involving a single issue. The IRS sends you written questions about a perceived problem, and may request additional information and/or documentation. If you don't provide satisfactory answers or information, you'll be assessed additional taxes.

- **Office audits.** Office audits take place face-to-face with an IRS auditor at one of the 33 IRS district offices. These are more complex than correspondence audits, often involving more than one issue or more than one tax year. If you make less than $100,000 per year, this is the type of in-person audit you're likely to face.

- **Field audits.** The field audit is the most comprehensive IRS audit, conducted by an experienced revenue officer. In a field audit, the officer examines your finances, your business, your tax returns, and the records you used to create the returns. As the name implies, a field audit is normally conducted at the taxpayer's place of business; this allows the auditor to learn as much about your practice as possible. Field audits are ordinarily reserved for higher income taxpayers—a category many professionals fall within.

1. How Small Business Owners Get in Trouble With the IRS

When auditing small business owners, including professionals, the IRS is most concerned about whether you have:

- **Underreported your income.** Unlike employees who have their taxes withheld, business owners who are not employees have no withholding—and many opportunities to underreport how much they earned.
- **Claimed tax deductions to which you were not entitled.** For example, you claimed that nondeductible personal expenses, such as a personal vacation, were deductible business expenses.
- **Properly documented the amount of your deductions.** If you don't have the proper records to back up the amount of a deduction, the IRS may reduce it, either entirely or in part. Lack of documentation is by far the most common reason taxpayers lose deductions when they get audited.

2. Records Available to Auditors

An IRS auditor is entitled to examine the business records you used to prepare your tax returns, including your books, check registers, canceled checks, and receipts. The auditor can also ask to see records supporting your business tax deductions, such as a mileage record if you took a deduction for business use of your car. The auditor can also get copies of your bank records, either from you or your bank, and check them to see whether your deposits match the income you reported on your tax return. If you deposited a lot more money than you reported earning, the auditor will assume that you didn't report all of your income, unless you can show that the deposits you didn't include in your tax return weren't income. For example, you might be able to show that they were loans, inheritances, or transfers from other accounts. This is why you need to keep good financial records.

IRS Audit Technique Guides

Would you like to know what the IRS examiner is supposed to look for when you are audited? You may be able to find out. The IRS has created a series of audit technique guides to train its examiners how to audit many types of businesses, including some types of professional practices. Many of these guides are available on the IRS website at www.irs.gov/businesses.

The audit technique guides of interest to professionals are those for:

- architects (available at www.unclefed.com/SurviveIRS/MSSP)
- attorneys
- business consultants (available at www.unclefed.com/SurviveIRS/MSSP)
- partnerships, and
- veterinary medicine (also useful for medical doctors and dentists).

B. The IRS: Clear and Present Danger or Phantom Menace?

A generation ago, the three letters Americans feared most were I-R-S. There was a simple reason for this: the IRS, the nation's tax police, enforced the tax laws like crazy. In 1963, an incredible 5.6% of all Americans had their tax returns audited. Everybody knew someone who had been audited. Jokes about IRS audits were a staple topic of nightclub comedians and cartoonists.

In 2004, only 0.62% of all Americans were audited, and an IRS audit was a relatively rare event. There are several reasons for the change:

- **A decline in the IRS workforce**—between 1992 and 2001, the IRS workforce declined by 16%; the number of revenue agents dropped by 21%.
- **An increase in workload**—at the same time the IRS workforce was declining, its work load was increasing; it grew 16% between 1992 and 2001.

- **A new emphasis on taxpayer service, rather than enforcement.**
  Starting in the mid-1990s, the IRS began to emphasize taxpayer
  service rather than enforcement.
- **Legal changes**—Congress enacted new laws in 1998 that were
  intended to prevent perceived abuses by IRS agents and auditors.
  These new protections also made it more difficult for the IRS to go
  after tax cheats.

According to the IRS Oversight Board, the IRS does not have the
resources to pursue at least $30 billion worth of known taxes that are
incorrectly reported or not paid. In 2001, the nation's "tax gap"—the
total inventory of taxes that are known and not paid—was estimated at
between $312 and $353 billion.

Both the IRS and Congress are aware of the IRS's enforcement
problems and have taken some steps to ameliorate them. The IRS has
received moderate budget increases in the past few years and has placed
a renewed emphasis on enforcement. Staff has been shifted from
performing service functions like answering taxpayer questions to doing
audits. The president's 2005 budget proposal called for a greater than
10% increase in IRS enforcement funding, including the hiring of 5,000
new auditors, tax collectors, criminal investigators, and other staff.

The precipitous decline in audit rates that began in the mid-1990s has
been stopped, but audit rates remain at low levels. However, the IRS
Commissioner promises that audit rates will go up in the next few years,
with professionals one of the main targets. With huge federal budget
deficits yawning as far as the eye can see, it seems likely that this is one
government promise that will be kept.

Although the IRS is a troubled agency and audit rates are at or near
all-time lows, hundreds of thousands of people still get audited every
year. In 2004, the IRS audited 184,456 of the 15,285,000 tax returns
filed by Schedule C filers—the category that includes the majority of
professionals.

Moreover, high-income professionals—particularly doctors, dentists,
lawyers, and CPAs—are a perennial IRS audit target. Indeed, in 2005,
the IRS issued a press release touting its success prosecuting health care
professionals for tax fraud.

C. How Tax Returns Are Selected for Audits

It's useful to understand how tax returns are selected for audit by the IRS. (By the way, if you are audited, you are entitled to know why you were selected. You ordinarily have to ask to find out.)

1. DIF Scores

One way the IRS decides who to audit is by plugging the information from your tax return into a complex formula to calculate a "discriminate function" score (DIF). Returns with high DIFs have a far higher chance of being flagged for an audit, regardless of whether or not you have done anything obviously wrong. Anywhere from 25% to 60% of audited returns are selected this way. Because the DIF formula is out of date, fully one-third of audits conducted in recent years through the formula resulted either in no change or a tax refund. The IRS is in the process of revising the DIF formula to achieve better audit results. Exactly how the DIF is calculated is a closely guarded secret. Some of the known factors the formula takes into account are:

- **Where you live.** Audit rates differ widely according to where you live. In 2000, for example, taxpayers in Southern California were almost five times more likely to be audited than taxpayers in Georgia. The IRS no longer releases information on audit rates by region, but according to the latest available data, the state with the highest audit rate is Nevada; other high-audit states include Alaska, California, and Colorado. Low-audit states include Illinois, Indiana, Iowa, Maryland, Massachusetts, Michigan, New York (not including Manhattan), Ohio, Pennsylvania, and West Virginia.
- **The amount of your deductions.** Returns with extremely large deductions in relation to income are more likely to be audited. For example, if your tax return shows that your business is earning $100,000, you are more likely to be audited if you claim $50,000 in deductions than if you claim $5,000.
- **Hot-button deductions.** Certain types of deductions have long been thought to be hot buttons for the IRS—especially auto, travel, and entertainment expenses. Casualty losses and bad debt deductions may also increase your DIF score. Some people believe

that claiming the home office deduction makes an audit more likely, but the IRS denies this.

- **Businesses that lose money.** Businesses that show losses are more likely to be audited, especially if the losses are recurring. The IRS may suspect that you must be making more money than you are reporting—otherwise, why would you stay in business?

- **Peculiar deductions.** Deductions that seem odd or out of character for your business could increase your DIF score—for example, a psychologist who takes huge depreciation deductions for business equipment might raise a few eyebrows at the IRS.

- **How you organize your business.** Sole proprietors get higher DIF scores than businesses that are incorporated or owned by partnerships or limited liability companies. As a result, sole proprietors generally are most likely to be audited by the IRS. Partnerships and small C corporations are ten times less likely to be audited than sole proprietors.

2. IRS Income Matching Program

Your clients may have to report their payments to you to the IRS on Form 1099-MISC. IRS computers match the information on 1099s with the amount of income reported on tax returns. Discrepancies usually generate correspondence audits.

Not all payments to professionals for their services must be reported to the IRS. A 1099 must be filed by a client only if:

- your services are performed in the course of the client's business
- you are paid more than $600 during the year, and
- you are not incorporated (subject to exceptions).

A 1099-MISC need not be filed by a client when you perform services for a client's business—for example, a lawyer represents a company in a lawsuit, or an accountant audits a business. Nor does a 1099-MISC need to be filed when you perform personal services for a client or patient— for example, a doctor operates on a patient, a lawyer writes a will for a client, a psychologist gives therapy to a patient, or an optometrist fits a client with eyeglasses.

In addition, a 1099 must be filed with the IRS by a client only if the client pays you $600 or more during a year for business-related services.

It makes no difference whether the sum was one payment for a single job or the total of many small payments for multiple jobs. Payments for merchandise or inventory don't count for purposes of the $600 threshold.

If you've incorporated your practice, the general rule is that your clients need not file any 1099s, no matter how much you are paid. However, there are two big exceptions: Payments to medical corporations and payments to incorporated attorneys must be reported on Form 1099. But, remember, this is required only if the services are provided for a client's business.

3. Groups Targeted for Audit

Every year, the IRS gives special attention to specific industries or groups of taxpayers that it believes to be tax cheats. As mentioned above, IRS favorites include doctors, dentists, lawyers, and CPAs. The IRS also targets taxpayers who use certain tax shelters or have offshore bank accounts or trusts (see below).

4. Tips and Referrals

You could also get audited as a result of a referral from another government agency, such as your state tax department. The IRS also receives tips from private citizens—for example, a former partner or ex-spouse.

5. Bad Luck

A certain number of tax returns are randomly selected for audit every year. For example, the IRS announced in 2005 that it planned to audit 5,000 randomly selected S corporation returns from 2003 and 2004 as part of a National Research Program study to assess the reporting compliance of S corporations.

If you find yourself in this category, there's not much you can do about it. As long as you have adequate documentation to support your deductions, you should do just fine.

State Tax Audits Grow Increasingly Common

Although most people (and books) focus on IRS audits, audits by state income tax agencies are becoming increasingly common. Many states are facing deficits, and are, therefore, desperate to collect more taxes. For example, Idaho increased income tax audits by 25% in 2003, while Kansas upped them by 30%. Many states have increased fines and late-payment penalties. Others have adopted severe—and highly effective—punishments against delinquent taxpayers. For example, some states refuse to issue driver's licenses to people who owe back taxes. Others are hiring private tax collectors and publishing names of tax evaders online.

D. Tax Shelters, Scams, and Schemes

Abusive tax shelters, scams, and schemes have been much in the news lately, and are a growing preoccupation of the IRS and Congress. High-income professionals are prime targets for promoters of questionable tax shelters and schemes, and many have gotten into tax trouble for participating in them.

The basic rule for avoiding abusive tax shelters and tax scams is simple: If it sounds too good to be true, it probably is. Before you invest or participate in any shelter that promotes substantial tax benefits in return for a minimal investment, obtain expert advice from a tax professional not involved in selling the shelter. Do not rely on legal opinions provided by the shelter's promoter.

For more information on tax shelters, visit the IRS website at www.irs.gov.

1. Tax Shelters

A tax shelter is any investment designed to reduce or avoid income taxes. There is nothing wrong with sheltering your income from taxes, people do it all the time. You'll have no trouble with the IRS so long as your shelter is legitimate. A legitimate tax shelter not only reduces taxes, it also has a real business purpose. Often, a tax shelter comes with an opinion letter by an attorney stating that it is legal (although this won't help you if the IRS decides it is not).

An investment in low-income property that provides rental income is a good example of a legitimate tax shelter. Such an investment can save you taxes through depreciation and other tax deductions, but tax savings are not the only reason for the investment—you also own a property from which you receive rental income. The investment involves a risk of loss that is proportionate to the expected tax benefits—for example, you might have trouble renting the property and end up losing the money you've invested.

What the IRS doesn't like are "abusive tax shelters." Tax professor Michael Graetz devised the best definition of an abusive tax shelter: "A deal done by very smart people that, absent tax considerations, would be very stupid."

An abusive tax shelter is an investment or transaction entered into solely to obtain tax deductions or other tax benefits. There is no legitimate business purpose. Signs that a tax shelter is abusive include:

- The shelter's promoters promise investors a larger tax write-off than the amount invested; often much greater than two-to-one after five years—that is, after five years, you'll save more than twice as much in taxes as you invested in the shelter.
- The shelter involves the purchase of assets at grossly inflated prices so that investors can claim larger deductions for depreciation, interest, and other items.
- The shelter is heavily promoted or marketed to the public by salespeople who earn substantial commissions.
- Investors must sign confidentiality agreements promising not to tell anyone about the shelter.
- The shelter includes a money-back guarantee—a promise in writing that the promoter's fees will be fully or partially refunded if the investor doesn't receive all the projected tax benefits from the shelter.
- The investment is very complex, but actually involves little risk, despite outward appearances.

An example of a very simple abusive tax shelter involves investment in a motion picture. The investors purchase a film for a grossly inflated price. They make a cash down payment for what the film is really worth, and enter into a loan agreement for the remaining balance due. The loan has to be repaid only if the investors earn money from the film. The investors obtain substantial tax deductions by depreciating the film at its inflated price, and from investment tax credits. It's highly unlikely that the investors will ever earn a profit from this transaction, but their tax deductions will far exceed the cash they invested.

Many more examples of abusive tax shelters can be found at the following website which tracks all kinds of tax scams: www.quatloos .com/tax_shelters_scams.htm.

The IRS has begun to wage war on abusive tax shelters and has established the Office of Tax Shelter Analysis (OTSA) to coordinate its efforts. A major focus is disclosure of "potentially abusive" tax shelters to the IRS so it can prevent them from being widely used. Expanded disclosure rules require tax shelter promoters to provide statements to the OTSA describing potentially abusive tax shelters, and maintain lists of the clients that buy them. The OTSA is creating databases from these disclosure statements and other sources to enable it to cross-check information reported on tax returns filed by investors in abusive tax shelters.

In addition, the IRS has identified many tax shelters as abusive and listed them in IRS notices and on its website (www.irs.gov).

The organizers and promoters of potentially abusive or listed tax shelters must register them with the IRS. Each shelter is given an identification number. Anyone who invests in a registered tax shelter must include the identification number on his or her tax return. This will often lead to an audit, with the taxpayer required to pay more tax, plus penalties and interest.

2.   Tax Scams and Schemes

Tax scams and schemes involve outright fraud or other forms of illegal tax evasion. This is in contrast to tax shelters which involve investments that could arguably be legitimate. Scam artists and scheme promoters often prey on busy professionals who don't have a lot of time to focus on their finances. As a result, the IRS says that it has seen an increase in tax fraud in the professional community, especially by health care professionals.

Common tax scams and schemes marketed to professionals include:

Abusive trust schemes. Abusive trust schemes involve a series of domestic and/or foreign trusts layered upon one another. The scheme gives the appearance that the taxpayer has given up control of his business to a trust and progressively reduces the income distributed to the trust beneficiaries by charging administrative or other expenses at each level. The reality is that nothing ever changed. The taxpayer still exercises full control over his business and assets. A network of promoters, who may charge $5,000 to $70,000 for their trust packages, market these schemes.

International business corporations. The taxpayer establishes a corporation in a foreign tax haven. This corporation has the exact same name as the taxpayer's incorporated business in the United States. As the taxpayer receives checks from clients, customers, or patients, he sends them to the foreign country to be deposited in his foreign corporation's bank account. This way, the taxpayer avoids reporting income to the IRS.

False billing schemes. A taxpayer sets up a corporation in a tax haven country with someone else as the owner, usually the scheme's promoter. A bank account is opened for the corporation, with the taxpayer listed as a signatory. The promoter then issues invoices to the taxpayer's business for goods allegedly purchased by the taxpayer. The taxpayer sends payments to the corporation which get deposited into the joint account held by the corporation and the taxpayer. The taxpayer takes a business deduction for the payments to the corporation, thereby reducing his taxable income and safely placing the unreported income into the foreign bank account.

Investors in abusive tax schemes are liable for taxes, interest, and civil penalties. Violations of the Internal Revenue Code with the intent to evade income taxes may also result in a civil fraud penalty or criminal prosecution. Civil fraud can include a penalty of up to 75% of the underpayment of tax attributable to fraud, in addition to the taxes owed. Criminal convictions of promoters and investors may result in fines up to $250,000 and up to five years in prison.

San Diego Doctor's Tax Scam Results in Prison Sentence

Rick Shacket, an incorporated San Diego doctor, and his attorney thought they devised a great way to hide Shacket's income from the IRS. They formed a sham corporation in Oregon called King Medical and created a false identity for Shacket. Shacket diverted over $540,000 in corporate funds from his practice to King Medical, and then used his false identity to take the money out of the corporation without the IRS tracing it back to him. Eventually, he got caught, tried, and convicted. Shacket was sentenced to 33 months in prison for conspiring to defraud the IRS and paid the government $370,000 in back taxes.

E. Ten Tips for Avoiding an Audit

Here are ten things you can do to minimize your chances of getting audited.

Tip #1: Be Neat, Thorough, and Exact

If you file by mail (as you should), submit a tax return that looks professional; this will help you avoid unwanted attention from the IRS. Your return shouldn't contain erasures or be difficult to read. Your math should be correct. Avoid round numbers on your return (like $100 or $5,000). This looks like you're making up the numbers instead of taking them from accurate records. You should include, and completely fill out, all necessary forms and schedules. Moreover, your state tax return should be consistent with your federal return. If you do your own taxes, using a tax-preparation computer program will help you produce an accurate return that looks professional.

Tip #2: Mail Your Return by Registered Mail

Mail your tax return by certified mail, return receipt requested. In case the IRS loses or misplaces your return, your receipt will prove that you submitted it. The IRS also accepts returns from four private delivery services: Airborne Express, DHL Worldwide Express, Federal Express, and United Parcel Service. Contact these companies for details on which of their service options qualify and how to get proof of timely filing.

Tip #3: Don't File Early

Unless you're owed a substantial refund, you shouldn't file your taxes early. The IRS generally has three years after April 15 to decide whether to audit your return. Filing early just gives the IRS more time to think about whether you should be audited. You can reduce your audit chances even more by getting an extension to file until August 15 or October 15 (the latest extension you can obtain). Note, however, that filing an extension does not extend the date by which you have to pay any taxes due for the prior year—these must be paid by April 15.

Tip #4: Don't File Electronically

The IRS would like all taxpayers to file their returns electronically— that is, by email. There is a good reason for this: it saves the agency substantial time and money. Every year, the IRS must hire thousands of temp workers to enter the numbers from millions of paper returns into its computer system. This is expensive, so the IRS only has about 40% of the data on paper returns transcribed. The paper returns are then sent to a warehouse where they are kept for six years and then destroyed. The IRS makes its audit decisions based on this transcribed data. By filing electronically, you give the IRS easy access to 100% of the data on your return instead of just 40%.

Tip #5: Form a Business Entity

Audit rate statistics show that partnerships and small corporations are audited far less often than sole proprietors. In 2004, for example, the IRS audited 0.26% of partnerships, 0.19% of S corporations, and only 0.22% of regular C corporations with assets worth less than $250,000. In contrast, 3.15% of sole proprietors earning less than $25,000 were audited. The majority of professionals in solo practice are sole proprietors, but no law says they have to be. Incorporating your practice or forming a limited liability company will greatly reduce your audit risk. However, you must balance this against the time and expense involved in forming a corporation or LLC and having to complete more complex tax returns. Moreover, in some states—most notably California—corporations and

LLCs have to pay additional state taxes. (See Chapter 2 for a detailed discussion of business entities for professionals.)

Tip #6: Explain Items the IRS Will Question

If your return contains an item that the IRS may question or that could increase the likelihood of an audit, include an explanation and documentation to prove everything is on the up and up. For example, if your return contains a substantial bad debt deduction, explain the circumstances showing that the debt is a legitimate business expense. This won't necessarily avoid an audit, but it may reduce your chances. Here's why: If the IRS computer gives your return a high DIF score, an IRS classifier screens it to see whether it warrants an audit. If your explanations look reasonable, the screener may decide you shouldn't be audited after all.

Tip #7: Avoid Ambiguous or General Expenses

Don't list expenses under vague categories such as "miscellaneous" or "general expense." Be specific. IRS Schedule C lists specific categories for the most common small business expenses. If an expense doesn't fall within one of these classifications, create a specific name for it.

Tip #8: Report All of Your Income

The IRS is convinced that self-employed people, including many home business owners, don't report all of their income. Finding such hidden income is a high priority. As mentioned above, IRS computers compare 1099 forms with tax returns to determine whether there are any discrepancies. Of course, much income professionals receive is not reported to the IRS on Form 1099 because 1099s are filed only when your client is a business. Thus, for example, a person who has his teeth fixed by a dentist won't be filing a 1099 with the IRS reporting how much he paid the dentist. However, if you are audited, the auditor may examine your bank records to see whether you received any unreported income.

Tip #9: Watch Your Income-to-Deduction Ratio

Back in the 1990s, a statistics professor named Amir D. Aczel got audited by the IRS. The experience proved so unpleasant that he decided to conduct a statistical study of how and why people get selected for IRS audits. He carefully examined more than 1,200 returns that were audited and reported his findings in a book (now out of print) called *How to Beat the IRS At Its Own Game* (Four Walls Eight Windows, 1995). He concluded that the key factor leading to an audit was the ratio of a taxpayer's expenses to his or her income.

According to Aczel, if your total business expenses amount to less than 52% of your gross business income, you are "not very likely" to be audited. If your business expenses are 52% to 63% of your business income, there is a "relatively high probability" that the IRS computer will tag you for an audit. Finally, if your expenses are more than 63% of your income, Aczel claims you are "certain to be computer tagged for audit." Of course, this doesn't necessarily mean that you *will* be audited. Less than 10% of returns that are computer-tagged for audit are actually audited. But being tagged considerably increases the odds that you'll be audited.

Whether Aczel's precise numbers are correct or not is anyone's guess. However, his basic conclusion—that your income-to-deduction ratio is an important factor in determining whether you'll be audited—is undoubtedly true. (A former IRS commissioner admitted as much in a CNN interview in 1995.)

Tip #10: Beware of Abnormally Large Deductions

It is not just the total amount of your deductions that is important. Very large individual deductions can also increase your audit chances. How much is too much? It depends in part on the nature of your practice. A $50,000 deduction for equipment would likely look abnormal for a psychologist who works from home, but not for a doctor with his own office.

Chapter 20

Record Keeping and Accounting

W hen you incur business expenses, you get tax deductions and save money on your taxes. But those deductions are only as good as the records you keep to back them up. Failure to keep proper records is by far the most common reason taxpayers lose deductions when they are audited by the IRS.

This is what Dr. Maureen Polsby, a sole proprietor neurologist, found out when she got audited. Dr. Polsby frequently drove from her home office to the Social Security Administration office in Baltimore to review disability claims. She claimed a $7,011 car expense deduction. Unfortunately, she failed to keep adequate records such as a diary or mileage logbook to document her business trips. As a result, the IRS and tax court completely disallowed her deduction. (*Polsby v. Comm'r*, T.C. Memo 1998-459.)

Any expense you forget to deduct (or lose after an IRS audit because you can't back it up) costs you dearly. For example, if you're in the 28% federal income tax bracket, you'll have to pay $28 more in federal tax for every $100 deduction you fail to take, not to mention additional state income taxes and self-employment or employment taxes.

Luckily, it's not difficult to keep records of your business expenses. In this chapter, we'll show you how to document your expenditures so you won't end up losing your hard-earned business deductions.

A. Recording Your Expenses

Recording your expenses is what we normally think of as "keeping the books." Every business should have a record of what it spends and what it earns. Without this information, it will be impossible for you to know how much profit your practice earns (if any); and it will be much more difficult to prepare your taxes.

Most professionals use accountants or bookkeepers to perform these recording functions. However, if your practice is small, you may choose to do it yourself and save the money.

For an excellent overall guide on how to do small business book-keeping yourself, refer *to Small Time Operator,* by Bernard B. Kamoroff (Bell Springs Press). A good (and fun to read) introduction to basic accounting principles is *The Accounting Game: Basic Accounting Fresh from the Lemonade Stand*, by Darrell Mullis and Judith Handler (Sourcebooks).

1. Your Accounting System

Your practice should have an accounting system that allows you to keep track of all the financial information you need to do your taxes and make good business decisions. Keeping track of your expenses is just one part of this system. An accounting system for a service business ordinarily includes a series of journals and ledgers (or their computerized functional equivalents).

Journals

A "journal" is a place where financial transactions involving your practice are recorded on a day-to-day basis. They are typically kept by your staff, by an outside bookkeeper, or by you if you have a small practice and do everything yourself. You should make sure that your accounting system includes all of the proper journals for your type of practice. These ordinarily include:

- an income journal that lists the date, amount, and source of all receipts
- an expense journal containing the date, amount, and description of all payments. You should also indicate whether the expenditure will be charged to a client.
- a general journal that contains all necessary supporting documentation for your deductible business expenses. (This supporting documentation is described in Section B.)
- if the practice has employees, including corporate owner employees, a payroll journal that reports wages and withholding for each pay period for each employee.

Additional journals may be needed for various types of practices. For example, attorneys are usually required to keep separate journals to record withdrawals and deposits of funds in their client trust account.

Ledgers

Journals record all your financial transactions. Ledgers are used to summarize this information to make it easier to use. Ledgers are a "snapshot" of your practice at a particular point in time—they can be created monthly, quarterly, or yearly.

The most important ledger is the "general ledger," a summary of all your journals, showing a complete picture of your practice's finances. The general ledger is used to prepare an income statement and a balance sheet that help determine the profitability of the practice and prepare tax returns. A balance sheet is a financial statement that shows assets, liabilities, and ownership interests of your practice at a point in time. An income statement shows the income your practice earned and expenses it incurred for a fixed period.

2. Accounting Software

All the information described above can be kept in handwritten books called ledger books. However, today most professionals use computerized accounting systems that perform the same recording functions that used to be done on paper. Many different types of accounting software are available.

There are a number of generic programs that are designed to be used by any type of business. The simplest financial programs are those like *Quicken* and *MS Money* that work off of a computerized checkbook. More sophisticated accounting software includes *MYOB Account Edge* and *Plus* by MYOB, *Peachtree Accounting* by Peachtree Software, and *QuickBooks* and *QuickBooks Pro* by Intuit. This software can accomplish more complex bookkeeping tasks, such as double-entry bookkeeping, tracking inventory, payroll, billings, handling accounts receivable, and maintaining fixed asset records.

However, you'll probably be better off using a program specially designed for your type of practice. Such a program will probably cost more than generic software, but it won't require as much customizing for your particular needs. There are specialized accounting programs available for every profession. Consult your accountant or bookkeeper about which program to use.

If you're doing your bookkeeping yourself, it is a good idea to initially do a set of manual records as well so you can verify that you are using the software correctly.

3.   Chart of Accounts

Your books should include an expense journal, in which you record the date, amount, and description of all payments (disbursements) made by the practice. This is the information you'll use to deduct your business expenses on your tax return. Your payments and receipts should be recorded by category. The list of all your categories is called a chart of accounts. You want your chart of accounts to be as complete as possible.

What categories you need depends on the nature of your practice. Many practices have dozens or even hundreds of categories. For example, a dentist's expense categories could include:

- accounting fees
- amortization
- auto expense
- bank charges
- business taxes & licenses
- cleaning
- cleaning supplies
- consultant fees
- continuing education
- credit card fees
- dental supplies
- depreciation
- dues & subscriptions
- electricity and gas
- employer taxes
- equipment
- equipment lease
- health insurance
- interest expense
- lab fees
- lab supplies

- landscaping
- legal fees
- life insurance
- mass mailing
- meals & entertainment
- nitrous/oxygen expense
- office rent
- office supplies
- other professional fees
- outside services
- paper products
- payroll expense
- postage and delivery
- repairs & maintenance
- retirement plan
- staff salaries
- telephone
- travel expenses
- water
- Web hosting
- workers' comp insurance
- Yellow Page ad.

Accounting software comes with its own "canned" categories. The categories in a specialized program for your type of practice may be sufficient. The categories in generic accounting software will likely have to be modified to suit your needs.

Hiring an Accountant

You should hire an accountant experienced with your type of practice to set up your accounting system. After that, a much less expensive bookkeeper or staff member can perform routine recording functions and balancing accounts. But the accountant should be available to handle any problems that come up. See Chapter 21 for more on hiring tax professionals.

B. Documenting Your Deductions

The IRS lives by the maxim that "figures lie and liars figure." It knows very well that you can claim anything in your books and on your tax returns, because you create or complete them yourself. For this reason, the IRS requires that you have documents to support the deductions you list in your books and claim on your tax return. In the absence of a supporting document, an IRS auditor may conclude that an item you claim as a business expense is really a personal expense, or that you never bought the item at all. Either way, your deduction will be disallowed.

You can hire an accountant or bookkeeper to record your deductions in your books, but you must document your deductions yourself. You need to learn the IRS's documentation rules and live by them each day. The most common business deductions—travel, meals, and entertainment—require especially good documentation.

1. What Supporting Documents Do You Need?

The supporting documents you need to prove that a business deduction is legitimate depend on the type of deduction involved. However, at a minimum, every deduction should be supported by documentation showing: what, how much, and who. That is, your supporting documents should show:

- what you purchased for your practice
- how much you paid for it, and
- who (or what company) you bought it from.

Additional record-keeping requirements must be met for deductions for local transportation, travel, entertainment, meal, and gift deductions, as well as for certain long-term assets that you buy for your business. (Section 3, below, covers these rules.)

You can meet the what, how much, and who requirements by keeping the following types of documentation:

- canceled checks
- sales receipts
- account statements
- credit card sales slips

- invoices, or
- petty cash slips for small cash payments.

Documentation for Expenses Reimbursed by Clients

You need exactly the same documentation for an expense that is reimbursed by a client as you do for an expense you pay yourself. Unless you provide your client with an adequate accounting for the expense and follow the accountable plan rules discussed in Chapter 17, any reimbursement you receive must be included in your taxable income. An "adequate accounting" includes providing the client with proper documentation of the expense. The client is supposed to keep your documentation for any entertainment expenses it reimburses you for.

Canceled Check + Receipt = Proof of Deduction

Manny, a sole proprietor architect, buys a $500 digital camera for his practice from the local electronics store. He writes a check for the amount and is given a receipt. How does he prove to the IRS that he has a $500 business expense?

Could Manny simply save his canceled check when it's returned from his bank? Many people carefully save all their canceled checks (some keep them for decades), apparently believing that a canceled check is all the proof they need to show that a purchase was a legitimate business expense. This is not the case. All a canceled check proves is that you spent money for something. It doesn't show what you bought. Of course, you can write a note on your check stating what you purchased, but why should the IRS believe what you write on your checks yourself?

Does Manny's sales receipt prove he bought his camera for his business? Again, no. A sales receipt only proves that somebody purchased the item listed in the receipt. It does not show who purchased it. Again, you could write a note on the receipt stating that you bought the item. But you could easily lie. Indeed, for all the IRS knows, you could hang around stores and pick up receipts people throw away to give yourself tax deductions.

However, when you put a canceled check together with a sales receipt (or an invoice, a cash register tape, or a similar document), you have concrete proof that you purchased the item listed in the receipt. The check proves that you bought something, and the receipt proves what that something is.

This doesn't necessarily prove that you bought the item for your practice, but it's a good start. Often, the face of a receipt, the sales slip, or the payee's name on your canceled check, will strongly indicate that the item you purchased was for your business. But if it's not clear, note what the purchase was for on the document. Such a note is not proof of how you used the item, but it will be helpful. For some types of items that you use for both business and personal purposes—cameras are one example—you might be required to keep careful records of your use. (See Section 4, below.)

Credit Cards

Using a credit card is a great way to pay business expenses. The credit card slip will prove that you bought the item listed on the slip. You'll also have a monthly statement to back up your credit card slips. If you're a sole proprietor, you should use a separate credit card for your practice. If your practice is organized as a corporation, LLC, LLP, or partnership, it's best that the card be in the practice's name. That way, you avoid paying for business expenses with your personal funds and then having to go to the trouble of being reimbursed by your practice.

Account Statements

Sometimes, you'll need to use an account statement to prove an expense. Some banks no longer return canceled checks, or you may pay for something with an ATM card or another electronic funds transfer method. Moreover, you may not always have a credit card slip when you pay by credit card—for example, when you buy an item over the Internet. In these events, the IRS will accept an account statement as proof that you purchased the item. The chart below shows what type of information you need on an account statement.

Proving Payments With Bank Statements	
If payment is by:	**The statement must show:**
Check	Check number Amount Payee's name Date the check amount was posted to the account by the bank
Electronic funds transfer	Amount transferred Payee's name Date the amount transferred was posted to the account by the bank
Credit card	Amount charged Payee's name Transaction date

2. Automobile Mileage and Expense Records

If you use a car or other vehicle for business purposes other than just commuting to and from work, you're entitled to take a deduction for gas and other auto expenses. You can either deduct the actual cost of your gas and other expenses or take the standard rate deduction based on the number of business miles you drive. In 2005, the standard mileage rate was 40.5 cents per mile for the first eight months of the year and 48.5 cents per mile for the last four months. The standard mileage rate for 2006 is 44.5 cents per mile. (See Chapter 5 for more on car expenses.)

Either way, you must keep a record of:

- your mileage
- the dates of your business trips
- the places you drove for business, and
- the business purpose for your trips.

The last three items are relatively easy to keep track of. You can record the information in your appointment book, calendar, or day planner. Or, you can record it in a mileage logbook—you can get one for a few dollars from any stationery store and stash it in your car glove compartment.

Calculating your mileage takes more work. The IRS wants to know the total number of miles you drove during the year for business, commuting, and personal driving other than commuting. Commuting is travel from home to your office or other principal place of business. If you work from a home office, you'll have no commuting mileage. (See Chapter 5 for more on commuting and automobile expenses.) Personal miles other than commuting include all the driving you do other than from home to your office—for example, to the grocery store, on a personal vacation, or to visit friends or relatives.

Claiming a Car Is Used Solely for Business

If you use a car 100% for business, you don't need to keep track of your personal or commuting miles. However, you can successfully claim to use a car 100% for business only if you:

- work out of a tax deductible home office
- have at least two cars, and
- use one car just for business trips.

If you don't work from a home office, your trips from home to your outside office are nonbusiness commuting, so the car you take from home to your office is not used 100% for business, even if you drive it only for business after you get to your office and then drive straight home.

There are several ways to keep track of your mileage; some are easy, and some are a bit more complicated.

52-Week Mileage Book

The hardest way to track your mileage—and the way the IRS would like you to do it—is to keep track of every mile you drive every day, 52 weeks a year, using a mileage logbook or business diary. This means you'll list every trip you take, whether for business, commuting, or personal reasons. If you enjoy record keeping, go ahead and use this method. But there are easier ways.

Tracking Business Mileage

An easier way to keep track of your mileage is to record your mileage only when you use your car for business. Here's what to do:

- Obtain a mileage log book and keep it in your car with a pen attached.
- Note your odometer reading in the logbook at the beginning and end of every year that you use the car for business. (If you don't know your January 1 odometer reading for this year, you might be able to estimate it by looking at auto repair receipts that note your mileage.)
- Record your mileage and note the business purpose for the trip every time you use your car for business.
- Add up your business mileage when you get to the end of each page in the logbook. (This way, you'll only have to add the page totals at the end of the year instead of all the individual entries).
- If you commute to your office or other workplace, figure out how many miles you drive each way and note in your appointment book how many times you drive to the office each week.

Below is a portion of a page from a mileage logbook.

Mileage Log

Date	Business Purpose	Odometer Reading Begin	End	Business Miles
5/1	Visit Art Andrews—potential client	10,111	10,196	85
5/4	Delivered documents to Bill James in Stockton	10,422	10,476	54
5/5	Picked up office supplies	10,479	10,489	10
5/8	Meeting—Acme Corp.—Sacramento	10,617	10,734	117
5/10	Lunch with Stu Smith—client	10,804	10,841	37
5/13	Meeting—Acme Corp.—Sacramento	10,987	11,004	117
5/15	Breakfast—Mary Moss—client	11,201	11,222	21
5/15	Lunch—Sam Simpson—potential client	11,222	11,247	25
5/15	Attend sales seminar—Hilton Hotel	11,247	11,301	54
5/17	Bank	11,399	11,408	8
5/18	Meeting—ABC Company	11,408	11,436	28
5/20	Sales presentation—Smith Bros. & Co.	11,544	11,589	55
Total				603

At the end of the year, your logbook will show the total business miles you drove during the year. You calculate the total miles you drove during the year by subtracting your January 1 odometer reading from your December 31 reading.

If you use the actual expense method, you must also calculate your percentage of business use of the car. You do this by dividing your business miles by your total miles.

> **EXAMPLE:** Yolanda, a fundraising consultant, uses her car extensively for business. At the beginning of the year, her odometer reading was 34,201 miles. On December 31, it was 58,907 miles. Her total mileage for the year was therefore 24,706. She recorded 62 business trips in her mileage logbook for a total of 9,280 miles. Her business use percentage of her car is 37% (9,280 divided by 24,706 = 0.366). Yolanda commuted to her office every day, 50 weeks a year. She determined that her office was ten miles from her home. So Yolanda had 5,000 miles of commuting mileage for the year.

Record Your Mileage Electronically

If writing your mileage down in a paper mileage logbook seems too primitive, you can keep your records in electronic form with an electronic device such as a Palm Pilot or computer. There is special software available for recording business mileage. However, be warned: Although the IRS's official policy is that electronic records are acceptable, many IRS auditors are old fashioned. They like to see paper and ink mileage records because they are much harder to alter, forge, or create in a hurry than electronic records.

Sampling Method

There is an even easier way to track your mileage: use a sampling method. Under this method, you keep track of your business mileage for a sample portion of the year and use your figures for that period to extrapolate your business mileage for the whole year.

This method assumes that you drive about the same amount for business throughout the year. To back up this assumption, you must scrupulously keep an appointment book showing your business appointments all year long. If you don't want to keep an appointment book, don't use the sampling method.

Your sample period must be at least 90 days—for example, the first three months of the year. Alternatively, you may sample one week each month—for example, the first week of every month. You don't have to use the first three months of the year or the first week of every month; you could use any other three-month period or the second, third, or fourth week of every month. Use whatever works best—you want your sample period to be as representative as possible of the business travel you do throughout the year.

You must keep track of the total miles you drove during the year by taking odometer readings on January 1 and December 31 and deduct any atypical mileage before applying your sample results.

> **EXAMPLE:** Tom, a doctor, uses the sample method to compute his mileage, keeping track of his business miles for the first three months of the year. He drove 6,000 miles during that time and had 1,000 business miles. His business use percentage of his car was 17%. From his January 1 and December 31 odometer readings, Tom knows he drove a total of 27,000 miles during the year. However, Tom drove to the Grand Canyon for vacation, so he deducts this 1,000 mile trip from his total. This leaves him with 26,000 total miles for the year. To calculate his total business miles, he multiplies the year-long total by the business use percentage of his car: 17% x 26,000 = 4,420. Tom claims 4,420 business miles on his tax return.

Keeping Track of Actual Expenses

If you take the deduction for your actual auto expenses instead of the standard rate (or are thinking about switching to this method), you must keep receipts for all of your auto-related expenses, including gasoline, oil, tires, repairs, and insurance.

Use a Credit Card for Gas

If you use the actual expense method for car expenses, use a business credit card when you buy gas. The monthly statements you receive will serve as your gas receipts. If you pay cash for gas, you must either get a receipt or make a note of the amount in your mileage logbook.

Parking and Tolls

Costs for business-related parking (other than at your office) and for tolls are separately deductible whether you use the standard rate or the actual expense method. Get and keep receipts for these expenses.

3.   Entertainment, Meal, Travel, and Gift Expenses

Deductions for business-related entertainment, meals, and travel are a hot button item for the IRS because they have been greatly abused by many taxpayers. You need to have more records for these expenses than for almost any others, and they will be closely scrutinized if you're audited.

Whenever you incur an expense for business-related entertainment, meals, gifts, or travel, you must document the following five facts:

- **The date.** The date the expense was incurred will usually be listed on a receipt or credit card slip; appointment books, dayplanners, and similar documents have the dates preprinted on each page, so entries on the appropriate page automatically date the expense.
- **The amount.** How much you spent, including tax and tip for meals.
- **The place.** The nature and place of the entertainment or meal will usually be shown by a receipt, or you can record it in an appointment book.
- **The business purpose.** Show that the expense was incurred for your practice—for example, to obtain future business, encourage existing client relationships, and so on. What you need to show depends on whether the business conversation occurred before, during, or after entertainment or a meal. (See Chapter 4 for more on deducting meal expenses.)

- **The business relationship.** If entertainment or meals are involved, show the business relationship of people at the event—for example, list their names and occupations and any other information needed to establish their business relation to you.

The IRS does not require that you keep receipts, canceled checks, credit card slips, or any other supporting documents for entertainment, meal, gift, or travel expenses that cost less than $75. However, you must still document the five facts listed above. This exception does not apply to lodging—that is, hotel or similar costs—when you travel for business. You do need receipts for these expenses, even if they are less than $75.

⚠ The $75 rule applies only to travel, meals, gifts, and entertainment. The rule that you don't need receipts for expenses less than $75 applies only to travel, gift, meal, and entertainment expenses. It does not apply to other types of business expenses. For example, if you go to the office supply store and buy $50 worth of supplies for your business and then spend $70 for lunch with a client, you need a receipt for the office supplies, but not the business lunch. If you find this rule hard to remember, simply keep all of your receipts.

All this record keeping is not as hard as it sounds. You can record the five facts you have to document in a variety of ways. The information doesn't have to be all in one place. Information that is shown on a receipt, canceled check, or other item need not be duplicated in a log, appointment book, calendar, or account book. Thus, for example, you can record the five facts with:

- a receipt, credit card slip, or similar document alone
- a receipt combined with an appointment book entry, or
- an appointment book entry alone (for expenses less than $75).

No matter how you document your expense, you are supposed to do it in a timely manner. You don't need to record the details of every expense on the day you incur it. It is sufficient to record them on a weekly basis. However, if you're prone to forget details, it's best to get everything you need in writing within a day or two.

Receipt or Credit Card Slip Alone

An easy way to document an entertainment, gift, travel, or meal expense is to use your receipt, credit card slip, invoice, or bill. A receipt or credit

Proof Required for Travel, Entertainment, and Gift Deductions				
Records must show:	**Amount**	**Time**	**Place or Description**	**Business Purpose and Relationship**
Travel	Cost of each separate expense for travel, lodging, meals. Incidental expenses may be totaled in categories such as taxis, daily meals, and so on.	Dates you left and returned for each trip, and the number of days spent on business.	Name of city, town, or other destination.	Business purpose for the expense, or the benefit gained or expected to be gained.
Entertainment (including meals)	Cost of each separate expense. Incidental expenses such as taxis, telephones, etc. may be totaled on a daily basis.	Date of entertainment.	Name and address or location of place of entertainment. Type of entertainment, if not otherwise apparent. For entertainment directly before or after business discussion: date, place, nature, and duration.	Nature of business discussion or activity. Identities of people who took part in discussion and entertainment. Occupations or other information (such as names or titles) about the recipients that shows their business relationship to you. Proof you or your employee was present at business meal.
Gifts	Cost of gift.	Date of gift.	Description of gift.	Same as for Entertainment.

card slip will ordinarily contain the name and location of the place where the expense was incurred, the date, and the amount charged. Thus, three of the five facts you must document are taken care of. You just need to describe the business purpose and business relationship if entertainment or meals are involved. You can write this directly on your receipt or credit card slip.

> **EXAMPLE:** Mary, a consulting engineer, has lunch with Harold, president of Acme Technologies, Inc., to discuss doing some programming work for Acme. Her restaurant bill shows the date, name, and location of the restaurant, the number of people served, and the amount of the expense. Mary just has to document the business purpose for the lunch and identify who it was with. She writes on the receipt: "Lunch with Harold Lipshitz, President, Acme Technologies, Inc. Discussed signing contract for engineering services." All five facts Mary must prove to document her meal expense are on the receipt. This is all Mary needs. She need not duplicate the information elsewhere—for example, in an appointment book or dayplanner.

```
GREENS RESTAURANT
FORT MASON, BLDG A
    SF, CA 94123
   (415)771-6222            05/26/2005
                             12:35 PM
                               30005
Server: LES
Table 28/1
Guests: 2                       6.50
                               12.00
Bowl of soup                   19.75
Sampler                        21.00
Filo
Ravioli                        59.25
                                5.04
Sub Total
Tax                            64.29

Total                         64.29

Balance Due
                        $10.00 tip

Lunch with Harold Lipshitz,
president, Acme Technologies, Inc.
Discussed signing contract for
engineering services.
```

Receipt Plus Appointment Book

You can also document the five facts you need to record for an expense by combining the information on a receipt with entries in an appointment book, dayplanner, calendar, diary, or similar record.

> **EXAMPLE:** Assume that Mary, from the above example, saves her receipt from the restaurant where she had her business lunch. She writes nothing on the receipt. She still needs to document the five facts. Her receipt contains the date, name, and location of the restaurant, and the amount of the lunch. She records who the lunch was with and the business purpose by writing a note in her appointment book: "Lunch—Harold Lipshitz, President Acme Technologies, Inc. Discussed signing contract for engineering services."

	Appointment Book	
19	Thursday	232/134
7		
8		
9		
10		
11		
12	Lunch—Harold Lipshitz, President, Acme Technologies. Cesar Restaurant.	
1	Discussed signing contract for engineering services.	
2		
3		
4		
5		
6		
20	Friday	233/133
7		
8		

Appointment Book Alone

If your expense is for less than $75, you don't need to keep a receipt (unless the expense is for lodging). You may record the five facts in your appointment book, dayplanner, daily diary, or calendar or on any other sheet of paper.

> **EXAMPLE:** Assume that Mary, from the above example, doesn't keep her receipt from her lunch. Because lunch cost less than $75, she does not need it. Instead, she documents the five facts she needs to record in her appointment book. She writes: "Lunch—Green's Restaurant, with Harold Lipshitz, President, Acme Technologies, Inc. Discussed signing contract for engineering services. $45." This short entry records the place of the lunch, who it was with, the business purpose, and the amount. She doesn't need to add the date because this is already shown by her appointment book.

Receipts to Keep	
Type of Expense	**Receipts to Save**
Travel	Airplane, train, or bus ticket stubs; travel agency receipts; rental car; and so on.
Meals	Meal check, credit card slip.
Lodging	Statement or bill from hotel or other lodging provider; your own written records for cleaning, laundry, telephone charges, tips, and other charges not shown separately on hotel statement.
Entertainment	Bill from entertainment provider; ticket stubs for sporting event, theater, or other event; credit card slips.

4. Listed Property

Listed property refers to certain types of long-term business assets that can easily be used for personal as well as business purposes. Listed property includes:

- cars, boats, airplanes, motorcycles, and other vehicles
- computers
- cellular phones, and
- any other property generally used for entertainment, recreation, or amusement—for example, VCRs, cameras, and camcorders.

Because all listed property is long-term business property, it cannot be deducted like a business expense. Instead, you must depreciate it over several years or deduct it in one year under Section 179. (See Chapter 9 for more on deducting long-term assets.)

Special Record-Keeping Requirements

With listed property, the IRS fears that taxpayers might claim business deductions but really use the property for personal reasons instead. For this reason, you're required to document how you use listed property. Keep an appointment book, log book, business diary, or calendar showing the dates, times, and reasons for which the property is used—both business and personal. You also can purchase logbooks for this purpose at stationery or office supply stores.

> **EXAMPLE:** Bill, an accountant, purchases a computer he uses 50% for business and 50% to play games. He must keep a log showing his business use of the computer. Following is a sample from one week in his log.

Usage Log for Personal Computer			
Date	Time of Business Use	Reason for Business Use	Time of Personal Use
5/1	4.5 hours	Prepared client tax returns	1.5 hours
5/2			3 hours
5/3	2 hours	Prepared client tax returns	
5/4			2 hours

Exception to Record-Keeping Rule for Computers

You usually have to document your use of listed property even if you use it 100% for business. However, there is an exception to this rule for computers: If you use a computer or computer peripheral (such as a printer) only for business and keep it at your business location, you need not comply with the record-keeping requirement. This includes computers that you keep at your home office if the office qualifies for the home office deduction. (See Chapter 7.)

> **EXAMPLE:** John, a psychiatrist, works full time in his home office, which he uses exclusively for his practice. The office is clearly his principal place of business and qualifies for the home office deduction. He buys a $2,000 computer for his office and uses it exclusively for his psychiatric practice. He does not have to keep records showing how he uses the computer.

This exception applies only to computers and computer peripheral equipment. It doesn't apply to other items such as calculators, copiers, fax machines, or typewriters.

5.   How Long to Keep Your Records

You need to have copies of your tax returns and supporting documents available in case you are audited by the IRS or another taxing agency. You might also need them for other purposes—for example, to get a loan, mortgage, or insurance.

You should keep your records for as long as the IRS has to audit you after you file your returns for the year. These statutes of limitation range from three years to forever—they are listed in the table below.

To be on the safe side, you should keep your tax returns indefinitely. They usually don't take up much space, so this is not a big hardship. Your supporting documents probably take up more space. You should keep these for at least six years after you file your return. Keeping your records this long ensures that you'll have them available if the IRS decides to audit you.

Keep your long-term asset records for three years after the depreciable life of the asset ends. For example, keep records for five-year property (such as computers) for eight years.

IRS Statute of Limitations	
If:	**The limitations period is:**
You failed to pay all the tax due	3 years
You underreported your gross income for the year by more than 25%	6 years
You filed a fraudulent return	No limit
You did not file a return	No limit

6. What If You Don't Have Proper Tax Records?

Because you're human, you may not have kept all the records required to back up your tax deductions. Don't despair, all is not lost—you may be able to fall back on the *Cohan* rule. This rule (named after the Broadway entertainer George M. Cohan, involved in a tax case in the 1930s) is the taxpayer's best friend. The *Cohan* rule recognizes that all businesspeople must spend at least some money to stay in business and so must have had at least some deductible expenses, even if they don't have adequate records to back them up.

If you're audited and lack adequate records for a claimed deduction, the IRS can use the *Cohan* rule to make an estimate of how much you must have spent and allow you to deduct that amount. However, you must provide at least some credible evidence on which to base this estimate, such as receipts, canceled checks, notes in your appointment book, or other records. Moreover, the IRS will allow only you to deduct the least amount you must have spent, based on the records you provide. In addition, the *Cohan* rule cannot be used for travel, meal, entertainment, or gift expenses, or for listed property.

If an auditor claims you lack sufficient records to back up a deduction, you should always bring up the *Cohan* rule and argue that you should still get the deduction based on the records you do have. At best, you'll probably get only part of your claimed deductions. If the IRS auditor disallows your deductions entirely or doesn't give you as much as you think you deserve, you can appeal in court and bring up the *Cohan* rule again there. You might have more success with a judge. However, you can't compel an IRS auditor or a court to apply the *Cohan* rule in your favor. Whether to apply the rule and how large a deduction to give you is within their discretion.

Reconstructing Tax Records

If you can show that you possessed adequate records at one time, but now lack them due to circumstances beyond your control, you may reconstruct your records for an IRS audit. Circumstances beyond your control would include acts of nature such as floods, fires, earthquakes, or theft. (Treas. Reg. 1.275.5(c)(5).) Loss of tax records while moving does not constitute circumstances beyond your control. Reconstructing records means you create brand new records just for your audit or obtain other evidence to corroborate your deductions—for example, statements from people or companies from whom you purchased items for your practice.

C. Accounting Methods

An accounting method is a set of rules used to determine when and how your income and expenses are reported. Accounting methods might sound like a rather dry subject, but your choice about how to account for your business expenses and income will have a huge impact on your tax deductions. You don't have to become as expert as a CPA on this topic, but you should understand the basics.

You choose an accounting method when you file your first tax return for your practice. If you later want to change your accounting method, you must get IRS approval. If you operate two or more separate businesses, you can use a different accounting method for each—for example, a dentist who also operates a separate lab business may use separate accounting methods for each business. (A business is separate for tax purposes only if you keep a separate set of books and records for it.)

There are two basic methods of accounting: cash basis and accrual basis. Most professionals use the cash basis method.

1. Cash Method

The cash method is by far the simpler method. It is used by individuals who are not in business and by most small businesses that provide services and do not maintain inventory or offer credit. However, if you sell merchandise and keep an inventory, you might have to use the accrual method.

The cash method is based on this commonsense idea: You haven't earned income for tax purposes until you actually receive the money, and you haven't incurred an expense until you actually pay the money. Using the cash basis method, then, is like maintaining a checkbook. You record income only when the money is received and expenses only when they are actually paid. If you borrow money to pay business expenses, you incur an expense under the cash method only when you make payments on the loan.

> **EXAMPLE 1:** Helen, a marketing consultant, completes a market research report on September 1, 2006, but isn't paid by the client until February 1, 2007. Using the cash method, Helen records the payment in February 2007—when it's received.

> **EXAMPLE 2:** On December 1, 2006, Helen goes to the Acme electronics store and buys a laser printer for her consulting practice. She buys the item on credit from Acme—she's not required to make any payments until March 1, 2007. Helen does not record the expense until 2007, when she actually pays for the printer.

When Is an Expense Paid?

Although it's called the cash method, a business expense is paid when you pay it by check, credit card, or electronic funds transfer, as well as by cash. If you pay by check, the amount is paid during the year in which the check is drawn and mailed—for example, a check dated December 31, 2006 is considered paid during 2006 only if it has a December 31, 2006 postmark. If you're using a check to pay a substantial expense, you may wish to mail it by certified mail so you'll have proof of when it was mailed.

Constructive Receipt

Under the cash method, payments are "constructively received" when an amount is credited to your account or otherwise made available to you without restrictions. Constructive receipt is as good as actual receipt. If you authorize someone to be your agent and receive income for you, you are considered to have received it when your agent receives it.

> **EXAMPLE:** Interest is credited to your business bank account in December 2006, but you do not withdraw it or enter it into your passbook until 2007. You must include the amount in gross business income for 2006, not 2007.

No Postponing Income

You cannot hold checks or other payments from one tax year to another to avoid paying tax on the income. You must report the income in the year the payment is received or made available to you without restriction.

> **EXAMPLE:** On December 1, 2006, Helen receives a $5,000 check from a client. She holds the check and doesn't cash it until January 10, 2007. She must still report the $5,000 as income for 2006 because she constructively received it that year.

Prepayment of Expenses

The general rule is that you can't prepay expenses when you use the cash method—you can't hurry up the payment of expenses by paying them in advance. An expense you pay in advance can be deducted only in the year to which it applies.

However, an important exception to the general rule, called the 12-month rule, went into effect in 2004. Under this rule you may deduct a prepaid expense in the current year if the expense is for a right or benefit that extends no longer than the earlier of:

- 12 months, or
- until the end of the tax year after the tax year in which you made the payment.

EXAMPLE: You are a calendar year taxpayer and you pay $10,000 on July 1, 2006, for a malpractice insurance policy that is effective for one year beginning July 1, 2006. The 12-month rule applies because the benefit you've paid for—a business insurance policy—extends only 12 months into the future. Therefore, the full $10,000 is deductible in 2006.

EXAMPLE: You are a calendar year taxpayer and you pay $3,000 in 2006 for a business insurance policy that is effective for three years, beginning July 1, 2006. This payment does not qualify for the 12-month rule because the benefit extends more than 12 months. Therefore, you must use the general rule: $500 is deductible in 2006, $1,000 is deductible in 2007, $1,000 is deductible in 2008, and $500 is deductible in 2009.

To use the 12-month rule, you must apply it when you first start using the cash method for your practice. You must get IRS approval if you haven't been using the rule and want to start doing so. Such IRS approval is granted automatically.

2.   Accrual Method

In accrual basis accounting, you report income or expenses as they are earned or incurred, rather than when they are actually collected or paid. The accrual method is not favored by professionals because (1) it can be complicated to use, and (2) it can require them to pay tax on income they haven't actually received.

When Income Is Received

With the accrual method, transactions are counted as income when services are provided, an order is made, or an item is delivered, regardless of when the money for them (receivables) is actually received or paid. As a result, you can end up owing taxes on income you haven't been paid. This is particularly bad news for professionals because they often have to wait a while (sometimes a long while) before they are paid for their services by their clients.

EXAMPLE: Andrea, an architect, uses the accrual method of accounting. She is hired by a client to design a house. She finishes the job on December 15, 2006 and bills the customer for $25,000 that same day. However, the client turned out to be a slow payer. By April 15, 2007, Andrea still hadn't received her fee. However, because she's an accrual basis taxpayer, she must include the $25,000 as income on her 2006 tax return and pay tax on it. Under the accrual method, the $25,000 became taxable income the year Andrea earned the money by completing her architecture services. It's immaterial that Andrea has not actually been paid.

Obviously, if you have many clients who owe you money, you could end up having to pay substantial taxes on income you haven't received. If it turns out that a client will never pay you, you may deduct the amount you're owed as a bad debt. But this will just wipe out the income you've already paid tax on in a prior year.

When Expenses Are Incurred

Under the accrual method, you generally deduct a business expense when:

- you are legally obligated to pay the expense
- the amount you owe can be determined with reasonable accuracy, and
- you have received or used the property or services involved.

EXAMPLE: The ABC Medical Corporation borrows $100,000 from its bank to help pay its business operating expenses. It signs a promissory note on December 15, 2006 and receives the money the same day, but doesn't start making payments to the bank until the following January. ABC can deduct the entire expense in 2006 because on December 15, 2006 it became legally obligated to pay the expense by signing the note, the amount of the expense can be determined from the note, and it received the money that day.

Thus, when you use the accrual method, you can take a deduction for an expense you incur even if you don't actually pay for it until the following year. You can't do this under the cash basis method. There are obvious advantages to getting a tax deduction this year without actually having to shell out any money until a future year. However, for most professionals these advantages do not outweigh the disadvantage of having to pay tax on income that hasn't been received.

Businesses That Must Use the Accrual Method

The IRS likes the accrual method. Any business, however small, may use it if it wants to. But, as explained above, few professionals want to.

Unfortunately, some types of businesses are required to use the accrual method—for example, partnerships with average annual gross receipts exceeding $5 million that have C corporations as partners. Ordinarily, C corporations with average annual gross receipts exceeding $5 million must also use the accrual method. However, personal service corporations may use the cash method even if they earn this much. Most corporations formed by professionals qualify as personal service corporations (see Chapter 2).

Businesses that sell, produce, or purchase merchandise and maintain an inventory are ordinarily required to use the accrual method. Thus, in the past the IRS required some professionals, such as optometrists and veterinarians who sold merchandise, to use the accrual method. However, an important rule change took effect in 2001 that permits most professionals to use the cash method, even if they carry an inventory.

The rule change created two big exceptions to the requirement that businesses with inventories use the accrual method:

- **Exception #1—Businesses that earn less than $1 million:** Even if you deal in merchandise, you may use the cash basis method if your average annual gross receipts were $1 million or less for the three tax years ending with the prior tax year.

- **Exception #2—Some businesses that earn less than $10 million:** Even if your practice earns more than $1 million per year, you may use the cash basis method if your average annual gross receipts were $10 million or less for the three tax years ending with the prior tax year, and your principal business is providing services. (Rev. Proc. 2001-10, Rev. Proc. 2001-21.)

So, as long as your practice earns less than $10 million per year, you can use the cash method even if you sell clients merchandise as well as provide them with services. However, you may deduct only the cost of inventory that you sell during the year.

Obtaining IRS Permission to Change Your Accounting Method

You choose your accounting method by checking a box on your tax form when you file your tax return for the first year you are in business. Once you choose a method, you can't change it without getting permission from the IRS. Permission is granted automatically for many types of changes, including using the 12-month rule to deduct prepaid expenses (see Section 1, above). You must file IRS Form 3115, *Application for Change in Accounting Method,* with your tax return for the year you want to make the change (if the change is automatically granted).

Automatic approval can also be obtained to change to the cash method if you've been using the accrual method and come within one of the exceptions discussed above. However, this type of change can have serious consequences, so consult a tax professional before doing so.

D. Tax Years

You are required to pay taxes for a 12-month period, also known as the tax year. Sole proprietors, partnerships, limited liability companies, S corporations, and personal service corporations are required to use the calendar year as their tax years—that is, January 1 through December 31.

However, there are exceptions that permit some small businesses to use a tax year that does not end in December (also known as a fiscal year). You need to get the IRS's permission to use a fiscal year. The IRS doesn't like businesses to use a fiscal year, but it might grant you permission if you can show a good business reason for it.

To get permission to use a fiscal year, you must file IRS Form 8716, *Election to Have a Tax Year Other Than a Required Tax Year.*

Chapter 21

Help Beyond This Book

There are many resources available to supplement and explain more fully the tax information covered in this book. Many of these resources are free; others are reasonably priced. The more expensive tax publications for professionals are often available at public libraries or law libraries. And, a lot of tax information is available on the Internet.

If you have a question about a specific tax deduction or any other tax-related matter, you can:

- consult a secondary tax source (see Section A)
- review the tax law (see Section B), or
- see a tax professional (see Section C).

You can do these suggested steps in any order you wish. For example, you can see a tax professional right away instead of doing any research yourself. This will save you time, but will cost you money.

 Before you try to research tax law on your own, we recommend that you learn how to do legal research first. An excellent resource is *Legal Research: How to Find & Understand the Law,* by Stephen Elias and Susan Levinkind (Nolo); or you can go to Nolo's Legal Research Center at www.nolo.com.

A. Secondary Sources of Tax Information

Going straight to the tax code when you have a tax question is generally not the best approach. The tax code itself can be dry and difficult to decipher—particularly if you're trying to figure out how a particular law or rule applies to your situation. Instead of diving right into the code books, your best bet is to start with one of the many secondary sources that try to make the tax law more understandable. Unlike the primary sources listed in Section 3, below, these sources are not the law itself or the IRS's official pronouncements on the law. Instead, they are interpretations and explanations of the law intended to make it more understandable. Often, you'll be able to find the answer to your question in one or more of these sources. You can also learn about topics not covered in this book—for example, what constitutes income for tax purposes, how to complete your tax returns, or how to deal with an IRS audit.

1.   Information From the IRS

The IRS has made a huge effort to inform the public about the tax law, creating hundreds of informative publications, an excellent website, and a telephone answering service. However, unlike the regulations and rulings issued by the IRS, these secondary sources of information are for informational purposes only. They are not official IRS pronouncements, and the IRS is not legally bound by them.

Reading IRS publications is a useful way to obtain information on IRS procedures and to get the agency's view of the tax law. But keep in mind that these publications only present the IRS's interpretation of the law, which may be very one-sided and even contrary to court rulings. That's why you shouldn't rely exclusively on IRS publications for information.

IRS Website

The IRS has one of the most useful Internet websites of any federal government agency. Among other things, almost every IRS form and informational publication can be downloaded from the site. The Internet address is www.irs.gov.

The IRS website has a special section for small businesses and the self-employed (www.irs.gov/businesses/small/index.html). It includes:

- answers to basic tax questions and a calendar of tax deadlines
- online access to most IRS forms and information booklets
- industry-specific tax information for certain industries like construction and food service
- tips to avoid common tax problems
- announcements of new IRS policies and procedures of particular interest to small businesses
- links to court opinions and to rulings and regulations on specific industries
- links to non-IRS sites for general tax information, and
- links to helpful small business resources.

IRS Booklets and CD-ROM

The IRS publishes over 350 free booklets explaining the tax code, called IRS Publications ("Pubs," for short). Many of these publications are referenced in this book. Some are relatively easy to understand, others are incomprehensible or misleading. As with all IRS publications, they only present the IRS's interpretation of the tax laws—which may or may not be upheld by the federal courts.

You can download all of the booklets from the IRS website at www.irs.gov. You can also obtain free copies by calling 800-TAX-FORM (800-829-3676) or by contacting your local IRS office or sending an order form to the IRS.

IRS Telephone Information

The IRS offers a series of prerecorded tapes of information on various tax topics on a toll-free telephone service called TELETAX (800-829-4477). See IRS Publication 910 for a list of topics.

You can talk to an IRS representative on the telephone by calling 800-829-1040. (It is difficult to get though to someone from January through May.) Be sure to double check anything an IRS representative tells you over the phone—the IRS is notorious for giving misleading or outright wrong answers to taxpayers' questions, and the agency will not stand behind oral advice that turns out to be incorrect.

Free IRS Programs

In larger metropolitan areas, the IRS offers small business seminars on various topics, such as payroll tax reporting. You can ask questions at these half-day meetings, which are often held at schools or federal buildings. Call the IRS at 800-829-1040 to see if programs are offered near you and to get on the IRS small business mailing list. The IRS also has an online tax workshop for small businesses. It can be found at the online classroom on the IRS website. You can also order a free CD-ROM with a video presentation of the workshop through the IRS website.

2. Other Online Tax Resources

In addition to the IRS website, there are hundreds of privately created websites on the Internet that provide tax information and advice. Some of this information is good; some is execrable. A comprehensive collection of Web links about all aspects of taxation can be found at www.taxsites.com. Other useful tax Web link pages can be found at:

- www.willyancey.com/tax_internet.htm
- www.abanet.org/taxes
- www.natptax.com/tax_links.html
- www.el.com/elinks/taxes.

Some useful tax-related websites include:

- www.accountsworld.com
- www.unclefed.com
- www.smbiz.com/sbwday.html
- http://aol.smartmoney.com/tax/filing
- www.taxguru.net.

Nolo's Website

Nolo maintains a website that is useful for small businesses and the self-employed. The site contains helpful articles, information about new legislation, book excerpts, and the Nolo catalog. The site also includes a legal encyclopedia with specific information for businesspeople, as well as a legal research center you can use to find state and federal statutes, including the Internal Revenue Code. The Internet address is www.nolo.com.

3. Tax Publications

If you're a person who likes to read books, you'll be happy to know that there are enough books about tax law to fill a library. Tax publications vary from the broadly focused to the highly detailed. You can find answers to most tax questions in one or more of these resources.

Publications for the Nonexpert

There are many books (like this one) that attempt to make the tax law comprehensible to the average person. The best known are the paperback tax preparation books published every year. These books emphasize individual taxes but also have useful information for small businesses. Two of the best are:

- *The Ernst and Young Tax Guide* (John Wiley & Sons), and
- *J.K. Lasser's Your Income Tax* (John Wiley & Sons).

J.K. Lasser publishes other useful tax guides, many of which are targeted at small businesses. You can find a list of these publications at www.wiley.com/WileyCDA/Section/id-103210.html.

Tax guides designed for college courses can also be extremely helpful. Two good guides to all aspects of income taxes that are updated each year are:

- *Prentice Hall's Federal Taxation Comprehensive* (Prentice Hall), and
- *CCH Federal Taxation Comprehensive Topics* (Commerce Clearing House).

Nolo also publishes several books that deal with tax issues:

- *Stand Up to the IRS*, by Frederick W. Daily (Nolo), explains how to handle an IRS audit.
- *Tax Savvy for Small Business*, by Frederick W. Daily (Nolo), provides an overview of the entire subject of taxation, geared to the small business owner.
- *Working With Independent Contractors*, by Stephen Fishman (Nolo), shows small businesses how to hire independent contractors without running afoul of the IRS or other government agencies.
- *Working for Yourself,* by Stephen Fishman (Nolo), covers the whole gamut of legal issues facing the one-person business.
- *Every Landlord's Tax Deduction Guide,* by Stephen Fishman (Nolo), provides detailed guidance on tax deductions for small residential landlords.
- *IRAs, 401(k)s & Other Retirement Plans*, by Twila Slesnick and John C. Suttle (Nolo), covers the tax implications of withdrawing funds from retirement accounts.
- *What Every Inventor Needs to Know About Business & Taxes*, by Stephen Fishman (Nolo), covers tax aspects of inventing.

Publications for Tax Professionals

Sometimes, you'll have a question you can't answer by looking at websites or tax publications for the layperson. In this event, you can consult one or more publications for tax professionals: accountants, CPAs, and attorneys. These are the most detailed and comprehensive secondary sources available.

There are six main publishing companies that publish reference materials for tax professionals:

- Business News Association (BNA); www.bna.com
- Commerce Clearing House (CCH); www.cch.com
- Klienrock Publishing; www.kleinrock.com
- Research Institute of America (RIA); www.riahome.com
- Tax Analysts; www.taxanalysts.com, and
- West Group; http://west.thomson.com.

These publishers produce an incredible volume of tax information, ranging from detailed analyses of the most arcane tax questions to brief, one-volume guides to the entire federal tax law. Among their publications are:

- **Tax services.** These are highly detailed discussions of the tax law, organized by IRC section or topic and updated frequently—every week, or every month. The most authoritative is *The Law of Federal Income Taxation*, published by West Group (it's also called "Mertens" by tax professionals because it was originally edited by Jacob Mertens). Other tax services include the *United States Tax Reporter* (published by RIA) and *Standard Federal Tax Reporter* (published by CCH).

- **Tax treatises.** Tax treatises provide in-depth, book-length treatment of a particular tax topic. Among the most useful are the Tax Management Portfolios, a series of paperback booklets published by BNA. If you're looking for information on a very precise tax issue, you might find what you need in a portfolio.

- **Tax citators.** Tax citators summarize tax cases and compile and organize them by subject matter and IRC section. By using a citator, you can find all the tax cases that have addressed a specific tax topic. Both CCH and RIA publish citators.

- **Tax deskbooks.** CCH publishes a well-known one-volume tax "deskbook" called the *Master Tax Guide* that provides an overview of the tax law. It's updated each year.

You can find a good discussion on how to use these tax materials in *West's Federal Tax Research* (South-Western College Publishing).

All of these publications are available in print form, on CD-ROMs, and on subscriber websites maintained by the publishers themselves or commercial databases (notably Westlaw and Lexis, subscriber databases containing legal information). As you might expect, they are generally very expensive. You can also find them in a law library, some large public libraries, or a tax professional's office.

Trade Association Publications

There are hundreds of trade associations and organizations representing every conceivable occupation—for example, the American Society of Home Inspectors, the Association of Independent Video and Filmmakers, and the Graphic Artists Guild. Most of these have specialized publications and newsletters that track tax issues of common interest. You can learn about specific tax issues in your industry that even your tax professional might not know about—perhaps a new case or IRS ruling. Also, you can often find speakers on tax topics at programs offered to members at conventions and trade shows.

If you don't know the name and address of an association relevant to your business, ask other businesspeople in your field. Or check out the *Encyclopedia of Associations* (Gale Research); it should be available at your public library. Also, many of these associations have websites on the Internet, so you may be able to find the one you want by doing an Internet search.

4. Tax Software

Today, millions of taxpayers use tax preparation software to complete their own income tax returns. The best-known programs are *Turbotax* and *TaxCut*. These programs contain most IRS tax forms, publications, and other tax guidance. Both have helpful websites at www.turbotax.com and www.taxcut.com.

B. The Tax Law

If you can't find an answer to your question in a secondary source, you might be able to find help in the tax law itself. Or, you may want to consult the tax law to verify (or clarify) what you've learned from secondary sources.

The "tax law" of the United States comes from several sources:

- the Internal Revenue Code
- IRS regulations
- court cases, and
- IRS rulings, interpretations, and tax advice.

Every branch of the federal government is involved in creating the tax law. The Internal Revenue Code is enacted by Congress (the legislative branch), IRS regulations and rulings are issued by the IRS (a department of the executive branch), and taxpayers may appeal the IRS's actions to the federal courts (the judicial branch).

The Tax Law Versus *War and Peace*	
	Number of pages
Internal Revenue Code	3,653
IRS Regulations	13,079
War and Peace, by Leo Tolstoy	1,444

1.   Internal Revenue Code

The Internal Revenue Code (IRC) is the supreme tax law of the land. The IRC (also called "the code" or "the tax code") is written, and frequently rewritten, by Congress. The first tax code, adopted in 1913, contained 14 pages. Today, the tax code is more than 3,600 pages long.

The IRC is found in Title 26 of the United States Code (USC for short). The USC encompasses all of our federal laws. "Title" simply refers to the place within the massive USC where the IRC is found.

The entire tax code covers income taxes, Social Security taxes, excise taxes, estate and gift taxes, and tax procedure. It is organized by category and broken down into subtitles, chapters, subchapters, parts, subparts, sections, subsections, paragraphs, subparagraphs, and clauses. The income tax laws are in Chapter 1 of Subtitle A of the Tax Code. Most of the laws dealing with tax deductions are found in Parts VI and VII of Subchapter B of Chapter 1.

For our purposes, the most important thing to remember about the organization of the tax code is that each specific tax law is contained in a separate numbered section. For example, Section 179 covers first year expensing of long-term business assets. For the sake of convenience, tax professionals will often refer to these numbered sections of the tax code.

> **EXAMPLE:** "IRC § 179(b)(4)(A)" means that this particular tax law is found in Title 26 of the USC (the Internal Revenue Code), Section 179, subsection b, paragraph 4, subparagraph A.

The tax code is published each year in a two-volume set (usually in paperback). You should be able to find it in the reference section of any public library. You can also purchase a set from various tax publishers, such as Commerce Clearing House and Research Institute of America. A complete set of the tax code costs over $80. You can also purchase a one-volume abridged version for much less. This will likely contain all the tax code provisions you'll want to refer to. The entire United State Code (including the IRC) is also available on CD-ROM from the Government Printing Office for under $40.

Fortunately, the IRC is available for free on the Internet. You can get to the entire IRC from Nolo's Legal Research Center—go to www.nolo .com. Portions are also available on the IRS website (www.irs.gov) and several other websites.

Make sure your tax code is current. The IRC is amended every year; in recent years, these amendments have made major changes to the law. Make sure that any copy of the IRC you use in your research is current.

2. IRS Regulations

Even though the Internal Revenue Code contains over 3,600 pages, it does not provide adequate guidance for every situation that arises in real life. To supplement the IRC, the IRS issues regulations, called "Treasury Regulations," "Regulations," or "Regs." Although written by the IRS, not Congress, these regulations have almost the same authoritative weight as the tax code itself.

While the tax code is usually written in broad and general terms, the regulations get down and dirty, providing details about how tax code provisions are intended to operate in the real world. Regulations are slightly easier to read than the tax code on which they are based and often include examples that can be helpful. The regulations cover many (but not all) of the tax code provisions.

To see if a particular IRC section is supplemented by a regulation, start with the number of the IRC section. If there is a corresponding regulation, it will bear the same number, usually preceded by the number "1."

> **EXAMPLE:** "Reg. 1.179" refers to a Treasury regulation interpreting IRC Section 179.

The regulations are published in a multivolume set by the Government Printing Office and tax publishers such as CCH and RIA. These are available in law libraries and may also be found in some large public libraries. Many regulations can be downloaded from the IRS website.

3. Court Cases

When a dispute arises between a taxpayer and the IRS, the taxpayer may take the matter to federal court. The courts are the final arbiters of tax disputes. A court may overrule the IRS if the court concludes that the IRS applied the tax code in a manner contrary to the United States Constitution or differently from what Congress intended.

Tax disputes are tried in three different courts: a special tax court that handles only tax disputes, the regular federal trial courts (called U.S. District Courts), and the Court of Federal Claims. If either the taxpayer or the IRS doesn't like the result reached at trial, it may appeal to the federal appellate courts (called the U.S. Court of Appeals), and even to the United States Supreme Court.

Decisions of these courts are published, along with explanations and discussions of the tax law. These court decisions provide valuable interpretations of the tax laws. Many, but not all, of these court interpretations are binding on the IRS. Thousands of court decisions dealing with tax law have been published, so chances are good that there is at least one decision on the issue that interests you.

To locate a published court decision, you must understand how to read a case citation. A citation provides the names of the people or companies involved on each side of the case, the volume of the legal publication (called a reporter) in which the case can be found, the page number on which it begins, and the year in which the case was decided. Here is an example of what a legal citation looks like: *Smith v. Jones*, 123 F.3d 456 (1995). Smith and Jones are the names of the people in the legal dispute. The case is reported in volume 123 of the Federal Reporter, Third Series, beginning on page 456; the court issued the decision in 1995.

Opinions by the federal district courts are in a series of reporters called the Federal Supplement, or F.Supp. Any case decided by a federal court of appeals is found in a series of books called the Federal Reporter. Older cases are contained in the first series of the Federal Reporter, or F. More recent cases are contained in the second or third series of the Federal Reporter, F.2d or F.3d. Cases decided by the U.S. Supreme Court are found in three publications: United States Reports (identified as U.S.), the Supreme Court Reporter (identified as S.Ct.), and the Supreme Court Reports, Lawyer's Edition (identified as L.Ed.). Supreme Court case citations often refer to all three publications.

Many, but not all, of these legal decisions are available free on the Internet. Tax court decisions and tax decisions from other courts from 1990 to date can be accessed for free at www.legalbitstream.com. Tax court decisions from 1999 to date can also be accessed at www .ustaxcourt.gov., which contains links to all types of law-related websites. Virtually all legal decisions are available on the subscriber websites Lexis.com and Westlaw.com. You may be able to access these websites through a library or tax professional's office.

Hard copies of published decisions by the United States Tax Court can be found in the Tax Court Reports, or T.C., published by the U.S. Government Printing Office. Tax court decisions can also be found in a reporter called Tax Court Memorandum Decisions, or T.C. Memo, published by Commerce Clearing House, Inc. Decisions from all federal courts involving taxation can be found in a reporter called U.S. Tax

Cases, or USTC, published by Commerce Clearing House, Inc. These are available in law libraries.

For a detailed discussion of how to research court cases, see *Legal Research: How to Find & Understand the Law*, by Stephen Elias and Susan Levinkind (Nolo), or go to Nolo's Legal Research Center at www.nolo.com.

4. IRS Rulings, Interpretations, and Tax Advice

It might seem like the tax code, regulations, and court decisions would provide everything anyone ever wanted to know about tax law. But even more IRS guidance is available. The IRS publishes several types of statements (besides Regs) of its position on various tax matters. These pronouncements guide IRS personnel and taxpayers as to how the IRS will apply specific tax laws.

Unlike the tax code and regulations, these statements do not have the force of law. Rather, they are the IRS's own interpretation of the tax law, which is not necessarily binding on the courts (or on you, should you choose to challenge the IRS's interpretation in court). However, they give you a good idea of how the IRS would handle the situation involved.

Revenue Rulings

IRS Revenue Rulings (Rev. Rul.) are IRS announcements of how the tax law applies to a hypothetical set of facts. The IRS publishes over 100 of these rulings every year. These rulings represent the IRS's view of the tax law, and the IRS presumes that they are correct. If an auditor discovers that you have violated a revenue ruling, you will probably have to pay additional tax. On the other hand, if you can show an auditor that a revenue ruling supports your position, you probably won't have to pay more tax. If you have violated a revenue ruling, all is not necessarily lost. Revenue rulings are not binding on the courts, which can (and do) disregard them from time to time. Thus, it's possible you could win your case on appeal.

You can download free copies of all IRS Revenue Rulings from 1954 to date from: www.taxlinks.com. Revenue rulings also appear in the weekly *Internal Revenue Cumulative Bulletin*, which is published by the U.S. Government Printing Office. Tax book publishers Prentice-

Hall, Commerce Clearing House, and Research Institute of America also reprint IRS Revenue Rulings. They are indexed by IRC section and subject matter.

> **EXAMPLE:** "Rev. Rul. 03-41" refers to IRS Revenue Ruling number 41, issued in 2003.

Revenue Procedures

Revenue procedures ("Rev. Procs.") are IRS announcements dealing with procedural aspects of tax practice. Rev. Procs. are used primarily by tax return preparers. They often explain when and how to report tax items, such as how to claim a net operating loss on a tax form or return. Revenue procedures are contained in the weekly *Internal Revenue Cumulative Bulletin*, which you can find in larger public and law libraries, and also are reprinted by tax book publishers and on the IRS website. You can obtain free copies of many revenue procedures at www.legalbitstream.com.

> **EXAMPLE:** "Rev. Proc. 99-15" refers to a published Revenue Procedure number 15, issued in 1999.

Letter Rulings

IRS letter rulings are IRS answers to specific written questions from taxpayers about complex tax situations. The only person who is entitled to rely on the ruling as legal authority is the taxpayer to whom the ruling is addressed; even if you find yourself in a similar position, the IRS is not legally required to follow the guidance it gave in the letter. However, letter rulings offer valuable insight into the IRS's position on tax treatment of complex transactions. Since 1976, letter rulings have been made available to the general public. You can access free copies of many letter rulings at www.legalbitstream.com. They are also published by tax publishers.

> **EXAMPLE:** "Ltr. Ruling 9913043 (April 3, 1999)" refers to a letter ruling issued on April 3, 1999. The first two numbers of the seven-digit identifier show the year it was issued, the next two indicate the week of the year, and the last three show the ruling for that

week. Thus, this letter ruling was the 43rd issued during the 13th week of 1999.

IRS General Guidance

From time to time, the IRS gives general guidance and statements of policy in official "announcements" and "notices" similar to press releases. They appear in the weekly *Internal Revenue Cumulative Bulletin*. It doesn't usually pay to search IRS announcements or notices because they are too broad to answer specific questions. You can access many of these for free at www.legalbitstream.com.

Internal Revenue Manual

The *Internal Revenue Manual* (IRM) is a series of handbooks that serve as guides to IRS employees on tax law and procedure. The IRM tells IRS employees (usually auditors or collectors) how specific tax code provisions should be enforced. The manual is available on the IRS website.

The IRM is revealing of IRS attitudes in certain areas—for example, Section 4.10.3 of the *Manual* describes the techniques IRS auditors are supposed to use when they examine the depreciation deductions claimed by a business.

IRS Forms and Instructions

IRS forms are well known to us all, especially Form 1040, the annual personal income tax return. There are more than 650 other IRS forms, listed in Publication 676, *Catalog of Federal Tax Forms*. You can get them free at IRS offices or by calling 800-829-FORM or 800-829-1040. You can also download them from the IRS website at www.irs.gov. Many IRS forms come with instructions and explanations of the tax law.

C. Consulting a Tax Professional

You don't have to do your own tax research. There are hundreds of thousands of tax professionals (tax pros) in the United States ready and eager to help you—for a price. A tax pro can answer your questions, provide guidance to help you make key tax decisions, prepare your tax returns, and help you deal with the IRS if you get into tax trouble.

1. Types of Tax Pros

There are several different types of tax pros. They differ widely in training, experience, and cost:

- **Tax preparers.** As the name implies, tax preparers prepare tax returns. The largest tax preparation firm is H&R Block, but many mom and pop operations open for business in storefront offices during tax time. In most states, anybody can be a tax preparer; no licensing is required. Most tax preparers don't have the training or experience to handle taxes for businesses and, therefore, are probably not a wise choice.

- **Enrolled agents.** Enrolled agents (EAs) are tax advisors and preparers who are licensed by the IRS. They must have at least five years of experience or pass a difficult IRS test. They can represent taxpayers before the IRS, and in administrative proceedings, circuit court, and, possibly tax court, if they pass the appropriate tests. Enrolled agents are the least expensive of the true tax pros but are reliable for tax return preparation and more routine tax matters. They can be quite adequate for many small businesses.

- **Certified Public Accountants.** Certified public accountants (CPAs) are licensed and regulated by each state. They undergo lengthy training and must pass a comprehensive exam. CPAs represent the high end of the tax pro spectrum. In addition to preparing tax returns, they perform sophisticated accounting and tax work. CPAs are found in large national firms or in small local outfits. The large national firms are used primarily by large businesses. Some states also license public accountants. These are competent, but are not as highly regarded as CPAs.

- **Tax attorneys.** Tax attorneys are lawyers who specialize in tax matters. The only time you'll ever need a tax attorney is if you get into serious trouble with the IRS or another tax agency and need legal representation before the IRS or in court. Some tax attorneys also give tax advice, but they are usually too expensive for small businesses. You're probably better off hiring a CPA if you need specialized tax help.

2. Finding a Tax Pro

The best way to find a tax pro is to obtain referrals from business associates, friends, or professional associations. If none of these sources can give you a suitable lead, try contacting the National Association of Enrolled Agents or one of its state affiliates. You can find a listing of affiliates at the NAEA website at www.naea.org. Local CPA societies can give you referrals to local CPAs. You can also find tax pros in the telephone book under "Accountants, Tax Return." Local bar associations can refer you to a tax attorney. Be aware that CPA societies and local bar associations refer from a list on a rotating basis, so you shouldn't construe a referral as a recommendation or certification of competence.

Your relationship with your tax pro will be one of your most important business relationships. Be picky about the person you choose. Talk with at least three tax pros before hiring one. You want a tax pro who takes the time to listen to you, answers your questions fully and in plain English, seems knowledgeable, and makes you feel comfortable. Make sure the tax pro works frequently with small businesses. It can also be helpful if the tax pro already has clients in businesses similar to yours. A tax pro already familiar with the tax problems posed by your type of business can often give you the best advice for the least money.

■

Index

U

V

W

■

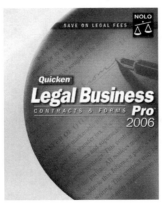

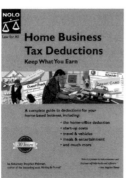
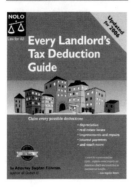

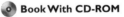